MARSHALL: Citizen Soldier

GEORGE CATLETT MARSHALL, Jr.

General of the Army; Chief of Staff, 1939-1945; the President's Special Envoy to China, 1946; Secretary of State, 1947.

Signal Corps Photo

MARSHALL
Citizen Soldier

By
WILLIAM FRYE

... still am I slave
When banners flaunt and bugles blow,
Content to fill a soldier's grave
For reasons I shall never know.

THE BOBBS-MERRILL COMPANY
PUBLISHERS
INDIANAPOLIS • NEW YORK

COPYRIGHT, 1947, BY THE BOBBS-MERRILL COMPANY
PRINTED IN THE UNITED STATES OF AMERICA

First Edition

For
MARY

ACKNOWLEDGMENT

The friendly interest and generous co-operation of the Secretary of War, Robert P. Patterson, alone have made possible even so limited a study as this of General Marshall, and it is with both gratitude and affection that I confess my great debt to the Judge.

John J. McCloy, formerly Assistant Secretary of War, was generous enough not only to contribute valuable material, but to assume the burden of reading the manuscript. Robert A. Lovett, formerly Assistant Secretary of War for Air, has been most helpful, as has Howard C. Petersen, Assistant Secretary of War.

The General of the Armies John J. Pershing has graciously permitted use of a personal letter and a portion of his account of the Meuse-Argonne fighting in World War I.

I am particularly indebted to Alex Mead and to Mr. and Mrs. Clyde B. Miller for guidance in assembling material for the chapter on the Marshall family in Uniontown; to Major General Philip B. Peyton, U.S.A. Retired, to Leonard K. Nicholson, and to Colonel William B. Couper, Historiographer of the Virginia Military Institute, for material in the chapter on the V.M.I.; and to Colonel Henry Hossfeld, U.S.A. Retired, and to Perry E. Thompson, G. W. Mathews, John T. Morton and J. W. Willey, formerly enlisted men of the 30th Infantry, for information about General Marshall's first assignment in the Philippines.

Colonel Joseph I. Greene, editor of the *Infantry Journal*, gave me invaluable assistance in locating sources of information, as well as permitting use of pertinent material from the *Journal*. To Brigadier General Charles T. Lanham, U.S.A., I am indebted not only for contributions to the text, but for permission to use a fragment of his poem, "Soldier," as inscription on the title page. My thanks are due also to Katherine Tupper Marshall for her generous permission to use material from her book, *Together*.

So many others have helped in the preparation of this volume that it would be impossible to list them here, even if most of them had not asked me to make no public reference to their contributions. I hope that each of them will accept this general acknowledgment as personal thanks.

WILLIAM FRYE

CONTENTS

CHAPTER		PAGE
I	DUELISTS AND SOLID CITIZENS	15
II	A GENERAL IS BORN	25
III	FROM RAT TO FIRST CAPTAIN	44
IV	MANIFEST DESTINY	65
V	STAR IN HIS POCKET	84
VI	TACTICS IN THE TROPICS	97
VII	THE FIRST CONVOY TO FRANCE	114
VIII	SWEATING ON THE STAFF	128
IX	TRIUMPH AND FRUSTRATION	147
X	LESSONS OF VICTORY	166
XI	CHINA—AND TRAGEDY	186
XII	DEBUNKING THE DOCTRINAIRES	202
XIII	STAR ON HIS SHOULDER	219
XIV	MARSHALL SPEAKS HIS MIND	236
XV	FIGHTING FOR AN ARMY	256
XVI	THE BLOW FALLS	279
XVII	GRAND STRATEGY	299
XVIII	GLOBAL ATTACK	317
XIX	TOO GOOD FOR COMMAND	334
XX	CODE OF A CITIZEN SOLDIER	353
	INDEX	377

LIST OF ILLUSTRATIONS

George Catlett Marshall, Jr. . . . . *Frontispiece*

	FACING PAGE
George Catlett Marshall, Jr.	30
V.M.I. Cadet Officers	31
Second Lieutenant Marshall	64
Elizabeth Carter Marshall	65
First Lieutenant Marshall	96
Temporary Colonel	97
Victory Parade	128
Aide-de-Camp	129
Staff Conference	160
Official Society	161
Marshall and Stimson	192
Eisenhower and Marshall	193
Casablanca Conference	224
At Casablanca	225
Quadrant Conference	256
Thanksgiving Day in Cairo	257
Teheran Conference	288
Beachhead in Normandy	289
Italian Front	320
French Tribute	321
Haircut at Potsdam	352
Katherine Tupper Marshall	353

MARSHALL: Citizen Soldier

I

Duelists and Solid Citizens

THEY held their ancestry high, the Marshalls. Some thought they flaunted it, but it was not so. Heirs of the South's high pretension, its cultivated manner, and habit of command, its tangled skeins of sib and kith, they bore the unmistakable mark of easy assurance. It was an aura, not natural but cultivated, yet so many generations old it was second nature, and unconscious. The Marshalls could not have shed it had they tried, and it would never have occurred to them to try; but they never smeared it over with condescension.

Their pride notwithstanding, they were liked from Stockton Hill to Haiti—pronounced Het-eye in Uniontown, Pennsylvania. If most of their close friends were among the West End swells with whom they were neighbors, that was only the natural result of comparable backgrounds and related tastes. They were not lacking in friends among the humbler citizens.

It may be that a faint suspicion they were snobs lingers in the town's memory of them because great reserve in a woman can be mistaken for haughtiness, and a talkative man may seem sometimes to brag. Mr. Marshall talked a very great deal indeed, and like most Marshalls before him and few since, he found his own family an extraordinarily interesting topic of conversation.

If Mrs. Marshall talked less of family, it was not because pride of birth was lacking on her side of the house. She was Laura Bradford, and her mother was Maria Louisa Stuart, a name sufficient to indicate how that family felt about its ill-starred but heady blood.

Laura's father, Dr. Jonathan Johnson Bradford, was a planter's son and an eminent physician, and the younger brother to whom he gave the beginnings of a medical education, Dr. Joshua T. Bradford, returned to Kentucky after completing his medical studies in Philadelphia to become a celebrated specialist in ovarian surgery. The two doctors, moreover, were the grandsons of Governor William Johnson of Maryland, a great patriot and a friend of General Washington.

But for all that, even the memory and name of a royal house and distant kinship with the Confederacy's most famous cavalryman, Laura was a member of no such family as her husband's.

It was small wonder the Marshalls found themselves interesting. They were more tribe than family, and the genealogical tree displayed some rich and curious specimens, from a roistering rogue of a colonial gentleman suspected of being Blackbeard in disguise, to the second and most famous chief justice of the United States.

Soldiers, they were, and planters; and doctors, judges, preachers, congressmen, and ambassadors. Marshalls with an excess of piety and evangelical fervor were balanced by Marshalls who scorned all revealed religion. There were gentle and kindly students and celebrated duelists, including one who achieved the ultimate swagger of contemptuous refusal to shoot his opponent.

If the vague tradition of descent from Strongbow and William the Marshal failed to take into account the sober verdict of historians that the great Earl Marshal's male line ended with his sons, the tradition persisted nonetheless as the explanation of how the Marshalls were Irish. Family traditions are much pleasanter and more romantic than such records as those which show that the Earl of Pembroke who came back from the Irish wars to marry the Princess Eleanor, daughter of King John, had no children at all.

However the Marshall name got to Ireland, it remained there in some obscurity for several centuries. It was more than three hundred years after Pembroke's departure that Captain John Marshall showed up a long way from home to win distinction and get himself badly wounded at the siege of Calais in 1558, then disappeared again into the mists of the green sweet island beyond the Irish Sea.

A century later his descendant, another Captain John Marshall, fought for the king against the Roundheads at Edgehill. He was an Anglican who liked the road to Rome no more than he liked the Lord Protector's psalmistry—who more violently Protestant than an Irish Protestant? He could not abide the Puritans, but the religious direction of the royal exile was not the way for him, and so he brought the Marshall name to Virginia.

It was in 1650 that he came to Jamestown, no doubt in a cockleshell of a ship full of refugee cavaliers. Not much later he left the fevers and contentions of the island in the James behind him, and crossed the York and the Rappahannock to the Northern Neck where he settled in Westmoreland County on the Potomac, had Lees and Fitzhughs and Washingtons for neighbors, is said to have fought notably against the Indians, and indubitably left a son, Thomas.

Thomas was a farmer who died in 1704, and he had two sons. William, the elder, can be forgotten. With John, the younger, born the first year of the eighteenth century, the family began to flourish. John Marshall of The Forest was a man of substance and importance, and a captain of the colony's militia. The Forest was no wood lot, but a plantation of twelve hundred acres.

His wife Elizabeth bore him nine children, and brought to the Marshall line its raciest ancestor. Her father, John Markham, was one of those rogues who fill family cupboards with skeletons. As long as they are alive their families wish them dead, but as soon as they die the families abandon the bitten lip and other signs of suppressed indignation, begin to smile and then to chuckle, and end by taking a kind of perverse pride in their outrageous behavior.

Markham was a handsome, swashbuckling, fortune-hunting wolf of a man, who rather liked the Devil and had no fear of God. He kept tongues wagging in Virginia. Some said he had a bankrupt peerage, others swore he was Teach the Pirate, with the black beard shaved off to help him elude the hangman. He married a wealthy widow of the colony, ran through her fortune, and deserted her. Back to England he went, to incur the impotent fury of his kin by selling a small estate the family had owned since before the Conquest. Apparently his colonial dame died, whether of disease or chagrin or rage tradition does not say, for Markham next eloped with a seventeen-year-old girl in England and brought her back to Virginia with him. The family records do not show whether Elizabeth was the daughter of the Virginia widow or the English maiden, but in either case she bestowed the stormy blood of her father on the Marshalls.

Of the nine children of Elizabeth and John Marshall of The Forest, two became the ancestors of an extraordinary succession of distinguished men. One of these two was Colonel Thomas Marshall, whose fifteen children included Chief Justice John Marshall. The second was the Reverend William Marshall, great-great-grandfather of General of the Army George Catlett Marshall, Jr.

Since the soldier and the preacher were friends as well as brothers, and their families honored the tribal ties long after the degrees of kinship had reached those baffling intricacies of distance that only Southern aunts and grandmothers can trace without charts, the legends of each line are inextricably bound to those of the other, part of the whole bright fabric of family memory. As each new generation became aware of it, there was no careful disclaimer of ancestry that might be collateral, so long as it was Marshall.

Colonel Thomas Marshall, then—to take the collateral ancestry first—as a child went to school with George Washington to the Reverend Archibald Campbell in Westmoreland County. With the young man Washington, young Marshall surveyed some of the endless Fairfax lands. Again like the master of Mount Vernon, he was a colonel of the Virginia Militia, and a member of General Braddock's disastrous expedition.

Moving from Westmoreland to Fauquier County, he built Oak Hill, the plantation home which he gave later to his son the chief justice. He became high sheriff of the county, a member of the House of Burgesses, one of the Culpeper Minute Men in the Revolution, a member of the council which asserted Virginia's independence, was at Valley Forge, fought at Germantown, and commanded the 3d Virginia Regiment at Brandywine.

It was Colonel Thomas, also, who took the Marshall family to Kentucky. He was appointed, in 1780, as surveyor general of the lands beyond the mountains which Virginia had appropriated for her officers and soldiers in the Revolution, and in 1785 he brought his family out there, making the last part of the journey by flatboat down the Ohio. Leaving Oak Hill to John, Colonel Thomas built Buckpond in the new state, and settled down to politics and pioneering. Obviously, the Marshall pioneering was not the primitive, hard-scrabble process usually associated with clearing the forests and tilling new lands.

His son John wrote of the colonel that he was a greater man than any of his children, but the children had their points. Louis, for instance, the youngest son, who received Buckpond as a wedding gift in 1800, nearly lost his head in Paris for joining the revolutionary mob when the king's justice still could reach him. His brothers, John and James—the latter married Robert Morris' daughter Hester— saved him from execution by arranging diplomatic intervention. Early an agnostic and late a Presbyterian elder, Louis studied medicine in Edinburgh and Paris, had a school at Buckpond and became fourth president of Washington College, now Washington and Lee University. There he was the central figure around which eddied and whipped an academic storm provoked by his bizarre notions of relaxing student discipline. Worsted, he went back to Kentucky, where eventually he became president of Transylvania College. A strange, complex and erratic person, Louis bore all his life the scars of his many duels in France. Pistol shot as well as swordsman, he killed a man in a duel in Kentucky, and scornfully refused to shoot General Thomas Bodley in another. Yet his choice of profession was not the medicine he had studied, but teaching; and the piety of his later years led him to expound the Bible with great earnestness to his students. He became so obsessed with Biblical prophecy that he even fixed a date for the destruction of the world. And—strange complex for a Kentuckian—he had a notable and very vocal hatred of whisky.

His brother James, a captain in the Continental Army and son-in-law of the Philadelphia financier Robert Morris, ran against John Brown for Congress in 1790, and lost. The campaign nearly included a duel over Marshall's charge that Brown was plotting to deliver Kentucky to Spain, but his cousin and brother-in-law, Humphrey Marshall, by a ruse prevented the pistol-shooting satisfaction which Brown's younger brother demanded. In all probability Humphrey had provided the content of James's challenged statement, and so felt honor-bound to get his cousin out of the trouble he was in; for Humphrey certainly had no squeamish objections to settling an argument with pistols at twenty paces.

He was the son of John Marshall, brother of Colonel Thomas and the Reverend William, and he came out to live at Buckpond to take advantage of the educational opportunities offered by what amounted to a family school, in which all who knew anything were teachers for the others, and all were students as well.

Son of a younger son, Humphrey's early prospects were not exactly wealthy, but he got a four-thousand-acre grant for his Revolutionary Army services, and died one of Kentucky's greatest landholders, so rich he was rumored to measure his money by the peck like Ali Baba's wife. Humphrey scorned revealed religion, had what was most inadequately described as extreme candor, and no shred of tact. His words, spoken or written, cut like a stiletto. In spite of these things, or—Kentucky being Kentucky—because of them, he was elected senator. There he ruined his popularity by voting for the Jay Treaty of 1794 with Great Britain. When he came home, he narrowly escaped a ducking in the Kentucky River, and did get stoned out of Frankfort, as Alexander Hamilton was stoned in New York for speaking in the treaty's defense.

He suspected the motives of Aaron Burr when that gentleman took his charming and ambitious way through the Ohio Valley on his journey south with a dream of empire, and was instrumental in exposing him. Writing under the pseudonym, "Observer," in the *Western World*, Humphrey undertook, as part of his campaign against Burr, to lay bare the dealings of sundry Kentuckians with Spain. His articles drove Judge Benjamin Sebastian from the state's highest bench, and got Humphrey involved in a feuding series of lawsuits with Harry Innes that ended only when both men signed a public agreement to stop attacking each other. Already at odds with Henry Clay over the Burr business, Humphrey insulted Kentucky's favorite son on the subject of a resolution of Clay anent the wearing of homespun, and the two then crossed the Ohio at Louisville to settle the matter with an exchange of shots. Despite all this, Humphrey still found the time to write the first formal history of Kentucky.

His grandson, another Humphrey Marshall, was a graduate of West Point, a successful lawyer, and an influential Whig member of Congress who became President Fillmore's minister to China. Finding on his return to the United States that the Whigs had ceased to exist as a party during his absence in the Far East, he joined the Know-Nothings, went to Congress again, and in the Civil War became a brigadier general of the Confederate Army.

If the first Humphrey Marshall was at odds with Clay, it did not keep his cousin Thomas Alexander Marshall from marrying Clay's niece. This Marshall was another lawyer, who lived in Frankfort and then in Louisville, became a member of Congress, supreme judge of Kentucky, and a member of the Kentucky Court of Appeals for twenty-one years.

Such were some of the Marshalls whose life centered around Colonel Thomas and his wife Mary as they made their patriarchal progress from Westmoreland County to Oak Hill, then to Buckpond, and finally to The Hill, at Washington, Kentucky, the home of their son Thomas, a Revolutionary Army captain who was with his father at Valley Forge. The men of the family were so spectacular that little is said of the great colonel's wife, but she must have been a patient and winning and noble woman who deserved better of her descendants than the epitaph on her grave at The Hill—"Mary Randolph Keith. Born 1737. She was good, not brilliant, useful, not ornamental, and the mother of 15 children."

Leaving the collateral ancestors and cousins many times removed of the General of the Army, it is startling to find behind the "reverend" title of his great-great-grandfather William a youth who was a tall, graceful, dark-eyed, handsome rakehell who rode like a centaur, fought like a devil, played at cards and dice, danced divinely and drank like a gentleman—more than was good for him, but carrying his liquor well. A little startling, unless it be remembered that this was John Markham's grandson.

He was born at The Forest, and was married in 1766 to Mary Ann Pickett, a lass with a name already proud enough, and destined to achieve a tragic immortality at Gettysburg a century later. They were living with the other Marshalls in Fauquier County when the dashing William got religion. This was a period of extraordinary evangelical revival in America, and the eloquent appeals of the New Light preachers made a profound impression on young Marshall. He joined the Baptist Church, and within a short time was preaching himself, preaching so earnestly, with such a torrent of words and flashing of eyes and more than vigorous gesturing that the county people thought him demented, and locked him up for a madman. His brother the colonel got him freed, and he resumed his preaching, no less earnestly, but apparently in somewhat less spectacular fashion. In 1780 he took his family to Kentucky, where he lived for another twenty-nine years, becoming in that time an important, if rather careless, landholder. A year before his death he divided great tracts among his children, but they soon lost most of the land because the titles were defective. Only a few hundred acres remained to be divided by his will in 1809.

His son Martin, who began his seventy-six years of life in Fauquier County in 1777, was married in 1803 to Matilda Taliaferro. If the previous marriages of the Marshall clan left them unrelated to any of the first families of Virginia, the alliance with the Taliaferro name remedied the defect. Among others, it added to the Marshall veins a few drops of the blood of that most fabulous of colonial Virginia gentlemen, "King" Carter of Corotoman.

Matilda Taliaferro's husband appears to have been an altogether admirable and likable person, and one of the young men who read law in his office in Augusta, Kentucky, is warrant for the statement that unlike most of the Marshalls, he never talked about his ancestry.

"He was reticent and dignified," this former pupil wrote, "and at the same time he was courteous to others, and of gentle manners."

Martin studied law with Captain Thomas Marshall, brother of the chief justice, at Washington, Kentucky, and even if he did not dwell on the family glories in conversation, was the one child of the Reverend William Marshall who maintained a close and affectionate relationship with his Uncle Thomas' family, visiting them frequently, and bestowing their names on some of his own children. He was a successful lawyer, but preferred a simple and quiet life at home to the bitter frenzies of Kentucky politics. His one venture into public office was as a member of the state legislature in 1805 and 1806.

His son, William Champe Marshall, had more of a taste for public preferment. Born at Augusta in 1807, he was educated at Augusta College, the Methodist Church's original institution of higher learning, and then read law in his father's office. Six times a member of the Kentucky legislature, he was also a member of the state convention of 1849, and later commonwealth's attorney for Bracken County and mayor of Augusta. His wife Susan Myers, daughter of an Augusta merchant, bore him nine children. The fifth was given the name George Catlett.

It was a pleasant town in which George Catlett Marshall grew up. The mighty river swept westward below its high bank, making the harbor that gave Augusta importance as a shipping point for tobacco, and inland the bluegrass hills rolled away toward Lexington. There was leisure, and agreeable society, and a college to give the boys their formal learning. The section was rich in tradition—hadn't Simon Kenton once owned most of the land of the town?—and the Marshalls themselves were a part of that tradition, a thing that had considerable influence, making their place and their dignity in the community something beyond question.

But the peace and the old ways were rent by the war. William and Susan, like many of their neighbors, seem to have leaned strongly toward the Southern cause, but there were Marshalls on both sides, and theirs was not the only family with divided loyalties. Whatever their feelings in the matter, young George, seventeen or thereabouts, appears to have been pressed into the Federal Home Guards by Major (they called him Colonel, later) Joshua T. Bradford, who in a few years would be his uncle-in-law, but now commanded the Home Guards in Augusta and was a determined Union man. Still a schoolboy, George must have been one of that band of warriors young and aged, of various degrees of enthusiasm and reluctance, who fought for Bradford a notable battle against General Basil W. Duke and a detachment of Morgan's Cavalry.

The fight raged through the streets and buildings of Augusta, as Duke drove for a crossing of the Ohio and a raid on Cincinnati, and the redoubtable Bradford contested the way with his nondescript militia. Duke won the battle, and burned some of the buildings in doing it, not to mention sending the Federal gunboats at the landing scurrying for safety when he turned his guns on them; but the Morgan men had lost so many of their number taking Augusta that the general had to abandon his Cincinnati expedition and retire again into Kentucky.

When the war was over, George was able to complete his schooling, and then to start looking around for something to do for a living. His parents were hardly wealthy, and even a modest fortune would have been strained to give plenty to nine children. There was financial help for a start, but not to underwrite idleness.

In 1869 George visited his sister Elizabeth, who had married John Ewing and was living in Pittsburgh. There he became interested in the iron industry, and decided he would seek his fortune in the industrial hills of western Pennsylvania. By summer he had found a job with the Dunbar Iron Company, a pioneer concern in the region southeast of Pittsburgh where the great Connellsville vein gave the steel furnaces the world's finest coking coal. That vein of coal would give him, directly or indirectly, such wealth as he was to have.

II

A General Is Born

CHARACTER springs from hidden sources. Even those who concern themselves deliberately with its formation rarely chronicle their efforts. Moreover, and to a far greater extent than they know, they build unconsciously and without intent.

It is relatively easy to identify the chief sources: parents, teachers, clergymen. To touch the vanished essence of them with the mind is another matter. Even with such aids as letters and personal reminiscences, much has to be left to conjecture. Lacking these, one can only examine the character which resulted and surmise what must have been some of the influences that shaped it.

The impact of the lesser sources of what a man becomes—the forgotten or inaccurately remembered ancestors, the playmates, the unconscious heroes and unconscious villains of the piece the town is forever playing unaware before its children's eyes—is lost in hint and guesswork.

In a Pennsylvania coal town, during the last two decades of the nineteenth century, in an unbalanced social atmosphere which mixed piety with greed, rigid ethics with ruthless fortune-building, homely virtues with the purchase of European titles, cockfighting with Sunday school, something fixed inside the form of a boy those qualities of integrity, devotion, zeal, and selflessness that, accompanied by profound intelligence, mark such greatness as appears only once in several generations.

Many people had a part in molding the character of General Marshall; but two emerge, however nebulously, from the welter of legend, trivial fact, and doubtful anecdote as of greater importance than the others. One was the Reverend John R. Wightman, rector of St. Peter's Parish in Uniontown. The other was the General's mother, a woman of great reserve, uncommon serenity, and spiritual force.

It is astonishing how little is remembered of the Marshalls in the city where they lived for more than thirty years. That impression of Mrs. Marshall as a woman of great depth and strength is general, but the words and actions which created it are lost. Her close friends have left no firm record of what she said and did. Her children are themselves a record, but of the kind that satisfies a philosopher rather than a chronicler. It has already been remarked that the latest generation of Marshalls has abandoned the singing of tribal praises practiced by its forebears.

Laura Bradford was born in Augusta, and passed her childhood there, but she had been living for several years with her Aunt Eliza Stuart at Monongahela City, Pennsylvania, when she was married in 1873 to her childhood sweetheart, George Marshall. Mr. Marshall was, at twenty-eight, a prospering young man with a business of his own, and an established position in Uniontown's upper social stratum.

It was his friendship with A. W. Bliss which brought his decision to live in Uniontown when he first got his job with the Dunbar Iron Company. Bliss was his partner in the new Dunbar Manufacturing Company, which produced firebrick for the coke ovens. So close was the friendship that the first home of the newly married Marshalls was with the Blisses in the old Gilmore place in the West End.

Mrs. Marshall and Mrs. Bliss, who was old Judge Gilmore's daughter, soon developed a friendship as close as that of their husbands. But Laura discovered also, and happily, that the town had a number of families of means and congenial background who had welcomed her husband, and now welcomed her. As a handsome young bachelor, with easy graceful manners, impeccable dress, and a flow of small and great talk that managed to convey the impression he was well informed on any subject mentioned, Mr. Marshall had established a firm niche in the community to which he brought his bride.

Because he talked so much, there is a livelier memory of Mr. Marshall than of his wife in Uniontown. Even of him, however, the limning is not portrait but sketch, and superficial. If much of his talk was idle chatter, more of it was not, and the impression remains of a gregarious individual with little vanities, but also with considerable ability and probity who, like most of the Marshalls, usually knew what he was talking about.

The town and the country around it, of course, had an imponderable share in shaping the new lives that Mr. and Mrs. Marshall brought into them. It was a picturesque and romantic land, this Pennsylvania hill country, although its face already was changing, scarred by tipples and mills and smoke. Braddock's grave was near by. Fort Necessity had stood guard here. Albert Gallatin had lived in the county, and Coulon de Jumonville was a local legend.

The National Pike was the central thoroughfare. It had carried the wagon trains of land-hungry pioneers and the postriders toward the Ohio country and the prairies beyond when Main Street was Elbow Street and Uniontown was called Beeson's Town, where the first lots were sold at public auction on the very day the Declaration of Independence was signed in Philadelphia.

Even Dunbar Furnace had a history already old. Its great cast sugar kettles had been wagoned to the Youghiogheny and floated down the twisting rivers on flatboats and rafts to boil the sugar out of cane from Louisiana plantations long before the War.

But Marshall's past was not here. The past that Marshall remembered, the romance he talked about, was the past of Kentucky and Virginia; of the punctilious gallants in plum-colored coats with fine linen ruffled on their chests (they were paladins, and very devils with the ladies, and himself not least among them, in his telling); of the ladies in crinolines against Corinthian columns and pedimented doors with fanlights, with a speech as soft and warm as the southern sun; of blooded horses on the bluegrass meadows—all the swords-and-roses fantasy that Southerners have wrapped around the South since the forgotten reality ended and the legend began at Appomattox.

This was the past that Marshall talked of, but what he came seeking in Uniontown was the present and the future. A new romance was waiting for the man with wit to see its possibilities, and boldness to risk what he had for what he hoped to gain. The empire of slaves and tobacco and cotton was ended, the empire of wage slaves and steel beginning to take shape. That was what brought George Marshall to Pennsylvania, not the past but the future. The face of this land was changing, and he would help to change it more.

If already the beehive ovens were beginning to fill the air with smoke and lay their fine black film on everything, there would be more of them, and the atmosphere considerably darker, before this business was finished. There was money to be made, and the glowing mouths of a bank of coke ovens had a beauty no less alluring because it differed from the beauty of wisteria trailing from a gallery. Here was the coal for the finest coke, the Pittsburgh furnaces and mills had expanding appetites, and labor was plentiful and cheap. There were the Irish, who had come in with the railroad building; and the Welsh, who came to the mines; and now the land was beginning to see the rough fair men and their shawled women, with the round faces and the ready smiles and the Slavic names that twisted the tongue and struck strangely in the ear.

For three years, young Mr. Marshall worked for a salary at Dunbar Furnace, learning the needs and the ways of the growing business around him, gauging risks and chances, watching for opportunities. Then, in 1872, he and Bliss formed the partnership that was to last their lives.

The initial enterprise of Bliss and Marshall was establishment of the Dunbar Manufacturing Company, the first producer of firebrick set up in the Connellsville region to supply the builders of coke ovens. The young partners had made a first-rate start. They did more than just manufacture firebrick to meet a growing demand. After some careful study, they produced an improved beehive coke-oven design that rapidly became the standard type throughout the area. The twenty thousand dollars they invested began to pay well, and within a few years the little company was employing fifty or more men, and turning out four and a half million bricks a year.

Once embarked in a business of his own, Mr. Marshall waited only long enough to be reasonably sure it was a successful venture before he took a wife. Just one year after the firebrick company was established, he was married to Laura.

The old Gilmore place, where the Marshalls found temporary domicile with the Blisses, overlooked Uniontown from a hill beside the National Pike. The brick mansion had started life in simple, rectangular Georgian dignity, but assorted additions and remodelings in the Victorian Gothic manner had given it a disconcerting appearance of mixed frivolity and sobriety, like paint and patches and spit curls on the face of a Quaker grandmother.

The Marshalls soon moved from its vast, square, marble-manteled rooms to a hotel in the town, and then to the large but unpretentious brick house in the hollow at the foot of Main Street, with its green lawns separated from the Gilmore place only by the small waters of a stream with the unlovely name of Coal Lick Run.

The year that Mr. Marshall and Laura were married, the already prospering partnership of Bliss and Marshall began to expand its business interests, leasing the Frost Works, a mining and coking concern near Uniontown. They operated it on a leasehold until 1879, when Marshall bought it for the partnership at a sheriff's sale. To operate and expand it, they formed an additional partnership with Major A. B. de Saulles and Maurice Haley, calling it the Percy Mining Company. When it was incorporated later, Marshall became president and Bliss secretary of the company.

In 1879, too, Bliss and Marshall acquired the Oliphant Furnace, built about one hundred and fifty coke ovens, purchased some additional coal properties, developed and expanded the lot, and then resold to the H. C. Frick Company, which was beginning to collect the important properties in western Pennsylvania which would be the foundation of a huge steel empire.

Eleven years in Uniontown, and George Marshall was one of the city's important citizens. The old brick house on Main Street sheltered, in horsehair and walnut elegance softened by Morris chair comfort, a growing and happy family. There were tree-shaded green lawns side and back, and a gallery in the ell where George and Laura sat on summer evenings, while Stuart romped in copper-toed boots, and Marie played and prattled beside them. There had been another child, whose brief infancy was by now a softened grief and a tenderness which somehow touched each of the more lively hopes and anticipations centered around the expected arrival of Laura's fourth baby.

Mr. Marshall was not getting rich, like J. V. Thompson across the street, who was getting so big that one of these days he would get the badly mistaken idea he was big enough to challenge the icy, calculating Henry Clay Frick. It was fairly evident by 1880 that Mr. Marshall was not going to be one of the country's financial titans; there is, however, no shred of evidence he ever thought he would be, or even desired enormous wealth. A lot of the savor of a simple and satisfying life would have disappeared if Mr. Marshall had abandoned the Masons, Democratic politics, the church vestry, and the delightful, time-wasting, conversational foregathering of cronies in the hardware store and the drugstore up the street, in order to concentrate on rapacious fortune-building as some of his neighbors were doing.

Not only did Mr. Marshall spend something less than all his waking moments accumulating wealth, but there is evidence that he was apt to be hasty and careless when large investments were concerned. In small things he was not prodigal. Some even called him "tight." But the sweeping gesture, figuratively speaking, was part of his background, and sometimes he trapped himself, as when he signed a document in a transaction involving a hotel at Luray Caverns in Virginia with his personal signature instead of adding the "President" which would have made it a corporate responsibility. That mistake removed several thousand dollars from the Marshall accumulation when the hotel burned and there was a litigious snarl over insurance liabilities.

If his fortune never reached imposing proportions, he got a lot of

GEORGE CATLETT MARSHALL, Jr.
The future Chief of Staff at the age of two.

V.M.I. CADET OFFICERS

Cadet First Captain Marshall is seated third from the left in this group portrait of cadet officers in 1901.

compensation from busying himself with the meetings of his lodge of Free and Accepted Masons. He was High Priest of the Royal Arch Masons, and he looked forward to being Eminent Commander of the Knights Templar. There were the vestry meetings at St. Peter's, and the convocations of the Brotherhood of St. Andrew. Mr. Marshall was a "joiner." He had a good time, and so did his family. Their financial condition was that vaguely prosperous state comfortably described as "well-to-do."

His wife apparently was content for it to be that way. If in her quiet, reserved manner she was a steadier person than her husband, more careful of money, a better "manager," there is no evidence that she showed any impatience with his easier way. The values which meant most to her and guided her household were not measured in money.

The petty vanities of success were no part of her conduct. Sometimes she had a servant, but frequently she did not. She was a careful and successful housekeeper, and she enjoyed that role. A tender and warm-hearted mother, she nevertheless instilled in her children remarkable qualities of self-discipline, and got them into such a habit of constant cleanliness that it quite astonished her friends, and theirs. There was another, inner cleanliness not so easily seen and commented upon, and she gave them that, too.

Not quite a week after Christmas, Laura's last pregnancy brought her to bed, and on the last day of 1880 the expected infant arrived at the house in the hollow, to usher in a new year with his squawling. He did not look at all like a soldier, and they had no way to guess how famous he would make it when they decided to give him his father's name.

Five months and five days old, the baby was clothed in tucked and gathered yards of petticoat and dress adorned with featherstitching, embroidery and lace, and taken on June 5, 1881, to the little plastered brick church of St. Peter, with its tall lancet windows and truncated tower, where the spire had collapsed in a storm.

There, prompted by the Reverend Richard S. Smith, Laura herself and James A. Searight, as godparents, renounced in the infant's name the Devil and all his works, the vain pomp and glory of the world, with all covetous desires of the same, and the sinful desires of the flesh, so that he would not follow nor be led by them. They also undertook to see to it that the infant learned the Creed, the Lord's Prayer, the Ten Commandments and all other things which a Christian ought to know and believe to his soul's health, and when they thought him sufficiently instructed, to bring him to the bishop for confirmation. After prayers, Mr. Smith reached out and took the infant from his mother's arms.

"Name this child," he said.

"George Catlett," Laura replied firmly.

Mr. Smith repeated the name, fixing it to the child he held, in the name of the Trinity, with a touch of water from the font.

For all his bearing his father's name, young George was Laura Marshall's son in looks and temperament. As the years passed it became increasingly evident that he had his mother's reserve, her great dignity, her steadiness, the same profound moral integrity, tempered perhaps by some of his father's easy manner and that indefinable quality which gentlefolk call "presence."

Such qualities suggest a rather formidable and unpleasant child, which George was not. In retrospect, in the occasional anecdote, the qualities revealed themselves early, but in truth George had a completely unremarkable childhood. Fun loving and active, he went through the normal succession of sand pile, playing Indians, collecting stray dogs, reading Wild West yarns, fishing, hunting, playing hookey, making average and sometimes less-than-average grades in school.

Uniontown was an interesting place for an active youngster with an inquiring and restless mind. A boy could hardly grow up in a house that faced a section of the old National Pike, with what had been a famous tavern just across the street with its four steep-roofed and dormered sections marching primly up the hill, and not be filled with tales of the Conestoga wagons and the stagecoaches, and the famous men who came and went, and stopped for a meal or a night at the White Swan.

Behind the White Swan, now just the Brownfields' home and butchering establishment, George Gadd's father had a blacksmith shop, where the glowing forge, the ring of anvils, the shoeing of horses and tiring of wagon wheels presented an endless prospect of complete enchantment. There was the carriage shop the Llewellyns had, next the Marshalls and up the hill a bit; and beyond that, and back from the street, the ancient gambrel-roofed mill of the Beesons', its wheels turned by water from the race that angled a mile and a half across town from the dam on Redstone Creek.

Before he prowled and watched and posed endless questions in these fascinating places, small George played in the sandbox under the big locust tree in the low, pretty yard of the Thompson home just across the street. He played with Andy Thompson, who was as fair and handsome as George was pug-nosed, freckled, and sandy; and he played with Andy's brother John, a little darker, a little more imperious and inclined to bully. Another playmate was Mary Kate O'Bryon, the pretty dark child who later gave George the nickname that did not stick, Flicker. It was a comment on the color of his hair, and somewhat overstated.

Later, the Thompsons' swing was a treasure, but it nearly cost the nation a future Chief of Staff when George, giddy with delight at the long sweeping rush, decided a jump at the end of the glide would be more exciting still. He landed in the beans in the Thompsons' kitchen garden, but very nearly impaled himself on the pickets that divided the garden from the lawn. Fortunately, all that the fence actually collected was the seat of George's pants.

As he grew older, the town grew smaller, or so it seemed, and the number of playmates larger and larger. By the time that Coal Lick Run was a moat for a castle or a mud fort, by the time small boys were Indians lurking behind the trees in the Marshalls' back yard, George and Andy and Alex Mead, who was Mrs. Bliss's nephew and lived in the big house on the hill, were being joined by George Gadd, and Will Wood whose father was a saddler and lived near the Thompsons, and Frank Llewellyn whose father ran the carriage shop, and perhaps at times, to their dismay or pleasure depending on the mood that was on them, by Mary Kate, and Helen Houston.

When George was six he was sent, as his brother Stuart had been sent before him, to Miss Thompson's school on Church Street. Inside that prim little narrow house, beyond its tall and lugubrious door and shallow high-latticed stoop, was a whole new world, bewildering and fascinating, of letters and numbers and pious songs and mottoes, of blackboards and slates and pencils, with Miss Alcinda Thompson, as prim and proper as her house, giving perhaps inadequate but unquestionably genteel instruction to the children of those who were willing and able to pay for a certain amount of distinction from the public schools. First day was exciting, and not the least of its discoveries was a new and firm friend. Assigned to share a double desk with O'Neil Kennedy, small-boy George eyed his deskmate closely, and liked what he saw. Billy Ewing and Jim Conrad came into the circle, too, as it widened for the schoolboy. Jim's father was ticket agent at the railroad station, not far from Miss Thompson's school. His mother, a pretty woman whose affection was easily claimed by small boys, particularly if they were Jim's schoolmates, was related to the New England Bradfords, and she and Mrs. Marshall used to get involved in long genealogical speculations, trying to figure out whether they might be kin.

The Conrads were "boardinghouse people," and Jim accordingly spent a lot of his time at the Marshalls' and the Thompsons' and the Blisses'. The summerhouse on the Blisses' front lawn, down the slope from the house, was a vine-covered center of play for all the neighborhood boys and girls. The stone washhouse at the back of the Marshalls' yard, when not in use as a laundry, was strictly the boys' domain. The little stove cooked more than one meal of chubs caught in the run, with potatoes and apples baked in the oven.

In the winters, the children coasted on Main Street, down the hill in front of the White Swan, until old Natty Brownfield, thinking of the horses, would sprinkle ashes on its glazed surface, thereby acquiring all unconsciously a reputation among the youngsters as a mean and heartless old guy. Then the coasting would shift to Gilmore's Hill, and the reckless and the older children, sometimes their parents too, would take their sleds to Hospital Hill.

There were chores to be done, but the boys seem never to have been saddled with such responsibilities with any degree of regularity. There must have been some shoveling of snow, and certainly there were lawns to be mowed, but even this usually was done at the Marshalls' by Mr. Marshall himself, who also looked after his cow, and kept a garden, and liked to putter in the yard. Some of the inside chores did not exist to as great a degree in the Marshall home as in others, because the family got to taking many of its meals at a hotel.

They had a horse, Old Billy, which was kept at a livery stable in town. Old Billy and the phaeton were used principally by Mr. Marshall for business, or by the family for Sunday drives, but usually the Marshalls walked to do their shopping, walked to church, walked ordinarily to pay their calls. At any rate, possession of Old Billy added nothing in the way of chores.

After Fred Hallow came to work for Mr. and Mrs. Bliss, he used to come down to the Marshalls' each Saturday to give the house a thorough cleaning, and to mow the lawn for Mr. Marshall. To Fred, as to many of his race, time more often than not was something to spend, not to save, and Mr. Marshall would betray exasperation.

"Fred, goddammit, where've you been? I thought you were coming this morning!"

Fred would look in astonished reproach at Mr. Marshall.

"Why, it ain't one o'clock yet, sir."

"Well, I've got the mower all sharp and set for you. Get that lawn done!"

And Fred would start cutting the grass, moving along the bank above the Run, keeping a wary and suspicious eye on the thick grass near the water. Suddenly he would jump and yell, and Mr. Marshall would laugh and call, "Fred, what the hell you afraid of?" But George would obligingly kill the snake for him, and the mowing would start again.

George, in partnership with Andy Thompson, kept the usual small boys' menagerie. They kept it, for the most part, in the Thompsons' yard, and it created a mild neighborhood flurry on one occasion when the report spread that the boys had a caged wildcat in addition to their less objectionable pets. At home, George kept no pets except dogs; but at one time he had quite a collection of those, and he used to go over to Mrs. Brownfield's to ask for butcher's scraps to feed them. Following a rich collection of the kind one morning, he went back in the afternoon for more.

"Why, George!" Mrs. Brownfield was astonished. "I gave you a lot this morning. What did you do with them?"

"Oh," he replied with complete and unabashed candor, "Mother made hash out of those."

The menagerie gradually disappeared until, about the time that George and Andy had gone as far as Miss Thompson could take them and so were transferred to the public education system at Central School, a block or so away, they became interested in gamecocks.

It was, of course, a completely illegal interest, but it flourished nonetheless all through Pennsylvania. The small boys were not immune to the fever which brought the sports from Pittsburgh and other places to the hills around Uniontown, where they gathered with their kind to match their lean and ugly birds for respectable stakes at some remote cockpit on the mountain.

George and Andy kept their "fightin' chickens" at the Thompsons' more or less hidden out of sight, although their elders seem to have made no strong objections. Alex Mead was one of the incipient fancy, too, and Jap Shepler and a lot of the others. They started out with game bantams, but graduated to the bigger birds, many of them—considering the youngsters' average low scale of income—of a deplorable state of excellence. Sid Bieghly, the tinner's son, used to run their hatchery for them in the basement of his home. On one disastrous occasion George went over for an anticipatory inspection to find that Sid's small sister Katheryn, deciding that a hatching of fluffy chicks showed a regrettable lack of color sense in being uniformly yellow, had improved the situation with some of her father's leftover paints and killed the lot of them.

Fightin' chickens, although they were something of an obsession for a time, were not the only matters that concerned George in his teens. He read voraciously, the books in his father's library as well as books which lacked parental sanction. He had a bicycle, and would go pedaling out the National Pike with Alex Mead, Herb Bowman, and Ed Hustead. He made friends with the new rector, the Reverend John R. Wightman, who liked this serious boy and found his quick mind able to leap the years between them and meet in a real friendship. George spent many hours with Mr. Wightman at the parish house, or in long hikes through the wooded hills in the spring and fall, happy in an extraordinarily fine companionship, stimulated spiritually and intellectually by a man who had the wisdom not to condescend, and the wit to recognize the superb qualities that were taking shape in this snub-nosed youth.

And there was, of course, school. In retrospect, it is strange that George Marshall should have left behind in Uniontown a reputation of being "dumb" in school. The rector of St. Peter's appears to have recognized abilities that others overlooked. Those who knew him best would not tag him scholar, but they remembered a quick, facile, and subtle mind. George certainly never encountered any particular difficulty learning anything he was interested in learning. Yet the belief that he was less than bright in school lingered in Uniontown. It appears to have begun with his transfer from Miss Thompson's to Central. On that occasion, he was quizzed by the public school principal, and he fared rather badly; by some accounts, so badly that his father was furious and would not speak to George for three days. That examination, and the reputation it gave George, may well have been only a part of the half-amused, half-petulant tolerance those who never attended Miss Thompson's school displayed toward that institution, even decades after it had vanished. Perhaps George had been able to outthink Miss Thompson with some consistency, and needed a strong and quick mind to impose some discipline on his own strong and quick intelligence. Apparently he found it in Professor Lee Smith, the principal at Central. Many years later, George recalled that Smith had told him he needed a licking; but he described the old teacher as both kind and considerate.

However his studies in textbooks progressed, his interest in how to do things did not flag. George had badgered Mr. Gadd the blacksmith with requests until Gadd at last agreed to let the youngster help him put an iron tire on a wagon wheel. Thus it happened that one morning George started out, apparently dutifully bound for school, but once in the alley behind the White Swan ducked into Gadd's shop where he was soon deeply and blissfully engaged in the delightful business of blacksmithing. Unhappily, his older sister Marie passed by on her way to school, and discovered George playing hookey for the first time in his life. She threatened to tell Father, promptly carried out the threat, and George was thrashed. It probably was not the only licking he ever got, since Mr. Marshall was not a notably even-tempered man, but it is the only one indisputably on record.

George and his friends had no regular allowances, but got odd bits of change from their parents as they could wheedle it in the immemorial fashion. George spent a lot of his nickels at Crane's Store, buying licorice candy. He had a passion for licorice sticks. He doted on the taste, and the results were so beautifully suggestive of chewed tobacco.

He also spent some of his change on *Diamond Dick*, *Nick Carter*, and other thrillers, which added their stimulus to an already active imagination. George's ability to visualize completely any suggested or described situation was to become one of his most valuable assets as an Army officer, and it showed up early.

There was, for instance, the occasion of Jim Conrad's twelfth birthday, in November of 1892, when Mrs. Conrad hired a rig and took Jim, with George Marshall, Andy Thompson, and Billy Ewing, out to Olwein's at Chalk Hill for a chicken and waffle supper. While they were there, a storm came up—a magnificent, howling, mountain storm with whipping rain and plenty of lightning and thunder. It was nine o'clock before the weather cleared, and the party could start back toward Uniontown. They had gone about as far as the hollow by Sam Brown's when the boys began to speculate about what it was like in the old days.

"Just think," said Jim, "what it must have been like when the Indians were around here."

"Yeah, the settlers must have been scared stiff!" This was Andy joining in. "They'd have an awful time gettin' out, through these thick woods, with the Indians yelling, and shooting arrows at them! And the tomahawks and——"

He didn't get a chance to finish. George, sitting on the front seat, turned around and said:

"Aw, shut up! Wait until we get up to where we can see the lights!"

The reading of penny thrillers did more than stimulate George's imagination. It got him fired from the job of organ boy at St. Peter's. There is nothing in the parish records to show that George was paid for this work, which probably was just a duty imposed on a boy who was the son of a vestryman and a friend of the rector, and obviously of the right age to be organ boy. He could not sing, and so he could not put the family piety to work in the choir.

The old church in which the Marshall children were christened had been torn down, and a new stone church erected on the site, its chancel located with canonical correctness in an apse at the east end. George's labors were performed in a small arched room on the south of the chancel. The light in there was excellent, and the rich sonorities of the Episcopal liturgy penetrated the room with insufficient volume to divert attention from a book. So George would sit and read, keeping an ear more or less cocked for his cue to start the sweep on its methodical back-and-forth mission of feeding air to the pipes.

But *Nick Carter* was altogether too absorbing one Sunday morning. Miss Fanny Howell pressed the keys and got no quiver of a response; there was no accompaniment for the astonished voices of the boys, Lew Bell and his wife and daughter, and Effie Cooper—

none of them prepared to sing *a cappella* on no notice at all—and George was fired by Miss Howell. Worse, he was in disgrace at home.

The disgrace was lived down eventually, and Jim Conrad must have been a very sympathetic friend while it was still keen and smarting. Jim was organ boy at the Presbyterian Church.

Meantime, the years moved along in a pattern that did not change much, year in and year out—school and books and cycling; swimming in the pond at the county farm; gathering in the Blisses' summerhouse on the lawn for lemonade and cookies in the late afternoon. Stuart was away at the V.M.I., and young men with slick clean faces were calling on Marie, and escorting her to the Fall and Winter and Spring Assemblies. Alex and Jim went away to Kiskiminetas, Alex to make quite a reputation as an athlete, Jim to prepare for Princeton and the study of medicine, which he never practiced because he lost his hearing. George had never been an athlete, although he used to go down to Gilmore's Field below the Marshall home and watch the Amateurs—a highly questionable name—practice and play, and get the thrill of his life when Harry Wilhelm would let him carry his bats.

But George was intense and quick and active. He was lithe, and even at the awkward age he was never awkward. Mrs. Kennedy came one day to call on Mrs. Marshall, bringing a basket with jellies and a bottle of homemade wine, and with Ralph trudging at her heels. Ralph, at seven, was profoundly impressed by the ease with which George, at thirteen, made his escape when the callers found him in the drawing room with his mother. He smiled, said, "How do you do, Mrs. Kennedy?" turned to the smaller boy with, "Hello, Ralph, how are you?" and then, with no lost motion or hesitation, said to his mother and her guests, "If you will excuse me, I have something I've got to do." Exit gracefully, even if to go no farther than his room, the east back room upstairs, to loll on the big dark bed with its high headboard, or sink back in the Morris chair and reach for a book from the shelves. He always knew what he wanted to do, and he usually had the finesse to do it in a way that caused the least possible fuss.

The last year before he went away to school was 1896. Early in that year, on February 7, the instruction that his mother and Mr. Searight had promised an earlier rector was deemed sufficient by the clergyman who was George's close friend, and the Reverend Mr. Wightman presented George to the Right Reverend Cortlandt Whitehead, Bishop of Pittsburgh, for confirmation.

When George had reaffirmed the pledge of faith given by his godparents, and the bishop had asked in his behalf for the gifts of grace— the spirit of wisdom and understanding, the spirit of counsel and ghostly strength, the spirit of knowledge and true godliness—the youngster knelt at the chancel rail in St. Peter's, and the bishop placed his hands on the bowed head and declaimed the stately and beautiful prayer:

"Defend, O Lord, this thy child with thy heavenly grace; that he may continue thine for ever; and daily increase in thy Holy Spirit more and more. . . ."

That same year witnessed William Jennings Bryan's memorable effort to reach the White House and start the free coinage of silver. The arguments were as heated, the appeals as impassioned, in Uniontown as they were anywhere else in the country. The Marshalls were Democrats, and the party had its marching club in town, less numerous than the Republican club, but still numerous enough to make quite a show as they paraded, George among them, wearing broad-brimmed, silvered, campaign hats. The opposition parade sported hats of gold. Rallies were frequent, and so were the parades, and between them, or perhaps while waiting for the school bell to ring, the boys from all parts of the city would gather at the railroad station, swinging their feet over the edge of the platform, and argue the fate of the nation, the virtues of the candidates, and the issues of the campaign, with limited understanding perhaps but with uninhibited enthusiasm.

Another year, and George was sixteen, and ready for college.

Where to send him was no problem. The Marshalls had been going to the Virginia Military Institute since Uncle Tom, who had moved from Kentucky down to Vicksburg before the War, had sent his son Martin there in time for the youngster to fight alongside the other cadets at the Battle of New Market and help to establish the V.M.I.'s most cherished and honored tradition. Stuart already had gone there, graduating in 1894 and coming back to Uniontown to be head chemist at Dunbar Furnace. George would go there, too, and although he did not know it then, Uniontown would never be home again as it had been.

He came back in the holidays, of course, walking stiffly down Main Street in his gray uniform and forward tilting little garrison cap, eyes straight ahead of him, a ramrod in his back. He was there, in fact, when they painted Main Street's pavement red, white, and blue, and the 10th Pennsylvania Regiment came back from the war with Spain and paraded through the town, while the slim cadet stood on the sidewalk in a cheering throng, his heart pounding and his blood tingling, and knew at last beyond question that he would be a soldier. He came back once more, when he had been a soldier in the Philippines, bringing his lovely wife to visit his parents.

But for all that, Uniontown was no longer home. The old folks were realizing it, too. Stuart got married, and young Dr. Singer kept coming to see Marie until finally no one else came, and he took her off to Greensburg with him. George was graduated from the V.M.I. and got his commission, and married a girl from Lexington. Mr. and Mrs. Marshall decided the house was too big, and they would take an apartment in the Skyscraper up the hill on Main Street. It was a wrench to leave the house, and to dispose of all the things that were in it that could not go into an apartment.

Laura set herself to that task, as she had set herself to so many tasks through the years. Up through the house she moved, room by room, cleaning out the accumulations of thirty years of housekeeping, getting at last to the attic. There she picked up something from the floor. She looked at it for a moment, then put what she had found firmly in the pile of discards.

"I don't think," she said wryly, "that George will find much use for these again."

"But, Laura!" Mr. Marshall had followed her through the house, aghast at the firmness with which she disposed of things so carefully saved through the years.

"But, Laura! You have no sentiment!"

They were George's first boots.

III

From Rat to First Captain

Spring in the Valley of Virginia, and a night without a moon. In the gloom of the First Stoop, a tall figure appeared silently at a silently opened door and stood motionless a moment.

In the starlight the form of the forlorn Rat stuck with sentry duty was faintly visible, walking stiffly down the far side of the quadrangle. No murmur came from any part of the darkened barracks. Taps had sounded, and the night had closed in. For the moment, at least, there was no hint of a bed-check inspection.

A mere dark wraith of movement, and the figure on the stoop had vanished. A moment later, from a window of the same room, it dropped quietly to the ground beside the outer east wall of the barracks. A quick glance to make certain no one had strayed, completely against all likelihood, to this deserted sector, and a tall, broad-shouldered, slim-hipped cadet walked quickly away from the building down the slope a little way, then swung right, circling the hill, hugging the deep shadows of the Mess Hall and Jackson Memorial Hall, avoiding the parade ground and the possibility of late-strolling faculty officers, striding through the dew-wet grass below the parapet, making for the vicinity of the Limit Gate. Cadet First Captain Marshall was "running the block."

Physically, it was simple enough to run the block, or break barracks. The single sentry inside the quadrangle could be eluded without difficulty, and even if he saw the offender he was expected, by time-honored custom of the Corps, to look the other way. The psychological hazards, however, were considerable. Not the least was the deliberate flouting of regulations by one whose schooling had stressed the regard of regulations, whose every hour was rigidly charted and sternly disciplined. In Marshall's case the offense was graver, because as First Captain he was primarily responsible for discipline in the entire Corps. There was, in addition, the knowledge that an inspection might be ordered at any moment; that it most certainly would be ordered at the first suspicion that any cadet was absent from his quarters without leave.

Caught running the block, Marshall would have been "busted." The chevrons which all but covered his sleeve from shoulder to elbow would be given to someone else, and the erstwhile First Captain would become a mere private in the ranks. Since that topmost rank in the Corps had been the one distinction he coveted, the blow would be a terrible one. Marshall calculated the risk, and took it. The lure was greater, and the reward for success a song in the heart and a hint of bliss.

For George was in love. It was first love, and it was for keeps. His goal this night was the quaint little green and white house on the lower side of Letcher Avenue, just outside the Limit Gate.

Every minute he was away increased the danger that he might be caught, but to whispered protest he could return murmured assurance. He would return to safety over the same route with no greater risk than when he came. Even if an inspection were started, Nick or Buster Peyton would get past the sentry and dash across the parade ground to shout a warning in time for him to be back in his room before the guard reached it.

Nevertheless, and all too soon, the moment came when Lily's protest was final. A last kiss, and he was gone, warily until he was once again inside the grounds, then boldly skirting the hill and regaining his quarters through the window, waiting open.

Inside, his roomates relaxed in relief that Pug's latest escapade was undiscovered, like the earlier ones, and in their relief called him fool and other uncomplimentary titles; but the words were just an unsuccessful effort to conceal the fact they loved him the more for what he had done. If Nicholson suggested he was making an ass of himself, or Peyton thought he could see Lily often enough without inviting reduction in rank, Pug Marshall knew they both were wrong. Furthermore, they knew it, too.

It had been almost four years since George, a Virginian come home despite a faintly alien air and a speech slightly harshened by the family's prospering exile, had seen for the first time the somewhat theatrical, crenelated, and turreted cluster of buildings, like a less than handsome castle on a hill, which was the Virginia Military Institute.

He had come through the Limit Gate, along the parapet and beside the parade ground to the barracks. He had walked through the sally port and, once inside, he became Rat Marshall, destined to suffer through Fourth Class year with his brother Rats, to learn the pride of the Baby Corps under the Stars and Bars at New Market, to feel his heart pound when a band played "Dixie," to discover the cadenced exaltation of disciplined ranks in close order on the parade ground, and to dream of a puritanical genius with a full black beard.

The constant verities maintained before the eyes and minds of the young men committed to the instruction of the V.M.I. are honor and devotion. Those who wish may read integrity for honor, but the old name still is current in a school which cherishes tradition, and it still suffices; what is meant does not change with the tag. As the instruments of maintenance, two things far outshine all others: the memory of the Baby Corps, the memory of Thomas Jonathan Jackson.

The pride in these is an intense and flaming cult, inculcated by the authorities, embraced with fervor by the cadets. It has a ceremonial aspect amounting almost to a liturgy, and is no mere vanity. Education, wrote Herbert Spencer, has for its object the formation of character. If most of the job has been done before a young man reaches college, it remains for the college to give the character spark, purpose, direction. To accomplish this, it is no hindrance that a youth knows with solemn exultation that he is a member of a Corps which once marched out as boys to make the sacrifice of men in battle; or that this Corps, these grounds, held the affection and knew for ten years the presence of a devout and righteous man whose superb talents were placed without question or hesitation at the service of a loyalty beyond self.

Stonewall Jackson! Manassas, the campaigns of the Valley, the Seven Days' Battle, Cedar Mountain, second Manassas, Harper's Ferry, Antietam, triumph and tragic death before Chancellorsville in the Wilderness—these the Corps studied and knew, as all military students must or count themselves no soldiers. But it was not just a military genius the V.M.I. held before its men and sealed in their hearts if it could; it was not even primarily a soldier. It was a desperately earnest, fanatically righteous, unflinchingly straightforward man, more deeply religious than even the noble Lee. It was the memory of an exalted quality of heart, a splendid ideal and practice of service, an attitude toward mankind and toward life reflected by the astonishing fact that, when just after the War between the States public subscriptions were asked for a monument to this Confederate general, the first came from a Negro Baptist congregation in Lexington for whom he had labored unobtrusively for a decade before the war which ended slavery. In the classroom, Jackson had been no great teacher; but he had taught in other ways, and he still teaches on the hill in Lexington.

Rat Marshall was a late arrival that September of 1897, and so he was directed, not to the topmost Fourth Stoop where Rats belonged and would rather be, but to Room 88 on the Third Stoop, which was taking some of the overflow of the largest Fourth Class in the school's history. It was next to the last room on the stoop, and it placed its Rat occupants at a decided tactical disadvantage: they had to risk the bloodthirsty whims of a good part of the Third Class to reach the relative security of their own quarters. They ran a gantlet, so to speak, every time they left their room or returned to it.

Three wary-eyed youths already occupied No. 88 when Marshall pushed open the door. John Gillum, near in age to Marshall, came from Rockville, Indiana. A second cadet, who came from New

Jersey, was older than his roommates and shocked them with his easy obscenities. The third was Leonard Nicholson, small and pleasant and friendly, whose home was in New Orleans.

Of the three, it was Nicholson who became Marshall's firm friend. They were to be roommates for four years, and in all that close association no fight or even small misunderstanding marred their comradeship. Gillum remained at the V.M.I. less than two years, the youth from New Jersey less than two months. The relationship with Gillum was amiable but without spark; that with the other an open antagonism. This cadet was bitterly unhappy. He hated the V.M.I., hated it for a damned prison, cursed the food, ridiculed the quarters, resented the discipline, blasphemed the traditions, and deliberately employed unsuspected resources of harsh manners and foul speech to punish his roommates. They gave him back a full measure of undisguised hatred, disgust, and contempt.

Between Marshall and Nicholson, however, the one reserved and intense and lashed by ambition, the other amiable and uncomplicated and unimpressed, there was from the start that unspoken recognition of kinship which fortunate young men know, a tie not of ideas but of understanding and deep instinctive attraction and loyalty. In their Third Class year it was enlarged to include Buster Peyton, a handsome and brilliant Virginian destined like Marshall to be a soldier, although at school he had no such intention.

There was much to be learned those first days, before the three upper classes returned to the hill, and while the tailors were getting the uniforms ready. There was more to be learned after the upper classmen returned, particularly concerning the very lowly position of Rats, and the sickening crack of a ramrod on the knuckles for a Rat who forgot to "fin out."

The entire school was busy getting ready for the trip to the Nashville Centennial Exposition in October; but there still was time for the Third Classmen to inflict on the Rats the regime of indignity from which they had themselves emerged so recently. The sadistic whimsy of hazing was sometimes brutal, and even when it did not take the form of individual torture it was a calculated process of constant harassment and shock, inevitably suggesting to the Fourth Class that the name "Rat" was a bitterly ironic overstatement of their miserably sunken place in the scale of animal life.

Forbidden by the Institute authorities under penalty of expulsion, hazing flourished nonetheless as a part, and the least easily defended part, of that hardening process by which the new cadet became in spiritual reality a member of a Corps which was a true unit, and ultimately once more an individual more sure of his individuality. At first only by force could he be made to function as one of a group; the discipline was imposed. By means not always subtle, the man whose mettle was fit for tempering grew from control to self-control, until in the end he imposed by his own desire those restraints upon himself which he could hardly brook when he first encountered them.

For all that, and moreover for all that it exists at all schools in all lands, the physical brutality which is the most obvious form of hazing is a savage thing and frequently dangerous. There was one particularly dangerous form employed by upperclassmen at the V.M.I., and only luck or a watchful providence preserved Rat Marshall from the indicated possible destination of "sitting on infinity."

For this devilishly ingenious tableau, a bayonet was placed on the floor, point up. Rat Marshall then was directed to squat over it, and it was up to him to keep the sharp point of the waiting weapon from contact with his posterior as long as his Third Class tormentor chose to keep him there. The inevitable fatigue crept up, and he sagged.

The bayonet gashed its victim, there was a spurt of blood, and a thoroughly frightened second-year man entered upon the terror of waiting for his expulsion from school as Rat Marshall limped off to find the post surgeon—the "gim." In this case, however, there was no expulsion. Rat Marshall refused to be an informer.

The "gim" found a superficial wound, but it was a near thing. Had the course of the bayonet varied by so much as one inch, it would almost certainly have been fatal. Because Marshall would not make a report, there is no record of the incident at the Institute, although it is probably the explanation of an entry in Marshall's file which shows that on September 24, 1897, Cadet Marshall was excused from duty, and that for three days following he was excused from ranks. The victimized Rat, of course, won the regard of the Corps for his silence. There was a more tangible result, as well: a chastened collection of upper classmen declared an armistice which exempted all the occupants of No. 88 from any hazing for the remainder of their Fourth Class year.

By October 10, Marshall was marching with the rest of the Corps at sundown to board "one of the Chesapeake and Ohio's magnificent vestibuled trains" for the trip to Nashville. The train, bedecked with lettered bunting which proclaimed to depot loafers along the route that it carried the "Cadets of the Virginia Military Institute" in its six cars, reached Nashville twenty-four hours later.

From the station, the Corps marched over the mud-coated granite cobbles of Broad Street to the Military Café on the exposition grounds, and then to the tent camp already set up for them. Within a half-hour the details were made, the sentinels posted, and most of the cadets were free to explore the wonders of the show, from the lath and plaster reproduction of the Parthenon, to the Casino and its chorus of bosomy beauties.

To give the trip more of a holiday aspect, taps was moved up to midnight, and reveille to seven. Breakfast was at eight and then, after guard mount at nine, the cadets were mostly free until dinner at three in the afternoon. Having crammed their interiors full of heavy food, they changed into the tailless coatees, crossed belts and shakos for dress parade at four o'clock. Since it was October in Nashville, they paraded that week either in rain and mud, or in a blazing sun like nothing the Shenandoah Valley knew.

All things considered, the first parade went off fairly well. There were some mishaps and uncertainties. Some of the older cadets, feeling quite grown-up and devilish, had been doing some surreptitious drinking, and appeared to experience considerable difficulty keeping their plumed or pompom-ed shakos on their heads. And Colonel Price, the commandant, brought a most unmilitary roar of laughter from the assembling Corps by falling off his horse.

But the formations were drawn up with commendable promptness nonetheless, and the five companies paraded before the admiring throngs, each cadet wondering if the girls were properly impressed, while a particularly critical audience—the officers and men of the 3d Cavalry, United States Army—praised the snap and precision of their rhythmic gray-clad ranks. Even the thirty-day Rats, Marshall and Nicholson included, reflected creditably the intensive close order drill they had been getting in preparation for the trip.

On the next day the Corps in full dress marched to the station and back again as guard of honor to a visiting governor. The usual film of black mud covered the streets, but the sun was out with midsummer force as the five companies stood rigidly at present arms outside the New York Building, mentally cursing the governor and the endless parade of carriages bringing notables to his reception. Straight and romantic and silent they stood, and three of them fainted from the heat. The band played "Dixie."

There was action and excitement, with blank cartridge fire and rebel yells, when the cadets took the part of Pickett's men against the regulars of the 3d Cavalry in a sham battle, re-enacting Gettysburg. But all such things cut into free time and fun, as did Colonel Price's discovery of a display of new ordnance. That was a heaven-sent classroom opportunity, and to the extreme annoyance of several hundred young men who would rather have been somewhere else, the colonel insisted on using it as such.

The expedition ended at last, and on Saturday, eight days after they had started out, the cadets marched once more through the Limit Gate and back to their barracks. Once more, the bare walls of No. 88 enclosed the room's ill-assorted inhabitants. The guns went back in the rack, the fine new Springfields the Institute had acquired the year before. Pug Marshall's was spotted easily. He had paid Sergeant Wolf two dollars and a half to give its walnut stock the fine lustrous polish that only the old Regular Army noncom knew how to put on, and that only cadets seriously bucking for military preferment bothered to buy.

Clothes went back on the shelves—no luggage in the room. No

pictures on the walls, either. Just the big square study table, the cots, the few hard straight chairs, the gunrack, the washstands and basins and buckets, the neat shelves, the neat or otherwise cadets.

Marshall was clean. No crust of dirt and soap curds in his washbowl to vie with others in the perennial contest of the Institute for the most heavily encrusted container. His speech was clean, too, and his mind and heart full of serious and lofty purpose.

Nicholson was a drawling and easygoing Southerner, as unconvinced as anyone could be that there was anything real and earnest about the whole business, unimpressed by the forms or by authority, conforming but not ambitious. If Marshall was a model of military neatness, headed for military distinction in the Corps, Nicholson was a "slack" private, to remain a private for four years, one of that group—slack, sloppy, and slimy—who took a perverse pride in seeing how much they could get away with in untidy appearance. But he had intelligence, breeding, and manners, and despite his family's wealth and prominence, no more trace of snobbery than Marshall had.

One day was very like all other days at the V.M.I. Reveille sounded at 6:20 A.M., and the cadets had five minutes to fall in. That explains why they slept in their underclothes, and may explain why there was never a shirt worn under the blouse. The starched white line that showed above the stiff braided collar of the blouse was simply a buttoned-in band.

Following roll call, the cadets came back to their rooms to finish dressing, and get down to the mess hall for breakfast at 7:00. After breakfast the rooms were policed, and classes began at 8:00. They continued, with a break for dinner, until 4:00 o'clock, and after classes the Corps fell in for an hour of drill. There was a period then of fifteen or twenty minutes to shift into coatee, shine shoes, put on the crossed belts, breastplate, polished buckles, and leather cartridge box for dress parade before supper. After supper, there was free time for a half to three-quarters of an hour before the study period began at 7:00. Taps were sounded at 10:00.

On Saturday, classes ran only until 1:00 P.M., and the cadets were not required to have dinner that day in the mess hall, but could fall out and go into downtown Lexington if they wished, getting back to the hill for dress parade at 5:00. It was their one opportunity to go downtown during the week, but that was no great restriction. The business section of a sleepy village offered little except the opportunity for simple and necessary purchases.

Sunday there was neither class nor drill, but the entire Corps was required to attend church services in the morning. Cadets might go with their own companies, which attended the town's four churches in rotation; or they could attend the church of their choice, falling in with the company which was taking its turn at the chosen house of worship that morning. This matter of choice was not always based, as intended, on faith and traditional communion. Matters having nothing to do with reverence sometimes dictated the choice. If the object was to get home as quickly as possible after the service, the Methodist Church was favored, being closest. The Baptists got the attention of an increment of cadets who elected to enjoy the shouting of a brimstone and sulphur sermon. The theological dialectics of the Presbyterian Church attracted those who chose to listen to "pompous preaching," and the Episcopal service drew the fatigue detail.

"If you were tired, you went to the Episcopal Church," one classmate of Marshall recalled. "Old Whistling Mac, the rector, had a lisp, and he could put anybody to sleep. George used to sleep with the rest of us on the cushioned pews."

With many cadets, of course, a more compelling reason than any of these was the presence at one of the churches of a Lexington belle who held, in pledge for the moment, a cadet heart.

After church, and after dinner, the cadets could spend two hours as they chose—that is, if they chose not to go downtown. East Lexington and the residential portions of the town were open to them, but the cadet discovered in the business district on Sunday afternoon was in an unhappy position.

The caste of classes was rigid, elaborate, and carefully defined at the V.M.I., but no other caste was recognized. Each man suffered as a Rat, inflicted suffering as a Third Classman, swaggered as a Second Classman, and if he lasted to reach the giddy eminence of the First Class, luxuriated—relatively speaking—in certain traditional privileges, such as the right to stay away from breakfast if he wanted to, imposing on some Rat the duty of bringing him a slice of cold corn bread and a bottle of coffee, concealed under a Rat blouse. A First Classman also had quarters on the First Stoop, which meant that he had the shortest distance to travel to fall in at reveille, and the easiest route to run the block.

Even for Rats, all was not sternness and discipline at the V.M.I. There was, for instance, nothing stern about a Molly Hole. Beneath a loosened floor board were hoarded such delicacies as might be sent in boxes from home, or bought in the sutler's shop with the limited money allowance. One birthday present received by Pug Marshall from Uniontown provided the material for a whole succession of secret feasts. His parents sent him a case of canned pork and beans, which he loved only slightly less than licorice sticks, and Marshall, Nicholson, and Peyton promptly concealed the cans in the Molly Hole. After taps, a prearranged signal tapped on the radiator pipes would bring the chosen few sneaking in surreptitiously through the darkness. A couple of cans would be extracted from beneath the floor and heated on the radiator, and then the cadets, whispering and snickering in the blackout, would attack a repast which had a savor Lucullus never discovered.

The most prized of such dainties in Marshall's Rat year were the oysters sent to John Fleming from Portsmouth. Fleming's father packed them in an ice cream freezer and sent them up by special express. Unhappily for Rat Fleming, they were of a perishable nature which could not be subjected to Molly Hole concealment, and a horde of hungry brother Rats descended on the hapless son of the sea-food dealer as soon as another freezer arrived. Fleming seldom got more than two or three oysters himself.

At the sutler's shop the cadets could buy candy, and wiener sausages, and occasionally fried rabbit. They could also purchase tobacco, and Marshall and Nicholson, self-consciously seeking the reflective pleasures of smoke, sent off to a famous dealer for extravagantly fancy pipes, silver-mounted, with amber stems. They would puff at these, enjoying their aromatic contribution to relaxed good fellowship, in that brief interval of free time between supper and studies. In their own room, Pug would strum not too expertly on a mandolin, accompanying the baritone of Buster Peyton and the voices of others who drifted in for songs and talk.

Vacation was strictly a summer phenomenon at the V.M.I., and the rest of the year knew no extended holidays. Thanksgiving, Christmas, Lee's Birthday, New Year's Day—these were days of special liberty, but additional holiday time neither preceded nor followed them.

On one of these rare holidays, Marshall tackled his classmates just after breakfast, proposing that the day be used for a hike. The top of House Mountain, the peculiar, flattened eminence like a verdant mesa which was the most noticeable feature of the landscape around Lexington, would be the goal, and they were to be back in time for dress parade. He was persuasive, but even so, only two of his classmates accepted the challenge. One was Nicholson, who for once and remarkably had no demerits to walk off; and Rooster Johnson also agreed to go along.

Once well started, Pug unfolded the rest of his plan, which was to determine whether the long hike could be accomplished in the regulation infantry step and marching cadence without stopping a single time for any cause whatever until the round trip had been completed. He was faced with mutiny at once, but kept his companions marching, and refused to be softened by their first protest or by the increasingly sarcastic and bitter protests as the hike proceeded.

The trip was completed, and on the basis laid down by Marshall, but seldom have six human feet displayed such a collection of blisters as those possessed by Cadets Nicholson, Johnson, and Marshall by the time they strode back through the Limit Gate that afternoon. Nicholson and Johnson "rode the gim" for a week, but Marshall, disdaining to see the surgeon, took his blistered feet to every formation with neither limp nor murmur.

The most solemn ceremonial day at the V.M.I. was May 15, the anniversary of the Battle of New Market in 1864, during Grant's Wilderness campaign. After a forced march up the Valley from Lexington, the cadets with the 62d Virginia Regiment, C.S.A., had held the center of the line, and had participated, with heavy losses, in an attack that forced General Sigel to withdraw his Union forces back across the Shenandoah River.

Ten cadets had been killed or mortally wounded in that engagement, and every year since, the name of each had been called at every roll call on the anniversary of the battle. When the name of one of the dead of the Baby Corps (they ranged in age from fifteen to twenty-four, those cadets) was called, one of his successors in the Corps stepped forward, saluted, and replied:

"Died on the field of honor!"

This began at first call, and was repeated at every formation through the day. The muster roll of the battle dead was not all, however. The occasion always was marked by oratory, usually dull, and then there was a dress parade before the spot where some of the ten lay buried on the grounds of the Institute. For some years their bones have rested in a common grave beneath a monument sculped by one of the Baby Corps, but in Marshall's day there were separate graves in a small cemetery. As the Corps presented arms, each member of the First Class stepped from his place, took a red rose from a bouquet, and placed it on one of the graves. Then came a salute of eight minute guns, and after the battalion fired three volleys, a bugler sounded taps.

This legend of heroism, and the proud and ceremonial memory kept alive at the V.M.I., made a tremendous impression on Cadet Marshall. His cousin, Martin Marshall, had been a member of the Baby Corps, and wounded at New Market. It was not, however, the fact of a cousin at New Market, nor the annual ceremony for those

> Sleeping but glorious
> Dead in fame's portal
> Dead but victorious,
> Dead, but immortal

which gripped the sixteen-year-old Rat Marshall. It was the blazing vision of glory, caught by an imagination which grasped and understood the courage and endurance that made the march up the Valley from Lexington to the crossroads village in Massanutten's shadow, the proud, elated understanding that even a Baby Corps—which, be it said, although tender in years was hardly composed of such babes as legend remembers—could fight with superb skill and drive, could maintain unbroken the quick and lively and unquestioning discipline without which there can be no victory.

This cadet was a soldier in the making. All the romantic trappings of military appearance at the Institute were less to him than this one brief fact of actual soldiering. He was, for four years, a member of a corps which not only had produced soldiers, but once as a Corps had *been* soldiers. It was a kinship, and he claimed it immediately and made it his own. Long before his first experience as a Rat of the May 15 ceremonies, he had crammed into his eager mind every scrap of information that survived of the Battle of New Market, and of the Corps' part in it. It was a lesser thing to most of his fellows, however proud they might be, however their eyes might well with tears at the muster roll and the dress parade, however their throats might choke with sentiment when taps were sounded over the moldering bones of heroes. How much it meant to Rat Marshall, his companions in No. 88 discovered after supper the evening of May 15, 1898.

Back in the room, Marshall diagramed the positions of the V.M.I. cadets and of all the other troops engaged on both sides, and proceeded to expound every maneuver of the battle to his roommates, who were first astounded, then aghast, then dismayed. But they could not escape. For days Marshall lectured them, trapped them into argument, interrupted their studies, hounded them so with his lore of history and tactics that for years afterward the mere mention of "New Market" was enough to make any one of them look furtively around for a route of flight.

Each summer, except that of 1900 when it was dispensed with because the previous autumn's typhoid outbreak had interrupted school for six weeks and extended the term by half that long into the summer, the cadets moved out of their barracks and spent two weeks in tents just down the hill from their own parade ground. This was the summer encampment, complete with target practice, company exercises, and sham battles. There being then no horses at the V.M.I., the Rats were pressed into service as artillery nags, dragging the guns into position. Marshall seemed to thrive in camp, probably because it was another approach to realism, but most of the cadets were inclined to take a jaundiced view of rain, mud, and assorted discomforts within sight of the barracks.

The extent to which a military college fosters militarism is indicated by the fact that, of one hundred twenty-two youngsters who started the Class of 1901 at the V.M.I., six became professional soldiers. When a man born for military leadership appeared, however, the Institute was ready with meat for him to feed on; he waxed able on it, and strong.

He thrived, did Marshall, throughout his four years at the V.M.I. When, in their First Class year, Pug Marshall became interested in football and went to the training table for his meals, Nicholson first entertained the ungenerous suspicion that the explanation was to be found in the better food supplied to the stalwarts of the playing fields. The suspicion was routed rapidly, however, in the remembrance that unlike Nicholson, Marshall had never found the Institute's generally lamentable food a distress.

Whatever the reason for it, Marshall's belated entry into team athletics was accompanied by brilliant success. With a fifty-yard run for a touchdown, he helped incite riot on November 17, 1900. The V.M.I. on that date trounced its next-door neighbor, Washington and Lee University, 40 to 0, and by the time the game was over, the cadets and the "minks" of Lexington's two campuses were viciously and pugnaciously unfriends. The town got a thoroughgoing demonstration of just how ungentlemanly young gentlemen can be on occasion.

The real glory, however, came from the Thanksgiving Day game with Virginia Polytechnic Institute at Roanoke, before a crowd of five thousand. The 5-to-0 victory over V.P.I. made the V.M.I. eleven state champions, and the reception they got when their train reached Lexington Friday evening was the kind reserved for kings and heroes, the entire Corps meeting them with cheers, half the young ladies in town at the station or lining the route to the Limit Gate, and a procession in carriages lighted by skyrockets and Roman candles.

The word of Marshall's prowess at left tackle had preceded him, and he found himself one of the idols of the Corps. Then, for all to read, came the report in the next issue of the Rockbridge *County News:*

". . . The tackling of G. Marshall in breaking up the interference was of the highest order, and a prominent University of Virginia athletic man said he was the best tackle in the South. . . ."

Then back to calculus, to tactics and field fortifications, to descriptive geometry, ordnance and gunnery, analytical mechanics, English and languages, to drill and guard mount and parade, to the business of completing this year with no demerits to spoil a perfect record.

For George Marshall accomplished the miracle of completing a four-year course at the V.M.I. without a single demerit. The most prolific single source of demerits for any cadet, of course, was the condition of his room when he happened to be room orderly. How Marshall managed to clear Rat year without any marks against him is hidden, but probably had to do with fanatically thorough and careful work. How he survived the rest of the course without room demerits is no mystery at all—he made a deal.

Beginning with their Third Class year, Marshall and Nicholson and Philip B. Peyton were roommates. Marshall and Peyton wanted cadet rank. Nicholson wanted as little work as possible. Thus it came about that, for three years, the name of L. Nicholson was posted every single week as the orderly of their room. Marshall and Peyton swept the room every morning, rolled and stacked the mattresses, folded the cots, saw that everything was clean and in its proper place—beds, chairs, tables, buckets, books, guns, clothing, accouterments. Nicholson did not turn his hand to do so much as flick away a fluff of dust; but if the room received demerits for any failure, Nicholson took them, and walked them off on penalty tour, one hour of sentry fashion marching with a rifle on his shoulder for each five demerits.

All of this was behind Marshall the morning of June 26, 1901, as the rolling, ponderous phrases of Judge Saunders rumbled through Jackson Memorial Hall, beating on the eardrums of the rigid cadets and their proud families, swirling in the still hot air heavy with the promise of storm, gilding the lily of Stonewall Jackson's memory with all the stately romantic flourishes that a Southern orator and gentleman deemed appropriate to an important occasion.

Old General Shipp already had handed out the diplomas to thirty-four cadets of the one-hundred twenty-two who had started the course four years earlier. They had, he averred, been zealous, faithful, and efficient in the performance of their academic and military duties. They had been a good class.

Cadet Charles Summerville Roller, Jr., sometime second-color sergeant and quartermaster, graduated fifth in his class, had delivered the valedictory by nomination of his classmates. He had done it with something less than the masterful assurance that Captain Roller displayed on the football field, something less than the glib facility that Editor Roller paraded in the pages of the *Bomb*. Valedictorian Roller was a little stiff and self-conscious about the discipline and training of the V.M.I. as an aid to a life of accomplishment and good citizenship. Still and all, it was a good speech, and in the accepted tradition of valedictories. Now it was Judge Saunders' turn.

". . . When the great captain died, thousands wept over the grave where genius and goodness and valor slept with him. . . ."

Nobody expected anything new to be said about Jackson, not after forty years. The Jackson-Hope medals, as prized as the diplomas themselves, had to be presented, and the judge was presenting them this year to Cadets St. Julien Ravenel Marshall, graduated first in his class, and Robinson Moncure, graduated second.

No, it was not expected of Judge Saunders that he say anything new about Jackson. Every cadet already knew more than he could have told them, and those of their families and guests who did not know, also did not care. It was just that the forms must be observed, and particularly that at the V.M.I. the forms concerning Jackson must be observed. Least of all did anyone, the judge himself included, think that prophecy would lodge in his labored phrases.

". . . When the time comes that another Jackson is demanded, the Institute will furnish him!"

It was another of the things he might have been expected to say, the occasion and the place being what they were. The words rang through the hall, but the ladies kept right on fanning themselves, and no one present even looked at Marshall—unless, perhaps, it was Lily Coles.

There was neither envy nor regret in George Marshall as two others received the medals for excellence in scholarship. He was graduating fifteenth in a class of thirty-four; but the distinction he had coveted he had won. He was Cadet First Captain. In a military college, he was first in military proficiency. Not yet twenty-one, he was already very much a man, and the President had sent him formal notice that appointment as a Second Lieutenant in the U. S. Army was waiting for him. And he was engaged to be married.

At the final german on Monday night, his partner had been Miss Nina Armistead of Baltimore. She wore white silk and carried American Beauty roses, and on her breast was Marshall's newly acquired Kappa Alpha pin. That pin was merely a token, the compliment of a gentleman to his dancing partner of the evening. The gentleman's heart was elsewhere, and firmly pledged.

His wooing of Lily Coles had been intense and impetuous. The ladies watched and commented, not always kindly, as another callow and snub-nosed moth fluttered around the devastating flame—or so they thought. They were mistaken. Snub-nosed he was, and less than handsome; but his boyhood had been outgrown and discarded. He did not flutter around Lily Coles; he claimed possession, and made good the claim.

Elizabeth Carter Coles was one of the most beautiful women in the Valley of Virginia, and since her own breathlessly lovely first youth she had been for ten years the reigning belle of Lexington. She was eight years older than George Marshall, but her discernment was as great as her beauty, and she gave her heart away entirely for the first time when this slender, assured cadet gave his in exchange.

The wit that was enough to send a cluster of beaux into gales of laughter was enough also to find the superb qualities and noble spirit which animated the tall and rangy form of George Marshall, and to love them. On his part, George found in Lily not only such beauty as sets young men to writing verse, but a gay and keen intelligence that was a perfect leaven for his intense and driving mind, as her wit was a foil for his quieter humor. And he found and loved a courage that touched and strengthened his devotion, adding a poignant tenderness to all the years they were to have together.

For Lily Coles was already nearly an invalid, and never would be strong. That was why George escorted someone else to the final german. Lily did not dare to dance. A thyroid condition had affected her heart, and sudden death was a realized possibility every day of her life. When she came into George's life, that fear came with her and made itself a part of their life together. There would be always the concern about exertion, the gauging of excitement, the consideration of climate in an Army household liable to assignment in any kind of climate. There was not, of course, an ever-present consciousness of the fear. People examine such facts, accept them, and make such arrangements as they can to ignore them. They do, that is, if they are people of courage and devotion, whose wish is to give intensely rather than to cling and claim meanly, and Lily was such a person. The things she could not do, why, she could not do, and need one talk about them or make a point of them?

This was the woman who made George Marshall's last year at the V.M.I. a year of excited bliss and exquisite torment. His free hours were spent at the Coles home at the Limit Gate, or walking with Lily beneath the trees and past the shuttered brick and clapboard fronts of the drowsy Southern town.

They were to be married as soon as George took up his Army commission, but that had to wait for his twenty-first birthday. Also, he had to be examined by a board of officers before the appointment could be confirmed.

Since he would not be twenty-one until the last day of 1901, he looked for a job to fill the months between, and found one as commandant of cadets at the Danville Military Academy, a preparatory school not too far from Lexington. On September 23, he appeared before the examining board at Governors Island, thought he had answered their questions rather well, but got no indication from them what they thought.

When December arrived, with the important birthday less than a month away, and still no word from the Army, George's nervous hopes and fears got the best of him. There was so much at stake—not only the one career that he wanted, but an early fulfillment of the love that had possessed him for a year. So, on December 5 he sat down and wrote to the Adjutant General of the Army. Did the fact he had received no communication from the War Department mean that he had failed in the examination and lost his appointment?

The reply was prompt, and completely reassuring. The board had found him eminently suitable for appointment to the Regular Army, and recommended that he be commissioned in the Artillery. Since he had told the board he would not be twenty-one until December 31, his commission would not be issued to him until after that date.

With that letter in hand, George and Lily could make definite plans for their wedding. In February, George took up his commission—it gave him his rank from February 2, 1901, the date on which the Army expansion bill which created the vacancy became law; and because there were no vacancies in the Artillery, he was commissioned in the Infantry. On February 11, 1902, Second Lieutenant George Catlett Marshall, Jr., U.S.A., and Miss Elizabeth Carter Coles were married, at eight o'clock in the evening, in the home of the bride's mother on Letcher Avenue beside the Limit Gate. Andy Thompson came down from Uniontown to stand with George when his childhood friend got married. Mr. and Mrs. Marshall were there, of course, and Marie and Stuart.

Lily's sister was present, and the bride, in white and carrying violets, was given in marriage by her brother, Edmund Pendleton Coles. In addition to the two families and Andy, only a few close friends from Lexington were present for the wedding and the supper which followed it. At ten-thirty, Lieutenant and Mrs. Marshall left by train for Washington, where they spent their honeymoon at the New Willard Hotel while the lieutenant awaited his orders from the War Department.

The orders came soon, to the 30th Infantry in the Philippines. That meant separation, for the Army was not sending officers' wives to a newly acquired outpost still flaming with insurrection. They had two months together, two brief months, before Lily stood on the dock and watched the U.S.A.T. *Kilpatrick* move out toward the Golden Gate, taking George to the other side of the world.

Then she went back to Lexington, to the house at the Limit Gate, to begin the long months of waiting. They were learning early, these two, what sacrifices the Army lays upon its own in order that it may serve the need of the republic.

War Department Photo

SECOND LIEUTENANT MARSHALL

The student officer at Fort Leavenworth posed in his dress blues for this photograph shortly before his graduation from the Staff College.

Photo Courtesy E. P. Coles
ELIZABETH CARTER MARSHALL
A rare portrait of the General's first wife taken several years after their marriage, probably during their stay at Fort Leavenworth.

IV

Manifest Destiny

Two things of extraordinary importance happened to the United States Army in February of 1902: Elihu Root moved boldly to equip it with the General Staff it did not want; and it acquired George Marshall, who was to nurture his career in the growing staff system and become the towering master of its belated flowering forty years later.

The Army, all of it, was very much aware of Mr. Root's move. It was the most drastic change proposed in the American military establishment since the foundation of the Republic, and it precipitated dissensions that ceased to be dangerous only when the General of the Armies John J. Pershing came back from France and used his great prestige to modernize the staff organization and fix it firmly in a pre-eminent position safely beyond attack or even question.

The Army paid not the slightest attention to its acquisition of Lieutenant Marshall. That was natural, and it was just. It was odd of Destiny to give the Army at one time the system, and the system's greatest master; but of the two, the system was vastly more important. Not even a Marshall could have accomplished the near-miracles of 1940 to 1945 without the instrument ready forged, and waiting for the hand which could wield it. It is overly simple, but generally true, to say that battles are won by the courage, ingenuity and suffering of soldiers, but wars are won by staff work.

Why is it true? The reason is the reason why a general staff exists. The decision is committed at last to the hands of riflemen, tankmen, artillerymen, pilots, naval gunners, bombardiers; but even before any one of these was mustered into the service, the high command knew, in general if not specific terms, where and when he would be committed to action, what weapons he would use, what clothing he would wear, how much ammunition he would need, what his chances were of being killed or wounded, what medical attention he would require, how he would be fed, even how his mail would be collected and delivered in the theater of action; all of this, and more, the high command knew, and it knew because of the staff.

That is to say, the high command knew these things in World War II. In World War I, the knowledge and the planning were something less than perfect, to put it gently; but they shone gloriously in comparison with the tragic and scandalous shortcomings of the Army and the War Department in the War with Spain. It was the fantastic and all but incredible chaos which characterized the conduct of that war which led Elihu Root to the general staff idea, and the inevitable debates over who won the war against the Axis should accord more than cursory attention to the contribution of that statesman, whose work as Secretary of War placed him in the very first rank of American public servants.

The Army which George Marshall entered in 1902 was held in considerable affection and esteem by the public, which thought of it largely in terms of the volunteers who had been its eager, usually valiant, and woefully abused majority. The public, elated and exultant over the crushing of Spain, gulping eagerly the triple-distilled dangers of imperialism and "manifest destiny," did not realize that Spain was a decadent power which would have experienced difficulty in resisting the attack of a well-organized metropolitan police force.

Moreover, the excited adulation accorded its largely volunteer army was more than counterbalanced by the wrath the public poured on the War Department, and—to the extent it comprehended its implication—on the Regular Army, for the mismanagement of the war and the incompetent handling of the troops, not in battle but in preparation.

The public was quite aware that men had died by thousands of typhoid and other diseases in badly planned and worse administered Army camps, that soldiers had been dispatched to the tropics wearing winter woolens, that embalmed beef had been supplied for rations. It had read of the incredible confusion at the embarkation port of Tampa, where freight cars loaded with supplies and equipment were backed up as far as Columbia, South Carolina, and—invoices and bills of lading not being received—the only way officers knew what was in them was to break the seal on each car and examine its contents; where nobody knew what units were to use which transports (there were not enough to accommodate the expedition ordered to Cuba), and unit commanders actually rowed out in midstream, boarded incoming empty ships, and held them for their own men by force of arms against the claims of other units.

Such conditions resulted from the fact that nothing even resembling a plan for war existed in the Army or the War Department at the outbreak of the conflict with Spain. That lack of plan was due in part to the fact that the military establishment, the Congress, and the public alike had forgotten that the primary function of an Army is to prepare for war, and for decades a money-starved and dwindling regular force had been scattered in small garrisons, largely on Indian patrol; even more, however, it was due to a system of dual control which effectively prevented anything resembling efficient direction of the Army.

This organization, which Secretary Root told Congress "would irretrievably ruin any man who was Secretary of War" when a conflict started, was based on this paragraph in Army Regulations: "The military establishment is under the orders of the Commanding General of the army in that which pertains to its discipline and control. The fiscal affairs of the army are conducted by the Secretary of War through the several Staff Departments."

The Commanding General, exercising complete control over the organization, training and operations of the field forces, was all but independent of the Secretary of War, and sometimes even asserted complete independence. He had, however, no shadow of control over the Staff Departments, collectively known as the General Staff, the most important being the Adjutant General's office. The Adjutant General, as well as the Quartermaster Department, the Ordnance Department, the Subsistence Department and other bureaus reported direct to the Secretary of War, and brooked no interference from the Commanding General. The situation was made worse by the fact that there existed at the top neither a planning nor a co-ordinating agency of any kind, and the duties and prerogatives of the various staff departments were fixed in great detail by statute.

This made overlapping of duties and consequent jealousies inevitable, and the bickerings and jurisdictional disputes were intensified by the system of promotion, which was confined to the staff or line branch up to and including the grade of colonel. Promotion within the Quartermaster Department, for instance, depended on the death or promotion of officers within that branch alone. Obviously, promotion was faster in some branches than in others, which did not exactly foster a co-operative spirit. Just as obviously, promotion was faster if the branch were enlarged so that it needed more officers—no branch overlooked a chance to expand its activities at the expense of others, or failed to lobby in Congress against any proposed curtailment of its size and mission.

The Secretary of War in those days, like the Secretary of the Navy to the present day, had his choice of two unsatisfactory courses of action: he could either attempt to regulate and co-ordinate the affairs of the various bureaus, bogging down in such a mass of detail that he lost the large view of national security; or he could let the bureau chiefs go their various ways unhampered.

The solution was obvious to any mind with even a glimmering of administrative idea: the Secretary of War should be the unquestioned head of the Army under the President, and there should be no military commander independent of him in any sense at all. The solution had occurred to a number of secretaries, and they had included recommendations in their reports. The recommendations were ignored. Root would not be ignored. He had been appointed to clean up a mess, and he cleaned it up. He had public indignation and concern as a weapon, but he had also determined and persistent opposition from the Commanding General and from the bureau heads. They had vested interests they would not surrender without a fight.

Exactly twelve days after George Marshall's commission as a second lieutenant was confirmed by the Senate, and three days after his marriage, the bill embodying Root's reorganization proposals was introduced in Congress. He had built up understanding for more than two years through a careful and shrewd public relations campaign to educate both public and the Army. Nevertheless the reaction was violent. The plan proposed to abolish the office of Commanding General, substituting that of Chief of Staff. The man who held this position would be the principal military adviser of the Secretary and the President. The chain of command would go from the Secretary through the Chief of Staff to all components of the Army. Most important, the bill would create a new kind of General Staff, without command or administrative duties or authority, to assist the Chief of Staff in planning, co-ordinating and supervising all Army activities. Importantly, this new General Staff was to have no permanent list of officers, but was to be filled by detail from the line and the old staff bureaus.

Marshall and his bride were still on their honeymoon in the New Willard Hotel, waiting for the lieutenant's orders to his first assignment, when the Commanding General of the Army, General Nelson A. Miles, appeared before the Senate Military Affairs Committee to lead the charge of the opposition.

Bristling with indignation, the wrathy old traditionalist, regarded by Congress and the nation as America's foremost military expert, betrayed his lack of understanding of the problem Root was tackling with the astonishing statement that, "as far as a plan of campaign is concerned, that must depend on the circumstances, and if a general is not able to make a plan and carry it out *instantly*, he is not competent to command an army, or a division, or a corps."

That, however, was not his big salvo. Looking at the senators, all veterans of the Civil War, he spoke as a soldier to brothers in arms, conjured up a brief vision of the genius of Washington, Steuben, and

Hamilton, hinted militarism and monarchy lurked in the very name of a general staff.

"The scheme," roared the general, "is revolutionary, casts to the winds the lessons of experience, and abandons methods which successfully carried us through the most memorable epochs of our history."

If anyone doubts the efficacy of such arguments, let him read over the testimony of Navy witnesses forty-three years later on the proposal to unify the War and Navy Departments. Then, as more recently, it had the intended effect. Members of the committee notified Root the bill could not be passed. But Root had a few trumps left in his own hand. He presented Lieutenant General Schofield, former commanding general of the Army who had been for a brief period Secretary of War. Major General Wesley Merritt, (Ret.), backed up Schofield's views. A letter from Brigadier General George W. Davis, then commanding the 7th Brigade in Zamboanga, Philippine Islands, undermined still further the position taken by Miles.

Root also intensified his publicity campaign, and finally in December published his annual report containing the classic statement of the duties of a general staff. This capped the brilliant series of papers which led Lord Haldane to say in 1906 that "the five reports of Elihu Root made as Secretary of War in the United States are the very last word concerning the organization and place of an Army in a democracy." This statement of Root's accomplished a very great deal to swing support in Congress to the general staff idea, and get the bill approved early in 1903. Root explained:

The duties of such a body of officers can be illustrated by taking for example an invasion of Cuba, such as we were all thinking about a few years ago. It is easy for a President or a general acting under his direction, to order that 50,000 or 100,000 men proceed to Cuba and capture Havana. To make an order which has any reasonable chance of being executed he must do a great deal more than that. He must determine how many men shall be sent and how they shall be divided among the different arms of the service, and how they shall be armed and equipped, and to do that he must get all the information possible about the defenses of the place to be captured and the strength and character and armament of the forces to be met. He must determine at what points and by what routes the place shall be approached, and at what points his troops shall land in Cuba; and for this purpose he must be informed about the various harbors of the island and the depth of their channels; what classes of vessels can enter them; what the facilities for landing are; how they can be defended; the character of the roads leading from them to the place to be attacked; the character of the intervening country; how far it is healthful or unhealthful; what the climate is liable to be at the season of the proposed movement; the temper and sympathy of the inhabitants; the quantity and kind of supplies that can be obtained, and a great variety of other things which will go to determine whether it is better to make the approach from one point or another, and to determine what it will be necessary for the Army to carry with it in order to succeed in moving and living and fighting.

All this information it is the business of a general staff to procure and present. It is probable that there would be in such case a number of alternative plans, each having advantages and disadvantages, and these would be worked out each by itself, with the reasons for and against it, and presented to the President or general for his determination. This the general staff should do. This cannot be done in an hour. It requires that the general staff shall have been at work for a long time collecting the information and arranging it and getting it in form to present. Then at home, where the preparation for the expedition is to be made, the order must be based upon a knowledge of the men and material available for its execution; how many men there are who can be devoted to that purpose, from what points they are to be drawn, what bodies of troops ought to be left or sent elsewhere, and what bodies may be included in the proposed expedition; whether there are enough ships to transport them; where they are to be obtained; whether they are properly fitted up; what more should be done to them; what are the available stocks of clothing, arms and ammunition, and engineers' material, and horses and wagons, and all the immediate supplies and munitions necessary for a large expedition; how are the things to be supplied which are not ready, but which are necessary, and how long a time will be required to supply them.

All this and much more necessary information it is the business of a general staff to supply. When that has been done the order is made with all available knowledge of all the circumstances upon which the movement depends for its success. It is then the business of the General Staff to see that every separate officer upon whose actions the success of the movement depends understands his share in it and does not lag behind in the performance of that share; to see that troops and ships and animals and supplies of arms and ammunition and clothing and food, etc., from hundreds of sources come together at the right times and places. It is a laborious, complicated, and difficult work, which requires a considerable number of men whose special business it is and who are charged with no other duties.

It was the lack of such a body of men doing that kind of work which led to the confusion attending the Santiago expedition in the summer of 1898. The confusion at Tampa and elsewhere was the necessary result of having a large number of men, each of them doing his own special work the best he could, but without any adequate force of officers engaged in seeing that they pulled together according to plans made beforehand. Such a body of men doing general staff duty is just as necessary in time of peace as it is in time of war. It is not an executive body; it is not an administrative body; it acts only through the authority of others. It makes intelligent command possible by procuring and arranging information and working out plans in detail, and it makes intelligent and effective execution of commands possible by keeping all separate agents advised of the parts they are to play in the general scheme.

Root was determined to have an organization which would enable the Army to carry out its primary function of preparing for war. He wanted no more of the Gilbert and Sullivan aspect implied in the comment of the Commissary General of the Army in 1898 that his office "was running perfectly until the war disrupted and disorganized it." What he wanted he got. The bill creating the General Staff was signed by President Theodore Roosevelt on February 3, 1903.

On that date, Lieutenant Marshall was experiencing the dullness of routine garrison duty with Company G, 30th U. S. Infantry, at Santa Mesa Barracks, and finding Manila a blissful contrast to the long and dreary months in fever-ridden Mangarin. It would, of course, have been even more blissful had Lily been there also.

The Army Transport *Kilpatrick*, having touched at Honolulu

and Nagasaki on the way out, delivered Lieutenant Marshall at Manila on May 13, 1902. Two days later orders were issued assigning him to Company G, and on May 21 he debarked from the old interisland contract transport *Isla de Negros* at Calapan, on the Island of Mindoro.

There he reported to Captain Charles I. Bent, a busy and harassed young man, who found himself at the moment in command of all U. S. forces on Mindoro, and found those forces threatened by an epidemic of Asiatic cholera which was raging throughout the islands. There was a detachment of fifty men of Company G stationed at Calapan, and the burden of its command was promptly transferred by Bent to the fresh and willing shoulders of Lieutenant Marshall.

This being a Regular Army regiment, the Lieutenant found his detachment operating smoothly enough under the stern regimen imposed by such stalwarts as Sergeants Shiebert, Smith, Brown, and Gebhard, abetted by Corporals Allen and Donaldson. The chief problem in discipline was to make the men conform to the emergency regulations imposed by Captain Clark I. Wertenbaker, the post surgeon, and his assistant, Contract Surgeon Fletcher Gardner, in an effort to keep the cholera from spreading from the native population to the troops. The efforts were, by and large, successful; but one of Marshall's men, Private William E. Rice, died of the disease in the post hospital on June 8, and was buried at Calapan.

Maintaining discipline, as Marshall knew, is less a matter of issuing strict and arbitrary orders, than of keeping men busy and interested. Accordingly, when Bent gave the newest arrival the job of planning a Fourth of July program for the men stationed at Calapan, Marshall planned a celebration using to the fullest the limited means available in this less than prepossessing outpost of empire.

One of the events he planned was an obstacle race, over a course laid out in the town's plaza—not a very imposing plaza, for all that Calapan was the capital of Mindoro—and employing such barriers and hazards as temporary fences, wagons, wheelbarrows, and other items ready at hand. Before the race began, Marshall gathered the several contestants together and gave them explicit instructions on traversing each of the obstacles. The last was a tarpaulin laid flat on the ground at the finish line. They were to crawl under it.

Private John W. Willey of Company M—no one guessed then that he was to stay in the Islands, grow prosperous, and in the end lose health, fortune, and part of a beloved family in Santo Tomas when the Japanese came—was first at the finish line, and far ahead of any competitor. But instead of crawling under the tarpaulin, he ran across it. Marshall said nothing, and waited. One by one the others came panting up to the line, and one by one they ran across the tarpaulin instead of crawling under it. When the last man stumbled in, the group gathered around the master of ceremonies, who proceeded to lecture them on listening to instructions and following them explicitly.

"Private Willey is the winner," he told the abashed group, "but if the last one of you to reach this line had remembered to crawl under that tarpaulin instead of running over it, he would have won the event."

There were other events, among them a foot race around the square containing the church and the jail, along streets recently renamed for American notables, including President McKinley; and a carabao race. The latter was won by a lad who had been inquisitive or observant enough to discover that the only way to make a carabao show even a faint desire for speed is to reach back, grab his tail, and pull it forward. Few Europeans knew that trick, and Marshall undoubtedly quizzed the winner about how he discovered it.

Marshall was forever asking questions. Private John N. Morton of Company F had been suspicious, then scornful, when the new Lieutenant, a couple of days after his arrival at Calapan, had interrogated Morton about some peculiarities of native behavior. Morton was an old hand in Mindoro, and the native behavior so well known it seemed obvious, and he suspected a trap, but he gave an answer. Marshall listened, nodded, and walked off, leaving Morton to continue guarding his prisoners. Later, when he discoursed on the stupid question to his fellows, Morton learned that most of them had been questioned about one thing or another by Marshall since the latter reported in Calapan. The new Lieutenant was not trying to trap anyone, he was just constantly in search of information, and went about getting it in the most direct manner he knew.

A week after the Fourth of July celebration, Marshall turned over his detachment to Lieutenant Henry Hossfeld, and the next day left Calapan to take command of the entire Company G at its headquarters at Mangarin. This desolate spot at the head of Mangarin Bay was inhabited by the members of Marshall's command, a handful of malarial natives, and what seemed to be half of all the world's mosquitoes.

Second Lieutenant Marshall took command of the company on his arrival July 13, but First Lieutenant Edward R. Stone retained command of the station until his departure July 29. Then Mangarin became Marshall's world, station and troops and civil responsibilities, cut off four weeks at a time from all contact with civilization, its only communication with home and the rest of the Army being the *Isla de Negros* or some other interisland transport, which was supposed to drop anchor there every month, but did not always arrive on schedule. There were no roads, no telegraph.

At his first guard mount, Marshall threw two men into the guardhouse—probably for imbibing too freely of tuba—and then began looking over his command. He found and liked the tough and competent First Sergeant, William H. Carter. Quartermaster Sergeant Frederick A. Sims, he decided, was a smart youngster and likable, but inclined to be fresh. Sergeant August Torstrup was a quiet, steady, dependable Swede. The privates seemed to be a clean and spirited group of average young Americans, with a surprisingly high state of morale, considering the dismal spot they inhabited.

The command was looking him over, too. What they saw was a rangy young man with an easy stride, a clear, light complexion, penetrating blue eyes, and sandy hair, immaculately uniformed and exuding authority. His words were quick, and very much to the point, enunciated calmly and firmly in a pleasant voice. The Lieutenant did not find it necessary to employ any strident shouting; but there was never any doubt about who was in command. Marshall was a strict disciplinarian, and the men decided he was a hard boss; but they sensed also that the hardness had a purpose, and that beneath it there was a very human young man who placed the welfare of every one of them ahead of his own.

Mangarin was the least attractive and most unhealthy spot on the entire island of Mindoro, but it had been selected as an Army post in order to provide protection for the establishment and property of the *Recoleto* Friars at San Jose, three miles to the north. The insurgents and the ladrones had made a habit of stealing cattle from this vast and neglected estate, but the Friars asked and received protection for what remained.

Thus it was that one of the first persons encountered by Lieutenant Marshall when he arrived at Mangarin was Padre Isidro Sanz. Padre Sanz was a lay brother, who knew the island of Mindoro as he knew the back of his own hand, understood both language and habits of the Mangyan natives of the interior, was useful as an interpreter, and to help a lonely man through lonely evenings could play cards, or strum the mandolin, or sing Spanish songs of a bawdiness truly Rabelaisian. Quite incidentally, he also looked after the interests of the Friars—a kind of liaison officer.

Even more useful, Lieutenant Marshall found, was a spraddle-toed old native named Eduardo Lualjadi, the Presidente of Ilin, a village on the island of the same name, which was separated by a narrow strait from Mindoro, and protected Mangarin Bay from the weather of Mindoro Strait and the China Sea. The Presidente Lualjadi was carpenter, farmer, sailor, boatbuilder, procurer of *cargadores* and other labor, handy man, and informer. He was a very useful person, and most important, he was faithful. That was something to cling to in a land where armed bands of ladrones still robbed and looted, where there was still considerable reason to believe the recent declaration that the insurrection was ended might have been a little premature.

But however the Moros might revolt in the southern islands, and remnants of insurrection be found or suspected in Luzon, on Mindoro life was pretty routine and humdrum. There were patrols to be made in the sector around Mangarin, and at frequent but irregular intervals to Ilin and smaller offshore islands, but they seldom turned up anything more exciting than a change of view. Occasionally reports would come in of raiding bands of ladrones, and then Marshall would take a detachment out in pursuit. In September such an alarm took them off by boat to Bulalacao, where for two days they searched the mountains before returning in disgust to Mangarin. Another report in December brought them sailing to the island of Semirara for another two-day bushwhacking expedition. But in each case the offending bandits had faded into the jungle and the inscrutable native throng long before the impotent vengeance of the Army came in view.

If nothing else, these expeditions gave Marshall a chance to see a little of the beauty of this island country. The mountains of Mindoro were picturesque, if difficult; and the narrow channel which separated Ilin from Mindoro presented a rare and fascinating sight: a curious accident of tide lines divided the water sharply into two sections, one a deep emerald green, the other an intense blue. He discovered but certainly did not love the village of Pandarukan, at the north entrance to Mangarin Bay, which consisted of one rambling house of wood and a dozen nipa huts; and he inspected the more impressive charms of Sablayan, which boasted two parallel streets, a church, and some relatively prepossessing houses, surrounded by extensive coconut groves, and presiding over a small bay with a bottom of beautifully colored coral.

As to the population of Mindoro, Marshall discovered that Mangarin, like the other coastal towns, was peopled by Tagalogs, the second-largest racial group in the Philippines, who had come to Mindoro from other northern islands, chiefly Luzon. Inland, the native Mindoro tribes were the Mangyans, whose lives consisted largely of being exploited or dodging exploitation by the Tagalogs; and the Batanganis, a very small group. These, incidentally, turned out to be the people identified with a legend that deep in Mindoro there lived a primitive white race, with one woman of the tribe so beautiful that any man who saw her once never came back from Mindoro. In sober fact, the Batanganis were the darkest-skinned natives of the entire Philippine archipelago. The small and chocolate-colored Mangyans were a primitive and timid people, afraid of the whites, but pleasant enough once the shyness was penetrated, and possessed of an easily aroused sense of humor. For clothing they wore nothing much but breech clouts, plus a red *bejuco* cord wound several times around the waist by way of ornament.

There was little enough contact with these primitive peoples of the interior of the island. Most of the military life was passed in the garrison village, where Marshall represented the majesty of governmental authority, and took his military duties very seriously indeed. Since he was for several weeks the only officer at Mangarin, these were not inconsiderable. He was commanding officer, adjutant, quartermaster, and civil governor of the district until the arrival of Captain Eames in the middle of September.

It was a tragically lonely assignment. The line between officer and enlisted man was very sharply drawn. Their welfare kept him busy most of the time, but their society for relaxation was forbidden. Marshall had to rely on the dubious pleasure of the company of Padre Sanz, or more frequently on close application to the limited number of books he had brought with him.

For the company, there was a limited amount of drill each day, and some target practice on a range near the post. The quarters were rather comfortable. They were substantial buildings, once used by the Friars of San Jose, looking for the most part not unlike plaster and half-timber work, but set up on bamboo or heavy timber piles to leave a good six feet of space between ground and floor, and roofed with a steep thatch of nipa palm. The hospital, of similar construction, was next to the barracks and connected with it by a roofed veranda where the convalescents lolled in reed chairs. There was a commissary building, and a long nipa shack for the mess hall. A secondary barracks, cookshack and guardhouse stood near by, along with smaller nipa shacks for the artificer, baker, tailor, and quarters for some of the noncommissioned officers. These smaller buildings trailed off almost indistinguishably into the nipa huts of the village.

The officers' quarters, which Marshall occupied in solitary state until Captain Eames arrived, were of the same variety as the other buildings of the post, but stood several hundred yards away from them at the south edge of the wide parade ground from which there was a sweeping view of Mindoro Strait (the post was across the river from the old village of Mangarin, and lay between the Strait and Mangarin Bay).

The Lieutenant had a native *muchacho* who performed the multiple duties of cook, houseboy, and personal valet. Beginning with his first guard mount at Mangarin, Marshall selected a man at each such ceremony as orderly to the commanding officer, but this was strictly to help him with military business. He never had a "dog robber," or "striker," as personal orderlies were called. Soldiers, in Marshall's mind, were not meant to be personal servants or messenger boys for officers, and even when he was Chief of Staff years later, he never had an aide.

At intervals, one of the contract transports of the Quartermaster Corps would arrive with supplies and mail, providing the one link with the rest of the world. Once in two months it was supposed to bring the paymaster from Manila, but that gentleman did not always put in his scheduled appearance. During the insurrection, the men had gone as long as six months without pay, and even after Marshall's arrival they experienced one period of four months without their wages. The plight of most of the officers in the Calapan garrison when Marshall reported in May was financially most unhappy, and the young Lieutenant, having arrived quite well heeled, made many and generous loans. With some, he discovered recovery was not entirely easy.

The supplies brought by the *Isla de Negros* consisted of prunes, dried apples, canned tomatoes, canned emergency rations and corned beef, rice, potatoes, canned salmon occasionally, and bacon which frequently attracted a population of worms. It usually brought a supply of beer, too, and a shipment of fresh beef. Sometimes there was a little ice, but frequently there was not, and when the ice was lacking, the fresh beef was consumed in fantastic feasts—steak-eating contests—in the first day or two after the transport's visit. This occasional treat was supplemented between boat arrivals with tough and stringy native beef, and the diet was varied also with native vegetables, turtle eggs hunted on the beach, fish from the teeming waters near the post, or some game from a hunting trip inland. Marshall may have hunted, while stationed at Mangarin, that rarest of big game animals, the timarau of Mindoro.

Getting the supplies ashore from the *Isla de Negros* was backbreaking work, but the men did not mind too much. When the sea was too rough for the transport to unload on the beach, and that was true on most of its visits, it would pull as far into the bay as possible, lighter the supplies to shoal water in lifeboats, and then the soldiers and native workers would wade out through the surf and carry the stuff ashore. From the beach, the things were dragged up slides to the post.

Delivery was only part of the job, however. The transport had to take on coal as well as put supplies ashore, and because the contract made by the Quartermaster Department in Manila specified that that the crew would not handle the coal until it reached the transport's deck, Lieutenant Marshall's men had to sack it, take it out in boats, and heave it to the deck.

Years later, pleading with a Congressional committee for authority to build the Army into an efficient machine and the money with which to do it, Marshall was to recall that coaling job, and cite it as an example of the indignity to which penny-pinching subjected soldiers, and also of the meaning of discipline.

The Quartermaster's money-saving contract which protected the crew from handling the fuel until it was on deck, said Marshall, "passed the buck to the soldiers, as someone had to handle that coal."

"Their pay was thirteen dollars a month," said the General recalling the second lieutenant and his men. "They worked from the coal pile on the edge of the jungle to a little flat-bottomed boat—we had only one—and rowed that through three-quarters of a mile of heavy surf to the ship, and laboriously transferred the coal to the deck of the ship.

"One day while working in a torrential rain a tall, lanky soldier from the mountains of Kentucky paused in the middle of his shoveling job, with his comment: 'I didn't see nothing like this on that damned recruiting circular.' My old first sergeant suppressed a laugh, and flashed back the order to 'keep your mouth shut and shovel coal—that's your job!' That gave me a lasting impression of the Regular Army; what discipline meant, what dependability meant in times of difficulty.... There is always a certain degree of grousing that seems to be inherent in the soldier ... but there are times when the leader must command, 'Keep your mouth shut and shovel coal; those are the orders!' "

As the weeks passed at Mangarin, the men of Company G realized that this reserved and crisp young officer was more than just a "hard boss." They discovered that if he was exacting, he was also scrupulously just, and even interested and sympathetic. Even punishment for infractions of discipline somehow was administered with such restraint of manner that it was not accompanied by ill will or personal indignity. They found that the line which separated commissioned officer from enlisted man, although firmly maintained by Lieutenant Marshall as an essential part of the equipment for keeping discipline, was not marked by any failing in courtesy.

They found, also, that Marshall believed that it was his responsibility, and the responsibility of every man in his command, to do the job assigned to them with such equipment as was provided. If the government failed to supply necessary means, they had to be improvised. If the rations did not arrive, then they lived off the country. He would not tolerate failure of himself or of his command to do the job assigned, whatever the shortcomings might be elsewhere.

Recreation was decidedly limited at Mangarin. There was swimming, if one wanted to brave unclothed the hordes of ravenous mosquitoes. Card games, checkers, or an occasional stray magazine or book helped pass the dull, candlelit evenings. In the daytime, hunting in the swamps for alligators or cranes, in the jungles for monkeys and birds, provided some sport, and there was usually an opportunity to bet on the natives' matches of gamecocks. Marshall had a surge of nostalgia when he saw those! And there was a fairly consistent imbibing of tuba, the not very potent fermented juice of native palms.

On December 22, 1902, the company had been ordered to Manila, and Captain Eames left with fifty-nine of the men on the U.S. Army Transport *Ingalls*, leaving Lieutenant Marshall in command of a detachment of twenty-six to remain at Mangarin until a relief detachment of Philippine Constabulary arrived. So Marshall spent Christmas in an outpost that was quieter and lonelier than ever. On December 27 the old *Isla de Negros* dropped anchor in the bay, and Marshall and his men went aboard. They reached Manila on December 30—at least the Lieutenant had lights and plenty of companionship for his twenty-second birthday.

At first the company was quartered in a hospital barracks, but toward the end of January they joined two other companies of the 30th Infantry at Santa Mesa, three miles east of the city. There they sweated out the routine of garrison life for several months, while Marshall sometimes played tennis with other officers, pored over maps and official reports and crammed himself full of the facts of the war in the Philippines and the insurrection which followed, or went to bed with a siege of malaria. Perhaps he went out to inspect the new post, still under construction, and not yet named Fort McKinley. In May he had a week of detached service assignment at Tanay, Rizal. In September Marshall commanded the company for a week while Captain Eames had a bout with malaria. The captain recovered in time to go with the company when it moved September 21 from Santa Mesa to Malahi Island Military Prison at Laguna de Bay, becoming part of the prison guard detachment. Two days later, Marshall went back to bed to stay nearly two weeks. Quinine and rest put him back on his feet in time to take command of the company again October 5, when Eames left to return to the States.

Meantime, the papers had been full of reports from the various islands of murderous attacks by ladrones, including one attack in which the marauders overwhelmed the native garrison of Calapan and shot a number of women and children in the Mindoro capital.

The men read these accounts avidly and fearfully—fearfully because this kind of thing, if it got out of hand, would mean that they would be ordered back to outpost service instead of going home, as they expected to do. One day in March they saw the sky obscured by dense clouds of grasshoppers, and they watched fascinated and horrified as the natives caught, cooked, and ate vast quantities of them. Two months later the sky was obscured again, this time by smoke as more than two thousand five hundred nipa dwellings of the city were destroyed in a conflagration.

But November came at last, and on the first day of the month the 30th Infantry assembled in quarantine at Mariveles on Bataan. Twelve days later they boarded the U.S.A.T. *Sherman*, which steamed over to Manila, and then on November 14 headed out past Corregidor, homeward bound. Some of the officers had their families with them, there were a few civilian families, and one or two Army nurses aboard, so pleasant shipboard companionship was not lacking, and the stops at Nagasaki and Honolulu were long enough for a little sightseeing, and buying of gifts and souvenirs for those waiting at home.

Even here, however, the intensely serious young Lieutenant Marshall could not relax entirely. He had handled his first assignment well, and it had included the most important command he would hold for thirty years—commander of a company and an outpost district. He had been achingly lonely, but he had not allowed his own morale or that of his men to sag. He might have been expected to sink into a deck chair, relax completely, dream of Lily, and forget labor entirely; but Lieutenant Hossfeld found him one day hard at work, arranging his orders and other official papers neatly in a book. Hossfeld teased him good-naturedly about such meticulous care of such routine affairs. The blue eyes turned coldly on Hossfeld.

"Look, Heinie," Marshall retorted levelly, "if you expect to get anywhere in the Army, you had better keep track of your orders and all your business!"

Lieutenant Marshall never thought official business, even routine official business, was either funny or trivial.

V

Star in His Pocket

CAPTAIN CLARENCE O. SHERRILL viewed the mutilated and wilted remains of his pride and joy, and cursed—not too softly.

Behind his half of the comfortable duplex quarters at Fort Leavenworth, in the generous green lawn shaded by noble elms and oaks, a lettuce bed had been thriving mightily under his doting care until a prisoner, detailed to trim the captain's grass, had systematically disposed of the lettuce also with the lawn mower. The sergeant in charge of the working party had wet his shirt with sweat and been voluble in self-excusing explanation, but the lettuce bed was gone.

Lieutenant Marshall, honor and distinguished graduate of the School of the Line and of the Staff College, and now an instructor with Captain Sherrill in the Engineering Department at both schools, heard the tale of woe and tch' tch-ed in sympathy. Then he teased.

"Shaggy," he inquired, dead-pan, "did you ever think about weeds?"

As Shaggy Sherrill's unwilling ears took in this blasphemy, the Lieutenant continued in thoughtful and soothing tones:

"I had a garden of weeds, once." He paused, then added softly, "You'd be surprised what you could do with them."

Leaving Sherrill to gather what comfort he could from this recital, the Lieutenant—with the faintest hint of a wicked gleam in his eye, and a casual parting salutation—wandered off toward his own quarters, two doors away.

This was not, really, a new Marshall, for all that there was a sly wit, a frank and zestful gaiety, that would have astonished those who had known him in the Philippines six years before. But some of the intensity had vanished from the surface of the ambitious young man, and the sternness had been softened. The ambition was there still, and the reserve; but it was as though, a little older, a little more sure, he could trust himself to open just a little the curtain he never quite removed entirely from between himself and the world.

Much of this was his wife's doing. Wherever that charming young woman went, there was gaiety and pleasure. Her wit was keen and irrepressible, her very presence a graciousness, and the Marshalls were decidedly a social success in the Army. Not that there was elaborate or frequent private entertaining; there was almost none. Parties usually were post affairs; but more and more friends delighted in dropping by the Marshall's quarters, and three or four guests for dinner occasionally added savor to the simple society of an army post.

Moreover, Lily's minor genius for the unexpected and biting phrase, her pleasant skepticism, seemed to be a solvent for the shell which encased her husband when the lieutenant was away from her. With her, he was complete and at ease; without her, troubled and lonely. The two of them had paid a visit to George's parents in Uniontown and attended his sister Marie's wedding in St. Peter's Church when the Lieutenant got four months' leave in the autumn of 1905, and after they left, Mrs. Marshall confided to a friend that she thought Lily "is good for George."

So she was; and it was not only that her wit and grace were perfect counterpoint for his intensity and drive. Marshall was one of those controlled and disciplined people who find both incentive and reward deep within themselves, who require neither urging nor applause from many men. Such people are terribly alone, without the release most find in the easy sharing of mind and heart with many people. For all their self-sufficiency, they are incomplete; and if they are fortunate, they find completion in one or two others. There are not more than two, usually—the heart opened to a lover, the mind to a friend.

George Marshall was blessed with rare good fortune; both heart and mind could be placed in trust with one person. His wife was his complete confidante, and his only one. For all the pleasure he took in dancing, in tennis, in dinner parties at the officers' club, in drag hunts, his many companions in such pleasures knew that they never penetrated a certain reserve. Only his wife received the full measure of what he had to give; only his wife was permitted to see all the burden he carried, and help to carry it.

The length of the road ahead, and the goal at the end of it, had come into view here at Fort Leavenworth. Here, George had become one of the "Morrison men." Here, the stamp of Major General J. Franklin Bell was placed on him. Here, he taught Captain John McAuley Palmer, and first came under the influence of that profound and noble and merry little man. Here, the consciousness that they were companions of greatness first struck his colleagues, and they began to tell one another that someday George Marshall would be Chief of Staff.

Return from the Philippines in November 1903 had meant Christmas and birthday in the States, and assignment with his company to Fort Reno, Oklahoma Territory. There, George had noticed the presence of some Negro troops, and lectured his own men carefully on the behavior he expected of them to prevent even a hint of racial clash. Then he and Lily had settled down to two and a half years of not very exciting garrison life.

From June 1904 until the following June, his company duties had been varied by the additional jobs of Engineer and Ordnance Officer for Fort Reno. A military mapping project then took him down to Fort Clark, Texas, for about four months, and that was followed by four months of leave. At the end of January 1906, he returned to Company G, 30th Infantry, at Fort Reno, and for a couple of months he commanded the company and acted as adjutant of the post. Then he was detailed as Post Quartermaster and Commissary Officer until the end of June, when Major W. R. Abercrombie, commanding Fort Reno, sent him off to the School of the Line at Fort Leavenworth, and entered on his efficiency report the comment that "this is a first-class all around officer."

When the new General Staff became a fact in 1903, few senior officers of the Army understood its true function, or realized that it would require officers carefully trained and schooled in the whole art of war—highly educated specialists. There had been schools in the Army for many years, but they had been, by and large, narrow and uninspiring institutions. One of them was the Infantry and Cavalry School at Fort Leavenworth.

Like most of the others, this had been closed during the War with Spain, but after the collapse of the Philippine Insurrection, General Bell had came home and reopened it. Bell was full of energy and ideas, and his prestige in the Army was very great indeed—his services during the Spanish War had been so brilliant that he was jumped from captain to brigadier general. Here at Fort Leavenworth, terminus of the Oregon and Santa Fe Trails, rich in traditions of the old Army, he turned his talents to the creation of an intellectual center for the new Army.

Instead of boning up on drill regulations and other necessary but petty matters, students who came to the new school found themselves concerned with tactics, strategy, and logistics. They studied military history, minor tactics, military hygiene, the organization of armies, weapons, law, and languages in the School of the Line. If they were in the upper half of the graduating class there, they went the next term to the new Staff College, where they took up broader aspects of their former studies, and added the duties of a general staff, tactical and strategic problems, field fortifications, and the problems of fortress warfare, map maneuvers, and other subjects, and learned as well such things as the methods of historical research.

They had to work, these students. The courses were stiff, the standards exacting, and the competition for standing intense and constant. It was not unusual for some of the student officers to suffer a physical or nervous collapse from the strain, and this finally resulted in an order to give each student his grades confidentially, instead of posting all grades for all to see.

Bell had gathered around him some of the Army's most brilliant military students, men who had made their profession a matter of serious and constant study during the lean years when study was not fashionable in the Army. To Leavenworth came Colonel Arthur L. Wagner, who deserves more credit than any other single officer for the revitalizing of the entire Army school system. Here came Major Eben Swift, Captain Arthur Thayer, and—most inspiring and beloved of them all—Major John F. Morrison. Morrison became Senior Instructor in Military Art and Assistant Commandant of the Leavenworth Schools, and the men who were fortunate enough to be students at Leavenworth while he was there took pride in calling themselves "Morrison men."

This atmosphere of enthusiastic intellectual renaissance in the Army, this ferment of ideas, this hard striving for grasp of problem and skill of solution found an eager recruit in George Marshall. He was fortunate to be there. In later years, a second lieutenant of Infantry stood about as much chance of a student assignment at Leavenworth as he stood to command an Army group. But in those first few years, the classes were filled with company grade officers— captains and lieutenants—and it wasn't until the realization of what was happening at the old post on the Missouri began to percolate through the Army as the graduates returned to their regiments that the senior officers began to ask for student detail there, and finally crowded the juniors out altogether. One of Marshall's classmates at Leavenworth was First Lieutenant Charles D. Herron, whose long and sober face completely belied the gay young bachelor he was. Herron, it developed, actually had been sent to the school as punishment by the colonel commanding his regiment because the bachelor lieutenant persisted stubbornly in ignoring plain hints that the colonel's homely daughter needed escort, and even courtship. Another of Marshall's classmates was John L. DeWitt, who more than thirty years later was to be a rival of Marshall for appointment as Chief of Staff. Stephen O. Fuqua, like the others destined to end a distinguished career as a general officer, was in the class also.

Marshall, the boy who had been "dumb" in school at Uniontown, the cadet who stood halfway down the class at the Virginia Military Institute, was first in his class at the School of the Line when the grades were examined in June of 1907. With that record, assignment to the Staff College for the next year was all but automatic. When the Academic Board met June 29, 1908, to survey the results of the year, they found George Marshall first in that class, also. Part of the Board's job was to make a report on each graduate, summarizing his abilities and suggesting the assignments he was qualified to hold.

The report of Marshall was more than twice as long as that on any of his classmates. It said:

Has shown marked proficiency in Field Fortifications, Topographical Surveying and Sketching. Has exhibited qualities which would appear to fit him especially well for the following professional employments: Topographical officer on marches, expeditions, and explorations. Aide-de-camp. Inspector General. Pay Department. Military Attaché. Quartermaster's Department. Ordnance Department. Adjutant General. Subsistence Department. Signal Corps. College detail. Recruiting officer. Organizing and commanding native troops. Staff officer with volunteer troops. Duty with organized militia (Governor's Staff). Line officer with volunteer troops, with advanced rank. Assistant Instructor, Army School of the Line, Military Art, Engineering. Chief of Staff in time of war for large tactical units. Duty with organized militia (special detail conducting field exercises in summer camps).

Appears well fitted for the following professional employments: Post Engineer Officer. Acting Judge Advocate of Department.

Especially recommended for War College Detail.

This was astonishing and extravagant praise for a lieutenant of twenty-seven. The indicated assignment which actually came his way was that of instructor in the School of the Line and in the Staff College. The last recommendation of the Academic Board, however, bears closer examination—that for detail to the War College.

The War College had been established in Washington in 1900 by executive order, when Secretary Root wanted an organization to substitute for a general staff until he could get the legislation he was seeking. After the new Staff came into being, the War College became a part of its Third Section, and its duties included those which under later reorganizations became those of the War Plans Division.

The name War College may be misleading to the average reader. It was, it is true, an institution for the higher military education of Army officers, but—as its President in 1903, Brigadier General Tasker H. Bliss, pointed out—in the old Latin sense of "collegium," implying a body of men associated together by a community of interest and purpose, to do something rather than to learn how to do it. The students at the Army War College worked, not at the examination and dissection of old problems and classic solutions, but at current and pressing problems of the Army and the War Department. Their class solutions were more than apt to show up in print as executive orders and Army Regulations. To be "especially recommended" for detail to this group was accolade, indeed!

As it turned out, Marshall never went to the War College as student, although years later he served a brief tour there as an instructor. In 1908, however, he began a three-year assignment as an instructor in the Engineering Department of the service schools at Leavenworth. Captain Edwin T. Cole was senior instructor in this department, and the four others included not only Marshall and his friend Sherrill, but also Marshall's old company commander in the Philippines, Captain Harry Eames.

Some highly important figures in the army of the future were absorbing the Leavenworth idea in those days. First Lieutenant Walter Krueger became instructor in German, having been graduated from the school. Even as a student he had been slaving away at translations of German military books to give Major Morrison more of the texts he needed. Morrison also had been using Sergeant Bell, another German scholar and a Regular Army noncommissioned officer, as a translator. Through the efforts of Morrison, Krueger and Bell, the Leavenworth men in those days knew more about German military organization and German military thought than either the French or the British staffs, who lived considerably closer to the threat.

Captain John J. Pershing, too busy fighting Moros in Mindanao and winning his promotion in one leap to Brigadier General to attend the Leavenworth classes, found out early what was happening there, and spent his spare hours cramming himself full of correspondence courses. Captain George Van Horn Moseley came as a student while Marshall was instructor, and so did Captain William Lendrum Mitchell of the Signal Corps, not yet the zealot and prophet of air power. Of all the students who came to Marshall's classes, however, the one who turned the tables eventually and became mentor of his teacher was Captain John McAuley Palmer.

Palmer—he was promoted to major while still a student in Lieutenant Marshall's classes—had a natural aptitude for historical research, and a brilliant and critical intellect. He was to become the most articulate of American military philosophers, and he was already well on the road to being the foremost champion of a cause that had few partisans in the Regular service—the citizen army, as opposed to the large professional standing force. When, in his old age, he surrendered the leadership of the cause, it was Marshall who took it over.

The first great study of American military organization written by an American Army officer was *The Military Policy of the United States* by Brevet Major General Emory Upton. He had already published a study of foreign military organizations, but the work on the American forces was unfinished when he died in 1881, and the manuscript was neglected and forgotten until Elihu Root found it and had it printed as a government document in 1904. Its effect on Army thinking was profound, and—for the most part—good. Upton's writings set the stage for the three-battalion organization for infantry and cavalry, the interchangeability of line and staff officers, examination as a prerequisite for promotion, establishment of a general staff, extension and development of the system of military schools. But the natural predilection of a highly competent professional officer for the professional army, confirmed by his incomplete researches particularly in the writings of George Washington, led him to condemn all militia systems as untrustworthy and therefore dangerous instruments of defense. From this he developed his thesis of the "expansive" or "expansible" army, a professional force sufficiently large that in time of war expansion of its enlisted strength could provide enough combat units officered entirely by professionals to meet the national need. As a second line, there would be volunteer organizations, and the third line would be the militia—little more, in fact, than a home guard. It was not a new idea, even in Upton's time, and it was never a sound one; but the professionals, since the war of 1812 and its abysmal militia failures, had been obsessed with the idea of getting along without the militia altogether. Instead, the solution—and this was to be John McAuley Palmer's crusade and triumph—was to hold the professional army to a minimum, and reorganize and train the militia, or National Guard as it is known now, so that it became an efficient force, and the true strength of the military establishment. Marshall, friend of Palmer, was to become the leader of the "citizen army" group within the regular establishment.

Marshall's position as an instructor at the Service Schools was a difficult one, because by 1908 the classes were composed almost entirely of officers senior to him. The Army was beginning to wake up to the importance of these schools. His great tact made him a success, and an impressive one. Marshall himself had been promoted to First Lieutenant just before his graduation from the Staff College, but virtually all his students were captains and majors—one class contained a single student of Marshall's own rank. Marshall succeeded so well that even his criticisms of student work never carried personal offense, and he won the respect and the liking of the older men.

They discovered, too, that Marshall's professional competence was matched by considerable thoughtfulness. Most of the schoolwork was done in classrooms, but there were field exercises and "tactical rides" also, and one of Marshall's classes was sent out on an exacting map-sketching expedition. It involved a grueling ride and difficult work on a very hot summer day. Arriving, sweating and fatigued, at the appointed terminal rendezvous, the class found their instructor waiting for them, and prepared to examine and criticize their work.

More important at the moment, however, was the fact that beside him was a supply of cold beer for all hands.

In addition to his duties as instructor, Marshall was associate editor—meaning Leavenworth correspondent—of the *Infantry Journal*, a semiofficial magazine, then as now one of the United States' foremost military publications. Of brief notes he may have contributed, of editorials he may have written, there is no record; but a single signed article appears in the *Journal* during the three years its masthead carried his name as one of the associate editors.

It is characteristic of Marshall that this one article bearing his name expounds no theory, engages in no argument. It is a lucid, straightforward account of the practical solution of a practical problem, economical of word and phrase, a concise explanation of method.

"A Combined Position Sketch made June 20, 1909, by the student officers of the Army Staff College at Fort Leavenworth," Marshall began, "is an excellent example of the practical system of combined position sketching, originated by Capt. E. R. Stuart, Corps of Engineers, and developed at the Fort Leavenworth Service Schools during the past four years."

That opening paragraph discloses another Marshall characteristic—his self-effacement and modesty. He gave the credit for originating the method where it belonged, but avoided mentioning the fact that the four-year development and systematizing at Fort Leavenworth was very largely the work of George Marshall. In fact, his own name is never mentioned in the article, and the only way the reader would know that he participated in the expedition was to realize that if he had not been there directing the job, he could never have written the detailed report.

The exposition of method is too long for quotation, but his statement of the problem and of the accomplishment is interesting as example of the practical work being accomplished in the revitalized Leavenworth schools:

The National Guard authorities of Missouri desired a detailed contoured map of the site for their new camp-ground near Nevada,

Missouri, and of the country in the immediate vicinity. Lack of funds and time prevented their having civilian engineers make the map. The War Department would not order engineer troops to do the work. The Missouri officers then appealed to the authorities of the Army Staff College for assistance. As a result of this it was decided that the staff class, composed of twenty-three officers and two instructors, should go to Nevada at the expense of Missouri and make a combined position sketch of the desired area.

The class left Fort Leavenworth by rail on the evening of June 19 and arrived in the town of Nevada at 7:00 o'clock the next morning. Breakfast was served at the station, and at 7:30 A.M. the officers drove off in six vehicles to the site of the encampment. The western border of the area was reached at 8:30 A.M. ... and the deployment of the sketchers at once began. The last man did not reach his place ... on the line of deployment ... until 9:30 A.M. At this hour all had started sketching. None of the sketchers had ever seen this terrain until the moment he started work. ...

At 3:30 P.M. the last sketcher had finished his work and the strips of celluloid, containing the sketch of the entire area, were put together on the ground. ...

The following is a résumé of just what had been accomplished: In seven hours 24 men had completely sketched an area of 27 square miles on a scale of 6 inches equal one mile, with 10-foot contours and all roads, fences, crops, woods, telegraph lines, houses, and even the plan of the camp water pipe line shown. At the close of this period the work was ready for immediate blueprinting, which means that completely serviceable maps could have been made available in a few minutes. ... Had this work been undertaken by an ordinary surveying party, it could hardly have been completed, ready for blue printing, inside of 30 days. ...

This, then, was a sample of what it meant to go to school at Fort Leavenworth in the days when Major Morrison, first under General Bell and then under General Frederick Funston when Bell went to Washington as Chief of Staff, was creating an intellectual center for military men, molding a corps of true professional experts, establishing a continuity of concept but particularly of method.

Meantime, life was very pleasant for the Marshalls at the old post. In the two years that George was a student, their social activity was rather limited. The faculty officers frowned upon student lieutenants who accepted too many invitations to dinner, or went to too many hops. George absorbed his studies eagerly, and suffered neither physical nor nervous strain from the intensive course; but he worked hard and consistently, and avoided most social activity while doing enough riding, or playing enough tennis or golf, to keep himself in trim.

Besides, the society of his wife was enough to satisfy him. His fellow students learned quickly that no one could compete successfully with Lily for George's attention. They learned, too, that after a class was dismissed at the far end of a long tactical ride, the surest way to get home in a hurry by the most direct route was just to follow Marshall. He was always in a hurry to get home, and always knew the shortest way.

After graduation from the Staff College, followed by a taste of field duty with troops at the National Guard camp at Gettysburg, George came back to Leavenworth as an instructor, and the pace was not quite so hard. The Marshalls began taking a more active part in all the post's social affairs, and George had a wonderful time. He liked dancing, particularly, and although his wife still could not dance because of her health, he never lacked for partners. As for the other officers, "sitting one out" with Mrs. Marshall became one of the most delightful of all reasons for going to a dance at all. Marshall also rode a lot, and took Lily on long drives through the rolling Kansas countryside in a buckboard. Hunting was another of his favorite pastimes.

For all that, the pastimes were never as interesting to Marshall as military problems, and he displayed a great aptitude for field problems in strategy and tactics. He was passionately fond of field duty with troops, and concerned always with the practical problems of handling men, both as individuals, and as troops in military problems and maneuvers. He worked with other students and instructors on various special studies, participating in the preparation of a highly technical small monograph on cordage and tackle, and contributing, along with Captain James A. Woodruff, to Sherrill's book on map making and topography.

Another of the Academic Board's recommendations of 1908 sent

Lieutenant Marshall off in the summer of 1910 to a series of one-week National Guard camps in New York and Massachusetts, and, at his own request, to the National Rifle Matches at Camp Perry, Ohio. He had got the idea into his head that too long an assignment at Leavenworth was removing him from the practical, shooting realities of the Infantry.

That summer of 1910 marked his departure from Leavenworth. After spending the month of August at Camp Perry, he took four months' leave, came back to another series of brief assignments, then settled down for a year as instructor with the Massachusetts National Guard. But the mark of Leavenworth was on him, and he had a star in his pocket. It was to be nearly thirty years before he could take it out of his pocket and put it on his shoulder as Brigadier General Marshall, but already his reputation was spreading through the Army.

An officer may not examine his personal file—the famous 201 file kept by the Adjutant General's Department—and may examine his efficiency file only in Washington, so it may have been years before Marshall saw what the guiding genius of the first years at the re-established Leavenworth school said about him:

"Lt. Marshall has one of the best minds I know. He is mentally very mature for his years. Possesses tact and good judgment. A most promising officer."

That was written on Marshall's efficiency report, when he was graduated from the Staff College, by Major Morrison. Marshall was, indeed, one of the "Morrison men." It was the highest praise a Morrison man could want.

Photo Courtesy E. P. Coles

FIRST LIEUTENANT MARSHALL

The date of this portrait is uncertain, but it was made some time after his promotion to first lieutenant in 1908.

TEMPORARY COLONEL

VI

Tactics in the Tropics

With heavy foreboding, Lieutenant Marshall telegraphed the Adjutant General of the Army on May 2, 1913, requesting immediate preference for assignment to the Philippines.

He had made one attempt to avoid Philippine service, because his wife was not well, and had been cautioned against the hardships of climate and service life in the islands. Neither of them could view with anything but distress and dismay the possibility of separation during a three-year foreign service tour.

Yet George's name was within a very few numbers of the top in the foreign service roster. There had been more than nine years of duty at home—with troops, as a student at Leavenworth, as instructor in the schools there, with the Massachusetts National Guard, then again with an Infantry regiment. He was slated definitely for another overseas tour.

So on April 10 he wrote to the Adjutant General, explained that his wife's health would not permit her to accompany him to the Philippines, and asked that he be ordered instead to any of the other foreign duty areas—Hawaii, Alaska, China, or Panama. The Adjutant General replied that the choices he had outlined were contrary to regulations laid down by the Secretary of War. The Army could not consider foreign service on a volunteer basis except in the Philippines.

In such circumstances, another man might have done nothing, hoping that luck would bring him the more agreeable assignment he was barred from seeking. Such a course would have been out of character for Marshall. Unhappily, but promptly and without hesitation, he telegraphed the Adjutant General requesting that he be ordered to the Philippines.

The three years between his departure from the Leavenworth schools and his return to the Philippines for his second tour of duty in the islands had not been entirely uneventful. Even before he left Leavenworth, the sudden death of his father had been the occasion for the last visit George was to make to Uniontown until after he became Chief of Staff thirty years later.

Mr. Marshall had been gravely ill in the late summer of 1909, but by the middle of September his convalescence had progressed so far toward complete recovery that his nurse had been dismissed and he was beginning to pick up the interrupted work of his business affairs. From his apartment in the Skyscraper, he was engaged in a telephone conversation with a business associate the morning of September 21 when his voice suddenly thickened, and faltered. He dropped the receiver, and then collapsed unconscious on the floor.

Mrs. Marshall summoned a doctor hurriedly. The diagnosis was apoplexy, and Mr. Marshall died that same afternoon without regaining consciousness. A funeral service was held in St. Peter's three days later, with his beloved Knights Templar sharing the ceremony for their friend and leader, and accompanying his body to Pittsburgh, where he was buried.

It was the end of the Marshall family in Uniontown. The house where they had lived so many years, the back yard with the twin pear trees between which small George had pitched a boy's tent and played soldier all by himself, already had disappeared and been replaced by a theater. After her husband's death, Mrs. Marshall went to Pittsburgh to live with the Ewings, and the break with Uniontown was complete. The last act was the filing with the Register of Wills of a paper in which the three children assigned all their interests in their father's estate to their mother. There was no will, and the total value of the estate was estimated in the probate accounting at something less than thirty thousand dollars.

The next year, after a series of one-week assignments as an instructor at various National Guard summer encampments and a month at the rifle matches at Camp Perry, Lieutenant Marshall asked for three months' leave, and early in September he and Lily went off for a tour of Europe. This was not work, but fun—a black-and-white London of hansom cabs, the strange and lovely luminosity of autumn in Paris, the tomb of imperial glory in the chapel of the Invalides, a Vienna still the seat of empire and still gay, a vanished Renaissance that somehow seemed to remain alive in Florence, the islands of the blue Mediterranean and the matchless remnants of the Acropolis, new empire and picturesque squalor and the incomplete, uneasy meeting of East and West in Algiers. They liked it so well that George asked, and got, a fourth month of vacation, and it was the end of January 1911 before they got back to New York.

For a few weeks, George was assigned to the 24th Infantry at Madison Barracks. Then he was shifted to San Antonio as assistant to the Chief Signal Officer and Adjutant of a battalion of Signal troops with a maneuver division assembling there. As the name indicates, the ostensible reason for this concentration of troops was to hold maneuvers; but the true reason was the government's desire to counter unrest below the border with a show of force.

The concentration was not entirely successful. The work of the yet new General Staff, it is true, made the operation a decided contrast to the chaos which characterized the Army's efforts in the Spanish War. However, even in 1911 there did not yet exist in the Army a single field division organization or headquarters, and the provisional division framework inaugurated for the three brigades of Infantry, the brigade of Field Artillery and brigade of Cavalry, and the necessary auxiliary troops converging on San Antonio required time and experience to develop efficiency. It was a lesson full of meaning for an intelligent and thoughtful observer who was also a participant, as Marshall was. The time would come when he would take almost desperate steps to test his organizations in maneuvers, and test as well the men from whom he must choose his leaders and their staffs.

General Leonard Wood, then Chief of Staff, made note in his

annual report that the San Antonio concentration, in which it took until midsummer to get the last regiment to its destination, disclosed the folly of keeping units under strength, proved the urgent need of reserve components to supplement the regular forces, the even more urgent need of reserve supplies and equipment and of established supply depots. The many and manifest shortcomings of this show of force on the border were, however, among the lesser burdens and worries of General Wood at the time.

Throughout 1911, Wood was engaged in the culminating episodes of a long feud in which the entire existence of the General Staff was at stake. Marshall, keen student and observer that he was, thorough and ambitious professional soldier, was fully aware of the schism that had developed in Washington, and conscious of its implications for the future of the General Staff and the Army in which already he hoped to rise to supreme position. Through the voluminous reports of the daily press and such especially interested publications as the *Army and Navy Journal,* much less studious and devoted officers than George Marshall followed with avid interest the rise and fall of Major General Fred C. Ainsworth.

This brilliant administrator and ambitious man had been undermining the general staff idea since its inception. Had someone less headstrong than Leonard Wood been Chief of Staff, someone less honorable and less certain of the issues than Henry L. Stimson been Secretary of War, Ainsworth's shrewd climbing might well have undone in 1911-1912 all that Elihu Root had accomplished in 1903.

When the general staff law was enacted, Ainsworth, a doctor turned administrator and Army officer, was a captain and chief of the Bureau of Records and Pensions, one of the old, permanent staff bureaus. Continuous residence in Washington gave these permanent bureau officers an opportunity not shared by line officers for close relations with members of Congress. They used the opportunity to protect and enhance the importance of their own duties, and no one was more canny or more adroit as lobbyist than was Ainsworth.

The original draft of the general staff bill gave the Chief of Staff, under the direction of the President and the Secretary of War, supervision over all line troops and the various administrative staff and supply departments. With no public hearing, Ainsworth achieved a change, so that the bill specified the bureaus over which the Chief of Staff exercised authority. The only bureau omitted from the list was the one Ainsworth headed. To clinch his independence of the new General Staff, he got a second clause inserted, limiting the Chief of Staff in general to supervision of military duties "not otherwise assigned by law." It would be doing that shrewd man a grave injustice to assume that Ainsworth did not realize this opened the door to any bureau chief with enough influence at the Capitol to obtain legislation specifying the duties and jurisdiction of his own bureau.

Ainsworth was bold, and he was ambitious, but for several years he played cautiously. He used every opportunity to advance himself, and to remove his office further from the jurisdiction of the Chief of Staff, but not until 1911 did he feel his position was strong enough for him to launch a direct assault on the entire general staff concept. It would be unfair to assume that Ainsworth was treacherous, or cynical; he was one of those gifted men who cannot understand that the general good is not necessarily served by policies and actions which enlarge their own responsibilities and enhance their own prestige. That he was an administrator of abilities far greater than the average is incontestable, and he instituted administrative reforms of lasting value in the War Department. Nevertheless, he came perilously close to wrecking the only instrument capable of making the United States Army an organization fit to implement the nation's policies.

Having exempted his own bureau from the supervision to which others were subjected in the new staff system, Ainsworth found his next opportunity in the desire of William H. Taft, who succeeded Root as Secretary, and the current Chief of Staff to get rid of the old name of Adjutant General. That officer, prior to the reorganization, had performed many of the duties now assigned to the Chief of Staff, and subtle suggestions of his former great power in the Army still clung to the title.

Ainsworth brought his gifts as an administrator to bear on the question, and suggested, among other things, that the now largely routine duties of the office of the Adjutant General be combined with the similar duties performed by his own office, achieving economy and efficiency by an administrative consolidation. The title proposed for the new office, "Military Secretary," suggests the function which Taft had in mind, and Ainsworth's merger proposal was approved readily.

The next move by the redoubtable doctor was to go quietly to his friends in Congress. The result was that the bill which established the office of Military Secretary specified, not by naming him, but by careful reference to seniority and the promotion list, that Ainsworth himself would be the first man to hold the new job. Furthermore, the law made him a major general, although all other bureau chiefs in the War Department held the lower grade of brigadier general. And, for a final and brilliant impudence, the bill directed that only the first Military Secretary should have the grade of major general—all who followed him in the office would be mere brigadiers.

When he had held his new office for a few years, Ainsworth was ready to seek real power. As a first step, he was able to get the title changed again. The Military Secretary became once more the Adjutant General, and precisely because Ainsworth knew that the old name still carried its connotations of power throughout the Army. Finally, in 1911, he challenged General Wood openly in a bid to restore his office to the pre-eminent position it had held prior to 1903.

The final clash came over the report of a board of officers on paper work in the Army. It was proposed to abolish the Muster Roll, a report with generations of tradition behind it, substituting a simpler form. Ainsworth insisted that the Muster Roll be kept without change, and wrote a series of memoranda climaxed by one in which, by insolent implication, he accused Secretary Stimson, General Wood, and all others who disagreed with him of being incompetent amateurs and dangerous meddlers in something that was none of their business. This memorandum challenged directly the competence of the General Staff and the validity of the staff concept.

Stimson, who would be Secretary again years later when Marshall was Chief of Staff, had allowed the controversy between Wood and Ainsworth to develop during twelve months of increasingly bitter cleavage. Why he did not take action sooner is not clear. A man of spotless integrity, he was nonetheless aware of political factors, and it may be that Ainsworth's well-known power and influence in Congress may have deterred the Secretary from action until there was insubordination of a character so grave it could not be ignored. Moreover, Stimson's great intellect worked slowly and deliberately. Swift to act when he had reached a decision, he reached that decision only after long and careful thought, concentrating upon a single problem to the exclusion of all others except routine matters. Whatever the reason for delayed action in this case, the final contumacious memorandum from the Adjutant General in February 1912 got action of a kind that Ainsworth certainly had not expected.

On February 14, Ainsworth received a letter from Stimson informing him that, by order of President Taft, he was relieved of duty as Adjutant General, but would remain in Washington, awaiting orders, until the President and the Secretary had determined what disciplinary action would be taken in his case. The incident exploded in Washington with the impact of a well-aimed bomb, and the whole Army rocked with the scandal. Ainsworth, however, knew when he was beaten. The next day, Senator Warren, chairman of the Military Affairs Committee, called President Taft from a cabinet meeting on the plea of "most urgent business." The senator had brought Ainsworth's request to be allowed to retire from the Army, and Taft approved the request.

Wood had emerged victor in the contest with Ainsworth, but it was a Pyrrhic victory. The removal of Ainsworth was to produce a violent Congressional reaction against Wood personally, and a lingering Congressional distrust of the General Staff. Nevertheless, the Staff survived, as it could not have done had Ainsworth remained Adjutant General.

When President Taft and his Secretary of War took action against Ainsworth, Lieutenant Marshall had been in Boston several months on detached service as inspector-instructor with the **Organized Militia of Massachusetts**. Completing that assignment in the late summer of 1912, he planned and directed some field exercises in a way that won the warm commendation of General Bliss, then commanding the Eastern Department.

On September 1, 1912, Marshall was assigned to the 4th Infantry at Fort Logan H. Roots, Arkansas. The regiment was commanded by Lieutenant Colonel Elmore F. Taggart, who gave his new lieutenant the job of organizing a course of study in the Garrison School for officers on duty at the post. How well Marshall handled the assignment is indicated by an Inspector General's report of his visit of inspection.

"I desire," wrote Major Eli A. Helmick, "to call attention to what I consider a model course of instruction which was prepared and carried out for the officers taking the post graduate's course in the Garrison School at this post.

"The instruction was very properly placed by Lieutenant Colonel Taggart in the hands of 1st Lieutenant George C. Marshall, Jr., who as a graduate of, and instructor in, the Army Service Schools, and as instructor inspector with the Massachusetts Volunteer Militia, is particularly well equipped for this class of work. Lieutenant Marshall has a natural faculty for the work of instruction and has cultivated it to a high degree."

Major Helmick's report was written just about a month before more unrest in Mexico brought the assembly of the 2d Division at Texas City and Galveston. The experience with the Maneuver Division two years before paid dividends this time, and a smoothly operating division headquarters had all the troops in the concentration area only a little more than a week after the first orders were issued.

Marshall's regiment was in the Galveston contingent, and while they were in Texas his commanding officer forwarded in March 1913 another glowing commentary on the outstanding abilities of this junior officer. Colonel Taggart told the War Department he thought Marshall should be entrusted with important duties, that he would consider his command fortunate to have Marshall in any capacity, that this lieutenant had a valuable fund of military information and an extraordinary capacity for imparting it to others, that—in short—he considered Marshall well qualified to command a regiment or a brigade.

This was all very fine, but it did not remove Marshall's name from the top of the foreign service list, nor relieve his worried mind of the fear of taking Lily to the Philippines. In the first week of July 1913, he sailed once again for Manila. Whether Lily had recovered by that time from the illness of the spring and went with him, or whether she came out later, is not clear; but at any rate, she joined him in the Philippines and they had, as it turned out, a completely successful and delightful three-year tour in the islands.

The climate, after all, was bearable, and living conditions were very pleasant indeed for young officers and their families. It was possible, even on a lieutenant's salary, to make quite a show of luxury, with roomy bungalow quarters on the post, and native servants plentiful and cheap. Of course, the show was apt to be more than the reality. The servants were not always as competent as they were plentiful, and it frequently required a sense of humor, some ingenuity, and considerable patience for an Army wife who spoke only English to manage servants who spoke only Spanish or Tagalog.

But there were delightful friends, and the pace was easy enough to allow considerable entertaining and being entertained, for all of Lieutenant Marshall's driving energy, and the passion for knowledge that would not let him rest. It was during this tour that Marshall collected maps, official reports, and histories, and with them visited every major Philippine battlefield of the War with Spain and the Insurrection, until he possessed the same encyclopedic knowledge of those campaigns that Cadet Marshall had displayed at the V.M.I. about New Market.

Nor was his thirst for learning confined to strategy, tactics, terrain, and supply. A few doors away from the Marshalls, Captain Laurence Halstead had his quarters. A few doors in the opposite direction were the quarters of Second Lieutenant Frederick Walker, who wanted to learn telegraphy. Captain Halstead, pleased by Walker's ambition, had agreed to practice with him. They installed a wire between their houses, and spent a portion of their leisure time tapping out messages to each other. During one of these practice sessions, both Halstead and Walker were startled when an unsuspected interloper broke in with a message of his own. They discovered that Lieutenant Marshall had heard about their arrangement, and being as eager as Walker to learn telegraphy, had simply tapped their line and installed a key in his own quarters.

Marshall, still a first lieutenant, probably knew as much about the Army as any officer of any grade in the Philippines at the time; and his colleagues in the 13th Infantry at Fort McKinley were finding out that, in an Army still very much concerned about forms and "spit and polish," this young Lieutenant was primarily concerned about the substance of things. This difference in viewpoint, and the penetrating mind of Lieutenant Marshall, brought about a wager, which in turn brought about a meeting with a senior officer who was to become one of his most enthusiastic admirers and advocates, Major Johnson Hagood.

Major Hagood had come out to Manila in the spring of 1913 on the staff of General J. Franklin Bell, who was commanding the Philippine Department. One day in the autumn, he heard of this wager made by Marshall—with whom, except that it was another lieutenant in his company, is not recorded—and the rumor took him out to McKinley to look up this man of whom he had never heard, but who obviously knew exactly what the United States Army was like in 1913.

It seems that Marshall's company was due for inspection, and Marshall bet his fellow lieutenant that he could name in advance three trivial faults the inspecting officer would find when he examined the formation; and that, moreover, when it came to the field exercise which was part of the inspection, Marshall would commit three grave violations of the most elementary tactical requirements, and none of them would be spotted.

The other lieutenant accepted the bet, and Marshall then wrote his predictions on a slip of paper which was placed in an envelope and sealed. After the inspection was over, the envelope was opened, the predictions were read against the report of the inspecting officer, and Marshall collected. He had won on all six points.

For the first half of the wager, it developed that Marshall had written that the inspecting officer would find one soldier who had not shaved for a couple of days, another with two buttons of his blouse unbuttoned, and a third who had forgotten his bayonet. All three showed on the inspecting officer's report of the formation.

For the second half, Marshall had written that when the company went out for its field exercise, a set problem involving an attack on an imaginary enemy position atop a hill, Marshall would first march the company, in a column of fours, straight up the road toward the hill until they were well within rifle range of the "enemy," instead of dispersing them in the fields for the approach; that as they approached the position, he would send a corporal out with a squad on patrol without giving them any instructions at all about where to go or what to look for; and, finally, a detachment would be sent up the face of the hill in attack, taking advantage of such cover as the rather bare slope afforded and crawling dutifully on their bellies through the grass, when in fact the attack should be launched through a thickly wooded ravine at one side which gave complete cover from observation and flanked the "enemy" position.

"I went out to McKinley and looked up this fellow Marshall, asked him about the wager, and he admitted that was the way it was," Hagood recalled years later.

"It taught me something. The lesson I learned, and I never failed to apply it during the rest of my career, was that the great thing in training soldiers is to get at the essentials, and—when you're inspecting—to look for the essentials."

It was a few months later that the professional attainments of this very junior officer, Marshall, were demonstrated in convincing fashion to the entire Philippine command during maneuvers involving between ten and fifteen thousand troops—all the strength on Luzon.

The episode has become one of the Marshall legends, embroidered at times past recognition, but in its bare facts an impressive episode needing no elaboration.

Even in those days, the fear of a Japanese invasion was a very real one, and coupled with the fear of another insurrection, contributed to the state of mind which resulted in the fact that soldiers of the Philippine Department slept with two hundred rounds of ammunition beside them. Defense against great force was considered impossible even then, but plans were drawn for delaying actions, and for defense against invading forces approximately equal in strength to the garrison on Luzon.

For purposes of the maneuvers which General Bell ordered for the two weeks beginning January 22, 1914, the forces on Luzon were divided into two approximately equal detachments. As one act of the maneuvers, Detachment No. 1 was to stage an amphibious attack in Batangas, and march toward Manila. Detachment No. 2 was to defend the capital city.

Captain Jens Bugge was named Chief of Staff, and First Lieutenant George C. Marshall, Adjutant, of Detachment No. 1. A day or two after the maneuvers started, Bugge went off to hospital with an attack of malaria and had to be replaced. General Bell was in Mindanao at the time, but his aide, Major E. E. Booth, who was in charge of training and maneuvers in the Department, had known Marshall at Leavenworth and on his own initiative named Marshall as Acting Chief of Staff to succeed Bugge.

Because of Marshall's youth and his junior rank, Booth expected the appointment to be criticized, and was not surprised by the outcry which followed. He stuck to his decision, however, because he knew Marshall's ability as a tactician. Equally important, Marshall was thoroughly familiar with the planned operations, and it would have been extremely difficult to find another officer who was both qualified and familiar with the plans. One senior officer of the detachment was told finally that he would accept direction from Marshall, or go before a retiring board.

The maneuvers began, and in the course of a few days Detachment

No. 1 was on the march through Batangas Province. The colonel commanding was an old-fashioned, shooting, hard-riding soldier unlearned in the Leavenworth lore. Umpires and observers, meeting the colonel as they rode over the area, watching every action, would call out, "What are you going to do, Colonel?" The doughty old warrior's unvarying reply was, "I'm going to turn their right flank!"

In all truth, the old colonel was not the only one engaged in the maneuvers who lacked the new schooling of Leavenworth. Few of the officers had it. The standard field order developed at Leavenworth was a mystery to most of them, in spite of the fact that it was designed to end mystery in field commands, and—more importantly—to guarantee against oversight of important factors. Every essential was part of the framework of the field order, and once an officer learned the form, he was most unlikely to neglect any part of it when issuing operational orders in the field.

Coming up to headquarters during the campaign, one of the company commanders in Detachment No. 1 arrived just in time to see the beginning of a legend. Lieutenant H. H. Arnold found the staff and unit commanders gathered around a figure, sprawled on his back against a fence in the shade of a clump of bushes, staring intently at a map spread on a board and fastened to a tree at a peculiar angle above his eyes. While Arnold and the umpires and observers watched, and the active participants wrote in longhand, Marshall began dictating his field order.

It was long, and it was complicated; but without reference to any notes, looking only at his map, Marshall dictated for several minutes without pause. When he stopped, the group around him was awed. He had dictated a complete and elaborate plan of attack. Every component of the maneuver detachment had its orders. Not one factor had been overlooked. Not one change was made—Marshall did not even read over the order. That was his plan, that was the detachment order; and the result was the complete routing of the defending detachment and a march straight into Manila.

Arnold, whose assignment in the same regiment was the beginning of a long and close friendship with Marshall that was to bear fruit in their teamwork during the war against the Axis, was astounded. When he returned home after the maneuvers, he described the incident to his wife, and added, "There's a man who's going to be Chief of Staff!"

Hap Arnold was not the only one impressed by Marshall's work during the maneuvers. Even those who had protested this important assignment for a youngster were won over, and the enthusiasm for Marshall was widespread and genuine. His unfailing courtesy and self-effacement, his manifest devotion to duty and his complete objectivity, had erased the sting which senior officers felt in taking orders from their junior. The chief umpire of Detachment No. 1, Lieutenant Colonel C. E. Dentler, praised the Lieutenant lavishly in his final report on the maneuvers.

"The orders issued from Headquarters, Detachment No. 1, were excellent," he wrote. "In several cases they are models that show a clear grasp of the situation and attention to every necessary point of tactics, and are so clear and definite as to be impossible to misconstrue."

Then he added:

"The sudden changes at Headquarters, Detachment No. 1, incident upon the relief of Captain Bugge as chief of staff on account of his illness and the detail of Lieutenant Marshall in his place, all occurring after the maneuver campaign was begun, greatly interfered with the organization of the headquarters for systematic work, and placed upon Lieutenant Marshall, who was thus promoted and at the same time handicapped, a severe task which he carried out successfully, and for which he deserves great credit."

General Bell returned while the maneuvers were in progress, and after they were completed, Major Booth wrote a full report of them for the General. In this report, Booth advanced the opinion that Marshall was the best leader of large bodies of troops in the entire American Army, without regard of age, rank, or previous experience. A few days later, at a luncheon for his staff, Bell said he regarded Marshall as the greatest potential wartime leader in the Army.

Whatever his potential rank, Marshall remained a first lieutenant, and went back to McKinley as adjutant of the post. On their return, he and Captain Halstead found that Mrs. Halstead had taken her two small sons and moved into the Marshalls' quarters for as long as the men were away. The fear of uprising and other vague native dangers prompted the move, and the same fear prompted Mrs. Marshall to welcome the move heartily.

"Doesn't it beat the Dutch," commented Marshall to Halstead with a grin, "how one scare plus one scare equals no scare?"

Marshall bought a typewriter and a bicycle from Halstead, and the bicycle he took apart and put back together again, just to demonstrate to himself that he could do it. There is no record that he felt such assurance about the typewriter. And he was shortly to acquire a more complicated and satisfactory method of transportation.

Captain Sherrill, his friend of the Leavenworth days, was transferred to Manila in the summer of 1914, and brought with him a new Model T Ford. The Sherrills and the Marshalls resumed with delight the close relationship they had enjoyed in Kansas, and so it was that when Sherrill, not much later, was transferred from Manila to Corregidor, where an automobile could not by any stretch of the imagination be considered necessary, he agreed to sell it to Marshall. To make delivery, Sherrill drove out from Manila, and he brought along in the tonneau a large can of oil. Chugging along one of the dikelike roads, he turned around to take a look at the oil can and make certain it still was upright, and drove off the road and into a rice paddy. Some Filipinos lifted the Ford, still occupied by Sherrill, back to the road, and he drove on with a car none the worse for its mud bath. Marshall took joyful possession of the vehicle, which he loved almost as much as his horse.

Apparently the vagaries of the service were as unpredictable then as later officers found them, and Sherrill's decision to sell his car may have been overhasty, for by the end of December 1914 the Sherrills were back in Manila. The last day of the month they went out to McKinley as guests at Marshall's birthday dinner, and to see the New Year in with George and Lily.

Suddenly, just before midnight, the lights went out all over the post, and the four friends chatting gaily on the veranda of the Marshalls' quarters were shocked into terror as the harsh tones of a bugle sounded the call to arms. Through the dusk and the starlight they could see the native employees swarming across the parade ground. Insurrection!

George dashed inside to get his sword, an essential part of his uniform, before running to headquarters. He was adjutant of the post, and the fastest he could get there would not be fast enough.

"Shaggy!" he shouted. "You take the women over to General Kernan's!"

Mrs. Sherrill called from the dark interior of the bungalow.

"I've got to go home!"

"You can't!"

"I've got to! The baby's with a native nurse in Manila!"

"You've got to get over to the general's! Come on out!"

Dancing with impatience, fuming at the delay, Marshall could see the Filipino boys still running off the post. He was supposed to be at headquarters, but he could not bring himself to leave his own place until he saw his wife and their guests started toward safety.

"Lily! Are you coming?"

"Well, George," the voice drawled out of the darkness, "I can't leave all my silver here!"

George exploded.

"Well, if you want to stay and be murdered for an old silver spoon, then stay!"

But in a very few minutes they were on their way. A car was found, and the Sherrills, in an agony of suspense, were driven back to town along roads crowded with muttering and shouting natives, to find on their arrival that their small son had not even been awakened by the hubbub. The insurrection proved to be no insurrection at all, but a kind of general strike by native workers. It did not last long, and things settled back quickly into the old pattern.

For all of 1915 the Marshalls remained at Fort McKinley, but on January 1, 1916, Lieutenant Marshall reported in Manila as aide to General Hunter Liggett, commanding the Department. He had only a few months to go before his foreign tour was completed, and they were spent living in the relatively impressive headquarters group known as the Military Plaza, a relic of the Spanish days.

In May the Marshalls returned to the States, speeded by Liggett's report that he considered Marshall an excellent officer of great ability, sound judgment and very practical sense, exemplary in habits and a hard student of his profession. He would need, and display again, all of those qualities very soon. A soldier's job is to prepare for war, and George Marshall was going home to prepare in deadly earnest for the war already in its second year in Europe.

VII

The First Convoy to France

On July 1, 1916, Lieutenant Marshall was promoted to Captain of Infantry, and reported to the Presidio of San Francisco as aide-de-camp to his old friend and mentor Major General J. Franklin Bell, commanding general of the Western Department.

The average civilian thinks of the aide to a general officer as a kind of glorified lackey, spending his very brief working hours executing gracefully certain menial or trivial tasks, and his much more extensive leisure hours gracing teas and cocktail parties.

Such aides-de-camp are not unknown in the military profession, even in the United States Army; but they are few. In most cases, the aide is in reality a kind of executive assistant to his chief. It was work of the latter kind that Bell exacted from Marshall, and he got it in a measure and of a quality that delighted him.

The summer of 1916 was a hectic and important one in the Army. When Marshall reached San Francisco the small but bloody encounter at Carrizal between two troops of the 10th Cavalry and some trigger-happy forces of President Carranza had sobered the Mexican chief of state considerably, and—although Brigadier General John J. Pershing and President Wilson could not yet be certain of it—grave hostilities on the border actually were at an end.

By this time, Pershing had a force of seventy-five thousand men along the border and in Mexico, and he had to hold them there while a joint commission arrived at a protocol under which the troops were withdrawn from Mexico in January 1917, with the revolutionary leader whose border depredations had started the whole thing,

Pancho Villa, still uncaptured. It was a delicate and trying job which had been given Pershing, and the concentration on the border, accompanied by the call of a number of National Guard units to Federal service, added tremendously to the administrative and supply problems of the several Army Departments, or territorial commands, within the United States.

With such difficulties complicating the normal Army problem of accomplishing very much with a minimum of means, the impetuous and headstrong old warrior Bell found the cool and assured young Marshall a steady and dependable assistant. Their work would have been heavy enough if the routine and the border tension had been all, but it was not. Most aspects of the National Defense Act of 1916 delighted the thoughtful officers of the "new Army," but it added a tremendous burden of reorganization to their duties. And, while President Wilson campaigned with his kept-us-out-of-war slogan, "preparedness" was another slogan that meant work for the Army.

The Act of June 3, 1916, marked the first time that the Congress of the United States had considered the Army as a whole, and attempted to frame a basic and over-all policy in a single law. Previous legislation had been largely fragmentary, arm by arm and service by service, producing an unbalanced aggregation of authorizations and appropriations that the most frantic efforts of the War Department had never quite been able to put together into something with an approximate resemblance to unity.

The 1916 National Defense Act established the Army of the United States, to consist of the Regular Army, the National Guard, and the Organized Reserve, supplemented by a Volunteer Army in time of war. Over a period of five years, the authorized peace strength of the Regular Army was to be increased to 220,000. Brigade and division organizations were approved. Closer Federal supervision of the National Guard was provided, commissioning of reserve officers authorized, and a Reserve Officers' Training Corps established. The planning of the General Staff had borne important fruit, although it came too late—the expansion was to take five years, and the country was destined to be at war in less than twelve months. And, unhappily, the General Staff itself very nearly received a death sentence in this legislation.

It was the last, and long-delayed, thrust from General Ainsworth, dismissed as Adjutant General more than four years earlier; and it was an indirect thrust, the result of the deep distrust of the General Staff engendered in the minds of Ainsworth's friends in Congress by his dismissal. Congressional resentment in 1912 had resulted in censure of Secretary Stimson by the House Military Affairs Committee, in a direct legislative slap at General Wood which specifically barred him from reappointment as Chief of Staff, and in a reduction of the General Staff itself from forty-five to thirty-six officers. Now, in 1916, Congress allowed an increase of eighteen officers over a five-year period, but by restrictive provisions actually reduced the General Staff on duty in the War Department to twenty officers. With a declaration of war less than a year away, the military planning and co-ordinating body for the entire Army was cut to twenty men! Furthermore, additional restrictive clauses in the law would have nullified the effectiveness of even this small group and restored the various bureaus to their old virtual independence had not the new Secretary of War, Newton D. Baker, had the vision of Root and Stimson, and by a skillful interpretation and wise regulation preserved the general staff concept.

These were important and fateful happenings, but another provision of the National Defense Act of 1916 was of more immediate importance to Captain Marshall. However the members of Congress might dislike Wood and resent the fate of Ainsworth, they were persuaded to recognize the value of Wood's obsession with modern tactical organizations, his unrelenting efforts for preparedness, and specifically his success with the Plattsburg training camp.

In his zeal to give civilians who were potential officers of a war-time Army the rudiments of military training, Wood, as commanding general of the Eastern Department, had opened at Plattsburg in 1915 a training camp at which civilians reported for a month's training on a volunteer basis, and without compensation. It was a small effort, pitifully small; its importance lay, not in its size, but in the attraction of public attention to the problem of training reserves. The 1916 legislation took up the plan seriously, and provided for the organization of such citizen training camps throughout the country.

Accordingly, General Bell, adopting the plan enthusiastically, had such a camp in operation at Monterey, California, by early summer of 1916, and had authority to organize two others on the West Coast. The Monterey camp, with about two thousand volunteer trainees, had been going two weeks under the command of a general officer when Lieutenant Colonel Johnson Hagood, then commanding an Army post at San Diego, received telegraphic instructions from General Bell to proceed at once to Monterey, stay at the camp for the remaining two weeks as an observer, and when the camp was over report to Bell in San Francisco. Hagood, as lieutenant colonels must when generals order, obeyed.

"Don't tell me about that damned camp," was General Bell's greeting when he walked in to report two weeks later. "I know it was rotten! I'm not going to have another one like that."

The old man leaned back in his chair, and grinned at Hagood.

"The next camp is going to be up at Salt Lake, up at Fort Douglas. I'm not going to send any general up there, like I did to this last one. I'm going to put you in command!"

Hagood said nothing, but he could not hide the gleam of satisfaction in his eyes, or keep from pulling himself an imperceptible fraction straighter before the general.

"And I don't want you to be too much puffed up about that, either," the general added with a malicious twinkle, "because I'm going to send George Marshall up there to be your adjutant. I picked you to be commanding officer because I knew you had sense enough to let Marshall run it!"

They looked at each other, and laughed. Each of them knew what the other thought about Marshall. The Army was the Army, and protocol was protocol, and a very junior captain commanding one of these camps was simply out of the question. But two very able senior officers, with character and warmth of heart beyond the average, could connive to make him commander in fact if not in name, and be delighted with each other in the conspiracy. It is the measure of Hagood that this story is known only because Hagood himself told it.

So Captain Marshall reported at Fort Douglas as adjutant, and on August 16, 1916, took over the training program that was to run a month. He had learned already from John McAuley Palmer that, whatever the theoretical desirability of a large professional force, the army of a democracy would always be a citizen army. In his work with the National Guard, he had come to know that these citizen forces, this much-maligned militia, if lifted out of the status of political football and state police and given proper training, could be the equal of any regulars in the world. He had thought a lot about the citizen army idea, and worked a lot with the citizen army reality; but, for all that, he was due for a lesson in zeal and enthusiasm at Fort Douglas.

They came pouring into camp from the cities and towns and counties of Montana, Idaho, Utah, and Washington. They were lawyers, merchants, bankers, doctors, teachers—about eight hundred of them; prosperous men, twenty-one to forty, who could afford to lose a month's income in the service of an ideal. They might have been expected to be soft, but Marshall was to find they could wear out their instructors, that he would be hard put to devise enough program to keep them busy. It was not a lark for them; it was not play, and many of them did need toughening; but they took the training seriously, they worked hard at it, and asked for more.

The trainees liked Marshall. So, for that matter, did the instructors. Marshall's tact and self-effacement were fully in evidence already, and the spirit animating Marshall and Hagood permeated the entire camp. Instructors came to Marshall for help, or sent requests that he come to their problems, and there was never any embarrassment, or loss of face; instead, the instructors were delighted when they could get a few minutes of his very busy hours.

The trainees were given target practice, taken on long marches, camped in the open, worked on small tactical problems—and minor tactics, not grand strategy, are the complicated part of the soldier's business. They were sent on scouting expeditions, and on patrols—and there was a lot of good-natured banter between Hagood and Marshall as it was made clear, this time, that each patrol was told where to go and what to do.

This was all field work, with no parade-ground foolishness. Marshall and his chief thought they had lined up a program intensive enough to make the trainees glad when the day's work was over, and there was time to relax. These businessmen had other ideas. They asked for instruction in bridge-building, and when it could not be included in an already full program, asked that it be given anyhow, after hours, when the scheduled program was over for the day.

The request was granted, and a drill in pontoon bridge construction across the lake at the camp was ordered. The first drill was a demonstration, a company of Engineer troops building the bridge while the trainees looked on. In the second drill, the trainees did the work while the Engineers directed them. In the third, the trainees did the job alone, and this time they broke the Army record for a bridge of that length!

When the camp closed, Hagood as commanding officer was required to make an efficiency report on the officers under his command. His report on Marshall contains what is probably the most remarkable tribute from a senior officer to a junior to be found in the history of the United States Army. The standard efficiency report contains this question, "Would you desire to have him under your immediate command in peace and in war?"

Colonel Hagood wrote in reply:

Yes, but I would prefer to serve *under his command*. . . . In my judgment there are not five officers in the Army as well qualified as he to command a division in the field.
. . . He should be made a brigadier general in the Regular Army, and every day this is postponed is a loss to the Army and the nation. [He is] The best officer in the Army below the grade of major, and there are not six better in any grade.
I have known this officer many years by reputation, and served

with him in the Philippine Islands during the Batangas Maneuvers. He is a military genius and one of those rare cases of wonderful military development during peace. He is of the proper age, has had the training and experience, and possesses the ability to command large bodies of troops in the field.

The Army and the nation sorely need such men in the grade of general officers at this time, and if I had the power I would nominate him to fill the next vacancy in grade of brigadier general in the line of the Army notwithstanding the law limiting the selection to colonels.

Then, to underscore his statement, Hagood added "He is my junior by over eighteen hundred files."

It was lavish and generous praise, but even if the War Department had been disposed to act on Hagood's suggestion—and there is not the slightest evidence of any such disposition—it could not have acted favorably on the recommendation for promotion. Officers in peacetime advanced in rank according to a rigid system of seniority, filling the vacancies created by the death or retirement of those at the top of the promotion list. Only after a man reached the grade of colonel was there selective promotion to the grade of general officer. In war, advanced rank was given by selective promotion, but it was temporary rank—when the emergency was over, the officer dropped back to his permanent grade in the promotion list of his arm or service.

Marshall went back to San Francisco, resuming his many duties as aide to General Bell and assistant adjutant of the Western Department. He remained there until December 31. Then, when General Bell was transferred to New York to command the Eastern Department, Marshall found himself at Governors Island, still aide to the general.

Here the mounting tension over Germany's submarine warfare, and the increasing certainty that the United States would be drawn into the war in Europe, was vastly more apparent than it had been in San Francisco. The mere being on the East Coast instead of the West made American participation seem more likely, and Captain

Marshall, as fully aware as any officer that the Army was not prepared to make a major contribution to the Allied effort, nevertheless began to think of France as the place where his acknowledged skill would be proved in battle, and win for him the position and the general distinction which the conditions of peacetime military service denied him.

With the fateful declaration of a state of war on April 6, 1917, his one obsession became that assignment to France. It was an obsession shared, of course, by virtually every officer in the Army, including General Bell. That splendid old fighter, casting over the possibilities, had already come to the conclusion that all the senior major generals of the Army would be passed over if an expeditionary force were sent to France, and that the newest Major General, John J. Pershing, would get the command. Having come to this conclusion, he sat down and wrote it to Pershing, and asked for an assignment under him. That letter was written early in April, and it was not until May 3 that Pershing received a cryptic telegram from Washington indicating that General Bell's guess had been very shrewd indeed.

It was small wonder that Pershing had been skeptical of his old friend's conclusion. There was no apparent decision by the government, when it declared war against the Central Powers, that it would send troops to Europe at all, or at any rate that it would send more than a small token force. The opinion was widespread, even in the Army, that the United States could supply effective help to the Allies in the form of its vast resources of raw materials and industrial capacity, but that creating an expeditionary force of important size was impracticable.

Such an attitude was easy enough to understand. The 1916 Defense Act had created the framework for a field army, but it had not created the army itself. The Army had no large tactical units in being, few weapons, a mere handful of officers and experienced noncommissioned officers, no experience with the trench warfare being fought in Europe, little training and very little strength. In Washington, the General Staff consisted of Major General Hugh L. Scott, Chief of Staff, and nineteen officers. There was an assortment of supply bureaus which were very shortly to start competing against each other for preference in the nation's factories and markets.

The picture was not entirely black, however. The exasperating troubles along the Mexican border the year before suddenly took on the aspect of fortuitous circumstance; because of them, the nation had approximately two hundred thousand men in service, including the National Guard units. And the hardening, discipline and schooling in the field which the troops on the border had received supplied the small but tough base on which the inverted pyramid of the National Army would be built.

Even the restricted and diminutive General Staff had been able to perform some of its essential functions. During the year following the passage of the 1916 Defense Act, the reduced staff had perfected regulations for the expansion of the Regular Army and establishment of the R.O.T.C., Officers' Reserve Corps, Enlisted Reserve Corps, and citizens' training camps. It had then gone farther, and produced a study of a system of national defense based upon universal liability to military training and service. When Congress, on May 18, 1917, approved the law calling for a wartime selective draft, this study by the General Staff became the basis for the actual organization of the National Army, with training cantonments and officers' training camps.

In May, also, Congress removed all restrictions on the size or duties of the General Staff, giving the President authority to provide all line and staff officers he found necessary. The damage, however, already had been done, as General Scott, the Chief of Staff, had pointed out in his report for 1916. The old soldier said he was certain the restrictions written into the 1916 act were based on a misconception of the duties of the General Staff and the Chief of Staff, and urged, not only that there be no further narrowing of the field, but that Congress be asked formally to reverse the direction taken in that law.

"This I hope it will do," he wrote, "by passing legislation which will sanctify by law the true powers of the Chief of Staff and remove all impediments to his command, subject to the Secretary's orders, of the line of the Army, and to his duty of co-ordinating the work of all the staff departments.

"The reasons which make this useful are to my mind quite evident and are not based upon any prejudice, or desire for power, or any lack of confidence in other corps and their chiefs, but solely upon elementary principles of military organization. . . .

"In any army unity of command is absolutely essential to secure prompt decisions and rapid execution of them."

When he read the Chief of Staff's report, it may have been the first time that Captain Marshall had seen that phrase—"unity of command." Within two years, he was to be aware of Pershing's insistence that what is essential for one army is just as essential for groups of allied armies operating against a single foe. And twenty-five years later, it was to be the central theme of Marshall's great contribution to the direction of allied armies, navies and air forces.

In the spring of 1917, however, Marshall was just another young officer, albeit more superbly equipped than most, quivering with eagerness to get across the Atlantic and put his fifteen years of thorough preparation to the practical service of his country. No doubt he hoped also—he knew the esteem in which he was held by many of his seniors with important influence in the Army, and would have been less than human had he not shared it—that, if he got to France, he would emerge from the war with the star of a brigadier general temporarily adorning each shoulder of his tunic.

Not long after the declaration of war, Captain Halstead—whose practice telegraph line had been tapped by Marshall at Fort McKinley—arrived one day at Governors Island to take an examination for promotion to major. He and Marshall had a brief reunion, and the conversation revolved around Marshall's intense desire to get to the front.

"I'd do anything!" Marshall told him. "I'd be an orderly!"

He was to get to France, but not as an orderly. The President and the War Department had decided to send at least one divison to France, and Pershing had been asked to furnish the units for it from the troops under his command in the Southern Department. The telegram from the Chief of Staff was the fourth communication Pershing had received indicating that the commander of the border mobilization and campaign was destined for bigger things.

The first had been Bell's letter. Next came the cryptic telegram from his father-in-law, Senator Warren of Wyoming, chairman of the Senate Military Affairs Committee, asking Pershing to "wire me today whether and how much you speak, read and write French." Following the telegram came a letter from the senator, explaining that Secretary Baker had hinted Pershing was being considered for a command in France, and had asked about the general's ability as a linguist. Between the telegram and the letter from his father-in-law, Pershing had received this message in code from General Scott:

"Under plans under consideration is one which will require among other troops, four infantry regiments and one artillery regiment from your department for service in France. If plans are carried out, you will be in command of the entire force. Wire me at once the designation of the regiments selected by you and their present stations."

Pershing called in his Chief of Staff, Colonel M. H. Barnum, and they agreed on the 16th, 26th, and 28th Infantry regiments and the 6th Field Artillery. These were ordered to the embarkation area in New York, where they were joined by two more artillery regiments, the 18th Infantry, and the necessary auxiliary units and became the 1st Division. Major General William L. Sibert was named to command it.

Late in June, Captain Marshall received orders detailing him to the General Staff Corps, and instructing him to report to General Sibert at the Quartermaster Depot in New York City. On June 26, he sailed for France aboard the first ship in the first convoy carrying American troops to the battlefields of the World War.

A month before he sailed for France himself, Marshall had met the commanding general of the American Expeditionary Force, who was to become his warm friend as well as the pattern of a leader to which

Marshall would seek in future years to cut the form of his own growth in the Army.

Pershing and his party had not reached New York until the day they were to sail for Europe on the British ship *Baltic*. On Pershing's staff were several with whom Marshall was to serve in close association in France, among them Major Fox Conner and Captain Hugh A. Drum, and at least one old friend, Major John McAuley Palmer. When the group reached General Bell's office, Bell warmly congratulated Pershing on his command, and then presented the members of his own staff. There was a brief conversation, and then Bell drove to the pier with Pershing. On the way, he reminded Pershing of his letter, and repeated the request for an active command. But Pershing knew that Bell was in failing health, and so remained noncommittal; the failure to see active combat service again was a bitter disappointment to the older man.

Between San Antonio and New York, Pershing had spent two hectic weeks in Washington, where he had learned, proudly but with considerable dismay, that he was to be commander in chief of an expeditionary force that was not yet more than a vague idea, instead of a division commander. Almost the only firm decision of major importance which had been made before he left Washington to sail from New York May 28 was that he was to resist French and British efforts to use American soldiers as individual or small unit replacements in their battered divisions, and insist on the integrity of American forces under American command. He selected the members of his own staff, but their organization was not worked out until they were on board the *Baltic*. It was on the *Baltic*, too, that Pershing arrived at the decision to ask the War Department to plan for an initial expeditionary force of one million men. Lesser decisions were made in Washington, however, and among them was the troop basis and organization of the 1st Division, with orders for its concentration in the New York area.

There is no record of how General Sibert came to select Captain Marshall as one of the staff of the 1st Division. The Captain's name probably was suggested by one of the Captain's friends, perhaps by

General Bell, and Sibert then called for Marshall's files, examining them and comparing them with those of other officers recommended to him. In that case, he would have seen Hagood's glowing recommendation, and also one from Bell covering Marshall's services as aide and assistant adjutant in San Francisco.

"That he is an officer of most exceptional worth and merit can hardly be questioned," Bell wrote. "I believe I am justified in saying that he is a good type of what a young soldier ought to be: well posted professionally, studious, able, conscientious, loyal, discreet, and industrious; courteous, considerate, neat and presentable; scrupulously honorable, thoroughly reliable, not afraid of responsibility, and possessed of sound judgment, excellent habits and an exceptionally bright mind, force and character.

"He was my aide-de-camp and assistant to the Department adjutant, in addition to his other duties. Has performed the duty of the Department adjutant with marked ability on several occasions during his absence. His duty as aide has been performed to my entire satisfaction. Is an exceptionally rapid, systematic worker. Never forgets, and is capable of accomplishing much in time available. Always cheerfully willing, never excited or rushed. Cool and level-headed—a good countervail for me."

He was about to demonstrate all the qualities that his superiors had been noting on his efficiency reports for years. Furthermore, he was about to discover that he would need every one of them. He has described in his own words the beginning of his experience as G-3, or operations officer, on the staff of the 1st Division—that division which had left its home stations as separate regiments and smaller units, and became a division only when it arrived at Hoboken just in time to embark.

Marshall told an Armistice Day audience years later:

I sailed from New York on the first ship of the first convoy, in June 1917. This was the 1st Division, a unit which eventually had 27,000 men in its ranks and suffered nearly 25,000 casualties in France. It went over with the first convoy, and it returned with the last in September 1919.

We embarked hurriedly in Hoboken, put out from the dock in the several boats, and anchored awaiting the completion of the installation of naval guns, and the preparation of convoy arrangements for crossing the Atlantic.

The staff of that division, of which I was a member, immediately got together—having assembled for the first time on the boat—to study our situation. We found, while anchored in the Hudson River, that the organization of the troops was entirely new to us, that there were four regiments of infantry in the division instead of the nine of our previous experience; that there were units of which we had never before heard, armed with weapons of which we knew nothing.

And like that expedition from San Francisco to the Philippines in 1898, with only 150 rounds per man, we were sailing three thousand miles from home to fight on foreign soil, and not until we arrived in France did the division commander and the members of the division staff learn that these new weapons were non-existent, and that the troops which on paper were charged with operating these weapons had never seen even a model of one.

We found that eighty per cent of the men in ranks were recruits, to many of whom rifles had been issued on the trains between the Mexican border and Hoboken. They were all good men, they were all splendid Americans—but they were not soldiers.

But they were going to be soldiers. It would take nearly a year, but they were going to be soldiers. Cantigny was ahead of these men, and St.-Mihiel, and the Meuse-Argonne offensive. It would be George Marshall whose plans would send them into battle, Marshall who would follow them along the muddy roads and into the trenches of the front line to be sure the thing was going according to plan, Marshall who would eat his heart out in a staff job because he was too good to be spared from the staff and given a command, Marshall who would find cold comfort in being told he was the most brilliant staff officer of the war, when all he wanted was to lead men in battle.

VIII

Sweating on the Staff

WHEN, in the autumn of 1917, Colonel Johnson Hagood went to General Headquarters at Chaumont-en-Bassigny and asked that George Marshall be promoted to full colonel and assigned to help him organize the Advance Section, Line of Communications, he was informed that the transfer was out of the question because "Marshall *is* the 1st Division!"

"I agree with you that Marshall's place is at the front, and not back with the Services of Supply," Hagood replied. "But if Marshall *is* the 1st Division, why don't you promote him to major general and put him in command?"

That shocking suggestion was even less possible than Marshall's transfer, Hagood was given to understand. Marshall was indispensable. Marshall could not be spared; but obviously he was much too junior for such advanced rank; the effect on senior officers would be most unhappy; moreover, Hagood certainly knew the restrictions imposed by regulation on promotion of officers detailed to staff duty. Hagood made an explosive comment, and went elsewhere for his Chief of Staff.

Pershing already had decided on a change in command for the division, however. It had been in France four months, and the Commander in Chief was far from satisfied with its progress. By the time Hagood made his unorthodox and unaccepted suggestion at Chaumont, Pershing already had told General Robert L. Bullard that he probably would get command of the division. Actually, General Sibert was not relieved until December 13, and Bullard took

National Archives

VICTORY PARADE

Pershing leads American troops beneath the Arc de Triomphe in Paris in 1919. Marshall may be seen in background, riding a white horse, between the second and third riders.

Signal Corps Photo

AIDE-DE-CAMP

Major Marshall, wearing the ribbons of his World War decorations, as a member of Pershing's staff in Washington.

command the next day. Sibert, with a brilliant record as a member of the Panama Canal Commission, was assigned to new duties in which his great skill as an engineer and an administrator could be employed more fully.

When the division headquarters, the headquarters of its two Infantry brigades, and the first contingent of troops sailed from Hoboken on June 14, General Sibert had commanded it for exactly five days, and the paper organization and assembly of the initial troops had been so hurried that even its name was provisional. It sailed as the First Expeditionary Division, and not until it had been in France nearly two weeks did it become the 1st Division, A.E.F.

Aboard the S. S. *Tenadores*, as this first convoy zigzagged across the Atlantic escorted by the cruiser *Charleston* and three torpedo-boat destroyers, there was considerable consternation as the staff realized how little they knew about this force they were to manage. Marshall and the others pored over the tables of organization, and picked each other's brain of knowledge, guess, and surmise. It was a peculiarly fitting irony that they arrived at St.-Nazaire, on June 26, in a fog.

By July 5, when this first contingent started moving up to the division's training area at Gondrecourt, the staff at least had learned what a Stokes mortar was, and had some inkling of the training job that lay ahead of them. So gigantic was the task, so great the time required, that already the officers were beginning to feel embarrassed at the wild enthusiasm with which the French greeted these first American troops, and the extravagant expectations of early victory, now that the Yanks had arrived. The movement to Gondrecourt alone would have been a fantastic impossibility for this first fragment of a division, without equipment or a functioning organization, except that the French military transportation system took over the job. The men made their first acquaintance with the unimpressive little continental freight cars, plainly marked to show a capacity of forty men or eight horses; but for all the skepticism of minds accustomed to the behemoths of American railway rolling stock, they admitted that the movement was accomplished with machine precision. The

French, after all, had been doing this kind of thing for three years.

Pershing had come down to St.-Nazaire when the convoy arrived, had made an inspection which gave him no reason to change his belief that it would be a long time before American troops made any effective contribution to an Allied victory, and had explained to the senior officers the problems facing them. Then, to bolster French morale and give the French capital an opportunity to see for themselves that the Americans had arrived, he ordered a battalion of infantry to Paris to share the parade and other ceremonies of an elaborate observance of Independence Day planned by the French government as a gesture of confidence and good will.

Paris went wild. The crowds cheered and laughed and sang. Women forced their way into the marching ranks of Americans and strode up the boulevards arm in arm with the men. The troops found themselves with wreaths of blossoms flung around their necks, bouquets stuck in their hats, flowers thrust into the muzzles of their rifles. Men and women even dropped to their knees, tears streaming down their faces, as the Yanks went by. But Pershing and his staff, and the commanders and staff of the 1st Division, were uncomfortably aware that the French and British officers who watched this show could not fail to see how completely awkward and untrained these troops were.

With this little morale assignment accomplished, the 1st Division got down to business. Gondrecourt, where division headquarters was established, lay above Neufchateau, near the St.-Mihiel salient. In the area around the town, the troops were billeted in villages and farms, and began learning all the things they had to learn about trench warfare under the tutelage of French 47th Division of Chasseurs. Even the rudiments of discipline had to be given a lot of these men, as well as the basic American training as riflemen who, in the American concept of open warfare, became in battle individuals dependent on their own resources of knowledge, skill, responsibility, and initiative. And even at the division level, the staff was discovering that it would be an uphill fight to maintain the aggressive spirit, the objective of break-through and maneuver, against the acceptance of siege warfare and immobile attrition prevailing throughout the French and British armies, which by this time had virtually no hope of taking the offensive successfully and hardly dared dream of administering a crushing defeat to the German armies.

For all the difference in viewpoint and ultimate aim, the Americans had much to learn before they could enter the line. They had to learn, first, how to dig trenches and live in them. They discovered that it was not enough to be a rifleman: the infantryman had also to be rifle-grenade man, hand-grenade man, light-machine gunner, heavy-machine gunner, Stokes-mortar man, something of an expert in the use of, and defense against, poison gas, sometimes a signalman, and on occasion even a second-class artilleryman. The problems met by the other arms and services were as many, and as varied. Training was a vital and inescapable preliminary to battle, for all the fact that nothing but combat is sufficient preparation for combat. Since these men had not been trained in the United States, they had to be trained in France. As the first contingent proceeded with its training, convoy after convoy brought additional units over. By September 1, most of the units had arrived, but not until Field Hospital 3 and Ambulance Company 3 arrived at St.-Nazaire December 22, 1917, was the entire 1st Division assembled in France.

Infantry, artillery, engineers, and signal troops were assembled by mid-August, however, and the rigorous training program was in full swing. Here, as at Fort Douglas the year before, Marshall was everywhere. As Operations officer—it came to be called G-3 when Pershing finally perfected his General Staff system on the French pattern—this program was to a large extent his responsibility. He pumped the French instructors and liaison officers dry with his interminable questions, absorbing their experience and knowledge and turning them into a rapidly growing competence which was reflected in the hardening of his division. He got his temporary promotion to major while acting as Chief of Staff of the division at the end of August, but that was no more than a minor incident in the busy days. There was not even time to be lonely.

Then, on October 21, battalions of the division's artillery and infantry moved into the line for the second phase of training—actual front-line duty, although in a quiet sector. The men were enthusiastic, despite the fact they were short of a lot of equipment, and even short of winter clothing. Thirty days were allotted for this part of the division's training, one battalion from each regiment going into the line for ten days at a time, alongside units of the French 18th Division.

The sector selected was that of Sommerviller, in Lorraine, just north of Lunéville. It had been inactive since 1914, when General de Castelnau halted the German advance on Nancy. On the Allied side of the line, peasants were occupying their homes ahead of the support positions, and on the enemy side people were living so close to the front-line trenches that the men brigaded with the French could watch them going to church on Sunday morning.

It was not precisely the horror of barrages and raids the doughboy usually associated with "front line," and it remained somnolent for two weeks after the Americans started occupying portions of the trench system. Then, on the morning of November 3, a company which had just moved into the line the night before and was finding its inevitable tension far from improving in a heavy fog followed by cold driving rain, was suddenly subjected to heavy bombardment. Major Marshall was at headquarters of the French 18th Division with its commander, General Bordeaux, when the first confused reports came in. Accompanied by the general, he headed promptly for the scene.

Major Marshall reported to the 1st Division Chief of Staff later that day in a hasty memorandum dated, "Einville, November 3, 1917, 2:30 P.M."

At 7:30 A.M. today I learnt at Division headquarters that there had been a very heavy hostile bombardment of the front line trenches from Aero to the south and that two soldiers of the 16th Infantry had been killed and two more of the same regiment wounded.

This information was telephoned by Lieut. Hugo and myself to Colonel King at Gondrecourt. I started out with General Bordeaux about 8:00 A.M. and went to Infantry headquarters at Einville. There we heard that one French soldier had been killed, in addition to the two Americans. We went on to Regimental Headquarters but learnt nothing new there. On our way up to the Artois Post of Command at Gypse we met an artillery major who had heard that some Americans were missing, but as there were no traces of a raid, it was thought that these men had been lost in the taking over of the sector that night.

At the Battalion P. C. we met the French Battalion Commander and Major Burnett, 16th Infantry. There we were told that three Americans had been killed and five wounded by the bombardment, etc., and that they were still investigating the absence of fifteen men, but had not yet located them.

We went forward and located the Commanding Officer, Co. F, 16th Infantry, Lieut. Comfort, whose company occupied the Artois Strong Point. He was still somewhat dazed by the shell shock of the bombardment. He conducted us forward. After reaching the doubling trench we met a French lieutenant who said that there had been a raid as they had found a German helmet and a German rifle. We continued on up to Lieut. McLoughlin's [Lieutenant William H. McLaughlin] platoon and found him slightly wounded in the face, his helmet bent by a shell fragment and he himself very much shaken by the bombardment he had experienced. The trenches had been badly knocked about, the communications trenches almost destroyed in several places. The general facts of the affair were still in much doubt, but a short investigation quickly cleared things up. The following is about what happened.

2. About 2:50 A.M., Nov. 3d, a heavy bombardment was delivered by the enemy on our line from Aero to the south, including Bures. In the vicinity of the Artois salient it was extremely violent. It lasted about fifty minutes. Apparently the tip of the salient was only lightly bombarded with 77 mms., as it was only slightly damaged.

The men generally sought shelter in their dugouts. Lieut. McLoughlin, commanding the platoon holding the salient, sought to get his men back to the doubling trench, but the latter was under the heaviest bombardment and he was knocked down several times by shell blasts. During this bombardment the enemy exploded long, gas pipe dynamite charges under the wire in front of each face of the tip of the salient.

When the bombardment lifted on the front trench about forty or fifty Germans rushed in from the two sides, killed or drove off the one or two soldiers who had come out of their dugouts, and carried off twelve of our men. Three soldiers of Co. F, 16th Infantry were killed. One had had his throat cut; one had been shot by a revolver as he stepped to the door of his dugout; and the third had had his head crushed in—whether by a club or a piece of shell fragment I do not know. The man with the cut throat was found, I understand, on top of the parapet.

I have not yet had an opportunity to question the wounded and I now understand that a German was wounded by the German barrage and has come into our lines, stating that the raid was planned in August and 250 volunteers called for, and that fifty participated in the raid. Everything regarding the German prisoner is new to me and as yet unchecked. Practically all the other details I found out for myself.

3. In order to get this off by the courier I have written it the moment I reached Einville and it is therefore disconnected and hurried. I will make a rough sketch to enclose. I am sending with this the list of names of killed, wounded and missing. Also the orders for that center of resistance, etc. The company had just taken over the sector about ten o'clock last night and only a few of the non-commissioned officers had ever seen the trenches in day light.

This report bore Marshall's rubber stamp signature, initialed "GCM" in pencil. It was followed by a second report, dated at Sommerviller later the same day, which contained additional details obtained from Marshall's questioning of the wounded Americans and the solitary German prisoner, but added nothing to the general picture he had already sent to headquarters.

The Major's apology for his "disconnected and hurried" report was hardly necessary. Hasty as it was, the memorandum was a concise and orderly report of the action in which the first American soldiers to die in France lost their lives. It is illuminating, moreover, for the insight it gives into Marshall's methods as a staff officer. Within an hour or two after he first heard of the bombardment, he was in the front-line trench talking to the platoon commander. Only seven hours after the first word reached him, he had completed a preliminary but thorough investigation, returned to Infantry headquarters at Einville, and written a report to his chief.

Two days later Marshall attended the impressive and moving ceremonies marking the burial of the first American dead of the war. Corporal James B. Gresham, Private Thomas F. Enright and Private Merle D. Hay were lowered into their graves in a field near Bathelémont between honor guards of French and American troops, while General Bordeaux saluted them. There was music from a French military band, and a lone American bugler sounded taps.

"Later in the day," Marshall wrote General Sibert, "I called formally on General Bordeaux and told him that if you had been present, I knew you would have expressed to him your appreciation of the honor he had paid to our first dead, and that your division, the entire American Army and the American people would always feel grateful for his action."

Considerable excitement was engendered throughout the small but growing American Expeditionary Force by this first taste of battle, and a full investigation was made by a special committee headed by Brigadier General James W. McAndrew. It was not, of course, an investigation accompanied by punitive intent. The entire A.E.F. was in training, and this was merely the first and one of the least of the combat experiences which would convert it into a war machine. The facts must be assembled, the lessons drawn, and the doctrine applied throughout the school system which General Bullard had been setting up since August.

On November 20, the last of the 1st Division units withdrew from the line for further training in the Gondrecourt area. This was the finishing process, the welding of the division into a battle team on the basis of its schooling and the actual experience its units, a battalion at a time, had now had.

General Bullard took command of the division on December 14, and sent out to create an administrative and command machine that would function regardless of the personnel manning it. He was imbued with Pershing's insistence upon the offensive spirit, and determined to resist the attitude of hopelessness implicit in the French acceptance of continued trench warfare as inevitable. Despite his own forebodings, his fear that the British and the French had been bled too much and too long to be capable of the vigorous action required for a clear-cut victory, Bullard also took his cue from the Commander in Chief's insistance that all the A.E.F. share President Wilson's expressions of general optimism, and act as if they were certain of early and complete triumph.

There was need for driving energy, that winter of 1917. The reports of Russia's collapse and revolution were followed by intelligence indications that Germany planned a great spring offensive in the west, and there was no reason to believe that the Allies could stop it unless American troops were ready to take an important part.

The last two weeks of 1917 the 1st Division's training included maneuvers that involved overnight marches, sleeping on the ground, standing in the open during hours of waiting, in drenching cold rains and biting winds. Nothing was allowed to interfere with the most rigorous training that could be devised. Much depended on this outfit. It was to be the first American division to engage the enemy, and more than mere prestige depended on its behavior when it finally collided with the German veterans. Few at the division level were concerned about Pershing's developing battle with the French and British to preserve the identity of the the American Army under American command; but Pershing was counting heavily on the performance of Americans in battle to clinch his arguments for him, and the first test would come with the 1st Division. They had to be good.

When, in January 1918, the division started moving to take over the Ansauville sector of the line, Bullard had reason to believe that it was ready for whatever lay before it. Brigadier General Frank Parker commanded his 1st Infantry Brigade, Brigadier General Beaumont B. Buck the 2d Infantry Brigade, which Bullard himself had brought to France. Colonel Stephen O. Fuqua was his Chief of Staff, and the key post on the staff, G-3 (Operations), was filled by Major George Marshall.

When the movement began on January 15, the troops had just finished the final two weeks of their trench maneuvers. The last five days had been particularly vicious, with the temperature freezing, and the men struggling through a morass of mud, snow, sleet, rain, and slush. Fortunately, the division had received some rolling kitchens, and hot food and coffee brought the men through the trial in better shape than the commanders and staff had thought possible.

The day they started for the front, the ground was covered with a sheet of ice. A morning snowfall had started melting, when a sudden drop in the temperature froze it solid. As if that were not enough, the freeze was followed by rain which turned the ice into a glassy hazard, filled the ditches with slush, penetrated the clothing of the men who marched forward in sodden, cold misery. The wagons of the supply train became a hopeless tangle, and many of the draft animals collapsed. All day and all that night the rain continued, but while the intense hardship of the march was a bitter reality still on the second day, the rain had at least cleared most of the ice off the roads by that time, and the column managed to move with some semblance of order.

Only the 1st Brigade of Infantry went into the line in the Ansauville sector, backed up by most of the division artillery. The American division was twice the size of a French division, so it was felt that half of the 1st was enough to accomplish the relief of the French 1st Moroccan Division. Furthermore, the staff guessed that when the Germans found out there were Americans in the line, the enemy would attempt to make their initial undertaking as uncomfortable as possible. They might need reserves, but there were none available yet in the A.E.F. Accordingly, the 2d Brigade was left in the Gondrecourt area to continue its training, and to be available as reserves for the 1st Brigade.

Division headquarters was established at Mesnil-la-Tour, about halfway between St.-Mihiel and Pont-à-Mousson. On the night of January 18, the Americans started moving into the front-line trenches as the Moroccans moved out. There was another Moroccan division on the right, and as the Americans moved in, the outfit on their right was engaged in evacuating about two hundred gas casualties. It served to emphasize that this was no longer a training detail, but the real thing.

As his division took over the sector, Marshall kept close watch on every movement. He also examined the position they were to occupy. It was not reassuring. Of course, it was a "quiet sector," but the terrain seemed to give every advantage to the enemy. The Allied trenches were in low ground, wet, and muddy. The Germans occupied high land, and in particular Montsec, a great bare hill opposite the left of the sector occupied by the Americans. Montsec dominated the entire landscape and gave the enemy a perfect observation spot from which to watch everything that occurred on the Allied side of the line. At the left, the American trenches terminated in an impassable lake; at the right, in a salient enclosing the village of Seicheprey and the splintered stumps of what had once been a small forest.

Despite the reluctance of the French to surrender the tactical command of the sector, Bullard insisted, banking on Pershing's firm policy that American divisions serve only under their own commanders, and on February 5 the tactical command of the Ansauville sector passed to Bullard (he remained under French corps and army direction, of course). The Americans decided to stimulate a little activity on this quiet front, and the German lines began receiving a considerably greater number of artillery shells and machine-gun bullets than they were accustomed to. The result was a German raid on the Seicheprey salient of the sector.

The Americans, however, were not caught napping. They had learned well from their French instructors during the months of training, and they recognized the signs when the raid was coming. When the enemy troops rushed the American first trenches after artillery preparation, they found them apparently deserted. Then, before they could get out, the Americans counterattacked. The Germans lost two or three of their flame throwers, one or two machine guns, and fifteen dead in the American lines, as well as several who got tangled in their own wire as they retreated and were killed by American riflemen as they hung there. It was not a great affair, since there were hardly more than two hundred men engaged on each side; but it put the entire division in fine spirits, and delighted their French neighbors in the line.

The division remained in the Ansauville sector until April 3.

Although a quiet sector, it saw considerable artillery activity every day, and an occasional raid. There were gas attacks, and plenty to learn about gas discipline. There was the constant drudgery of repairing and maintaining the trench system, particularly after such an attack as that of the night of February 28, when the division suffered a number of casualties although holding its positions and inflicting even greater losses on the Germans. Marshall reported three days later that the artillery barrage for this raid by the enemy had been so heavy that he was still unable to make anything approaching an accurate tally of American dead, or of the casualties suffered by the enemy. German shells had blasted craters thirty feet across and fifteen feet deep, he told GHQ at Chaumont, and trenches and dugouts along the part of the sector where the attack occurred had been obliterated.

The Americans, however, were not always on the receiving end of activity in the Ansauville sector. Their morale was excellent after they carried out some successful raids of their own, and in his daily operations report for March 6 the division G-3 included some German testimony as to the zeal and accuracy of American artillery.

It was a strange entry in the usually crisp and sober operations report, but Marshall had been amused by it, and slipped it into the paragraph on Infantry Activities:

"A sentinel in a listening post heard the enemy opposite Center H indulge in the following conversation (translation): 'Come here, come here, Fritz. Take this pick and pry that stone loose. Take this shovel and throw that dirt out. Those ——— over there, we work all night to fix these trenches, and they blow them to h—— in the daytime!' "

Watching the division in action, the staff was critical not only of performance, but of organization. Late in April, Major Robert Lewis, a liaison officer with the French for Colonel Fox Conner, the G-3 at GHQ, was writing to his chief that the French staff officers fround the American organization too big and overmanned—that an American battalion commander, given a sector he could control, had too many men and risked unnecessarily heavy casualties.

"I told Colonel Marshall of this conversation later in the morning,"

Lewis wrote, "and he said that the staff of the division had reached somewhat the same conclusion, and was considering the solution of the question in this particular case by the establishment of a divisional depot. Marshall said in addition that he thought the companies too large for the company commanders to handle with the amount of experience they have had."

Marshall apparently impressed the rest of the staff and his division commander also with this view, for two weeks later Lewis, in another letter to Conner, reported that "General Bullard gave the order this afternoon to reduce the strength of the Infantry companies to four platoons of 40 men each. . . . The personnel which is left over after the reduction in strength of the companies which will result from this reorganization is to be organized into Divisional School and Replacement Depot."

By the time this came about, the 1st Division had left the Ansauville sector and was facing Cantigny. The last campaigns had started, and there would be little rest in quiet sectors for any division until the war ended. The long-expected offensive was heralded in March by a series of savage German raids along the entire Western Front. The enemy was probing the lines, and trying also to mask his true intent. The blow fell on March 21, with a great offensive on the Somme which for a few days threatened to overrun the cathedral city and vital railroad center of Amiens. The 1st Division, which had been engaged in the backbreaking toil of digging a whole new system of trenches and emplacements for a complete reorganization of the defenses from a shallow, strongly held line only five or six hundred yards wide to an intricate deployment in depth of a mile or more, was hastily pulled out and sent northwest to the vicinity of Montdidier.

By mid-April, the division was approaching its new positions, and as its trains were arriving, Marshall reported at the heaquarters of General Debeney, commanding the French First Army, under whose orders the 1st Division was to fight. There, among other things, he learned that the elaborate defense in depth on which his division had been working when it was pulled out of the sector north of Toul had been vastly modified as a result of the fighting on the Somme.

Marshall was given the new method which the division was to use in its new sector, which was on ground only recently occupied, and lacking trenches.

The troops were hard at work on the new system when the second great push of the German spring offensive began on the Lys, and all but broke the British Fifth Army. Two weeks later, the defense system was altered again, throwing on Marshall and his Operations staff a tremendous burden of planning, and on the troops an even heavier burden of digging.

Marshall had other plans to occupy him, as well. Before the 1st Division stood the village of Cantigny, on a plateau which masked a valley beyond. Its capture was regarded by Debeney as an essential preliminary to the counteroffensive which the French high command planned against the exposed flank of the German salient south of the Somme, and the job was the first major combat assignment given to American troops.

This was no quiet sector, but an extremely lively one (even in the sector north of Toul, the 1st Division had suffered between three and four thousand casualties). Accompanied by the shelling, the raids, and the digging in, plans went forward for an attack. The 28th Infantry was selected to make the assault, and on May 22 it was pulled out of the line for a short course of intensive training. Between May 26 and 28 it was fed back into the line, and on May 28 it attacked. Colonel Marshall's daily operations report for that day began simply:

"I. General Characteristics of the Day:
 "We successfully attacked and took Cantigny.
"II. American Activity:
 "After a heavy destructive fire by our artillery the 28th Infantry advanced and took CANTIGNY in accordance with Field Orders No. 18. All objectives were taken and the ground is now being consolidated. 175 prisoners, of whom 3 are officers, have been counted. It is impossible to estimate the enemy's losses in killed and wounded, but they were very heavy. Our casualties are estimated to be about 300. Details will be furnished later."

The following day Marshall was able to report that the American positions in the village and on the heights of Cantigny had been consolidated, despite three vicious German counterattacks on the evening of May 28, and two more between 6:00 and 7:00 o'clock in the morning of May 29. Three days later, his report to GHQ disclosed that the division had expanded its front, taking over an additional sector previously held by the French 152d Division, and now had both Infantry brigades abreast in the line.

The success was complete, and there was elation at division headquarters, at Pershing's GHQ, and among the French; but it remained a local success only. The enemy had launched his third and most threatening drive of the spring, along the Chemin des Dames between Soissons and Reims, and the proposed counterattack against the German Somme salient never was undertaken.

Pershing had come up to watch the Cantigny attack, and was pleased with the dash displayed in this first major American attack, but appeared to take the success as a matter of course. It was, in truth, a limited affair; and Bullard, expressing satisfaction with the 28th Infantry's aggressive drive, also said the attack was so well prepared that it could not have failed. This was indirect praise, but still praise, for Marshall, since Marshall had prepared the plans. And if Pershing had assumed success at Cantigny, he was nervous about hanging on to it. Having left to return to his own headquarters, he turned around and came back to impress upon Marshall and the other division officers the absolute necessity of beating off all counterattacks.

The success of the attack might be a matter of course to Pershing and Bullard, but it was blood and agony to the Infantry who lost more than a thousand in killed and wounded in the attack and in the violent German counterattacks and artillery reaction which followed it. The cost of this battle, of any battle, was very real to Marshall as he followed the course and checked the results of the fight he had planned. He watched the American Infantry demonstrate its quality at Cantigny, the fighting heart of the American civilian temporarily forced to war, and the thing he saw would not be forgotten soon.

Meantime, the German army was thundering down between Soissons and Reims, driving its Chemin des Dames attack down to the Marne and Château-Thierry. That battle was no part of Marshall's problem, or of the problems of the 1st Division. But it provided one of their exasperations. Two weeks after it got started on its dangerous way, more instructions came down from French headquarters about those defenses in depth—how and where and why the Americans were supposed to dig themselves in. Marshall looked at these new orders. His troops had been digging since January, as well as doing a considerable amount of fighting, and getting rather badly mauled from time to time by German artillery and gas. And here were fresh instructions to start digging again, and in different fashion. Different? Well, it differed from the fashion of digging in vogue north of Toul through February and March; it differed from the fashion adopted after the enemy's offensive on the Somme; it differed, also, from the variation which became the approved form after the Lys offensive of the Germans. But—and this was what Marshall spotted instantly and with considerable annoyance—a translation of the latest French orders would have been found almost word for word in the Field Service Regulations of the United States Army for 1914!

"In other words," Marshall commented years later, "there had been no change in fundamentals, but during three years of trench warfare those fundamentals had been lost sight of, and now in that critical summer of 1918, we were back again to first essentials of warfare.

"To me that was an impressive lesson, and since then whenever changes are proposed, modern theories advanced, or surprising developments are brought to my attention, I automatically search for the fundamental principle involved in the particular matter at hand."

In June 1918 the particular matter at hand was to dig, or not to dig, defenses in depth. Headquarters of the 1st Division, A.E.F., notified its French superior headquarters that the 1st Division was prepared to do one of two things: it could fight or it could dig, but it was no longer possible to do both.

There were other problems, as well. Marshall, who throughout his career found the complication of military forms and orders a continual exasperation, heard that the planners at GHQ in Chaumont had decided to abolish the Topographical Section at all division headquarters. Having worked for months to get this section working properly at 1st Division headquarters, he was concerned, and got hold of Major Lewis, the GHQ liaison officer. The result of their conversation showed up in another of Lewis' breezy, highly informal reports to Colonel Conner.

"Colonel Marshall tells me," the major wrote, "that they have only just begun to be able to handle the operations orders, and maps and diagrams, efficiently since they got this section to functioning smoothly. There are so many things which can be shown so much more clearly and so much better by maps and diagrams than by long, complicated orders that the section is most necessary to the Division staff."

Marshall's hard work during the winter and spring did not go unnoticed by his commanding general. On June 6, Bullard recommended that he be promoted from lieutenant colonel to colonel because "he has had, of all officers of the General Staff up to the present, the widest experience in actual staff work in G-3. . . .

"That work, it seems to me, has been well up to the standard of the best armies with which the American Expeditionary Force is serving," General Bullard added. "I believe it would be a mistake to keep Lieutenant Colonel Marshall, with his experience and ability, in as low a grade or as low a place as he now occupies, and I recommend his promotion to the next grade as fitting to the higher place to which he is sure to be called."

The recommendation came back, disapproved because of the War Department policy that "a line officer detailed on staff duty will be promoted only when promotion becomes normally due him according to his place on the lineal list of his own arm."

Bullard was right, however. Marshall was sure to be called to a more important job, and the call would not be delayed much longer. There was not a great deal to do in the Cantigny sector. The division was alerted for the defensive when the enemy attacked the French First and Third Armies between Montdidier and Noyon, but participated in this defensive only to the extent of suffering from artillery barrages and a heavy enemy trench raid. No serious assaults were launched on the American lines.

On July 4, the Americans celebrated by shelling the Germans with every weapon they could bring to bear on the enemy. Then the Artillery Brigade had a horse show in the woods behind the Château de Tartigny, and in the evening Marshall and some of the other officers from division headquarters were invited to a big interallied dinner at French Corps headquarters in observance of Independence Day. Wine as well as food was plentiful, and when the French toasted the United States, Marshall responded with a speech in French that made the friendly evening a complete success.

The next night, two French divisions began the relief of the American 1st, and Bullard's headquarters moved to Nivillers, between Beauvais and Breteuil. Marshall was on the move again. The division was headed for the Forêt de Compiègne for a share in the Aisne-Marne operation, but Marshall was headed for Chaumont and an important assignment directly under Colonel Fox Conner in G-3 of GHQ.

How did Beauvais strike this tired man? Over the little city the towering abrupt mass of the unfinished cathedral is a compelling reminder to any man who sees it that if men failed here, it was not for lack of daring. It is not serene, Beauvais; the peace of other Gothic fanes is absent from this great vault flung against the sky. It is not a refuge, and one who seeks escape there will only be troubled. But there could hardly be found, for a soldier going from lesser battle to great campaign and new challenge, a more fitting benison than he would find in a few moments beneath those soaring arches. Broken and incomplete, Beauvais cathedral is the very form of courage, impetuous and bold.

Marshall went through Beauvais disappointed and bitter. He had made one last attempt to leave the staff, to get a command. He had done it in a brief, blunt, appealing memorandum on June 18:

"1. Request that I be relieved from duty on the General Staff and assigned to duty with troops.

"2. I have been on staff duty since February, 1915, and I am tired from the incessant strain of office work."

He handed this to his commanding general, and Bullard sent it forward to the Adjutant General of the A.E.F.

"I cannot approve," said Bullard's covering note, "because I know that Lieut. Col. Marshall's special fitness is for staff work and because I doubt that in this, whether it be teaching or practice, he has an equal in the Army today. But his experience and merit should find a wider field than the detailed labors of a Division Staff."

Marshall's request was turned down, and Bullard's recommendation accepted. Marshall went to the wider field occupied by the Operations staff of GHQ.

IX

Triumph and Frustration

When Lieutenant Colonel Marshall reported on July 13, 1918, at Chaumont for duty with the G-3 Section of General Headquarters, A.E.F., the bleak Allied outlook of the spring had changed to one of cautious optimism, even envisioning a possible Allied offensive that might achieve a clear-cut victory sometime in 1919.

Marshall had much to do, and much to learn. In the long, taxing, and dangerous year with the 1st Division, Marshall had won two promotions, been decorated by the French, and had been so absorbed by the problems of his own division that he had only a sketchy understanding of the general situation as it appeared at the high command level.

His own training and battle experience had been as rigorous as that of the line troops in the "Fighting First." There are staff officers who view their duty as calling them to nothing less comfortable than the environs of their maps, charts, desks, and swivel chairs; but Marshall was a staff officer of a different kind. To him, an army was not a machine, but a living organism. His plans moved, not pieces on a chessboard, but men in trenches, on parapets, through jungles of barbed wire, under artillery bombardment, in gas barrages, crawling through rain and mud, struggling against ice and snow, dragging their wounded through shell craters to safety, living men driving themselves about the world's most ghastly and terrible business.

If, as his new chief, Colonel Fox Conner, believed, Marshall was the best operations officer in the A.E.F., it was because this profound human understanding led Marshall to the perception that these forces were not mechanical, but living; that the units he manipulated were a throbbing synthesis of the sum of hope, courage, endurance, and agony, of the fear and cowardice and failure, of many men.

It had not been enough for Marshall, in these twelve months, to plan the movements and draft the orders, and then arrive at his judgment of success or failure, and seek the reasons for them, by perusing the reports that came back from the scene of action, whether that action involved a supply train moving up from the rear, or a raid by a handful of men to get prisoners for questioning. Having issued the orders, Marshall himself then went to the action. It was no love of danger that sent him there, no silly bravado. It was simply his passion to *know*. To plan battles that would end in victory, to draft orders that would be carried out, it was necessary to know how men reacted to every conceivable situation, how they behaved under all conditions, and the only way to know was to be on the spot when the reactions and the behavior could be observed. Accordingly, Marshall went. A year and a half after he left the 1st Division, he was cited in Division General Orders for superior professional attainments, tactical skill, and sound judgment, but also because by "his courageous conduct in obtaining information through personal visits to the most exposed lines, he contributed in a determining manner to the training, morale and operations of the Division. . . ."

All this preparation he brought to the gigantic tasks awaiting him at Chaumont. Moreover, when he arrived he already possessed the confidence of Colonel Conner, the able Chief of Operations at GHQ, with whom he had been in constant contact throughout the past year, and with whom he had had personal conferences every week or two. And he knew Pershing, and had the confidence of the Commander in Chief.

It was not yet the close association and deep bond of mutual esteem and affection it was to become, this acquaintance with Pershing. They had met in General Bell's office at Governors Island just before Pershing sailed for France, and casually on several occasions when Pershing visited the division headquarters in the months following arrivals. On one of these occasions, the meeting had been more than casual. Pershing had come up to watch some training exercises, and made a critical remark when they were completed. Marshall took issue with the general, and told him why he thought the commanding general had expected too much of these troops who had had in fact too little training for the type of maneuver ordered.

One of their more recent meetings had been at Mesnil-St. Firmin, near Cantigny, when Pershing had come over from Chantilly. He had just had another long argument with General Pétain, who was still trying to get Pershing to break up the American divisions and feed them by battalions into the French divisions as reinforcements.

It was May 19, and Pershing had spent the night with General Bullard. The next morning he briefed the division staff on the general situation on the Western Front, then went into a long conversation with Marshall. In great detail they went over the plans for the forthcoming attack on Cantigny. Pershing wanted to be certain this thing would go well. He told Marshall it was important for Allied morale that the Americans make their appearance in battle soon, and that it be a successful appearance. Closer to his heart, however, was the fact that a successful attack on Cantigny might help him persuade the French and British that the best way to use American troops was in large units under their own commanders, instead of destroying their identity to bolster the battered and faltering Allied divisions. The Commander in Chief took fresh hope from the enthusiasm which the division showed for its approaching test, and was impressed by the quiet mastery shown by Marshall.

Thus it was that the Commander in Chief knew the man who was called to Chaumont in July to familiarize himself with the operations at the top level, and then to set to work on the limited campaign to which Pershing had clung as his first American Army objective since his first month in France—reduction of the St.-Mihiel salient in Lorraine.

Lorraine had been selected as the area in which the American Army, if it ever came into existence, would take over its own front and operate as a national army. The locations of ports and rail lines clinched the choice, which had been indicated by the commitments and primary interest of the British and French in other sectors—the British were concerned with protecting the Channel ports, the French with guarding Paris. That left the area to the east of the main French efforts the logical choice for the Americans, and the choice was confirmed by the fact that the ports of Bordeaux, St.-Nazaire, Nantes, and Marseille could be used by the A.E.F., and they were served by rail lines into Lorraine which were not already pre-empted for British and French supply. Accordingly, the choice was Lorraine, and an understanding was reached between Pershing and Pétain that the first American offensive would be to reduce the triangular salient southwest of Metz and below Verdun which pushed its apex to the town of St.-Mihiel.

When Marshall started for Chaumont, the British and French still were seeking to replenish their own exhausted divisions with American troops in units no larger than a battalion, and there was no firm commitment from the Allied high command on a date or an area for the First American Army on which Pershing stubbornly insisted. Nevertheless, Pershing already had established a Corps, and was moving to set up his First Army and take personal command of it. He saw that the German offensives of 1918 had been stopped, and he guessed at least that the offensive now begun by the French against the Marne salient, the Aisne-Marne operation, would succeed and give the Allies the initiative for the first time in nearly four years.

The Americans possessed an offensive spirit, a determination to break through the trench systems and restore to this war the classic mobility of warfare, and an unwavering conviction that this could be accomplished. These attitudes were lacking in the military councils of the French and British; and small wonder that this was so, for the frightful losses in men had nearly wrecked the entire French government, and had created in British minds a horror that would trouble them for decades and cloud their strategic judgment in another and greater war twenty-five years later. America had not suffered comparably, and while it was to be the swelling stream of American production and the fresh vigor of American troops which swung the balance and made possible an Allied triumph, Britain and

France had borne the brunt and paid the cost in lives to stop the German armies in the west. American troops appeared in important strength only during the battles which marked the last effort of the enemy to force a decision and gain a German victory. The great American offensives were undertaken only after the Germans had lost the initiative and assumed the defensive on the Western Front. At that point, fresh American troops in growing numbers and increasing efficiency gave the Allies the advantage. The trench system, that elaborate network of field fortifications bearing such a startling resemblance to the seventeenth-century siege works of Vauban, would be ruptured; and the American insistence upon rupture and exploitation would prove once again, to Allies and to enemy, the continuing truth of Vauban's dictum, "Place besieged is place taken."

The day that Marshall left for Chaumont, the 1st Division began moving toward the Forêt de Compiègne to take its place as part of the French XX Corps in the main attack below Soissons against the Marne salient. This was the deep wedge driven into the Allied lines in May by the German offensive on the Chemin des Dames. Its farthest edge was on the Marne at Château-Thierry and Belleau Wood, where the American 2d and 3d Divisions had electrified the Allies by their gallantry and their success in June. The American 3d, 28th, and 26th Divisions strengthened the newly won Allied confidence in the American forces by their determined stand along the Marne when the Germans tried to widen the salient toward Epernay in July—it was here that the 38th Infantry of the 3d Division won its title, "Rock of the Marne," with its obstinate resistance which halted the German attack.

When the Germans began this Champagne-Marne assault July 15, plans were well advanced for the Allied attack on the salient to begin July 18. The two American divisions were hurried into the line southwest of Soissons through a torrential rain, along roads deep in mud and clogged with Americans moving forward, French and Moroccans moving back, and the supply trains of all three competing with artillery for possession of the crammed and tangled passage. Through the black night, the Americans came to their assault positions on the double, arriving just in time to push off as the attack started on July 18.

The 2d Division drove forward eight kilometers in the first twenty-six hours of the attack, capturing some three thousand enemy troops and a mass of artillery and other equipment; but it suffered approximately four thousand casualties itself, had made exhausting marches to reach the area from the rest sector to which it had only recently been sent after its desperate fighting at Château-Thierry, and accordingly it was withdrawn after the second day of the Aisne-Marne operation.

The 1st Division, which Marshall so recently had left, suffered some seven thousand casualties in the four days and nights it remained as one of the spearhead divisions of the French XX Corps's attack. Sixty percent of its Infantry officers were killed or wounded. In two of its Infantry regiments all the field officers except the colonels commanding were casualties, and in a third the colonel was included among the casualties. The division took three thousand five hundred prisoners from seven different German divisions which were thrown against it in the enemy's desperate efforts to check the assault; but the enemy efforts failed. The Fighting First broke through the entrenchments of the Germans' pivot position to a depth of eleven kilometers.

Meantime, the active front had been extended steadily southward by other corps of the French Tenth Army, with French Sixth Army maintaining pressure as the pivot at Château-Thierry. In the latter army was the American I Corps under General Hunter Liggett, containing the American 26th and French 167th Divisions on its front in the Château-Thierry sector. To the right, the French XXXVIII Corps was on the Marne with the American 3d Division among its units. On July 21 the attack plan was reversed, and this French Sixth Army became the main effort while the Tenth Army, having broken through below Soissons, became the pivot. Before the end of the month, five more American divisions were involved in the operation. Liggett's I Corps was the first American Corps to appear in battle in France—sixteen months after the United States had declared war on the Central Powers. Before the Aisne-Marne operation was ended, the American III Corps was in command of a sector also, under General Bullard.

The Germans conducted their withdrawal in this second Battle of the Marne with great skill, fighting bitter rear-guard actions by day and retiring at night. On July 28 they made a determined stand on the Ourcq River, a small stream running west through the salient about midway between the Marne and the Vesle. The hills on the north of the Ourcq commanded the country for miles, and made excellent delaying positions for the enemy. But on July 31 a breach was achieved in the hills, and the Germans began falling back again. There were no more naturally strong positions short of the Vesle, and it was on this stream that the line became stabilized again in the first days of August. When the battle ended here, the American 4th and 32d Divisions were in the line, and the two American Corps, I and III, held a continuous front of eleven miles, with bridgeheads on the north bank.

The Marne salient had been wiped out. The railroad from Paris to Nancy had been liberated, the threat to Paris itself removed. Most important, the Allies had gained their first victory of the year. A German offensive had been stopped, and then changed into a retreat. The Allies had regained the initiative, and the outlook was suddenly changed completely.

The battle was still in progress, but it success was assured, when Marshal Foch called a conference at his headquarters for July 24. Foch had been named in March, in the face of the mounting spring offensive by the enemy, to "co-ordinate" the activities of the various Allied armies. This co-ordination did not succeed too well, and by early April a session of the Supreme War Council in the Hotel de Ville at Beauvais was engaged in a furious discussion of what was meant and what was not meant by the authority to co-ordinate. Clemenceau was there, and Lloyd George, as well as Field Marshal Sir Douglas Haig, General (he was not yet a marshal of France) Foch, and Generals Pétain, Sir Henry Wilson, Tasker H. Bliss, Weygand and Pershing. There was considerable beating around the bush before Lloyd George asked Pershing's opinion. The American commander put it bluntly: unity of command was needed, unity of action was impossible without a supreme commander, co-ordination was a myth, and he thought Foch should be named Supreme Commander of the Allied Armies without further quibbling. The decision was made that day—after three and one-half years of war, unity of command was finally achieved by the Allies.

Now, in July, Foch was suggesting that the Allies give serious consideration to taking the offensive in earnest, looking to a victory over Germany in 1919. The latest German offensive of the year had been checked, and the Allied counteroffensive begun July 18 had turned it into a defeat. He proposed three preliminary actions as essential preparations for any general Allied offensive:

1. Release of the Paris-Avricourt railroad in the Marne region as the minimum result of the current Franco-American operation in the Aisne-Marne area.

2. Freeing of the Paris-Amiens railroad by a concerted action of the British and French.

3. Release of the Paris-Avricourt railroad in the region of Commercy by the reduction of the St.-Mihiel salient by the American Army.

In addition, he wanted the commanders and staffs to think of the possibility of another operation on the British front in the north which would recapture the important mining regions around Béthune and drive the enemy away from the Channel ports of Dunkerque and Calais.

More importantly from Pershing's viewpoint, the July 24 conference brought a reluctant agreement in writing, at long last, for the separate existence and operation of the First American Army. But it was the tentative decision for an American attack on the St.-Mihiel salient that meant work for Marshall.

Marshall had plunged into work soon after his arrival at Chaumont, studying the St.-Mihiel salient and approaches, getting ready for operational planning on the basis of the asssumption at GHQ that the attack would be undertaken. Friends who came to GHQ on other missions and seized the opportunity to find Marshall and have a brief visit discovered him tucked away in a small room, so arranged that they could not get much farther than his door, and from their deepest penetration could see none of the maps and charts with which he was working. Marshall would have no secrets leaking from his office.

In general, it astonished them also to learn that Marshall knew more than anyone else at headquarters about the locations and dispositions of American units. He kept one map that almost any officer could examine, and it got to be known that Marshall's information was frequently well in advance of the official reports. It was another reflection of the colonel's ability to get around. When work required it, he was at his desk. When he could be spared, he was out in the field, visiting headquarters, talking to men in the ranks, asking questions, finding out for himself what was going on. Conversations with second lieutenants in railway stations frequently meant new tacks on Marshall's map, and the lieutenants probably never knew how much they had disclosed to the interested and sympathetic young lieutenant colonel.

The nebulous character of the proposal to send the Americans against the St.-Mihiel salient made it necessary for Marshall to prepare, not one, but several plans. One would have been sufficiently difficult. The American troops were scattered along the Western Front from the Swiss border to the English Channel. They were powerful in infantry and machine gunners, but woefully deficient in artillery, aviation, transport, and other essential arms and services, due to British and French appeals that infantry replacements be rushed, using all available shipping to the exclusion of other troops, which the Allies undertook to supply when the Americans finally took the field as an army and needed them.

By the time a firm decision was made on St.-Mihiel on August 9, the First Army staff was completing its organization at La Ferté-sous-Jouarre, where Pershing had formally ordered it into existence late in July. General Hugh A. Drum was Chief of Staff, and when the St.-Mihiel decision became firm, his G-3 section was increased by the addition of Lieutenant Colonel Marshall and Lieutenant Colonel Walter S. Grant, who also had been at GHQ and concerned in the St.-Mihiel planning.

Taking cognizance of the presence of two American Corps on the Vesle, the First Army was given nominal command on that sector, and this step was given considerable public announcement and acclaim. In sober reality, the only concern the First Army had with that sector was to get any American troops it might have to St.-Mihiel when the time arrived, and the announcement was a "cover" plan to confuse the enemy. To add to the German uncertainty about American plans, particularly after considerable activity became obvious in the St.-Mihiel region, an elaborate hoax was devised indicating a forthcoming American offensive in the Belfort region to gain the left bank of the Rhine.

Marshall had an extremely complicated problem on his hands in directing the planning for the St.-Mihiel offensive. It contemplated not only the reduction of the salient, but the possibility of a rupture of the Hindenburg line and a developing campaign that would imperil the German positions at Metz and in the important Briey region. It was necessary not only to plan the movement of scattered American units over limited routes to the concentration area, but to plan in such a way that all movements occurred at night, and by day there would be no traffic on the roads or railroads to betray the concentration to enemy observation. This meant complete orders for each day's march by each unit. The plans had to include units to be supplied by the French, and even by the British. There were involved questions of co-ordinating the action with operations by the French on both sides of the salient, and for the participation of French divisions in the assault itself.

Then, at the end of August, Foch came up to Pershing's headquarters and proposed to the startled American Commander in Chief and his staff that the St.-Mihiel operation, scheduled for September 12, with its plans now virtually complete and troops moving into the area, be greatly reduced in scope and an entirely new plan for employment of the American Army be adopted.

What had happened was that the reduction of the various enemy salients had gone so far by this time that Foch was beginning to think in terms of major offensives that would end the war in 1918, instead of waiting until the following year. What struck the Americans at Ligny-en-Barrois, where First Army headquarters had moved on August 28, was that the plan proposed by Foch would once more split the American Army, and place its portions under French command.

Pershing rejected the proposal. When Foch asked him if he did not wish to participate in the battle, Pershing replied he most assuredly did, but with an American Army and in no other way. That Army, said Pershing, would fight in any sector of the line to which Foch chose to order it, but it would fight as an American Army, not as divisions lost in French armies. The verbal argument appeared to end with an agreement that after the St.-Mihiel attack, the American Army would make a major assault on the German positions between the Meuse River and the Argonne Forest. That decision was made final three days later, after further conferences between Pershing, Foch, and Pétain. Foch had wanted to start his big offensive not later than September 15, but agreed to postpone it in order to allow the St.-Mihiel operation to go forward as a desirable preliminary. The St.-Mihiel attack, however, was now restricted to a mere reduction of the salient, with no plan to exploit any advantage gained and try for a break-through.

With the decision firm, the operation went forward, and on the morning of September 12, more than five hundred thousand American and one hundred fifty thousand French troops attacked the salient which the Germans had held since 1914. By evening of the first day, virtually all the main objectives had been reached. Deep raids and bitter local fighting continued, but by September 16 the operation was completed. The Germans had been thrown into complete disorder by the unexpected assault, and it seemed to the disappointed American commanders that an opportunity for a complete breach of the German lines here was missed when the line was ordered stabilized along the restricted objectives.

But even before the St.-Mihiel attack began, Marshall had been pulled away to handle the even more complicated and vastly more important plans for the Meuse-Argonne offensive. A definite agreement had been reached by Pershing, Pétain, and Foch that the American First Army would begin its second offensive not later than September 25. It was one of three major offensives planned to force the Germans out of France by the end of the year, even if a complete Allied victory should elude Foch's armies until 1919. As the Americans attacked between the Meuse and the Argonne, supported on their left by the French west of the Argonne Forest, a Franco-British offensive was to be launched on the general line St.-Quentin-Cambrai, advancing between the Oise and the Scarpe, and a third Allied offensive was to be directed east of Ypres.

The primary objective was to breach the enemy's main lateral line of supply and communications, which ran through Carignan, Sedan, and Mézières, and the sector ahead of the Americans was the most critical, from the German point of view, because here the front lay closest to this main railroad-highway communications artery. Before the other offensives he could withdraw to a great depth before he was threatened vitally, but between the Meuse and the Argonne he must hold at all costs, or his forces in France would be split.

As soon as the decision was reached on September 2 to undertake the Meuse-Argonne offensive, Marshall had been put to work planning it. To begin the battle on September 25—the date later was extended one day, and the attack began September 26—Marshall had to figure how to get eleven French and Italian divisions, with two Corps headquarters, out of the line, and put fifteen American divisions with three Corps headquarters into it. Some of the Americans had to come from behind the British front, some from rest sectors in the Vosges; more than half were committed to the St.-Mihiel operation, and could not move toward the Meuse-Argonne front until the successful reduction of the salient was assured.

There were three standard gauge railroads available for the movement of troops and supplies in the area behind the American front. One ran east-west between Verdun and Ste.-Menehould, another north from Bar-le-Duc to Clermont-en-Argonne, and the third northeast from Bar-le-Duc through Commercy and St.-Mihiel to Souilly and Verdun. There were only three roads leading into the proposed battle area, which meant one for each Corps to be committed by the First Army. Even in good repair, they were barely adequate to supply the divisions that would depend on them, and elaborate plans had to be made to concentrate engineers and material to extend and maintain these vital routes.

Over these six lanes, Marshall had to withdraw 220,000 men, and advance 600,000 others, a total of 820,000 men to be handled in the plans and in the execution. It required the most meticulous preparation, including—as before St.-Mihiel—detailed daily march orders for each unit. The troop movements began September 12, the same day the St.-Mihiel battle started, and had to be completed by September 25. To screen the Allied intentions, it was necessary to leave the front line thinly held by the French and Italians until the last possible moment, and it was necessary to make all movements at night to preserve secrecy.

It was not only men that had to be moved over these limited and certain to be congested lines. There were nearly four thousand artillery pieces, forty thousand tons of ammunition to be concentrated before the start of the battle and three thousand tons moved daily after it started. Depots were established for ordnance, ammunition, gas and oil, quartermaster supplies, engineer supplies, water supply, chemical warfare supplies, medical, signal, motor, and tank supplies. There were thirty-four evacuation hospitals to be established and maintained, additional railway lines to be built, three thousand five hundred trucks to be handled, more than ninety thousand horses and mules.

The planning completed and the operation begun, Marshall was away from headquarters and in the field, spotting errors, solving problems as they arose, drawing on his prodigious memory and tremendous energy to keep this vast and complicated preparation moving on schedule, and in secrecy. The planning had been in the most precise and infinite detail, and only Marshall's exertions assured success, as Pershing himself testified.

Pershing wrote:

As in the concentration prior to St.-Mihiel, the route and length of each day's march for each unit had to be prescribed in order to prevent road congestion and insure the necessary daily delivery of supplies. It was a stupendous task and a delicate one to move such numbers of troops in addition to the large quantities of supplies, ammunition and hospital equipment required.

That it was carried out in the brief period available without arousing the suspicions of the enemy indicates the precision and smoothness with which it was calculated and accomplished. The battle at St.-Mihiel followed the plan so closely, however, that it was possible to withdraw troops exactly as intended. It seldom happens in war that plans can be so precisely carried out as was possible in this instance.

The details of the movements of troops connected with this concentration were worked out and their execution conducted under the able direction of Colonel George C. Marshall, Jr., of the Operations Section of the General Staff, First Army.*

So brilliantly did Marshall plan the concentration, so precisely did it occur under the assiduous supervision of this colonel who seemed to be everywhere at once and know everything that happened, that the enemy had no inkling of the pending attack until the barrage started which signaled its beginning. In the space of two weeks, nearly a million men and their supplies had been moved in absolute secrecy. It was recognized at the time, and the judgment has stood through the years, as the most magnificent staff operation of the war.

Marshall, of course, remained as Assistant G-3, and then—in October—as G-3, of the First Army throughout the Meuse-Argonne offensive, and the constant watch over operations and the drafting of orders for the three corps engaged were primarily his responsibility throughout that bloody and desperate struggle. For forty-seven days, the men of the First Army fought their way through the natural barriers and elaborate successive lines of fortifications which barred their way to the communications arteries which were the life line of the German armies in the west. Some of the imperishable

---

* From *My Experiences in the World War*, copyright 1931, by John Joseph Pershing, published by J. B. Lippincott Company.

Signal Corps Photo

STAFF CONFERENCE

The Chief of Staff at a 1941 meeting with Generals Gerow, Wheeler, Miles, Arnold, Haislip, Twaddle and Bryden of the General Staff.

Signal Corps Photo

OFFICIAL SOCIETY

Señor Felipe Espil, the Argentine Ambassador; Mrs. Marshall, Señora de Espil and the Chief of Staff at a War

epics of the Army occurred in the Argonne and on the heights between the forest and Meuse, among them the exploits of Sergeant Alvin C. York and Lieutenant Samuel Woodfill, and the tragic but heroic stand of Major Charles W. Whittlesey and the Lost Battalion. But these belong to the history of the infantrymen, the disciplined and dedicated foot soldiers who bore the terror and deserve such glory as may be found in battle, not to the narrative of the staff officer.

The battle began at dawn on September 26, along a front of twenty-four miles which gradually was extended until it stretched approximately ninety miles, from the Argonne Forest to the Moselle River. Some one million two hundred thousand men were used in all, and they drove the attack thirty-two miles north and fourteen miles to the northeast before the Armistice of November 11 halted the fighting. Their ultimate objective was a complete break-through, but particularly to sever the Sedan-Mézières railway and the road which paralleled it. The rail line was never reached, but it had been under artillery fire from less than two kilometers for five days when hostilities ended, and the important Carignan junction was only five miles from the American lines.

Pétain had expressed the opinion before the battle started that the terrible obstacles ahead of the Americans would prove almost insurmountable, and that the First Army would not get beyond Montfaucon during the autumn; but Montfaucon fell the second day, and the troops hammered slowly past it, and gradually left it far behind. By November 6, the retreat of the Germans before the Americans had become a rout. On that same day the rail line came under the fire of American guns—troops were not actually astride the tracks, but the main lateral communications of the German West Front in effect had been breached. That was the day the German high command asked Foch for an armistice.

In the words of the official operations report of the A.E.F., "two such coincidences are not the result of chance, and are, themselves, sufficient proof that the American soldier had borne his share in securing victory."

Not only was the railroad's usefulness to the enemy destroyed, and Carignan itself approached, but the city of Sedan had come within artillery range. It was decided, ultimately, to hold the Americans back and allow the French on their left to come up and enter Sedan, a city which had for the French an emotional importance even greater than its strategic value. But before this generous decision was made, Pershing had coveted for his own men the honor of first entry into the historic town, and this produced one of the most astonishing episodes of the war.

The First Army's I Corps was on the left, in contact with the French Fourth Army. The boundary between them ran a little to the right of Sedan, but the Americans were well ahead of the French and could easily extend their left to enter Sedan. The V Corps was on the right of I Corps. Foch had ordered unrelenting pressure on the enemy, and the French army commander had indicated to Pershing that he was willing for this to mean that the Americans might enter Sedan before the French arrived there.

By this time, Pershing had organized a Second Army, to the right of the First, under Lieutenant General Robert L. Bullard, had designated Lieutenant General Hunter Liggett to command the First Army, and was directing operations of both from GHQ as an army group commander. His operations chief, General Conner, went to First Army headquarters in the *mairie* at Souilly on November 5 to get Liggett's troops moving toward Sedan.

Liggett was away, and so was his chief of staff, General Hugh A. Drum, but Marshall was in the operations room, and he and Conner drafted a memorandum order to the commanders of the two corps, Major General Joseph T. Dickman of I Corps, and Major General Charles P. Summerall of V Corps. It read:

Subject: Message from the Commander-in-Chief.
1. General Pershing desires that the honor of entering Sedan should fall to the 1st American Army. He has every confidence that the troops of the 1st Corps, assisted on their right by the 5th Corps, will enable him to realize this desire.
2. In transmitting the foregoing message, your attention is invited

to the favorable opportunity now existing for pressing our advance throughout the night.

Conner then left to return to GHQ, and Marshall kept the draft of the memorandum on his desk until Drum returned to Souilly about 6:00 o'clock that evening after a visit to the front. Drum read over the draft, and then directed the addition of this sentence at the end of the second paragraph:
"Boundaries will not be considered as binding."
The memorandum was then signed "By command of Lieutenant General Liggett: H. A. Drum, Chief of Staff," and sent off by courier. It was also telephoned direct to I Corps and V Corps headquarters. About 2:00 o'clock the next afternoon, Summerall arrived in person at the headquarters of the 1st Division, which was part of his corps, and issued an oral order that the division was to march at once on Sedan, and to attack and seize the city. Under the command of Brigadier General Frank Parker, the division set off promptly, marching in five columns directly across the communications lines of the entire I Corps and into the area of the French Fourth Army, leaving unutterable confusion in its wake.

On the way, its patrols burst into the command post of a brigade of the Rainbow Division, and found Brigadier General Douglas MacArthur bent over a map with some of his staff. Even in those days, MacArthur affected a rakish and unorthodox cap, its appearance not unlike that of a German officer's headpiece, and he was hustled off by the patrol as a prisoner. He was released, of course, as soon as his "captors" presented him to an officer who could examine his credentials.

Beyond, the 26th Infantry, part of the 1st Division, found itself in front of the French 40th Division, right in the spot where General Laiguelot wanted to lay a barrage. The French general asked them to retire, but the regimental commander, Colonel Theodore Roosevelt, Jr., replied that his orders were to march on Sedan, and he proposed to do it.

Laiguelot, however, sent a message to First Army headquarters, and the complaint from the French was the first that General Liggett, or anyone at First Army headquarters, heard that Summerall apparently had placed an unexpected interpretation on the line which Drum had added to the memorandum order—"Boundaries will not be considered as binding." Liggett, exploding with rage, rushed to I Corps headquarters to try to get the situation straightened out, but was calmed down in the process of soothing General Dickman, beside whose purple wrath Liggett's rage was no more than a little spat of temper. In the course of a couple of days, the marching troops were withdrawn through the tangle they had created, and by 10:00 o'clock in the morning on November 9, the 1st Division was back in V Corps territory. The march had been the worst tactical aberration of the war, and if the Germans had been in any condition to launch a counterattack, it might have produced a disaster. Fortunately, the enemy resistance had all but collapsed, and instead of a tragedy, the A.E.F. had a comedy for its annals.

A complete investigation was ordered and begun, but the Armistice on November 11 soothed the ruffled feelings and dissipated the indignation on all sides, and the investigation was dropped.

Throughout the great Meuse-Argonne offensive, haggard and sleepless for days on end, Marshall had never quit hoping for a command assignment. He had been promoted in September to full colonel on General Drum's recommendation, in recognition of his preparation of the St.-Mihiel drive. Halfway through the Meuse-Argonne battle, Brigadier General Frank E. Bamford, temporarily commanding the 1st Division, had asked Pershing to assign Marshall to the command of the 28th Infantry Regiment. The request went forward with the endorsement of Colonel Malin Craig, Chief of Staff of I Corps. The assignment would have made Marshall happy. This was the regiment that took Cantigny earlier in the year, and Marshall was quite aware that Hanson Ely, who had commanded the regiment as a colonel at Cantigny, was already a major general and in command of the 5th Division. Promotion went to the combat commanders, not to the staff.

But the request was turned down. Instead, Pershing lifted Marshall out of a mere detail in the operations section, and assigned him as Chief of Operations for the First Army. That was on October 17, two days after Bamford's request was made; and on the same day, Pershing sent to the War Department his recommendation that Colonel George C. Marshall, Jr., be promoted to brigadier general.

To come so near the goal, and not to reach it! To win neither the command, nor the rank! The recommendation for promotion to brigadier general was lost when the War Department halted all promotions after the Armistice was signed. Marshall remained a temporary colonel, and instead of a command, he was given the job of chief of staff of the new VIII Corps, organized after the Armistice.

The war was over. Marshall had done superbly a job that probably no other officer in the Army could have done as well. He had achieved great distinction within the Army, and there was by this time hardly a single Regular officer in the entire A.E.F. who did not realize that this man had the capacity for greatness, and probably would become a dominant figure in the Army.

But the disappointment was great. The war had come and gone, and it was still the capacity that was recognized, not the achievement; a future of greatness, not greatness now. He had planned battles, better than anyone else could have planned them. And other men had taken his plans, and led men in battle. Marshall knew that his own chief talent was the understanding and leading of men. He knew, too, that after the plans are made, and the orders issued, the most difficult job remains to be done; that the supreme test of leadership is in command on a battlefield. That had been the one test he sought for himself, and the one test denied him.

X

Lessons of Victory

The *Leviathan* arrived in New York on September 8, 1919, bringing General John J. Pershing home to a triumphant reception by the public and a final contest with Major General Peyton C. March, the Chief of Staff.

It brought, also, Colonel George C. Marshall, Jr., aide-de-camp to the A.E.F. commander, who might with better luck have been one of the famous generals of the war, but was in fact completely unknown to the cheering public, and ignored by it. To Lily, however, his homecoming was a triumph, and this acclaim sufficed.

When any man comes home from war to the woman he left behind him, there is a little gulf of strangeness between them, not difficult to bridge unless they are frightened or disconcerted by it, but there nonetheless. The awareness of it comes fully in the instant of meeting; only at the moment of reunion does each realize how complete and how terrible the separation has been, and find the other something of a stranger.

With the Marshalls, what little trace of this there may have been was submerged in their deep joy that their divided life was whole again. Army wives of necessity school themselves in the acceptance of a marriage in episodes, and this was not the first separation the Marshalls had endured. It was sufficient bliss that their common being, suspended by two years of absence, was alive again; the process of enriching it by the discovery of what each had been and thought in the absence could be left with gay wisdom and deep understanding to the small revelations the weeks and months would bring.

Yet Mrs. Marshall could only have found the colonel a very different man from the captain who had sailed so eagerly for France. The months since the Armistice had been relatively easy, and Marshall was no longer haggard and drawn by sleepless anxiety as he had been during those weeks of the Meuse-Argonne offensive; but those weeks had left their mark. The unfamiliar, telltale lines around his eyes and mouth reflected the scars on his spirit; they were the visible signs of inner suffering. The other signs were there, as well. Tragedy is the food of mental growth and moral increase, and Mrs. Marshall found in her husband both greater assurance and more gentleness, and a subtle gain of thought and speech revealing the profound understanding which now enriched his professional competence and great integrity.

For Marshall had learned much in France. He had not yet learned, perhaps, that war is not the most terrible affliction of mankind, but the brutal result of things more terrible if less easily discerned. But fear and pain and death he had seen in frightful measure. These are things which at times are more terrible to see than to endure, particularly if the beholder feels himself in any slight measure responsible for the agony he watches; and Marshall, having drafted the orders which sent these men to death and maiming on alien soil for reasons they did not rightly comprehend, did not emerge unscathed. Even the bright flame of courage seen and understood was not compensation, but rather added burden; for the poignancy of heroism is more pain than glory, and that is the reason men find it difficult to talk about bravery.

He knew now what he had sensed before, that discipline is less a thing imposed by decree upon others than a restraint placed upon oneself. The decree is useless unless those to whom it is directed accept it with knowledge and understanding and without cavil. Ambition may be served only as long as it is subjected to the service of others; no man has the right to cast off the disciplines accepted by his fellows to serve his own ends at their expense, and in the knowledge they will mind the restraints he would abandon.

If, in the learning of that lesson, there was disappointment, there was certainly no anger. It had been his one hope that he would lead troops on the field, and the opportunity was denied him. How deeply he felt about it he had confessed to Buster Peyton, his V.M.I. roommate, when Colonel Marshall and Major Peyton found themselves seated beside each other at dinner one night at General Ely's headquarters. There had been some admiring talk about Marshall's work as First Army G-3, and Peyton mentioned it to his old friend. "I know," was the reply, "but I would rather have commanded a regiment than anything they could have given me."

"I know. . . ." Of course he knew. Marshall has been described, on many occasions and by many men, as "modest." If these admirers have meant by that to impute to Marshall an unawareness of his own abilities, an unconsciousness of the validity of the encomiums heaped upon him, then it is the wrong word. No man of extraordinary capacity, destined for greatness, lacks such knowledge of himself. Marshall knew his own quality as well as any admirer. He would not have wanted the command of troops so desperately had he not known how superbly he would have led them. The quality of leadership is palpable if unsubstantial, a rarer and greater quality than those of the orderly, rational, and perceptive mind which may be sufficient for even a very able staff officer. Marshall knew that he had that quality. What he did not know was that this quality in him had been reserved for a greater destiny, to serve a more urgent public need.

However disappointed he was that war had not brought to him the command role he had coveted, the regret did not for a moment swerve him from his fixed purpose to serve out his career in the Army. If public acclaim was missing, the same was not true within the military establishment. Within the higher levels of commands and staffs, and to some extent at the lower levels, Marshall's reputation had increased tremendously, and the word of his organizing abilities, of his administrative capacity, spread even outside military circles. There were opportunities in private business for men of his caliber. But Marshall had chosen the Army, and in the Army he would fight out his problems and satisfy his ambitions as best he could.

It is natural for all men to translate their experience of mankind into professional attitudes, to bend this wider knowledge to its applications within their own craft. Given a man as completely absorbed by his chosen career as Marshall was absorbed by the military art, who is as careful as Marshall was to screen his intimate thoughts and secret heart from all but his wife, and his professional expressions and attitudes become the only key to the man himself. What were the professional reflections, the memories of two years of war, which would mark his future service?

"Control of troops closely engaged with the enemy is the most difficult feat of leadership and requires the highest state of discipline and training," he was to write within a few months. The sentence appeared in an article written, in quite pedestrian prose, for the *Infantry Journal*. In that one sentence, which can be lifted out of its context and stand alone, appear the two ideas which were to preface every approach Marshall made to the problem of the military establishment and war—to discover and utilize that elusive quality of leadership, and to give all men destined for combat the training that would make them soldiers and not just cannon fodder.

How does one find leaders? There is only one way, and that is to put the candidates to the test. Just as the only way in which any person or group of persons can become fit to exercise the responsibility of citizens is to assume responsibility, exercise it, and suffer the social penalties for irresponsibility, so the only way that an army can select leaders is to give the most promising candidates an opportunity to demonstrate in the field whether they possess the quality. Only battle itself provides the ultimate test, but the job can be done with something approaching precision in maneuvers and training exercises.

These offer to training the closest approximation of combat conditions which an army can attain in times of peace. Training was to become an obsession, not only with Marshall, but with many others who went to France in 1917-1918. How could it be otherwise? The failure to reach objectives in the first two days of the Meuse-Argonne, the bewilderment of units which failed to recognize opportunity and convert it to capture and break-through, the mounting slaughter as the battle developed into a long and bitter struggle against the Kriemhild positions, the traffic jams on the inadequate roads, the shortcomings of liaison, the wasted courage and bitter death—these were the failures of green troops, the splendid men who were not soldiers because America had not trained them before she went to war, and because the compelling urgencies of the war itself demanded their use before they could be adequately trained even in France.

With agony of spirit, Marshall had watched the blood of the finest potential soldiers in the world run out at Montfaucon, on the heights of Cunel and Romagne, at Buzancy, in the Woëvre, because they had not been prepared for this thing before they were flung into it. That was tragedy, and Marshall's was a mind which comprehended tragedy.

Another idea had grown in the Meuse-Argonne, however. Marshall had watched these insufficiently trained civilians become in forty-seven days of battle an army of veterans skilled with weapons, shrewd in maneuver, canny in the brutal but exacting and infinitely various lore of the battlefield. When finally their great blow on November 2 had crushed the German fortifications and they stood at last above Sedan, the amateurs of September had become the finest instrument of war on the continent of Europe, vibrant and alive, disciplined and sure. But these were not professionals. They were civilians in uniform. When Marshall came back from France, he was definitely a member of the "citizen army" group within the Regular Army, opposed to the advocates of the large permanent force of professional soldiers. The division already was sharp within the Army. In a month, it would come to attention of Congress and the public.

More immediately, life was a matter of being deeply glad to be home and reunited with Lily, plus a hectic round of private and official affairs as he attended his chief in the heartwarming but burdensome welcome which the United States gave the Commander in Chief of the American Expeditionary Forces. For a few months after the Armistice, Marshall had served as chief of staff of VIII Corps in France. In January, he had been called back to GHQ to help in the planning for additional American troop movements into Germany, and then in March he had gone on a lecture tour. Accompanied by General Drum and Colonel Wiley Howell, he had been sent by Pershing on a trip to various headquarters in the major commands—First, Second, and Third Armies and the Services of Supply—as well as to such A.E.F. schools as the Staff College at Langres, to lecture on the "Organization and Development of the A.E.F. and the Operations of its Armies." The three officers had several enlisted men as assistants, operating the lantern slide and motion picture equipment to illustrate the talks.

Not long after this trip was completed, Marshall's disappointment over the failure to win a field command was softened somewhat by the award of the Distinguished Service Medal, highest decoration for noncombat service and preceded only by the Medal of Honor and the Distinguished Service Cross in the entire list of Army distinctions, in recognition of his outstanding performance and services on the Operations staff.

After his recall from VIII Corps to GHQ in January, Marshall had been thrown into almost daily contact with Pershing, and in May he became one of the General's aides. With Pershing, as with General Bell earlier, Marshall was a "working aide," not a social secretary. Some time after Marshall left Pershing's office, he found himself one day with another officer and a handsome but frivolous woman who had been a coquettish fixture in the Washington social scene while Marshall was there. It developed, in the conversation, that she had once asked Marshall to have tea alone with her.

"And you didn't come!" she reproached him archly. "And you an aide!"

"Maybe," retorted Marshall, with a meaningful look in his blue eyes, "I wasn't that kind of an aide!"

If there had been serious work with Pershing in France, and the serious work would be resumed in Washington, at the moment Marshall's assignment involved a series of affairs which undoubtedly contributed to Pershing's pride and elation, but which he faced with considerably less courage than he had shown toward the French and British commands on the subject of the integrity of American forces under American command.

The parade down Fifth Avenue in New York, leading the 1st Division, was not too bad; and it included a dramatic scene when Pershing halted the column as he reached the reviewing stand, dismounted, walked over to the bunting-hung structure and reached up to shake hands with Cardinal Mercier, who leaned over and grasped the strong brown hand of the American commander in his two frail white ones.

The tumultuous welcome, and another parade, in Washington were survived easily enough, too, and the general endured a mammoth reception at the Willard Hotel. The private invitations which deluged him, however, he declined firmly, and the news reporters, many of them with embarrassing questions (already there was the inevitable talk about Pershing for President), pursued him until he became almost psychopathic on the subject. He wanted to disappear for a while, rest a few days, find an opportunity to pull his thoughts together and face the strain imposed by custom on a hero who had returned and was expected to display himself.

The solution was provided by Mrs. Fox Conner—her father's hunting estate, Brandreth, in upstate New York. Huge, isolated, beautiful, it was the perfect spot. So, on October 7, the party started for the Adirondacks. After a month together, the Marshalls were to be separated again, for Lily did not go along—but this time for only a little more than two weeks. General Pershing, General and Mrs. Conner, Colonel Marshall, Colonel John G. Quekemeyer, another of Pershing's aides; Mrs. Conner's sister, Pauline Brandreth, their cousin, Elsie Robinson, and the Conners' young daughter Florence—that was the party, on a tract of twenty-seven thousand acres as remote from New York and Washington as if it had been on the moon.

At the railroad station seventy miles north of Utica, the group climbed into a three-seated buckboard to drive to the lodge. It was only seven miles, but the trip took two hours. Looking at this beautiful wilderness, gauging its inaccessibility with a critical eye, Pershing began to relax.

"I don't believe anybody's going to get me," he muttered. "I don't believe anyone can get me here!"

Mrs. Conner was startled, and intrigued.

"Who do you think is going to *get* you?"

"Reporters!"

They all laughed, the general included. Then they arrived at the lodge, an ancient log house, settled comfortably beside a clearing at the edge of a beautiful lake. Pershing looked around gratefully, flung his hat and coat on a chair, and announced firmly, "I'm never going to go home!"

They hunted almost every afternoon. The total bag is not of record, but Marshall got at least one buck, and Pershing—fittingly, being senior to his aide—a much larger one. And the general was to discover that even Brandreth was not as inaccessible as he had thought. One day two nuns arrived, on foot, from their sanitarium at Saranac, good Irish Sisters with their share of secular curiosity, and more energy than most.

"Sure," they explained happily, "we heard that General Pershing was here, and we didn't believe it, but we thought we'd walk in."

And walked they had, seven and a half miles. They saw the general.

Marshall wrote, dutifully but also eagerly, to his wife each day. One of the letters brought an apologetic comment from Mrs. Marshall to Mrs. Conner when the group had returned to Washington, and the Marshalls and the Conners were having dinner together. George, remembering the boating on the lovely lake, had told his wife that "every morning I have a row with Elsie Robinson." And Lily, thinking of tempestuous quarrels, said to Mrs. Conner, "I don't understand why George should have to have all those rows with Elsie!"

The return to Washington was a return to serious business. They discovered that Colonel John McAuley Palmer, a couple of days after Pershing's party left for Brandreth, had brought the citizen-versus-professional army cleavage into the open by informing the Senate Military Committee that he thought the military establishment proposal they were considering, the official plan sponsored by the War Department and the Chief of Staff, General March, was "not in harmony with the genius of American institutions." The remark precipitated the last great disagreement between Pershing and March. The latter had proposed a standing army of more than five hundred thousand regulars. Pershing, called to testify before a joint session of the Senate and House Military Committees, asserted that a Regular Army of two hundred seventy-five to three hundred thousand was ample. It was Marshall and Conner who collected the material which the general used in support of his statement, and briefed him for his appearance.

The latest disagreement between Pershing and March was the result of a profound difference in viewpoint on the fundamental structure of an American Army. Pershing and the group who came back with him and were closest to him, among them Marshall, Conner, and Palmer, while recognizing the superior efficiency of professional troops, held that the entire history of the United States proved that this nation would never tolerate the expense of a standing army large enough to serve its needs. They went farther, however, and saw that the superiority of the professional force was in reality no more than a difference in training; properly trained, the militia became the equal of the professional army, and in some respects surpassed it. It followed, in the minds of these able and thoughtful men, that the solution was not the establishment of a huge standing army and its inevitable and intolerable burden of cost, but the maintenance of a minimum professional force accompanied by a reorganization of the militia elements to assure their proper training and their immediate availability as part of the emergency or wartime national army. The regulars would garrison the overseas outposts, and supply enough for a small protective mobilization within the United States. Beyond that, the Regular Army would be no more than the essential minimum to maintain the necessary full-time attention to military developments, insure a continuity of doctrine and method, and supply the guidance in instruction for the citizen elements organized as reserves. The regulars would not even provide all of the instruction. Officers and noncommissioned officers of the reserve components would do the bulk of it. With the veterans of the World War to start with, there was the finest opportunity since the republic was founded to achieve a rational solution of the military problem in a democracy.

In the opposing camp, the advocacy of a large standing army was not based on any selfish desire to reserve military preferment and distinction to the professional. It was based, rather, on the many and well-known failures of the militia and the scandals of the volunteer system throughout the country's history, including the shortcomings of the National Guard and of the divisions of draftees in the latest war. It was a shortsighted view, in that it did not seek the reasons for the failure of citizen components and assumed that such failures were inevitable and inescapable in any but professional forces; but however shortsighted, it was neither selfish nor militaristic.

Soon after the Armistice of 1918, Pershing had been asked by the War Department to send someone home to represent him in the councils of the General Staff as it undertook to plan the postwar military establishment. Palmer was commanding the 58th Infantry Brigade, part of the 29th Division, when Pershing sent for him in December and assigned him to the Washington detail. So completely did Pershing know Palmer's views and so completely did he share them, that he did not bother to give him any specific or detailed instructions when Palmer reported to him at Chaumont. The younger man was simply to go to Washington and speak for the A.E.F. commander, and use his own judgment as to what he said and how he said it.

By the time Palmer reached the War Department, however, the War Plans Division of the General Staff already had completed its study and recommendations, and they already had been junked by General March. This able officer, as imperious as Pershing, had come home from France during the war to take over as Chief of Staff and bring some order out of the staff chaos in Washington. That job he had accomplished in thoroughgoing fashion; but he had also come into conflict with Pershing. Their quarrels had to do mostly with supplies, and with the flow and the training of men. Each accused the other of impossible attitudes and demands, each charged the other with failure to co-operate. This is not the place to examine in detail those disagreements, but broadly speaking both were victims of the fact that the United States went into the war unprepared for it. By the time March, who considered himself as Chief of Staff to be Pershing's superior, had ripped the War Department staff apart and put it together again as a functioning organization, Pershing had perforce worked out his own solution in France. He wanted no interference with his operating organization, and held the job of the War Department to be merely that of supplying the means which he found necessary for his assigned job.

Whatever his theory of the General Staff's function, in practice March expected it to be merely the instrument of his ideas and plans as long as he was Chief of Staff. Thus, he not only did not wait for Pershing's representative to be heard in the postwar planning councils of the War Plans Division; he rejected the work of that division itself, and drafted himself, with the aid of a small group of senior officers, the proposal that was submitted to Congress as the official War Department plan for the future of the Army. Briefly, it discarded the traditional citizen forces as a part of the national defense scheme, and proposed a standing Army of more than a half million. It was received with marked lack of enthusiasm at the Capitol, and members of the military committees let it be known they were reluctant to begin consideration of the permanent military establishment until the Armistice had been replaced by a treaty of peace.

With the job he had come home to share thus disposed of before his arrival, Palmer was assigned to the General Staff, as chief of a section of the War Plans Division. There he was working on rather routine duties when a letter from the Senate Military Committee to the Secretary of War, asking the Department's recommendations on a bill introduced by Senator New proposing universal military training, was referred to his division for study. Palmer, Colonel Tenney Ross and Colonel Allen J. Greer became a committee which buckled down to a thorough study of the question of universal training and its relation to military organization. The result of their study was a memorandum report recommending the establishment of a reserve army of forty-eight divisions, to be formed under the army rather than the militia clause of the Constitution, and with an initial membership composed of veterans of the wartime National Army who would be replaced gradually by the products of a universal training system. The committee made reference to the fact that such a scheme would permit reduction of the Regular Army far below the half-million of the War Department plan. Concurrences were obtained from other divisions of the General Staff, and the memorandum report then was sent in to March. He not only rejected it, but instructed the General Staff to confine itself in the future to perfecting details of the plan he already had submitted to Congress.

That plan was under study by the Senate Committee when Palmer, as chief of one of the subdivisions of the General Staff, was called before it as a witness the second week of October 1919. The senators, assuming they were getting just another rubber-stamp endorsement of the official position, gave him only cursory attention until Palmer dropped that remark about disharmony with American institutions. Chairman Wadsworth asked him just what kind of military system he favored. It took Palmer the better part of two days to give the committee the answer to that question, and when he had finished the committee asked for him to be assigned as its special adviser. The War Department agreed, carefully disclaiming any responsibility for the advice Palmer might give, in view of the things he already had said. That, of course, left Palmer a free hand, and he played it so well that Wadsworth was to say later the colonel was the real author of the National Defense Act of 1920.

The labors of Palmer and the committee, with the backing of Pershing and all the citizen army advocates, revolved around the question of what to do with the National Guard. In order to insure adequate supervision of the Guard's training, Palmer proposed that it be merged in a purely Federal reserve, using the army clause of the Constitution. This was a matter with considerable political implications, however. The National Guard already was touchy about the attitude displayed toward it by the Regular Army, and the committee was afraid that any such proposal as this would stir up enough opposition to defeat the entire bill. They chose instead a double reserve—the National Guard and the Organized Reserve—but adequate Federal supervision was assured by using the army instead of the militia clause of the Constitution as the basis of organization. Also involved was the disposition of the Guard units, many of them with records and traditions antedating the Revolution of 1776. Wadsworth thought this problem not only explosive politically, but virtually insoluble. Palmer, however, had the answer to that—let the solution be found by joint committees of Regular and Guard officers. The Guard would accept a solution to which it contributed, but would fight the imposition of a plan arrived at without the Guard's participation.

At the end of October 1919, Pershing appeared before the joint session of the House and Senate Committees and added his public testimony in support of the proposals which Palmer had been advocating. He asserted an army half the size proposed by March was adequate, and instead of scrapping the citizen-army structure, recommended a better training schedule for the National Guard to make it an efficient part of the first-line defense system. Pershing advocated also a single promotion list for the officers of the Army, ridding it of the separate promotion list for each arm and service which had been productive of so much jealousy and disunity.

There was, of course, a primary condition on which the citizen army advocates predicated their plans—universal military training. This was included in the bill which the Senate Committee drafted and introduced, but the public outcry was so great that Wadsworth and his colleagues eliminated it rather than jeopardize the entire measure. Further compromise was necessary to reconcile the conflicting House and Senate measures, but in its final form the National Defense Act of 1920 made the citizen-army idea a national policy, although it was to remain a policy less than half implemented for twenty years.

Except as he was called upon to prepare material for Pershing, Marshall was not directly involved in the battling and maneuvering for the National Defense Act. Indirectly, however, his concern was great, and his interest very much alive. When he was in Washington, he and Conner and Palmer, as well as other like-minded officers, would get together for long discussions of the proper military establishment, or the philosophy of the profession of arms in a democracy. Conner and Marshall were described as "a mutual admiration society," and Palmer was a full-fledged member of their club. On the aspect of the Army's place in society they were in hearty agreement: it was, and must remain, the instrument and not the framer of policy.

But during much of the time the National Defense Act was being debated in Washington, Marshall was not even in the city. Pershing was still Commander in Chief of the A.E.F., and all the country still wanted to look at him. Accordingly, at the end of November he set out to tour the country. Traveling in a special car, and accompanied by Marshall and a group of other officers, the general by Christmas Eve had visited Army camps and war plants in Virginia, South Carolina, Georgia, Alabama, Kentucky, Ohio, and a half-dozen other states. The group also had displayed itself to hurrahing crowds in dozens of cities and towns, and eaten its way through a staggering succession of elaborate official luncheons and dinners. After a break for Christmas, the journey was resumed, and they toured Texas, the mountain states, and the Far West. In some of the Western cities the jam of cheering and eager citizens was so great that Marshall had to spearhead a flying wedge formation of aides and orderlies to open a path for Pershing. Back to Washington at the end of the winter, they were off again in April for an inspection of the Panama Canal.

By June, they were once more in the States, and Pershing went to West Point to make a speech to the graduating class. Then Marshall scored a real triumph—from West Point, the general went to Lexington, and there the Commander in Chief of the A.E.F. distributed the diplomas to the class of 1920 at the Virginia Military Institute. He spent two days in Lexington, and endeared himself to the hill and the town by saying that he had always heard the V.M.I. referred to as "the West Point of the South," but after seeing the school and its spirit, he wondered why they had not called West Point "the V.M.I. of the North."

On June 30, Marshall's temporary wartime rank lapsed, and for one day he became once more Captain Marshall. On July 1, he was promoted to major in the Regular Army. It would be thirteen years before he once again displayed the eagles of a full colonel on his shoulders.

Back in Washington, with most of the required trips completed, Marshall set to work in earnest on the tasks Pershing assigned to him. With Conner, he went methodically through the records of the Operations Division of the A.E.F. staff, arranging them for the archives, and writing the final Operations report. More directly under Pershing's eye, he labored on the material for the final report of the First Army, A.E.F., and did a lot of the writing of it. This one did not go too smoothly—one draft, submitted for Pershing's study, came back with the comment that the general thought it more or less verbose in places, with a tendency to place too much emphasis on staff and not enough on combat troops; he was sending a corrected copy to serve as a basis for further discussion.

In August, both Pershing and his aide went off for holidays, Pershing to Brandreth again for a gay and sprightly house party, and Marshall and his wife to Lexington for an extended leave. There were parties in Lexington, too, but what Marshall enjoyed most was the long rides, three or four hours every day, through the beautiful hill country of the lower Shenandoah Valley.

The leave ended, Marshall returned to work on the First Army and G-3 reports. Since the latter is, in large part, Marshall's work, the section on "Military Lessons of the War," read in the light of the preparations Marshall was to achieve twenty years later, is illuminating:

The tactical lessons to be gained from the war are infinite, and even though it were possible it is not desirable to attempt their enumeration here. Their study is rather a matter for the future, and in such study we should avoid the error of assuming that our experiences within themselves, rather than the logical deductions from them and other experiences, are the lessons which we seek.

But our experience taught one great lesson that, while it stood out so prominently to the General Headquarters, is likely to be soon forgotten. That lesson is: The unprepared nation is helpless in a great war unless it can depend upon other nations to shield it while it prepares. Every scrap of the history of the American Expeditionary Forces bears this lesson, but it is only necessary to justify it by remembering a few of the facts brought out in this report:

More than a year elapsed after our declaration of war before we were able to undertake an offensive action, and then only one regiment of infantry was actually engaged.

Not one American-made gun of the most essential calibers appeared on the battle front in the 18 months from our declaration of war to the Armistice.

First the necessity of saving a defeat and, next, the possibility of winning the war in 1918, thereby saving American lives as well as the suffering of the world, required putting the American soldier into battle without the training, discipline and leadership which he deserved.

In the article written for the *Infantry Journal*, under the title, "Profiting by War Experiences," Marshall discloses the comprehensive nature of the intellect he brought to bear upon purely military questions.

The article begins with a broadside against critiques appearing in service journals, discussions at service schools and colleges, and even pamphlets published by the War Department which indicated to Marshall that the American military student of the World War was being led astray on the formulation of tactical questions and on organization, because the circumstances of incidents referred to were presented without sufficient detail to form a basis of judgment.

He wrote:

Furthermore, the majority of our officers had but a brief experience in battle and were so hard-pressed before, during, and immediately after engagements that it is difficult for them to make an accurate, critical analysis of the battle tactics involved, and it is well known that a single example is apt to prove a dangerous guide for future action.

French defense plans were undoubtedly too long, Marshall continued, but the American critic of those plans would do well to remember that in stabilized warfare some such defense plan was essential to co-ordinate the actions of neighboring divisions. Formations for attack might depend, not alone on the theoretical ideal for the front elements, but on such matters as how often the division could get hot meals to the men in the front line. Trained machine-gun officers probably knew more about their weapon than an infantry officer, but that was no reason to forget that "the determining phase of a battle is usually a melee in which the infantry battalion commander alone is able to make decisions in time to take best advantage of the constantly changing situation."

Marshall wrote:

A divided command on the battlefield is out of the question. Control of troops closely engaged with the enemy is the most difficult feat of leadership and requires the highest state of discipline and training. It would therefore seem that the machine guns should be an integral part of the infantry battalion.

Misuse of the "accompanying gun" was due primarily to lack of proper training of infantry regimental and battalion commanders, and exasperated field-artillery officers should not assume that the idea of the accompanying gun was a hopeless error from the start. Some of the orders presented to students as models had only one noticeable defect—they never reached their destinations in time to influence the action; whereas many apparently crude and fragmentary orders got to the front-line commanders, and made the plans of the higher command effective. Orders for the movement of troops ought to be studied with consideration for the time element involved—orders that looked excellent in the textbooks might, in fact, have forced the marching of the troops with too much discomfort and fatigue. Finally, most Americans in France got their experience at St.-Mihiel and the Meuse-Argonne, when the German armies were spent and already on the defensive, and should remember that the German army of a few months earlier was quite a different opponent.

Marshall concluded:

Many mistakes were made in the Argonne which the German at that time was unable to charge to our account. The same mistakes, repeated four months earlier in the war, would have brought an immediate and unfortunate reaction. It is possible that methods successfully employed in the Meuse-Argonne would have invited a successful enemy counterattack in the spring of 1918.

It is not intended by this discussion to belittle our efforts in the latter part of the war, for what we actually accomplished was a military miracle, but we must not forget that its conception was based on a knowledge of the approaching deterioration of the German Army, and its lessons must be studied accordingly. We remain without modern experience in the first phases of a war and must draw our conclusions from history.

It was hardly a brilliant paper, this 1921 effort by Major Marshall; and certainly it lacked both sparkle and finish as a literary effort; but it revealed fully his already well-developed skepticism of the glib solution, his complete unwillingness to accept military dogma, his distrust of established patterns and the rule book, his passion for complete and accurate knowledge, his deep concern with the realities of his profession.

This professional objectivity and his breadth of understanding were once more drawing attention to Marshall. He was requested by name in a letter from the Secretary of the Navy to deliver a lecture before the Naval War College on the Army's operations during the war. He refused a proffered assignment as an instructor at the Army War College. In the early winter of 1920 he went to Milton and Exeter, New Hampshire, to deliver another A.E.F. lecture. This time, Mrs. Marshall went along, and the jaunt included more festivities than business—the Marshalls were entertained at two luncheons, a tea, a supper party, and a lavish dinner.

In 1921, Pershing became Chief of Staff, and he reorganized the General Staff along the lines worked out in France for the A.E.F., fixing the pattern that was to remain until 1942. The Personnel Division (G-1) handled the staff duties relating to personnel policies of the Army; the Military Intelligence Division (G-2) was charged with the collection, evaluation, and dissemination of military information; Operations and Training (G-3) had the planning function for organization, training and normal operations of the military forces; Supply Division (G-4) supervised supply functions of the Army, and the War Plans Division (WPD) was in charge of planning for the employment of the Army in a theater of war.

The National Defense Act embodied, and Pershing and the entire Army were certain they were imbued with, the views of John McAuley Palmer on the nature and duties of a General Staff. As a result of his studies of the evolution of the staff system, Palmer was convinced that the use of the General Staff as a general supervisory group was wrong. They were, he held, specialists of the most restricted type, and the supervisory idea stemmed from a mistranslation from the German—instead of General Staff, it should have been general's staff, which carried the proper connotation of general's helper, charged with preparing orders, carrying on training, operating an intelligence service, supervising supply, but interfering as little as possible with the operating function of any arm or service.

The General Staff, in other words, was the eyes and ears of the Chief of Staff and the Secretary, advising them, but possessing no authority and exercising no command function. The National Defense Act enlarged the General Staff, and confirmed it on this basis. Yet the organization which Pershing had perfected in France was not alone a planning and advisory group. It was also, in a very real sense, an instrument of command, and of necessity it exercised command functions. The unhappy truth was that the planning function could not be separated from operations, and the careful distinction which Elihu Root had drawn between them in order to get a General Staff at all in the face of opposition from the old-line staff bureaus baffled the men who tried to maintain the distinction, and produced an organization which had to be scrapped in two great wars.

The manifold problems developing in the Army and the War Department as the country lapsed into the happy assumption that the war to end wars had really ended them meant that Marshall was busy throughout his tour with Pershing in Washington, but the years passed pleasantly, and the work was not arduous enough to keep the Marshalls from having a full and happy social life. Marshall served as recorder for staff boards, watched the tightening purse strings reduce the Organized Reserve to paper and the Regular Army to impotence, wrote speeches for the general. In 1923 he was promoted again to lieutenant colonel. In 1923 also he accompanied Pershing on a nationwide tour of the Citizens' Military Training Camps. They were in California when President Harding died suddenly after a trip to Alaska, and so became an official military escort on the funeral train which brought the chief executive's body back to Washington. Then, early in 1924, Marshall's detail as a staff officer expired, and he welcomed the return to duty with troops. On April 28, 1924, War Department Special Orders No. 100 carried this announcement:

"1. Lieutenant Colonel George C. Marshall, Jr., Infantry, aide-de-camp, is relieved from his present assignment and duties, Washington, D. C., and is assigned to the 15th Infantry, effective July 1, 1924."

The 15th Infantry was at Tientsin, China. Marshall was ordered to proceed by Army Transport from New York about July 12 for San Francisco, and from San Francisco by Army Transport to Chinwangtao. Pershing gave a farewell luncheon for the Marshalls at the Shoreham Hotel on June 8. The last preparations were made, the packing completed, and good-bys said, and in July the Marshalls sailed for China to begin the most interesting and most delightful three years of their life together.

XI

China—and Tragedy

The enchantment of the Orient has cast a spell on many Westerners, and Marshall was no exception. With his passion for facts, his probing mind, his clear perception, and the profound understanding and noble compassion which mark great men, he saw China without the veil of exotic illusion that clouds the usual American thinking about Cathay. In Marshall's case, love was not blind; but the spell was on him nonetheless.

The long sea trip from New York had been a fabulous delight, a journey over seas not desperate but serene, spiced at intervals with stops long enough for shore excursions and parties with old friends. In Panama, the Conners had welcomed the Marshalls with open arms, a big party, and seemingly unlimited quantities of champagne. Did Lieutenant Colonel Marshall meet Major Dwight Eisenhower at that party? Eisenhower was executive officer to Conner at the time, and had learned long ago that the highest accolade his chief could bestow was to tell him he had done some job just as Marshall would have done it.

There had been another stay in San Francisco, and at Honolulu, where the Marshalls were met by Major General and Mrs. Summerall, and had lunch with them at the Moana. Then the general turned his limousine over to his guests, and they drove for hours through the breath-catching beauty of Oahu. Back on the ship, Marshall escaped the leis and the gay clamor of his friends to write a brief note to Pershing. Just before he sailed from San Francisco, he had telegraphed "Adios" to his former chief, and the general's "Au revoir affectionately Pershing" had reached him by radiogram aboard the transport.

"Your wireless message was deeply appreciated," Marshall wrote. "Incidentally, it electrified the ship and quite dignified me...."

Then he described the welcome he and his wife had received from the Conners and the Summeralls, and added:

"No words can express the regret and loss I feel at the termination of my service with you. Few ever in life have such opportunities and almost none, I believe, such a delightful association as was mine with you. May all good things be yours. Goodbye—

"Affectionately,
"Marshall"

When Marshall arrived at Tientsin, the impression prevailed among the officers of the 15th Infantry that he had come to take command of the regiment. In fact, his orders directed him only to report to the Commanding General, American Forces in China, for duty; and Brigadier General William D. Connor assigned him as Executive Officer, 15th Infantry, and temporarily as acting commanding officer.

Taking over from Major E. F. Harding, the senior battalion commander of the regiment who had been exercising the temporary command for several weeks, Marshall directed the detachment until the arrival of Colonel William K. Naylor three months later. The other battalion at Tientsin was commanded by Major Joseph L. Stilwell.

China was in chaos, and it was a difficult and trying task which Marshall took over at Tientsin. The opportunistic intrigues of Dr. Sun Yat-sen had led him to a strange alliance with the celebrated Marshall Chang Tso-lin, war lord of Manchuria, to bring about the downfall of another war lord, Wu P'ei-fu, with whom both had been in alliance at one time or another, but whom both found objectionable at the moment. When Wu's army met that of Chang at Shanhaikwan in October, Chang and Dr. Sun had already arranged for Wu's defeat by persuading one of his confreres, the so-called Christian General Feng Yu-hsiang, to desert him in the battle. This "Christian" general's men had once gone into battle wearing armbands with the legend, "Trust in God and show no mercy." Feng played the traitor as arranged, and Wu was overwhelmed. His beaten and scattered troops started streaming south, and most of them seemed to be heading for Tientsin.

Marshall discovered that most of his officers were convinced, with weary resignation, that every time an army was defeated in this civil war—and that occurred fairly frequently—Tientsin was due for a horde of stragglers. Under the protocol between the foreign powers and the Chinese government—nobody was quite certain who or what was the Chinese government at the time, but Peking retained official recognition, and anyhow all sides clung to the protocol—Chinese troops were forbidden to enter the foreign concession areas of Tientsin, which lay a considerable distance west of the native city. The trick was to keep them out without becoming involved in a fight.

An outpost line was established several miles out, covering all approaches to the foreign city, to prevent the straggling Chinese military from approaching the concession area. This outpost line served the incidental purpose of protecting about two dozen native villages from the depredations of the wanderers, and the village officials got together later and erected a small marble tablet to the American troops in token of their appreciation. No effort was made to keep these broken troops from entering the native city. In fact, they were permitted to enter the concession area provided they surrendered their arms at the outposts.

There was seldom any trouble during one of these periods, but trouble was always a distinct possibility, and Marshall took the outpost line very seriously. The men—it was Major Harding's battalion during this particular episode—lived under field conditions, and Marshall made frequent inspections. On the first, he was critical—the men ought to make a smarter appearance, for prestige purposes. Less than two months in China, and Marshall already was thoroughly familiar with the value placed upon "face" by the East. From then on, the men at the outpost line looked as though they were on dress parade. The mark of Marshall was on another order, too: the footsore and hungry Chinese stragglers, before they were sent on to the native city with their arms or allowed into the concession area without them, were fed by the Americans.

By the end of January, Marshall was writing Pershing that he was enthusiastic about his assignment: "The officers of the regiment rate unusually high—as do their wives—and the training and school work is very interesting." But the job was not without its problems, and Marshall was still critical of elaborate paper work and unrealistic inspection policies in the Army.

Marshall wrote:

Today is "pay-day" and we are up against the problem of cheap liquor and cheaper women—Chinese, Japanese, Russian and Korean. I am relearning much about the practical side of handling men, but it seems much the same old problem. . . .

With only five months of experience to judge from, I am more and more firmly of the opinion I held in the War Department, that our equipment, administrative procedure and training requirements are all too complicated for anything but a purely professional army.

I find the officers are highly developed in the technical handling or functioning of weapons, in target practice, in bayonet combat, and in the special and intricate details of paper work or administration generally, *but* that when it comes to simple tactical problems, the actual details of troop leading, they all fall far below the standards they set in other matters.

I suppose this is due to the fact that the application of the principles of troop leading and tactics is largely a matter of judgment, therefore the War Department, through its inspectors and overseers, is more exacting about those questions which are matters of fact and can be determined in figures or percentages—or in matters of administration.

No one ever understood better than Marshall that the regimen imposed by order is the least part of discipline, and he made his active interest in the enlisted men of this regiment felt from the moment of his arrival. By the time winter arrived in Tientsin, he had seen to the construction of a covered ice-skating rink. He stimulated other athletics, for the officers as well as the enlisted men, and got the men interested in amateur theatricals. Within a short time, the companies found themselves vying with one another in a variety of amateur contests.

Nor did his concern stop with the provision of activity for their leisure hours. First priority, in fact, was given to vitalizing the training of the troops. Furthermore, Marshall was determined to have the most impressive regiment in Tientsin, and that took considerable tightening of discipline and sprucing of appearance, because there were some rather smart and showy foreign units stationed in the concession area. And, after about a year, he took over the Chinese language course for officers and started a similar course for enlisted men. Under his guidance, some excellent and simple textbooks were prepared and written for these courses.

Marshall himself had shown an astonishing ability to master this most difficult of languages, a spoken and written tongue of syllables, tones, and symbols without an alphabet. He had plunged into the study of Chinese as soon as he arrived in September, and six months later, presiding at a summary court martial, he took the testimony of a native witness without the help of an interpreter.

"If anyone had told me last summer that I would soon be able to grunt and whine intelligible Chinese I would have ridiculed the idea," he wrote Pershing.

Not because of his growing proficiency in Chinese, although that certainly made it simpler and was taken by them as courtesy and compliment, Marshall sought out Chinese officials and local citizens on every possible occasion. His eagerness for knowledge knew no more bounds than his universal human sympathy and understanding, and these people attracted him as people, as representatives of an ancient culture alien to his own, and fascinating. The range of Marshall's interests was extremely broad, and he would talk with equal avidity about Chinese politics, old porcelain and paintings on silk, or the degeneration of Taoism from the noble philosophy of Lao-tse to a cult of a million superstitions. The Chinese who met him responded to this man's interest, sincerity, and courtesy, and no foreigner in Tientsin was better liked.

The men of his command, officers as well as enlisted men, both liked Marshall and stood in awe of him. The awe was induced upon his arrival at Tientsin by the man's reserve, by his firmness and exacting standards however tempered with understanding and mercy, by a knowledge so comprehensive as to be slightly terrifying, and by his abrupt manner. That abruptness was never accompanied by discourtesy, even when it was accompanied by wrath; yet even those who became his close friends in Tientsin, who rode with him, played golf and tennis with him, swapped jokes, and were his companions in amateur theatricals never quite broke through the restraint that was between them. Always they remained conscious of a quality of great dignity, knew themselves to be companions of an extraordinary man. It was the quality noted by an officer who served closely with Marshall throughout the war against the Axis powers years later. This officer, groping for illustration, finally said that, not only had he never heard Marshall tell a dirty story, but the most frigid social atmosphere it had ever been his unhappy lot to experience was that which descended suddenly upon a room in which an unwary and less than sensitive officer ventured to relate a dirty story to Marshall.

For all the essential dignity of this man, and the slight awe of him that persisted in the regiment, the officers and their wives found the simple informality of the Marshall home and the warm welcome they received were attracting them there more and more frequently. Junior officers with troubled minds found themselves, to their astonishment, unburdening themselves to Marshall, and finding him interested, sympathetic, and helpful. They discovered, too, that Mrs. Marshall not only was an entertaining hostess and a very intelligent woman with ideas of her own about the problems all the garrison was facing, but that she was a dependable friend as well. Particularly, the junior officers found—and they liked it—if she had criticisms to make of their behavior, she made it to them, not to someone else.

"You always knew exactly what Mrs. Marshall thought about you, because she told you frankly," said one of these younger officers. "She was not one of those Army wives who carry tales to the commanding officer."

Marshall's best-loved recreation was riding. He preferred to ride in the tender light and sweet air of dawn, but any hour when he could get away was apt to see him cantering through the country around Tientsin. To give the men of the regiment another form of recreation, and also to endow the regiment with a more impressive appearance for ceremonial and parade occasions, he organized a mounted detachment of the 15th Infantry.

Horses were hard to get in China, and the regiment began getting some Mongolian ponies to replace the broken-down old mounts supplied to the officers. Marshall acquired a particularly handsome pair of these animals, and encouraged other officers to buy them. With other more or less enthusiastic horsemen, he would organize long rides through the countryside, varied sometimes by a paper chase followed by a "hunt breakfast."

During the winter of 1925-1926, a young cavalry officer on his way to Peking was stranded in Tientsin for several weeks when the most recent flare-up of civil war cut off the routes to the capital, and Marshall enthusiastically seized on him as a heaven-sent instructor in horsemanship. He bullied his fellow officers into taking advantage of this unlooked-for opportunity, and out they rode, day after day, at 8:00 o'clock in the morning in the bitter December weather. They got a lot of exercise which they probably needed, and certainly improved their horsemanship, but none save Marshall and the young cavalryman showed the slightest evidence of pleasure in the process.

A few weeks later the weather had moderated enough for a game of tennis, and Marshall, Harding, Chaplain Miller, and Captain Wagoner were riding home after a couple of sets of doubles. Marshall remembered that Harding had a considerable talent for light verse which enlivened most gatherings of the little Army colony.

"Harding," he said, "Mrs. Marshall and I are celebrating our twenty-fourth anniversary Friday. You and Mrs. Harding are coming, and I wish you'd do a poem for it."

Harding nodded. He had already been trying to write a verse expressing the amused resentment of the unhappy but devoted riding students, and decided to combine the two. The resultant effort was addressed to Mrs. Marshall, and read by Harding at the party.

Signal Corps Photo

MARSHALL AND STIMSON

". . . an almost perfect team of statesmen began to pull together."

EISENHOWER AND MARSHALL

Signal Corps Photo

"I've known the colonel a year or more," he began. Then he paused a moment before adding, in a tone eloquent of shocked but sympathetic dismay, "My God! *You've* known him for *twenty-four!*" He proceeded in the same vein, but most of the remainder was lost in laughter, led by Marshall's gleeful shouts.

The shipment of ponies for the mounted detachment inevitably included a few "outlaws" which could not be broken to the saddle, and these contrary beasts were turned over to the machine-gun company to pull its carts. Marshall was most particular that the training of these animals include no abuse, and he sent one day for Harding and ordered him to relieve a certain lieutenant from the training job. Marshall had seen him strike one of the ponies. Harding investigated, found the lieutenant had slapped the pony across the face with a piece of harness because it was the only way he could get him between the shafts of the cart, and went back to Marshall and told him he thought the lieutenant's action was justified. Marshall refused to alter his command, and the lieutenant was relieved of the duty. He took it rather well, and in truth was probably glad—it was a burdensome detail which no one wanted.

If the winters were unpleasantly cold in Tientsin, the summers were disagreeably hot, and the troops went to summer camp at Nantassu on the coast, for a little drill, a lot of firing practice, and even more recreation. The reservation had an excellent beach, and a rest camp was established there for the officers and their families. The first summer they spent in unadorned tents, but the next year Marshall saw to it that the tents had brick floors, and that brick walks were built through the area. It made a pleasant vacation spot for the entire command. Each battalion spent about six weeks in the camp, which opened before the weather got uncomfortably hot in Tientsin. Usually it was July or August before the officers' families came down there.

Just off the military reservation was an unprepossessing little shack, operated as a canteen by a Chinese who sold, among other things, beer. It was known as Denny's Dump, and "Dump parties" became the vogue for officers and their wives. The Marshalls entered into these affairs with enthusiasm—the beer, the singing, and the dumb crambo and charades.

Social life was gay—if somewhat less simple—in Tientsin, too, particularly after the new Country Club was opened in 1926. This was a rather lavish establishment, with tennis courts, a swimming pool, and an orchestra for dancing, and it had the added advantage for families on Army pay that, for all its elaborate scale and appearance, it was cheap.

Marshall was still busy, however. Not only was he executive officer of the regiment, but post-school officer and summary court officer as well, and at various times in temporary command of the regiment. General Connor had written a letter commending him for the prompt and efficient way he took hold of the situation and met the problems existing on his arrival. Later Colonel Isaac Newell, who arrived in 1926 to take command of the regiment, added another letter of official commendation, remarking that he had been impressed by the high standards of discipline and training in the regiment, and by the extremely smart appearance of the men. Marshall also kept himself in touch with the shifting politico-military developments in China. Many of them, in fact, he had to watch for their possible effect on his work. The killing of a Chinese worker in a Japanese-owned factory in Shanghai in the spring of 1925 had touched off riots and a bitterness against all foreigners in China that spread through the entire country and gained momentum steadily. On this, if on nothing else, the Chinese seemed to be in agreement. Since the 15th Infantry was in China to protect American interests, the rising tension kept Marshall alert.

The antiforeign agitation seemed to grow with the advance of the armies of the Kuomintang—which had established its "Nationalist" government in Canton—northward into the Yangtze Valley in 1926. These armies were led by a man whom Marshall had yet to meet, but with whom he would have much to do in the years to come— Chiang Kai-shek. The Kuomintang stirred up some interest in the United States, which up to that time had displayed no great general concern about revolution, counterrevolution, and the endless campaigns and intrigues of war lords in unhappy China. Pershing had written to Marshall in 1924 that, while he envied him the opportunity to be in China during an interesting period, in reality no one in the United States paid much attention to the Chinese revolution. By December 1926, however, Pershing's letter reflected a growing concern lest the Kuomintang surge northward become completely successful and spell the end of extraterritoriality in China. The same day that Pershing wrote this letter—it was the day after Christmas, 1926—Marshall wrote to the general from Tientsin:

How the Powers should deal with China is a question almost impossible to answer.

There has been so much of wrongdoing on both sides, so much of shady transaction between a single power and a single party; there is so much of bitter hatred in the hearts of these people and so much of important business interests involved, that a normal solution can never be found. It will be some form of an evolution, and we can only hope that sufficient tact and wisdom will be displayed by foreigners to avoid violent phases during the trying period that is approaching.

And yet it is expecting too much to believe that matters can be readjusted quietly and wisely, with continued public pronouncements by politicians such as Borah and Lloyd George. There may be truth in what they say, but you cannot yell such messages at an excited crowd without the danger of violent and unreasoning outbreaks.

We have a good example of the difficulties of the problem, here in Tientsin. Two editors are daily attacking each other in their respective editorial columns over the proper method of meeting each new crisis or question. One is an American, the brother of Fox of the Washington *Post*, and the other is an Englishman named Woodhead to whom Martin Egan gave me a letter of introduction.

They are 180 degrees apart in their views. Both are here on the ground and both are Anglo-Saxons and better informed than almost any other men in China. The first trouble is, one hates everything British and the other hates everything American. Woodhead talks China but is thinking about Shylock and war debts. Fox reacts in the opposite fashion. The Chinese read and rest assured that the foreign powers will never be able to meet on a common ground.

Speaking of war debts, the feeling of these Britishers here, also the Belgians to a more polite degree, is so bitter that intercourse with them is too difficult to be attempted. The British officers and the few higher bred or born compatriots of theirs out here are sufficiently agreeable, but the common run of business men, who make up the bulk of this rather large foreign community, are so openly rude and offensive, that it pays to avoid them unless one is willing to frankly mix it up with them, which an Army officer on foreign service hardly dares to do. Fortunately, we have such a large Army community and such unusually charming people that we have little or no time for outsiders.

This letter, leaving aside the immediate and personal comment on the way the old China hands were reacting to the war debts controversy, revealed in Marshall a more profound perception than was usual in Westerners of the powerful revolutionary ferment at work in China. Marshall certainly did not understand at that time that the chaos he was witnessing was merely the beginning of a long period of turmoil, which would require not decades but generations to adjust the ancient civilization of China to the impact of Occidental industrialism; but he saw very clearly that the problem was one of human rights and dignity, not alone of imperial privilege and the stability of foreign investments.

If his sympathies appeared to lie with the bedeviled government at Peking which held the capital and claimed legitimate lineage, that was but natural. And in protesting privately to a personal friend the speeches of a former British Prime Minister and a United States Senator whose sympathies were with the Cantonese government, and whose speeches were warnings to the Western powers not to embark on new imperialistic interventions in unhappy China, he did not say that their attitudes lacked reason—indeed, he said precisely the opposite—but reflected the inevitable concern of an American Army officer with the maintenance of civil order. After all, one of the peacetime uses to which the Federal government of the United States puts its Army is to preserve domestic tranquillity. Already, the state of China bore not even a faint resemblance to tranquillity, and it was nothing strange that an Army officer should be disturbed by statements which he felt might feed the flames of civil war. (It was perhaps symptomatic of China's future for many years to come that Chiang Kai-shek, the revolutionary of 1926, would become soon the chief of state, and then the symbol of stability—some would name it reaction—against whom the continuing ferment would be directed.)

The letter, an unusually long one for Marshall, went on to describe his two Mongolian ponies and how long it had taken him to win their confidence, and it told the general that Marshall had accepted a cabled request from General Ely to take detail as an instructor at the War College when he returned from China. Refusal might have been considered offensive—it was, after all, the sixth time since 1919 that the War College had asked for him. Marshall added that his wife "is radiant over the idea of a beautiful house at Washington Barracks."

Although Marshall had thus accepted a new assignment as early as Christmas 1926, his tour in China still had a few months to run. During these last few months, General Connor returned to the United States, to be succeeded by Brigadier General Joseph C. Castner in command of American Forces in China. Castner was an old rough-and-ready, and the diplomatic aspects of his new assignment did not appeal to him in the least. The command of the troops did appeal, however, and he had some very definite ideas about training. One of those ideas was that the regiment was no proper regiment unless it was prepared to make long marches, and demonstrated that capacity occasionally.

It was true that the regiment had done almost no extended marches for some time. There were several reasons, the primary one being that the unsettled conditions in China required the regiment to be at its station in Tientsin. The lack of good water and other problems posed by the question of sanitation in rural China also were to be considered. But Castner insisted on marching, and shortly after his arrival in the spring of 1927 he ordered a four-day hike of sixty miles.

The first day the regiment, officers, and men with Castner and Marshall at the head of the column, marched twenty-two and a half miles. To the general's astonishment, this supposedly flabby outfit lost very few casualties along the route. The next morning, the column formed for the second day. Castner looked them over, and made an announcement.

"Do a good march today," he said, "and we'll call it off at the end of these two days."

Then they started, and at a killing pace. Major Harding was bringing up the rear with a special battalion, including a service company of Filipinos. The smaller Filipinos could not keep up with the longer stride set by the Americans, and Harding's battalion would drop farther and farther behind, until he would order them into the double to catch up. They had been on the road about two hours when Marshall dropped back.

"How's the pace?" he asked.

"We're doing all right," Harding replied, "but it's going to knock these men out."

Marshall trotted back to the head of the column, and fell into step beside the general and the major who was setting the pace. He spoke to the major. "Cut the pace to one hundred and six to the minute." Castner glared his disapproval of this insubordinate interference with his pet project. Marshall ignored the look, and the pace was slowed perceptibly. Castner said nothing—there were times when even generals heeded certain expressions on Lieutenant Colonel Marshall's face.

But if officers and men were aware of the power held in leash by this man, awed and a little puzzled by the reserve that still was not aloofness, the dignity that had nothing of vanity or haughtiness, the same was not true of children. The children of the little Army colony isolated in China adored Marshall, and he returned to them a warm and simple affection. It was a tragedy to the Marshalls that they had no children of their own, but the youngsters in other Army families on any post where the Marshalls were stationed learned quickly, as children do, where trust could be placed and trust would be given. The Colonel could be sharp with misbehavior—when some of the boys at Tientsin ducked their obligations in one community affair, to the disappointment and chagrin of their parents, it was Marshall who dubbed them acidly the "Boy Scuts." But the way into young hearts was easy for Marshall, and how firm a place he had there was disclosed when he left Tientsin. At the railway station there was a group of officers' children, gathered to say good-by—not to the whole detachment of two hundred twenty officers and men that was going home—but to Marshall. Each small girl had to kiss the Colonel good-by, and then he gravely shook hands with each small boy until he came to the last and the smallest, a five-year-old. The youngster shook hands, but that was not enough. He wanted a kiss, too; and he got it.

The last autumn the Marshalls were in China, Marshall, Major Harding, and Captain Frank Hayne decided it might be fun to go down to the summer camp for a hunting trip. There was supposed to be plenty of game on the coast, geese, and ducks particularly. Marshall suggested the trip, and it was agreed that Harding and Hayne would go down as scouts. If they found the game there, Marshall would follow, bringing Mrs. Harding and Mrs. Hayne with him—Mrs. Marshall could not go because her physical condition forbade such exertions as were implicit in a camping trip.

The two scouts got down to Nantassu and surveyed the hunting prospects. The abundance of game, they decided, was a myth—there was nothing to be found. Moreover, it was cold on the coast, and the whole idea began to look less good. They telegraphed their findings to Marshall, and advised him not to come. But the Colonel was not to be deterred. Borrowing an oil stove to keep the two women from suffering from the cold, Marshall escorted Mrs. Harding and Mrs. Hayne to Nantassu. The five of them stayed about a week, and it turned out to be a lot of fun after all. They even managed to find about a half-dozen ducks, and one goose.

Just before their departure from Tientsin, the officers and their wives who were going home in the spring of 1927 were entertained at a party by the regimental commander, Colonel Newell. The evening included a skit about Army transports and the difficulties of customs inspections, for which Marshall himself wrote the words of one song dealing with the passion of Army wives for buying Chinese pottery and porcelain—"Every woman's trunk loaded up with junk," the participants chorused.

There were only five officers in the group that returned to the States that summer of 1927, and Colonel Marshall and Major Harding the only senior officers. Lieutenant J. E. McCammon and his bride were in the party, and Lieutenants E. C. Johnson and J. B. Pierce. The Marshalls were going to Washington, and the Hardings to Fort Benning—they had had a lot of fun together in Tientsin, they assured each other when the U.S.A.T. *Thomas* had delivered them in San Francisco, and they would miss each other now that their paths were diverging; but then the Army had a promising way of bringing old friends together again in new assignments. They were very gay and happy about it; but the Hardings were saying good-by to Mrs. Marshall for the last time.

Not long after they reached Washington, the heart trouble which George and Lily had managed to ignore most of the time for twenty-five years became suddenly and alarmingly worse, and Mrs. Marshall went to Walter Reed Hospital in Washington for treatment. For days on end Marshall endured an agony of fear, and during that agony brought himself finally to face with calmness the fact that his wife probably would not recover. Then, slowly, her condition began to improve, and toward the end of the second week in August she was released from the hospital temporarily, to return in a few weeks for more treatment.

Instead of moving into their quarters at the War College, they borrowed an apartment on Florida Avenue from their old friends, Brigadier General and Mrs. John McAuley Palmer. There they took new hope, and Mrs. Marshall, not yet strong enough to write, dictated a note to General Pershing thanking him for some flowers he had sent her. Marshall, sitting beside her, typed the note as she dictated. In September she returned to the hospital, and her health continued to improve, definitely and unmistakably.

On the morning of September 15, Mrs. Marshall was well enough to be up, and well enough to do a little writing. The doctors had told her, in fact, that she could go home the next day. She began a letter to her mother, who had been in China with her, and now was back in Lexington. A little later, a nurse entered the room and found her lying dead over the unfinished note. The heart which had served and tried her for so long—great belle, lovely bride, stunning woman, devoted wife—had failed at last.

Her death was a shattering blow to Marshall. Except for athletics, he had not developed those many and varied interests outside the home that most men know. To an extraordinary degree, his wife had satisfied every need of his mind and spirit, had absorbed every interest he had outside his profession and shared his burden in that. Now, suddenly and brutally, he was alone and adrift. A few weeks earlier, he had been prepared to face this, had known the imminence of death and disciplined himself to accept it. But as Mrs. Marshall's health improved, the fear departed, and when the blow struck him, his guard had been dropped completely. To Marshall, hurt and bewildered, it seemed that it was his own life and all its meaning that was buried in Arlington a few days and an eternity later.

XII

Debunking the Doctrinaires

IN A thicket above a ravine in a remote section of the reservation at Fort Benning, Georgia, First Lieutenant Charles T. Lanham was furiously at work. "Furiously" is used advisedly—the volatile young man was seething with rage.

Sensitive poet, exuberant playboy, intense and mercurial, he was a student in the Company Officers Course at the Infantry School, and at this particular moment in 1931 was inwardly cursing the Fates and anything else that came to mind because the Command Post Exercise on which he was engaged had become a foul trap, keeping him from his pleasures.

There are times when certain activities, for no discernible reason, seize upon the minds and hearts of a group or a community and become an obsession. At Fort Benning, in 1931, among the junior officers, the obsession was blackjack. Not just any form of gambling would do—it had to be blackjack. Furthermore, for the duration of the spell, blackjack acquired such proportions as to become one of the few really important things in life.

So, when the CPX—Command Post Exercise—was set up, the gang of whom Lanham was an impetuously enthusiastic member decided they would brush the work off in a hurry, and gather in the woods for a game. Now a CPX was one of those devices the Army figured out for training its officers during the lean years when it had officers, but neither men nor money for maneuvers. The command posts were set up along a theoretical line of battle, and staffed with the proper number of officers. They were given certain tactical problems, a complete communications system, and theoretical troops to carry out their plans and orders. The troops, however, remained strictly theoretical.

Lanham, designated S-1, or adjutant, at one of the command posts, agreed with his eager colleagues that "nobody looks at these papers anyhow," and promised to join the game. It would be simple. But then the S-2, or intelligence officer, became ill and could not participate in the exercise, so his job was given to Lanham as additional duty. At the command post after the exercise had begun, the S-3 (operations officer), scrambling down the bank of a near-by ravine, fell and sprained his ankle. So Lanham found himself S-1, S2, *and* S-3.

It takes a certain amount of time even to brush off all three of those jobs, and Lanham was in an explosive temper. He was scribbling furiously away, trying to get the minimum essential work completed and dash for the blackjack game which he knew had started already without him, when a quiet voice spoke out of the air from behind his left shoulder.

"Lanham," said the voice, "I'm very happy to see you working with your customary enthusiasm. I've been very disappointed at what I've seen around these other posts, with the officers gambling instead of pursuing their military duties. I shall not forget what I have seen."

Lieutenant Lanham, frozen rigid by the first words, had managed to get to his feet and face the visitor by the time the latter stopped speaking. He had been right when he thought he recognized that voice. The speaker was Lieutenant Colonel Marshall, Assistant Commandant of the Infantry School, who—as usual—was not waiting for student papers and official reports to tell him what went on, but was finding out for himself.

Marshall turned and walked away. Lanham's tongue was stuck firmly to the top of his mouth, and he could not have spoken a word had he tried. But he broke into a cold sweat as he watched the receding figure disappear among the trees, and he did not play blackjack that afternoon.

Marshall had been assigned to the Infantry School in 1927, after his wife's death. His friends, distressed by Marshall's grief, knew that he would like a change of assignment to take him away from Washington, away from the quarters he and his wife had shared at the War College. General Summerall was Chief of Staff now, and discovered that Brigadier General Edgar T. Collins, in command at Fort Benning, would be delighted to get Marshall there. So the transfer was ordered.

Marshall went to Benning as assistant commandant of the Infantry School. That meant, in effect, that he was actually in charge of the school, since the title of commandant belonged to the commanding general at the post, and he left the school to his assistant.

The Infantry School was one of that elaborate system of schools which had grown up in the Army under the impetus given to higher training by the Staff College at Leavenworth and its teachers and graduates. It gave junior officers intensive instruction, particularly in minor tactics and the leadership of small units, the most difficult of all military problems.

Marshall found several old friends already at Benning, and the first to hear of his assignment probably was Buster Peyton, who was chief of the Tactical Section. Collins saw Peyton one day soon after Marshall's transfer was ordered in the fall of 1927, and called to him.

"Who do you suppose I'm going to get to run this school for me? George Marshall!" The general had a note of triumph in his voice. "He has the soundest sense, the finest military background, and that rare thing, imagination—above any man I know. I'm going to get him to come down here and take that academic training out of a rut."

Apparently, the irascible "Windy" Collins did not have Marshall in mind the day he pounded his desk and roared at a group of officers in his office, "By God! We used to have characters in the Army, but we don't have them now!"

Peyton was not the only old friend that Marshall found at Benning. The Hardings were there, with Major Harding chief of one of the sections at the Infantry School, and Major Stilwell, another colleague from the China tour, was in the Tactical Section under Peyton. During Marshall's tour at Benning, a certain Major Omar N. Bradley would arrive for duty in the Tactical Section, and demonstrate such capacity that Marshall would assign him to head the Weapons Section.

Marshall found that General Collins was right—the Infantry School had got into an academic rut. Most of its instructors were quite conservative, and inclined to base their teachings on their own limited experiences in the World War—the very thing that Marshall had warned against in his article for the *Infantry Journal* in 1921. The tactical doctrine had developed a new orthodoxy, quite formalized, based to a large extent on the positional warfare which had characterized the conflict in France, and with firmly established precepts for problems of attack and supply. Instruction was by the regulations and the rule book, and the student who attempted innovation was likely to find that his grades suffered.

In part, this was the result of the inevitable tendency of all men to cling to the forms and the methods they know and have used. In greater part, it was due to the fact that the Army, suffering from the usual postwar reaction against military establishments, had sunk to its lowest state in years, and only exceptional men can escape the general and self-pitying apathy of a neglected group, remain devoted, alert, and vigorous in a restricted and frustrated organization.

The National Defense Act of 1920 had re-established the basis of the citizen army, and authorized a professional core of 280,000 men, enough to give the idea reality and efficiency. It had regularized the administrative and command machinery, establishing the combat arms—Infantry, Cavalry, Field Artillery, Coast Artillery, Air Service, Engineers, Signal Corps—as bureaus headed by general officers, in the same fashion as the old staff bureaus. True, it had abolished the system of detailing officers from the line to the administrative staff bureaus, but more than enough compensation was provided in the single promotion list for the entire Army.

The act had authorized the organization of brigades, divisions, and corps, so that for the first time the Army had peacetime authority to create the essential battle headquarters for its field forces. Corps

Areas were established on a geographical basis to simplify and decentralize the co-ordination of training and administration. R.O.T.C. units were authorized in unlimited numbers, provided a Regular Army officer was detailed to each as instructor, and there was no limit, either, on the authorized number of Citizens' Military Training Camps. The National Guard was a Federal force, an integral part of the defense establishment, although its units remained available to the governors for state militia needs; but its instruction was to be more closely supervised by the Regular Army, and its officers were required to meet certain minimum standards before they could be commissioned in the Army of the United States.

The framework was there, and the opportunity; but the appropriations were not forthcoming. As early as 1922, the simple process of cutting appropriations had reduced the Regular Army strength from the authorized two hundred eighty thousand to an actual strength of one hundred seventy-five thousand—more than six hundred regular officers had to be discharged summarily. The next year, legislation limited the total of regular officers to twelve thousand. There was no money for maneuvers, no money for airplanes, none for experiments with tanks, or development of new artillery. In 1926, Congress relented to the extent of authorizing the Air Corps to expand over a five-year period to a total strength of one thousand eight hundred planes, one thousand six hundred fifty officers, and fifteen thousand enlisted men; but this expansion was to be at the expense of the rest of the Army, and the next year the appropriations had the effect of allowing slightly more than ten hours a year flying time for Air Corps officers.

It was the era of the Kellogg-Briand Pact to outlaw war, of an all but universal belief in America that this nation's involvement in the World War had been the joint product of the trickery of diplomats and the greed of munitions manufacturers. Anything that smacked of military matters was obviously militaristic, and the Army was not exactly held in high esteem. In the circumstances, it was not surprising that a lethargy descended on the military mind, and that the prevailing mood was one of frustration and resentment. For the

Army, organization, training, weapons became once more, and of necessity, idea rather than fact, plan instead of experiment, command post exercises rather than maneuvers—a thing of papers, maps, sand tables, and short practice marches.

Soon after his arrival at Benning, Marshall went into a huddle with Peyton, chief of his Tactical Section. They discussed the problem at some length, and as they talked it became evident to Marshall that his task was to destroy the prevailing idea in the school that battle is a conventional thing, to make the instructors and the students understand that imagination and ingenuity play a very great part in combat.

"The whole faculty is indoctrinated with formalized defense," Peyton remarked as the session ended.

"Then," said Marshall dryly, "we'll just *un*-doctrinate them."

It was not Marshall's way to throw the school into an uproar. He took a few days to examine this new assignment thoroughly, talking with instructors, visiting the classrooms, watching the procedures and methods with a shrewdly appraising eye and mind, discussing the problems with the chiefs of sections. Then the attitudes of the new assistant commandant began to be felt at Benning.

To get at the heart of things, to understand the realities of battle—that was the aim. "Americans," Marshall remarked to some of his staff, "are the greatest elaborators in the world." He wanted instructions and reports reduced to their essentials. The men at Benning soon learned that Marshall was looking for results, not literary quality, in their orders, studies, and monographs. Instructors who had been in the habit of using the full fifty-five minutes of every class period, even when they had to indulge in stalling tactics to consume the time, were told to tell the students what they had to tell them, and then dismiss the class, even if it had required only thirty minutes.

He abolished the "set piece" demonstration maneuver by the 29th Infantry which had become an established part of the course. It was performed on carefully chosen terrain, and showed the students the perfect solution of a carefully thought-out problem. Marshall said students learned more from making mistakes than from watching a perfect demonstration, and put the 29th to "demonstrations" on unexpected problems over terrain selected at random. Before the end of his tour at Benning, the students were in command of these tactical exercises, instead of participating only as spectators.

This same obsession with reality, this concern with practice and test rather than learning by rote, was applied to the preparation of orders and training manuals. A few days after his arrival, he asked Peyton to prepare a plan for a tactical exercise. Peyton worked out a scheme of the type familiar to the staff at Benning, but he was sure that Marshall would not like it, and suggested when he gave it to him that it probably was not the kind of thing Marshall had in mind.

Marshall read it over. "No," he said, "this is not what I want. Here——" He took a map of Fort Benning, and with a pencil drew a line at random across a portion of the reservation. "That's the line. Plan it there." The carefully selected area, where ideal attack and ideal defense could be plotted, where roads were good and communications easy—that was not the way to teach lieutenants and captains how to be smart on the battlefield, how to lead men to victory through unexpected situations.

The young officers who came to Benning as students in those years were, as is normal for young men, skeptical of the mighty reputation the school and its assistant commandant were acquiring throughout the Army. The institution was referred to flippantly as Marshall's Military Academy on the Upatoie (the Upatoie was a creek which traversed the Fort Benning lands and flowed into the Chattahoochee on the military reservation, about eight miles from Columbus), and the tales they had heard of Marshall gave many of them, before they ever saw the man, the impression of a stuffed shirt.

The first glimpse most of them had of the Assistant Commandant was when the class of students gathered for opening exercises, and Marshall addressed them. They saw a tall, rangy man of plain features, whose nervous intensity was disclosed only by a distracting facial spasm as he began to talk. The grimace disappeared as he proceeded, and they became aware of the earnestness, the intense drive and assurance, and above all the simplicity of this man who was talking to them.

A vast gulf of rank separated a lieutenant from a lieutenant colonel in those days, and most of the students saw comparatively little of Marshall. Gradually, however, they came to know that he was keeping a close personal watch on everything that occurred at the school, that he was likely to show up at any class, at any time. One group in the fall of 1930 was attending a lecture on the psychology of leadership, and growing more and more bewildered as the instructor lost command of his subject, floundered in embarrassment as he sought to pull his lecture together again, and finally came to a stammering halt. When that occurred, Marshall was sitting in the back of the room. He walked forward, and said apologetically to the instructor that he would like to say a few words. He began talking, slowly, avoiding with great care anything that might add to the instructor's embarrassment, but gradually giving the young men before him such an inspiring discourse on the subject of leadership that everything they heard in the months that followed would seem flavorless beside it. The group had been given an insight into a breadth of vision and understanding which staggered them, and had observed a demonstration of tact and courtesy toward the embarrassed instructor that none of them would forget.

In the field exercises, as in the classroom, Marshall was apt to slip unheralded into a group of students to observe the work. Lanham was involved in one of these, an earlier episode than that in which he was lucky enough to be balked in his desire to play blackjack instead of working. The students had been at work on a platoon problem, the instructor had outlined the approved solution, and they had reached the comment stage. Lanham took issue with the announced solution, on the grounds that it was psychologically unsound—that troops would not, in fact, behave as the solution assumed they would. An argument developed, and Lanham stated his points in rather heated terms. The instructor brushed them aside airily, with no little condescension. And then the unexpected voice came from the edge of the group—"I would like to comment on Lieutenant Lanham's ideas, because I agree with them." It was Marshall, and he took over the discussion. Lanham, who had not even suspected that the Assistant Commandant knew his name, was understandably elated.

"That's the kind of thing," said Lanham later, "to crank up devotion in a first lieutenant."

It was also, of course, an excellent way to impress upon a group of young officers in dramatic fashion the belief of a veteran and superbly able officer that the rule book is a guide, not a solution containing all the answers; that past experience will not be repeated, and is useful to the student only if he subjects it to critical examination and intensive thought.

The most striking single product of the new emphasis on the realities of battle and the value of imaginative thought which Marshall injected into the training at Fort Benning was a book, called *Infantry in Battle*, written at the Infantry School under his administration. It was a textbook on the tactics of small units, and it was perhaps the most important single military textbook prepared in the United States up to the time of its publication in 1934. It was translated promptly into German, and used by the German Army—the first American military treatise adopted by the *Wehrmacht*. It had, moreover, a profound influence on the approach to training in all arms of the United States Army.

"The art of war has no traffic with rules, for the infinitely varied circumstances and conditions of combat never produce exactly the same situation twice." That was the opening sentence of this book, and it stated the theme which ran through all its twenty-seven chapters, dealing with such matters as scheme of maneuver and main effort, terrain, mobility, surprise, orders, control of units in combat, command, and communications, the infantry-artillery team, the advance to the attack, battle reconnaissance, counterorders, night attacks. The scheme of the book was simple: each chapter began with a general discussion of the problem; then came a series of actual examples from the records of the various armies—enemy as well as Allied—of the World War, each example followed by a critical discussion of its success or failure and the reasons therefor; and the chapter ended with a statement of conclusions—an assessment of the general principles to be deduced from these specific illustrations.

Marshall, of course, did not write the book. The War Department had asked him to prepare it, and he delegated the job to the Fourth Section at the Infantry School, headed by Major Harding. This was the military history and publications section, and it was Harding who planned the book and supervised its preparation. Much of the research was done by Captain John A. Andrews and Captain Robert H. Chance, and Major Richard G. Tindall wrote the original drafts of most of the chapters. Captain Russel B. Reynolds also participated in the book's preparation.

Then Lieutenant Lanham was ordered to the Fourth Section as an instructor. He had previously been ordered to the Tank School as a student, a detail he did not particularly want, but thought advisable for the sake of his future career, and was reluctant to accept the assignment to the Fourth Section staff. But Marshall wanted *Infantry in Battle* completed, and wanted Lanham to do it. He sent for the lieutenant.

"I would like you to stay here and do this book," Marshall told Lanham. "If you have no objection to having your orders changed, I promise you that I will see that you get, not only to the Tank School, but also to the Advanced Course."

Lanham accepted the assignment, and he was to have no cause to regret it. Several years later, when Marshall was Chief of Staff, he would learn how long Marshall's memory was, and how thoughtful the chief could be of the ambitions and desires of other officers. In 1940, a recent graduate of the Command and General Staff School at Fort Leavenworth, Lanham was on duty with the 8th Infantry at Fort Screven when he was asked to accept a detail to the General Staff in Washington. He declined, because of his desire to remain with troops, but for two months was uncertain what had become of the recommendation. Then Marshall came to Fort Screven for an inspection, and while he was there told Lanham he had killed the proposed staff assignment for the younger officer each of the three times it came to his desk for approval.

"I stopped it because of my own experience," the Chief of Staff explained to the grateful Lanham. "I had had two details involving writing, and I was due for a third. I did everything I could to stop it, and finally avoided it."

When Lanham reported in the Fourth Section at Benning and took over the completion of *Infantry in Battle,* the chapters had been outlined, the material assembled, and a first draft written by Tindall. However, much of the analysis remained to be done, many of the maps had to be redrawn, and some of the research checked, particularly the translations from the French sources used in the volume. Finally, the rewriting of Tindall's draft was begun and completed, and in 1934 the volume appeared. Marshall by that time had left Benning, but he wrote an introduction to the book which was a summation of his approach to training and the art of war.

Marshall wrote:

This book treats of the tactics of small units as illustrated by examples drawn from the World War. It checks the ideas acquired from peacetime instruction against the experience of battle.

There is much evidence to show that officers who have received the best peacetime training available find themselves surprised and confused by the difference between conditions as pictured in map problems and those they encounter in campaign. This is largely because our peacetime training in tactics tends to become increasingly theoretical. In our schools we generally assume that organizations are well-trained and at full strength, that subordinates are competent, that supply arrangements function, that communications work, that orders are carried out. In war many or all of these conditions may be absent. The veteran knows that this is normal and his mental processes are not paralyzed by it. He knows that he must carry on in spite of seemingly insurmountable difficulties and regardless of the fact that the tools with which he has to work may be imperfect and worn. Moreover, he knows how to go about it. This volume is designed to give the peace-trained officer something of the viewpoint of the veteran.

By the use of historical examples, the reader is acquainted with the realities of war and the extremely difficult and highly disconcerting conditions under which tactical problems must be solved in the face of an enemy. . . .

This work does not purport to be a complete treatise on minor tactics of infantry. The aim of its authors has been to develop fully and emphasize a few important lessons which can be substantiated by concrete cases rather than to produce just another book of abstract theory.

For all its importance, and for all that it was an official project in its inception, planning, and preparation, *Infantry in Battle* did not appear as an official publication. Probably because there were no official funds to pay for the printing, it was published as a commercial venture by the Infantry Journal Press. The peacetime munificence of the American public and Congress toward their military establishment is further indicated by the fact that during this period between the wars, there were not even any funds to publish a new edition of the official Infantry Drill Manual for something like nine years. The only edition in print was a commercial one published by the Military Service Publishing Company, and many officers and units had the manual for essential and required training use only because they spent their personal or unit funds to buy it.

With a program of such importance to engage his mind, the edge of his grief was dulled somewhat, but Marshall still was lonely. In January 1928, feeling the desperate need of an older friend to help him through the winter, he wrote inviting Pershing to come down to Benning for a visit, promising him he would find a good climate, horses, and fine riding trails, and agreeable people.

Pershing was unable to accept the invitation—he was getting ready for another trip to Europe. During the spring, Marshall himself considered Europe for his summer holiday, but later abandoned the idea. Instead, he decided to visit his mother in Pittsburgh, and then rest and loaf in Virginia, possibly going to New England in August. The end of August found him writing from Upperville, Virginia, that he had been resting the entire summer, with never a thought of work, and was ready and eager to return to the job at Benning.

Marshall's mother died on October 25, 1928, and his sister came down from Greensburg, Pennsylvania, to spend the winter with him. It was a godsend to Marshall to have someone so close and dear to him presiding over his household for nearly ten months, and Marie enjoyed the life on an Army post tremendously. During the spring, he declined the request of Secretary Davis that he accept appointment as Chief of the Philippine Constabulary—Mr. Stimson, then Governor General of the Islands, suggested Marshall to Davis—and he also declined the proffered post of Superintendent of the Virginia Military Institute. He did, however, go up to Lexington in June 1929 to make the commencement address at the V.M.I. His old friend Pershing approved his refusal of both jobs.

"Your future interest lies in your continued splendid service with the Army," the general wrote. "I hope things may come out for you much better in the near future than you now hope."

That summer of 1929 Marshall spent in Wyoming, riding a large part of every day, and regaining some of the weight that the recent troubled years had taken from him. He also read the manuscript of Brigadier General John McAuley Palmer's newest book, an important work on the historical continuity of the citizen army in the United States, and wrote enthusiastically of it to Palmer when he returned to Benning after his holiday. He had tested one chapter, he told Palmer, by reading it aloud to Mary Roberts Rinehart, who had the cottage next his, and she had been as enthusiastic as Marshall. The work was published in 1930, but never achieved popularity. To the general public indifference to military questions was added the sales resistance contributed by an unfortunately forbidding title—*Washington, Lincoln, Wilson: Three War Statesmen.*

Meanwhile, a new hope of personal happiness had been awakened in Marshall that winter when he met Mrs. Katherine Tupper Brown at a dinner party in Columbus. She was the widow of Clifton S. Brown, a Baltimore lawyer who had been killed in his office by a client in 1928. A handsome and gracious woman, she was a graduate of Hollins College, and once had been a Shakespearean actress, trouping with Sir Frank Benson.

These two mature and intelligent people liked each other at first meeting, and their mutual interest and sympathy grew into a deep affection. Marshall spent a part of his summer leave at Mrs. Brown's cottage on Fire Island, New York, and later in the summer wrote to Pershing to tell the general that he and Mrs. Brown planned to be married in the autumn. Pershing was his former aide's best man when they were married on October 16, 1930, in the chapel of Emmanuel Episcopal Church in Baltimore.

The Marshalls returned immediately to Fort Benning, and the night of their arrival the commandant honored the bride by presenting the military society of the post to her at an elaborate open-air reception and dance at his quarters. Anticipating the reception, Marshall had given his wife a thorough briefing on military affairs and Benning gossip so that she might appear well informed on local matters. Standing beside her at the reception, Marshall used a prompting system he had employed as aide to Pershing, muttering a pre-arranged cue word as each guest approached and the name was called out by the commandant. The system permitted Mrs. Marshall to greet each of them with some personal remark—thanks for a gift, mention of some long-ago association with the Colonel, reference to an honor or a promotion received recently. But there were more than a thousand guests, and the strain began to tell on the guest of honor. Finally, the approach of a late arrival provided the Marshalls with what was to become one of their favorite family jokes. As a woman recently and proudly the mother of triplets stepped up to shake hands with Mrs. Marshall, the Colonel murmured, "Triplets!" The bride, with her most gracious smile, held out her hand and said, "Thank you so much for your lovely triplets!"

The bride's arrival at Benning was marked also by another of Major Harding's verses. Addressed to Mrs. Marshall, it gave her a rough idea of the range of activities she would have to adopt if she were to share all her husband's interests, leaving entirely aside his professional career:

> If you rise with the dawn for a cross-country ride;
> If you stay up past midnight and dance;
> If you swim, and play golf, and shoot quail on the wing,
> And read through a book at a glance;
> If you're keen about horseshows, like amateur plays,
> And understand polo and art;
> If you sparkle at dinners (which I'm sure that you do)
> Then I know you're the Queen of his Heart.*

Mrs. Marshall did, in fact, share most of the indicated interests; and she settled quickly and graciously into the life of the post. For his part, Marshall accustomed himself with obvious relish and pleasure to the presence of a family; for with his bride came her three children, a daughter, Molly, and two sons, Allen and Clifton. By Christmas, Marshall was writing happily to Pershing that he had taken the younger of the two boys on an eighteen-mile wildcat hunt at 5:30 o'clock in the morning.

Marshall's close friendship with Pershing added little chores to his already full and busy life. Pershing was still, and would remain for several years to come, the dominant figure in the Army, and his favor was eagerly courted by those who sought preferment. Some of these who were also friends of Marshall made the approach to Pershing through the younger officer. On at least one occasion Marshall forwarded the request of a senior officer for Pershing's support in his desire to become Chief of Staff, although he would have only a year to serve in the office before he reached the statutory retirement age of sixty-four. Pershing replied unfavorably, because he thought the one-year term would establish a bad precedent.

But Pershing himself wanted some help and advice. For several years he had been devoting considerable time to the preparation of memoirs of the World War. Marshall, just before his marriage, had read a preliminary draft and suggested that it lacked color, to which Pershing retorted that it was possible for such works to contain too much color. In November the completed manuscript was sent to

---

* Quoted by permission of General E. F. Harding.

Marshall for reading and criticism, but the criticism was resented by Pershing, who informed Marshall his comments were not constructive. Marshall explained that he thought Pershing had shown great restraint during and after the war, and that his stature had grown accordingly. He repeated his belief that the lack of restraint in the general's manuscript, particularly in his criticism of the Allied commands and of the War Department, was ill-advised and added that he had been both frank and honest, which he thought was the best service he could offer his former chief. Later he went to Washington, and spent three days going over the manuscript with Pershing, but if the general was swayed at all by Marshall's arguments, the two-volume work which appeared the following March was itself evidence Pershing had failed to conform sufficiently to excellent advice.

In Tientsin, Marshall had devised a complicated, compact, and beautiful close-order parade maneuver for ceremonial occasions. This concern with ceremonial as a stimulant to pride of arm and service showed at Benning also, and Marshall planned a pageant which reflected all the many and interesting activities of this large post. Performed in a natural amphitheater on the reservation, the pageant became the showpiece for distinguished visitors. It was the climax of a reception for General Briant Wells, who once had commanded at Benning and retained a particular affection for the post, when he came visiting during Marshall's tour there. On this occasion, Marshall asked Major Harding to write a story about the pageant for the weekly post paper, chiefly to give the general a tangible memento of the visit.

Early in 1931, the long-standing policy of the Army, confirmed by the National Defense Act of 1920, that every officer must serve at least two years of every six with troops instead of on a detached service or staff detail, sent the generals of the Infantry scurrying for some means of keeping Marshall at the school. In the end a point was stretched, and he was assigned to duty with the 24th Infantry at Fort Benning, in addition to his other duties, to provide a technical compliance with regulations and keep him in charge of the Infantry School.

The next year, however, Marshall's preference for command assignments was satisfied, and he left Fort Benning for Fort Screven, near Savannah, Georgia, to take command of a detachment of the 8th Infantry there. He was already at Screven when a letter arrived from Major General Stephen O. Fuqua, Chief of Infantry.

Fuqua told him that for four and a half years he had held one of the most important posts in the Infantry—Assistant Commandant of the Infantry School. During that tour, Fuqua continued, Marshall had exhibited the highest qualities of loyalty, devotion to duty, judgment, and leadership; and these qualities, combined with his natural abilities as executive and instructor, and his fine professional attainments, had gone far to place the Infantry School on the high level it occupied in the Army's educational system. Brigadier General Campbell King, another World War associate who by that time had succeeded General Collins in command at Benning, added his praise of Marshall as one of the most highly gifted officers in the service, and "very exceptionally qualified for the grade of general officer."

Such praise was nothing new to Marshall, although of course each added compliment was a pleasant thing to receive; but what made Marshall happy in June of 1932 was the long delayed fulfillment of a cherished desire. For the first time since Captain Eames arrived at Mangarin and took command of the company there thirty years before, Marshall had command of a post and its troops. This was all he had ever really wanted in the Army, and at last it had been given to him.

XIII

Star on His Shoulder

On a Saturday morning in the late spring of 1932, Master Sergeant J. R. Dick walked toward headquarters at Fort Screven in a most apprehensive and unhappy frame of mind. He had been summoned by the new commanding officer, Lieutenant Colonel Marshall.

Marshall had arrived two days earlier, preceded by the inevitable flood of rumors which circulate on an Army post when a new C.O. is scheduled to put in his appearance. In this case, the rumors had dealt largely—more and more largely—with what an extremely tough guy this Marshall was.

Dick, approaching the presence with growing trepidation, was casting his mind back frantically over his eleven years in the Army, trying to remember all the things he should not have done of which he was guilty, all the things he should have done which he had neglected to do. Concealing his nervousness behind that utter lack of expression that only Army sergeants can achieve, he entered the Colonel's office and stood at attention before the desk.

"Good morning, Sergeant." The Colonel's voice was pleasant, but crisp. "I understand you're in charge of the post baseball team. Why haven't we been winning ball games?"

Sergeant Dick's vast relief was almost audible.

"Sir, I can't get the men out for practice," he explained. "I'm just a master sergeant, and they don't pay too much attention to me. It would be different if there were an officer in charge."

Did the sergeant have a suggestion about which officer? He did—Lieutenant Childs.

"And why do you suggest Lieutenant Childs?'

"Sir, he has just reported here for duty from the University of Georgia. He coached the ball team at Georgia."

"That will be done right away. Present my compliments to Mr. Childs, and ask him to report to me, Sergeant."

The lieutenant took over the Fort Screven ball team, and the team began to win games. More importantly, the regimental sergeant major had discovered that the "tough" Colonel Marshall had a sincere interest in the morale of the enlisted men of his command. It was an interest that would find expression in more important and tangible matters than the progress of unofficial athletics. The enlisted men, particularly the old Regular Army noncommissioned officers, learned that the new C.O. was of a different stripe from most of the commanding officers they had known, and the respect they accorded any commander gradually lost the tinge of cautious apprehension which marked their expectation of his coming and acquired an overlay of deep gratitude and affection.

After breakfast in his large and pleasant quarters with the capacious verandas which faced the ocean from the center of officers' row, Marshall began his day at Screven by combining his favorite recreation, riding, with a personal inspection of the entire post. By 9:00 o'clock he was in his office, and "officers' call" began—the daily conference with the officers of his command. The first things disposed of were the shortcomings Marshall might have discovered on his morning ride—and woe betide the individual responsible if the next morning's inspection disclosed the fault still uncorrected! Next came any orders or inquiries which might have been received from Corps Area headquarters in Atlanta, perhaps occasionally problems connected with the approaching visit of an inspector of one variety or another, the discussion of the troop training program with the officers, and the Colonel's request for suggestions from the officers on all phases of post activity. Marshall organized his time expertly, and by the time he returned to his quarters for lunch, most of the essential business of his headquarters had been disposed of. How he spent his afternoons depended to some extent on the season. Ordinarily, there was little training activity in the afternoons, but if any schools were in session on the post, Marshall visited them. If athletic teams, the baseball team particularly, were practicing or had a game scheduled, Marshall was certain to be there.

Under Marshall's aegis, a closer relationship was developed between the post and its civilian neighbors. Official and civic groups in Savannah, and even officials of the state government, found themselves invited by the commanding officer at Fort Screven to be the Army's guests on special occasions, and watch the parades and reviews. Governor Talmadge visited the post and Marshall ordered a review for him. Afterward, the Colonel had a reception at his quarters, and the noncommissioned officers as well as the commissioned officers were invited to meet the governor.

If the troops found a new excuse for the inevitable soldier grumbling in the fact that the new commandant worked them harder because he insisted on having a spotless post, they found more than ample compensation in the improvements made in their quarters, the renovation of the post gymnasium, the sprucing-up of the service club, the completion of the golf course, the construction of a recreational area. This last was complete with a swimming hole, achieved by damming a creek near the post; with barbecue pits, boats, small pavilions for shelters, and playground equipment for the children. Lifeguards were stationed around the pond, and more than one toddling small child of an enlisted man's family learned to swim at Screven. When one of the companies had a barbecue or an oyster roast at the recreational area, the Marshalls never failed to attend it; just as they never failed to attend the enlisted men's monthly dance at the service club. A captured rumrunner was obtained from the Coast Guard, and used for boating parties on the river, or to take groups over to Dufuskie Island for fishing and hunting trips.

The year 1933 brought a fifteen-percent pay cut in the Army, and as a further sacrifice to the need for economy, officers were forced to take extended leave without pay. It was characteristic of Marshall that the overload of work which fell to him as a result—for weeks at a time he was not only commanding officer, but post adjutant, recruiting officer, and assorted other details—bothered him very little, but the plight of the enlisted men, particularly those with families, distressed him.

Marshall ordered the company mess halls opened to the enlisted men's families for the noon meal. Because he knew the families would prefer to eat their meals in their own quarters, a bucket container was devised to hold a complete lunch. One serving of each item on the menu went into that container for each member of the family, and it made no difference how many members there were—the cost was fifteen cents, whether two or six were fed. He became more solicitous than ever in his inquiries about the men's families, and they were not routine inquiries. The Colonel knew the names, and asked specifically about them. And it had long since become known on the post that if anyone were ill in the quarters occupied by the enlisted men, the Colonel's wife would be there, to be certain that they lacked nothing they needed.

If most of Marshall's solicitous attention was for the enlisted men of his command during this trying period, he did not relax his supervision of other matters. One incident is remembered particularly by those who served with him at Screven. Among the junior officers at the post was one who was independently wealthy, and he and his wife gave a cocktail party in 1933 at which they served champagne cocktails. Marshall sought out the officer and remonstrated with him. Because of the economy program, the Colonel pointed out, the captain's fellow officers were on reduced pay, and could not afford to emulate his example or to return his hospitality in equally lavish fashion. There were no more champagne cocktail parties at Screven while Marshall remained there.

That same year, 1933, saw the creation of the Civilian Conservation Corps. Marshall was on his way with the regiment to Fort Benning for training exercises, and had reached Macon, Georgia, when he received orders to return to Fort Screven with his troops in order to be there when the first CCC company arrived. The march was reversed, and the regiment made the one-hundred-mile return trip by truck in one day. (One hundred miles is no problem for a single family in an automobile, but poses some obstacles for an entire regiment of infantry.) When the World War veterans who composed this first contingent of the CCC in that district reached Fort Screven, they found the Colonel commanding waiting to welcome them—not formally at his headquarters, but informally and personally at their barracks. It fell to Marshall to supervise the organization of the seventeen CCC camps in a district comprising Florida, a large part of Georgia, and a segment of South Carolina. If he shared the widespread Army resentment that it was the Army, whose privates were drawing $17.50 a month, which had to be housekeepers and administrators for the CCC, whose men drew $30 monthly, he never gave the slightest sign of it.

It is likely that Marshall never thought of the matter in such terms. He saw in these men the bewildered victims of a depression which had broken them financially and shaken their spirits, and they received from him the same sympathetic interest and close attention that he gave to troops. One of them told Colonel Peyton later that Marshall had done more, by his frequent visits and real interest, to improve the morale of the CCC men than anyone who had worked with them.

Bootlegging was the worst problem that confronted Marshall in connection with these camps. The dangerous and demoralizing flow of raw, cheap, corn whisky would find a channel into a new camp as soon as it opened. When the police and sheriff's office were unable to cope with the problem, Marshall went to the bankers and merchants and gave them two weeks to end the liquor traffic at the camp, or the camp would be moved. The monthly pay roll was an important commercial asset in the community, and the maneuver usually was successful.

Early in 1933 Marshall, who had gone to Screven to command a detachment of the 8th Infantry, was given command of the entire regiment, and began dividing his time between Screven and Fort Moultrie, South Carolina, which was the regimental headquarters. Soon he and Mrs. Marshall moved to Moultrie, and Mrs. Marshall has told how the colonel, about this time, made a diplomatic agency of the CCC. A French cruiser on a good-will tour had put in to Charleston, and the Marshalls came to the rescue of Mayor—later

Governor and Senator—Maybank, whose city treasury shared the depressed state of the nation in 1933, by entertaining at a dinner, reception, and dance at Fort Moultrie. The skipper of the cruiser then invited the garrison and many Charlestonians to a reception and dance on the ship.

"During the evening," Mrs. Marshall related, "George told the Captain that a CCC camp near Georgetown, South Carolina, was soon to be opened, across a narrow strip of water from the spot where Lafayette had made his first landing in America. He said he would like to name it Camp Lafayette and invited the Captain to raise the flag in the presence of his officers and crew. I looked a little astounded. The contrast between the reception on this brilliantly lit ship, decorated from stem to stern with flags, and a CCC camp seemed almost absurd. George, however, continued quietly to explain the CCC project, how the President had conceived it to meet a tragic financial condition in this country and what it was doing to alleviate the depression and put the poverty-stricken young men on their feet. The Captain was so interested that he talked late into the night. Long after his other guests had gone he was still asking questions and George was still explaining with astonishing enthusiasm."*

The captain not only accepted the invitation, but telegraphed the French Consul in Philadelphia to come down for the occasion. The captain and his party were received by the mayor of Georgetown, whose home was the house in which Lafayette had spent his first night in America, and escorted to the CCC camp. Mayor Maybank came over from Charleston, and the post band from Fort Moultrie. As the official party—including the entire crew of the cruiser—entered the camp, the band struck up "La Marseillaise." There was a standard CCC camp dinner under the live oaks. There were speeches, the raising of the French flag by the Consul and the American flag by the skipper, and the band played the "Star Spangled Banner." Then the CCC boys became guides for the visitors, showing them all over the camp.

"The dedication had been solemn, impressive," the Colonel's wife

---

* From *Together: Annals of an Army Wife*, copyright, 1946, by Katherine Tupper Marshall. Quoted by Mrs. Marshall's permission.

CASABLANCA CONFERENCE

Marshall stands directly behind the President in this official group portrait which includes Harry Hopkins (extreme left), General Arnold and Admiral King (at Marshall's right), Sir Alan Brooke, Chief of the Imperial General Staff (behind Churchill), and (to Brooke's left) Sir John Dill, Admiral Mountbatten, and General Somervell.

Signal Corps Photo

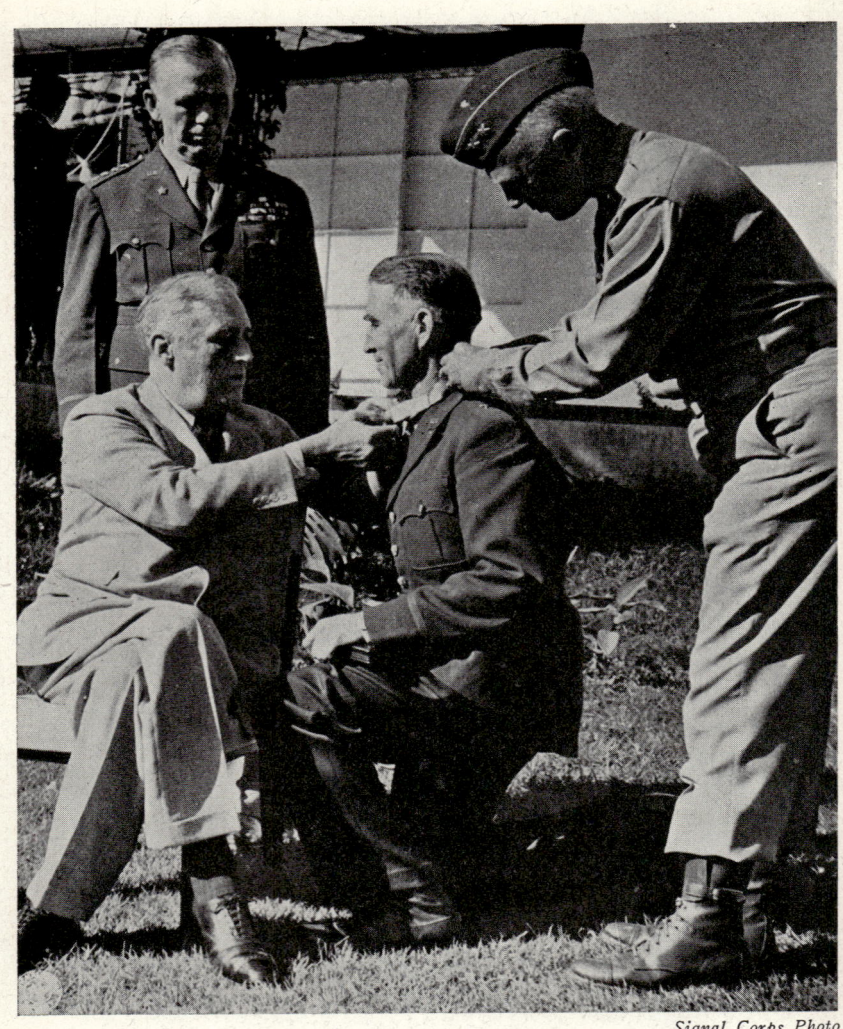

Signal Corps Photo

AT CASABLANCA

Marshall watches as General Patton helps President Roosevelt place the ribbon of the Medal of Honor around the neck of Brigadier General William H. Wilbur for extraordinary heroism in the North African invasion.

remembered, "but when the formalities were over everyone, young and old, entered into the spirit of the occasion. There was no depression at Camp Lafayette that day; for one afternoon at least all were joyously happy.

"Three months later Colonel Marshall received a copy of L'Illustration with several pages devoted to the ceremony at Camp Lafayette. Mayor Maybank had been awarded the decoration of the Legion of Honor."*

But Marshall and his wife had hardly settled into their new quarters at Moultrie—Mrs. Marshall had just hung the last yard of curtain on the forty-two French doors in the house—when Marshall received a letter from Major General James F. McKinley, Adjutant General of the Army, notifying him that General MacArthur, the Chief of Staff, had assigned him to the job of senior instructor with the Illinois National Guard.

It was a savage blow to Marshall, and he protested. Marshall wrote directly to MacArthur, and he wrote also to the Adjutant General, informing him he had taken the liberty of a direct appeal to the Chief of Staff, because he was reluctant to accept another staff detail when he had been expecting a command capacity. The letter to General McKinley closed with a reminder that, in all his career, Marshall had asked for only three things—duty with troops, duty in the Philippines, and duty in China.

MacArthur wrote to Marshall on October 6. What he said has not been disclosed, but on October 9 Marshall replied that "under the circumstances" he would be glad to undertake the assignment. So, in the late fall of 1933, Marshall reported in Chicago. The Century of Progress Exposition was in full swing, but the country was still in the throes of a depression, the military were out of favor, and Marshall himself had been shunted into what most of the Regular Army regarded as a dead-end street for anyone of his rank and brilliant professional attainments. The only really bright spot was that, at long last, he had got his "step" to full colonel. He was eligible, now, for promotion to brigadier general; but the man Pershing

---
* From *Together: Annals of an Army Wife,* copyright, 1946, by Katherine Tupper Marshall. Quoted by Mrs. Marshall's permission.

had called the finest officer of the World War would not become a general as long as Douglas MacArthur remained Chief of Staff.

The arrival of Marshall was awaited with keen anticipation in the office of Major General Roy D. Keehn, commanding the 33d Division, Illinois National Guard. The curiosity of this hearty, forthright, plain-speaking man had been sharpened to an unusual degree by a conversation with Charles G. Dawes, Chicago banker who as General "Hell 'n' Maria" Dawes had been an important figure in the Services of Supply in France, and then had been Vice-President of the United States.

Colonel John P. McAdams had completed a tour as senior instructor with the Illinois Guard, and Lieutenant Colonel Joseph C. Hatié replaced him on a temporary basis until some officer could be found to take the three-year detail. Keehn wrote to MacArthur, asking him to assign a certain officer who had been Chief of Staff of the 33d Division at one time during the World War. MacArthur declined, informing Keehn he had selected the officer in question for promotion, but that if Keehn would give him a few weeks' time, he would send the Illinois Guard one of the best, if not the best, officer in the Army. Then, on September 30, MacArthur telegraphed suggesting Marshall. Keehn had never heard of Marshall, but accepted MacArthur's proposal.

A day or two later, Keehn encountered Dawes in the lobby of the bank which occupied the ground floor of the building at 208 South LaSalle Street in which both had offices. He asked Dawes whether he knew an Army officer named Marshall—George Marshall.

"Yes," said Dawes. "Why?"

"MacArthur's sending him out to us for our senior instructor."

An expression of astounded incredulity appeared on Dawes's face, and he pulled the famous underslung pipe away from his mouth.

"*What?* He can't do that! Hell, no! Not George Marshall. He's too big a man for this job. In fact, he's the best goddammed officer in the United States Army!"

It should be noted that in the exchange of letters with Keehn, the

Chief of Staff had made much the same assessment of Marshall, that he was one of the best, if not the best, officer in the Army; but by implication, at least, he had also informed Keehn that the best officer in the Army was *not* slated for promotion to the grade of general.

Keehn was understandably curious about the instructor his division was getting. He liked him the moment they met, and as the weeks passed, he became firmly convinced that Dawes had not been guilty of overstatement. His enthusiasm for Marshall became boundless, and so outspoken at such official affairs as Army Day banquets that the colonel was embarrassed. After Marshall had been in Chicago a few months, Keehn made a trip to Washington. While there, he called on MacArthur, to tell the Chief of Staff that he should pull Marshall out of the National Guard instructor's task, promote him to brigadier general, and give him an assignment commensurate with his capacity. The answer he got elated him, and as soon as he got back to Chicago, he burst into Marshall's office.

"Do you know what MacArthur said to me?"

"No." Marshall looked up from his desk.

"He said, 'Don't you worry about Marshall. We've got one of the best jobs in the Army picked out for him. He's never going to be a brigadier. He's going to be the next Chief of Infantry.'"

The faintest hint of a small, ironic smile appeared on Marshall's face.

"Did he tell you when there would be a vacancy there?" the Colonel inquired.

Keehn, slightly taken aback, admitted the question had not occurred to him—when would there be a vacancy?

"Three years," said Marshall, and returned to his work.

Whatever may have been the opinion of the rest of the professional soldiers about the National Guard and a detail with it, Marshall regarded the Chicago assignment neither as dead-end street, nor as something unworthy of the best efforts he could give it. As in all his new details, he came into Chicago quietly, and took a little while to survey this new situation before he took any action. When the action came, it was nothing drastic.

But the division staff officers, nearly all of them prominent in business or the professions, suddenly realized that their somewhat desultory Monday night meetings had ceased to be the familiar, haphazard, floundering affairs of the past, that the entire staff had a goal in front of it, and each officer a definite job in which he was expected by Colonel Marshall to produce results. Even this mature group felt its morale rise when, one Monday night, they came in to find that Marshall had persuaded Keehn to rent an additional room at headquarters on the twentieth floor at 208 South La Salle Street, and in the room was a desk for each staff officer, with a name plate on the desk.

Marshall realized that the officers needed some intensive training, and he resorted to the established Army device for use when there is nothing but officers, pencils, paper, maps, and telephones to work with—the Command Post Exercise. Soon after his arrival in Chicago, he had planned an elaborate map maneuver for the winter, and the officers of the division worked their way through this problem, which for want of a better name was designated a War Game, on successive weekly drill nights over a period of about two months.

Marshall had realized that the basic shortcoming of National Guard training resulted from the lack of contact between the various headquarters units, the several arms, and the services, due to their physical separation. Each branch—whether division staff, Engineer battalion, Field Artillery regiment, aviation—tended inevitably to concentrate on the theoretical aspect of its own specialty, missing entirely the teamwork that is the first necessity of troops actually in the field.

Accordingly, he set up a trite theoretical situation of a regiment of infantry with artillery and cavalry attached, opposing a similar force. The designated commanders solved the initial situation as a map problem, their subordinates carried out the orders received as another map problem, and so down the chain of command until every unit had been brought into the first "maneuver." Marshall then studied their orders, arrived at a judgment of what would probably have been the actual results of troop movements under them, and issued this summary to the commands involved, along with the indicated intelligence reports of the "enemy." These became, in turn, the basis for new orders, and the process continued until the stage was reached at which, supposedly, the larger bodies of troops would soon be in contact on the battlefield. At this point, the opposing staffs and command organizations were assembled in two armories, connected by telephone, and the last phases were worked out under Marshall's supervision in a one-night Command Post Exercise.

A year later, the same technique was used, but on a more ambitious scale. A hurried deployment of the entire division was assumed to be necessary, and the plans and orders, originating at division headquarters, went down through the successive stages of brigade, regiment, and battalion, the commanders and staffs at each level working out the requirements for their portion of the problem and issuing the necessary orders to the lower echelon. For this exercise, the senior instructor used geological survey maps of an area about eighteen miles from Camp Grant, where the division went for its brief summer training period. Then, in the summer of 1935, the officers converted their War Game of the previous winter's armory drills into a terrain exercise on the ground, and checked their theoretical movements against the physical difficulties those movements would have encountered. The artillery units were not in camp; but all the others were there, and they learned a lot about the impossibility of some of the movements they had ordered.

Keehn watched the development of this experiment in training with mounting enthusiasm. This Chicago lawyer had never had any military experience when Governor Horner of Illinois appointed him commander of the 33d Division—the governor knew Keehn, respected his judgment and administrative capacity, and regarded him as a personal friend; moreover, he wanted to escape what he was certain would be the political embarrassment involved in selecting either of the two brigadier generals who were eligible. By the time Marshall arrived, Keehn had learned enough about military matters to know that his division was not all that it should be; and when Marshall had been there a few months, he was convinced that the

33d was well on the way toward being the best National Guard division in the United States.

Marshall's job involved the supervision of approximately thirty-five Regular Army officers and noncommissioned officers who were detailed as Guard instructors in Illinois, as well as the planning of the training program which they carried out. The Colonel was insistent upon strict discipline in the Guard units. He wanted the training, even if it could be only one night a week during most of the year and a two-weeks' camp in the summer, to be conducted in a smart military atmosphere, as business, not as fun. And he discovered, also, something of the meaning of politics in the National Guard (he had already had some bitter lessons about politics in the Regular Army). He appeared with Keehn before committees of the Illinois legislature, urging a more generous support of the Guard, and—after Keehn was elected president of the National Guard Association in October 1934—he went to Washington to back a delegation seeking funds from the Federal government for construction of armories. On that trip in April 1935, Keehn went first to MacArthur, outlining to the Chief of Staff the association's plans for new armories.

"That's fine," said MacArthur. "But come back next year—I'm trying to get an increase for the Regular Army this year."

"Well, that's fine," Keehn retorted, "but I won't be president of the National Guard Association next year. You don't mind if I try, on my own?"

"No, go right ahead," replied MacArthur.

So Keehn went to President Roosevelt, and laid the request for Public Works appropriations for armories before the Chief Executive. Mr. Roosevelt was sympathetic, but why call them armories? After all, there was so much pacifism in the country that anything even smacking of military matters ran into immediate opposition in the Congressional committees. Why not call them "community centers"? Keehn recognized the touch of political shrewdness when he encountered it, and the armories were built as community centers. They were, be it said, larger and more elaborate than the National Guard required, and actually were used as community centers.

It was the training of the Guard to which Marshall devoted most of his attention, however, and he had the satisfaction of seeing this segment of the citizen army improve perceptibly under his sympathetic and skillful direction. In his second summer with the division, when the units went to Camp Grant for the summer encampment, he put them through a three-day maneuver at the end of the period—the first time the division had actually moved off the camp reservation for field exercises. The attack on "Riley's Ridge" near the Wisconsin state line ended about 7:30 o'clock one morning, and by 9:00 o'clock he had assembled the officers under a huge, makeshift canopy constructed of tent flies at the highest point on the ridge. There he gave them a four-hour critique of the maneuvers they had just completed. Stenographers were there to take every word, and motorcycle couriers ran their notes to Camp Grant. There a written résumé of Marshall's critique was prepared and mimeographed, and by the time the troops marched back into camp, copies of the résumé were ready for distribution to them. The Colonel wanted every man in the division to know exactly what the purpose of the maneuvers had been, how the problem had been attacked and solved, what the shortcomings were—all the facts, and the reasons for them.

The climax of this training came in the summer of 1936, when the Second Army held maneuvers in Michigan. There, the 33d Division learned from Marshall by opposing him. Marshall commanded a brigade which outmaneuvered the division he had trained in at least one major phase of the exercises, but the Colonel had the enormous satisfaction of seeing his training pay dividends in the highly competent staff work and operations of the Guardsmen. On one occasion, the Guardsmen came very close to capturing Marshall and his headquarters.

At this stage of the maneuvers, Marshall had his command post in a schoolhouse. His entire brigade had only one airplane, which was used for observation purposes, but on this particular morning apparently failed to find an approaching party of the "enemy" until the force was almost within sight of Marshall's headquarters. The schoolhouse was abandoned hastily, and the headquarters went scuttling down the road. After about two miles, Marshall halted the flight, had his radio set up beside the road, and began trying to re-establish contact with his one plane.

A farmer and his wife were in the adjoining field, and the wife walked over to the fence and spoke to Marshall.

"Well," she said, "so they've got you on the run this morning?"

"Yes, ma'am—" Marshall grinned—"they certainly have."

"Well, if it was me, I'd stop 'em," she said.

"Oh," said the Colonel, "and just how would you stop them?"

"Well, *I'd* put some real bullets in them guns!"

Marshall laughed, but told her he thought he had better not resort to that extreme. The farmer's wife was typical of the residents in the maneuver area. All of them had become interested in the war games going on in the neighborhood, and Marshall took particular pains to stimulate that interest, and explain to any of them who spoke to him just what was going on. His headquarters were established in the barns and sheds of one farm for two or three days during the exercises, and part of Marshall's daily routine there was to give the farmer who owned the property a thorough briefing in the day's operations. The farmer then would summon his neighbors, and brief them on what he had just learned from the brigade commander.

As always with Marshall, there was no hint of condescension. His interest in people was very real, and very generous. His office staff in Chicago learned as the months passed that the Colonel had a list of people whom they came to call the "pensioners"—some of them old soldiers and noncommissioned officers who had served with him, some of them civilians with whom he had struck up an acquaintance somewhere. They would drift into Marshall's office occasionally, and he always saw them—not just five minutes for the sake of courtesy, but for long talks.

Staff Sergeant Frank Singer, who was chief clerk in the senior instructor's office and sometimes doubled as Marshall's adjutant when there was no commissioned officer on hand to do that job, came in one morning to find Miss Pearce, the receptionist, trying to discourage two very battered and dirty civilians who insisted on seeing the Colonel. They were young men, and one of them had only one leg. Singer went on in to Marshall's office and told him about the callers.

"Oh, yes," said Marshall. "Send them right in."

The unprepossessing visitors were ushered into the Colonel's office, and remained there for a half-hour. When they left, Marshall pushed the buzzer on his desk which summoned Singer.

"That couple of youngsters, the ones who were just here—I picked them up once, several years ago," Marshall said. "They never fail to call on me when they're in town. It usually costs me five dollars, but they're very interesting."

Marshall, of course, also had more distinguished visitors, and among them, to the undisguised excitement of everyone in the office, came the General of the Armies Pershing. Pershing, of course, was one of the most easily recognized figures in the country, and the attention he attracted wherever he went was not welcome to the old general. His visit was expected, and knowing how the general disliked being stared at and creating flurries of excitement, Marshall arranged for him to be ushered into his office through a back door. However, Marshall knew his office staff, too, and was determined that their curiosity would be satisfied. So, while the general was in his office, Marshall found an excuse to send in turn for every member of his office staff—stenographers, typists, receptionist, even the office boy—to do some errand, and while they were in the office, of course he introduced them to the A.E.F. commander.

This personal thoughtfulness was continually in evidence. The women in his office invariably received flowers or some other gift on their birthdays, and at Christmas. When Marshall organized a Command Post Exercise, as he did about once every six months, which began in his office on Saturday afternoon and ran straight through until Sunday night, he would insist that the stenographers—who had been kept very busy during the CPX—take the next day off and rest.

"But it's Monday—there will be a heavy mail!" they would chorus.

"But I want you to rest," the Colonel would reply.

When the officers, junior instructors with the Guard or others detailed to his establishment, appeared to be suffering from accumulated fatigue, he would order them to take a fifteen-day leave. Then he would telephone their wives, inform them of his action, and ask them to telephone him if their husbands attempted to do any work during the vacation he had ordered for them.

Meantime, if MacArthur and those around him were not disposed to lift Marshall out of the backwater in which he had been placed, others were more concerned. Out on the West Coast Major General Malin Craig, commanding the 9th Corps Area at San Francisco, would denounce the Army's promotion system occasionally, and cite George Marshall as the example of its worst failure. Pershing was reported to have gone to the White House and told President Roosevelt that if he did not promote Marshall soon, he would never be able to make him Chief of Staff in time to do the job that would have to be done. And down in San Antonio, Marshall's old friend Hagood seized an opportunity to speak to the Secretary of War.

Secretary Dern had come to San Antonio in 1935, and was the guest of Hagood, who was then commanding the 8th Corps Area. Dern asked him if he had any good colonels whom he could recommend for promotion to brigadier general.

"Mr. Secretary," Hagood replied, "I have a great many good colonels whom I could recommend, but the best colonel in the Army is not under my command. His name is George Marshall, and he is on some duty over in Chicago."

"Yes," said Dern, "I have heard that Colonel Marshall is a very good man. But he is too young."

Marshall was not quite fifty-five. He was also not quite one year younger than MacArthur, who had then been Chief of Staff for nearly five years. However, important shifts were coming in the Army high command. MacArthur, who had held the post of Chief of Staff longer than any other officer and was beginning to look more or less like a permanent fixture in the office, had been tendered, and had accepted with the approval of President Roosevelt, appointment as military adviser to the Philippine Commonwealth government, with the rank and title of field marshal in the Philippine Army, a handsome salary, lavish quarters, and the task of organizing the forces of the island commonwealth in preparation for the approaching independence of the Philippine Republic.

On October 1, 1935, General MacArthur was on his way to Manila to assume his new duties, in addition to those he already had as Chief of Staff. There was a widespread, if nebulous, understanding in the War Department that MacArthur would retain his Army title indefinitely, with some other officer—probably General Hugh A. Drum—taking over as Acting Chief of Staff during his absence. President Roosevelt was on the West Coast. Between his hotel at Coronado, California, and the Navy cruiser toward which he was being driven, with his usual escort of secretaries, Secret Service men, and news reporters, he signed the nomination of Major General Malin Craig to be Chief of Staff. So unexpected was the appointment that the new Secretary of War, Harry Woodring, received his first intimation of it when an officer came to his office in Washington with a report of the news stories coming in from California.

Just one year later, on October 1, 1936, Colonel Marshall was promoted to brigadier general and assigned to command the 5th Infantry Brigade at Vancouver Barracks, Washington. After almost thirty years, the star had come out of his pocket to rest on his shoulder.

XIV

Marshall Speaks His Mind

"AND if we then ask what kind of intellect is most closely associated with military genius, a glance at the subject as well as at experience will tell us that searching, rather than creative, minds, comprehensive minds rather than such as pursue one special line, cool, rather than fiery, heads are those to which in time of war we should prefer to trust the welfare of our brothers and children, the honor and safety of our country."

This description of the intellectual qualities needed in a military leader might have been written with Marshall in mind, but Karl von Clausewitz had been dead one hundred twenty-six years when Brigadier General George C. Marshall, clad in a double-breasted suit, polka-dot bow tie and Homburg hat, arrived at Vancouver Barracks on October 27, 1936, to take command of the 5th Infantry Brigade.

He was less than three years away from the most colossal responsibilities ever laid upon an American military officer. There is strong evidence, but no clear proof, that under the new dispensation in the War Department—Secretary Dern had died and been succeeded by Harry Woodring, and MacArthur had been replaced by Craig—the promotion of Marshall to brigadier general was merely the first step in a plan to bring him to Washington as Craig's successor.

There were hurdles yet to be cleared, and the political pressures, within as well as outside the Army, would become strong enough to produce some hesitancy and uncertainty even in General Craig. But that situation would develop in 1939, when Marshall already was Deputy Chief of Staff; and Secretary Woodring told certain officers at Fort Leavenworth as early as the summer of 1937 that Marshall would succeed Craig.

Colonel Henry Hossfeld, who had served with Marshall in the Philippines and now commanded the 7th Infantry, greeted the new brigade commander and his wife when they arrived at Vancouver after an automobile trip from Chicago. It was Marshall's first sight of Vancouver Barracks, and his wife's first trip to the Northwest. Both of them were delighted with the beauty of their new home, and the General quickly made himself an expert in the lore of the post, which was one of the historic garrisons of the Army. A few months after his arrival, Marshall wrote to General Keehn in Chicago describing his work in the Northwest:

In the first place I have three different jobs, the most immediate being the command of this post and the regiment and detachments stationed here. Vancouver Barracks is one of the old historic outposts of the army. Established in 1849 on the site of a Hudson Bay Company station, the traces of whose lookout station are still descernible in a tall fir tree, for more than fifty years it was the center for the development of the northwest. General Grant's log quarters are a part of the present post library building. Phil Sheridan left here a lieutenant to start his meteoric rise to fame. Pickett was a member of the garrison. My quarters were occupied by a succession of Civil War celebrities or Indian fighters. General Miles built the house, which was later occupied by Canby, Crook, Gibbon and Pope.

During the past thirty years there has been little change in the outward appearance of the post, but the interior of barracks and quarters have been modernized to a degree and made reasonably attractive and comfortable. Giant fir trees ornament the parade; every yard has its holly trees and a profusion of shrubs. The original apple tree of the northwest, planted in the yard of the old trading post, still lives and is carefully fenced against possible harm. In my yard is a cherry tree of reported antiquity, with three grafted varieties of the fruit. All is in delightful contrast to the institution-like appearance of many army posts.

The Columbia River, bordering our aviation field (we have four planes) in extension of the parade, emerges from its famous gorge a few miles above the post. In the distance the symmetrical cone of Mt. Hood stands covered with snow, summer or winter.

Another of my duties is the command of the 5th Brigade, one regiment of which occupies posts near Spokane, in Montana, and in North Dakota. The local regiment has two companies at Chilkoot Barracks in Alaska. Except for inspections, training policies and periods of concentration, there is little for me to do with the troops of the brigade not stationed here.

My most pressing duty concerns the command of thirty-five CCC companies scattered through Oregon and southern Washington. These camps are beautifully organized, and the supply system and weekly motor transport convoys operate from here, in a precise routine, under the capable direction of a staff of reserve officers.

The location of the camps contributes a great deal to the pleasure of my work, situated as they are along the coast, high in the mountains, on lakes, and at other points of scenic interest. Excellent fishing and hunting can usually be found in the vicinity of these camps—the steel head salmon are now running—but it is not necessary to go so far afield. A few evenings ago my orderly called attention to four cock pheasant and six hens roosting in a tree in the yard.

To reach a large section of my district in eastern Oregon I must traverse the Columbia River gorge, finally emerging from the dense green of the vegetation of the damp near-coastal region into the typical barrens of the dry western plains. In winter one passes, within a mile, from overcast skies, fogs or rain into the glare of cloudless skies. It is possible now, with the spring flowers blooming, to motor an hour and a half from here to the skiing slopes of Mt. Hood. Oregon is a region of contrasts.

The CCC companies are a source of keen interest. Near Pendleton, the scene of the famous annual "round up" or rodeo, is a company of Boston boys. Under Beacon Rock—except for Gibraltar, the largest monolith in the world, is a group of young fellows from the swamp regions of Arkansas. Providence, Rhode Island, has a company near Tillamook on the shore of the Pacific. Their road sign reads, "Tillamook 18 miles. Providence, R. I., 3100." We have groups from New York, Connecticut, New Jersey, Ohio, Kentucky, Minnesota and the Dakotas.

The boys all seem to like this country, and I imagine that this peaceful invasion will have a marked effect on the future development of the region, as many of these young men remain out here to marry and settle down. As a whole they are a fine lot, hard working, studious in following the educational courses we provide, and seeming to develop considerable ambition, along with the necessary energy and resolution.

I was very fortunate to find an old army friend in the Governor of Oregon, Major General Charles H. Martin, retired. He has done a great deal to help me in my contacts with the people of the state. I was also fortunate to find our old friend General Rilea at Salem. The Adjutant General of Oregon and the Commanding General of the 41st Division, General George White, has been most cordial. We served together on an examining board last month. He and I will command the opposing forces in the army maneuvers next August, and I am trusting him not to put a price on my head as you did in the 2d Army maneuvers in Michigan last summer.

The latter part of April we leave for a month of division maneuvers at Fort Lewis, some of the troops coming from as distant points as Salt Lake City and San Francisco. We will also have a brief joint maneuver with the Navy and Marine Corps, for which I am Chief Umpire.

June and July will be occupied with ROTC, CMTC, and Reserve regiment camps here and on our firing range fourteen miles away. And the last two weeks of August we return to the Fort Lewis reservation and vicinity for army maneuvers.

The town of Vancouver—some 15,000 people—adjoins the post. Portland is across the Columbia eight miles distant. The people are friendly and cordial. The country seems prosperous despite the recent prolonged maritime strike which inflicted heavy losses on the lumber people, the apple growers and many other industries of this vicinity.

I have just read the descriptions in the last *Guardsman* of the work of the Illinois National Guard during the flood. Colonel Davis and his command evidently did a magnificent job in a manner which should convince every citizen of the security guaranteed his home and his family by the maintenance of efficient state troops. The frequent employment of the National Guard in times of public disaster, to succor the distressed and to reestablish law and order, should have dispelled all feelings of hostility towards the military, and should win for it the determined support of citizens generally. It is the great non-political force in this country, state or federal, for the security of citizens.

I am deeply interested in the continued development of the 33d

Division towards combat team efficiency. As commanders, and particularly staffs, acquire facility in the expeditious conduct of training and handling of troops, the efficiency of the division will reach a state not now considered possible of achievement. Without increase in working time and with less effort they will be able to accomplish twice as much. You have a splendid personnel, and the sky is the limit.

This long letter—it is worth noting that Marshall did not dictate it to a secretary, but typed it himself—shows that the General was enjoying thoroughly his new command. There is more than that, however, to be discovered in it. The paragraphs about the young men in the CCC camps, particularly, reveal in Marshall's own words his interest in those under his command or supervision as individual human beings, not as units in a table of organization. And a glimpse of a fundamental and extremely important attitude in this man destined so soon to assume vast responsibilities is provided by the paragraph which commented on the Illinois National Guard's services in a disastrous flood.

That attitude was Marshall's conception of the military forces in a democracy as the servants of the public. Marshall was ambitious from his youth, no more proof than other men against the lures of fame and power, quite properly not content with any ultimate post which did not challenge and use his full capacity, but in that post content that his great abilities were used for the benefit of others, not his own advancement—not even in prestige. In the mind of Marshall, an American society in which the military would control or even exert pressure upon the civil government, instead of subjecting themselves to the civil will, was simply unthinkable.

It is an attitude rarely attributed to the military mind, and yet in all truth found quite generally among soldiers in the United States. Most American soldiers—and most civilians as well—lack the stature of Marshall, and accordingly they lack perhaps the profound insight and broad comprehension which in Marshall set that attitude upon an unshakable philosophical base. Yet, with rare exceptions, American soldiers confine not only their requests to the Congress and their advice to the civil executives but their statements to the public as well, to matters affecting the performance of the duties assigned to them—planning and effecting the military security of the nation. No career in America requires more constant sacrifice and devotion, and promises less reward, than the military service; yet able men have not been lacking in a career which throughout its history has been a poor route to any reward except the knowledge that one has served the public.

Marshall came at last to the topmost rank of his chosen profession, but if he knew when he went to Vancouver that the goal was in sight, it did not diminish his interest in the command he took over in the Northwest. He began his tour with a very thorough inspection of the entire post, going into places no one had thought for years that a general officer would bother with. He made the expected public appearances—such as occupying the reviewing stand with the mayor of Vancouver for the Armistice Day parade. He dropped in at the noncommissioned officers' quarters, and asked their wives how matters stood, and how the buildings might be improved with such means as he had at his disposal. He saw to it that Lieutenant C. N. Hunter, who had charge of Works Progress Administration projects on the post, used some of the money to convert a dilapidated theater of World War vintage into a basketball court and skating rink. The old gymnasium was remodeled and redecorated to become a club for noncommissioned officers. Still concerned that the men on his post have expert guidance to stimulate their efforts in athletics, Marshall made Lieutenant William Nave—"Spike" Nave, Army quarterback of the late twenties—post athletic officer.

When Mrs. Marshall's daughter Molly returned from her year and a half of traveling around the world and came to live on the post, the General's quarters became a center for the younger officers and their wives, and they found they were more than welcome. On Christmas Day, all the bachelor officers were invited to dinner by the Marshalls. The General and his wife could always be depended upon to show up at parties. And Lieutenant Hunter got a full demonstration of Marshall's "sternness" at one of the dances at the Officers' Club. During an intermission, some of the officers took over the instruments and started playing. Hunter was having a wonderful time with the drums when Marshall came up to him, said, "Move over, son!" and took control of the percussion array.

In June 1937 Marshall became involved in an episode which made him the target of some ill-natured comment in the local newspapers. The occasion was the transpolar flight of three Soviet airmen, who hopped off from Moscow intending to fly over the North Pole to San Francisco, but landed three days later at Vancouver, six hundred miles short of their goal. Marshall threw a guard around their plane, took the three men to his own quarters, and prevented the reporters from seeing them until the men had had the interval of privacy and rest they wanted. The reporters finally got their interviews, however, and watched Ambassador Troyanovsky receive a presentation sword as an official memento of the flight.

Troyanovsky, who had been awaiting the fliers at San Francisco, came up to Vancouver as soon as he learned they had landed there, and became a fourth guest at Marshall's quarters. He found that Marshall had discovered a Reserve officer who spoke Russian and acted as interpreter; that the General had opened up a direct telephone line to Washington in order to put the men in touch with the Soviet Embassy; that he had lent the fliers his own pajamas, and had a department store send around twenty suits of clothing and other apparel, so the men could select what they wanted without having to face the crowds that would besiege them as soon as they left his quarters. The "warm thanks" of the ambassador to the General were conveyed in person at Vancouver Barracks, and later in a formal note to the State Department.

Later that summer, Marshall commanded one of the opposing forces in the Third Army maneuvers, and outmaneuvered his "enemy," but appears to have made no important contribution to the art of war, unless it was his demonstration that he could take some of his noncommissioned officers, brief them quickly but thoroughly, and use them effectively as staff officers. It was something of a tour de force, and Marshall took vast pleasure in it.

In the autumn, Marshall went quietly down to Letterman General Hospital in San Francisco for a long-deferred thyroid operation. Few of the officers at Vancouver realized that his absence from the post was not just another inspection tour of CCC camps, or knew that the delicate and dangerous operation very nearly cost Marshall's life. Afterward, however, his friends noticed that his general health appeared to be greatly improved, and that the old nervous intensity had been replaced by an unfamiliar calmness.

Then, in the summer of 1938, he was ordered to Washington to head the War Plans Division of the General Staff. He came at a moment when the uneasy thought that war was a possibility had begun to creep beneath the curtain of willful blindness which the vast majority of Americans had hung between themselves and the rest of the world. In the minds of many of the country's leaders, and certainly among most of its military leaders, that possibility was viewed as a probability. They did not welcome the thought, these military men; there must, in fact, have been moments when they came close to terror at the realization of the complete—except for the Navy's fleet, almost absolute—lack of means to accomplish their sole mission of defense.

Hitler had announced to the world three years earlier that Germany was rearming. He had reoccupied the Rhineland two years before Marshall came to Washington to assume responsibility for America's war plans. The anti-Comintern pact was two years old, the Rome-Berlin Axis was nearing its third birthday. Intervention in Spain had tested the *Luftwaffe* and the panzers in battle, and shown the shape of things to come to a democratic world unwilling to see and unwilling to understand what it saw. In March 1938 Austria had been added to the Third Reich, and the expatriate Germans of the Sudeten region became the excuse for mounting pressure against the Republic of Czechoslovakia. Before Marshall had been in Washington three months, Edouard Daladier and Neville Chamberlain, prime ministers of the two great democracies of Western Europe, would go to Munich and publicly wash their hands of the blood of the one great democracy of Central Europe in order to achieve "peace in our time." The shame of that betrayal would shock Britain and France into a belated facing of facts and a fearful knowledge that they must fight. In the United States, however, the illusions of the selfish and cynical twenties would persist until France fell and Britain was at bay, and Americans began to understand at last that men cannot escape evil, but must seek it out and destroy it.

Nor had Japan been idle in those years. Through all the muddled ineptitude displayed by the United States in its foreign relations during its emergence as a world power, and the slow awakening of its people to the inescapable fact that wealth and strength bestow obligations as certainly as privileges upon their possessors, there had run two clear and consistent ideas. The first was the Monroe Doctrine, that Anglo-American concept of the inviolability of the two Americas by conquerors seeking empire; the second an unwavering insistence upon the territorial integrity of the vast and ancient but feeble state of China, and access by all nations on equal terms—the "open door"—to such needs and opportunities as China might present for investment and commerce. Yet, after the one ineffective protest by Secretary of State Henry L. Stimson against the seizure of Manchuria in 1931—a protest made ineffective by the United States' unwillingness to back it with force, and by a refusal of participation from a Britain unaware that it could not run with the fox and ride with the hounds of the Orient—the United States had done no more than indicate disapproval while Japan seized Jehol Province, bombed and seized Shanghai, occupied the area around Peiping, committed the rape of Nanking, bombed and sank the gunboat U.S.S. *Panay*—in short, waged open war in China.

This was the state of affairs when Marshall reported as Assistant Chief of Staff, War Plans, in July 1938. As usual, he made no abrupt changes in personnel or methods. The executive officer of the division was Lieutenant Colonel Leonard T. Gerow. Marshall sent for him soon after his arrival, and asked him to sit down and give the new division chief a brief but thorough orientation in the division's current work.

Marshall found, of course, that plans existed in the division for operations against virtually every nation in the world—against almost any conceivable combination of enemies, and with almost any conceivable combination of allies. Many of these studies were out of date, however, and during his tour with WPD a large part of its labor was the revision of these plans. Particular attention was paid to Europe, and the closest study was given by Marshall and his staff to plans which involved this country's most likely foes, the Axis Powers. The possibility that the United States might became involved in a war in both the Atlantic and Pacific Oceans was not overlooked, but later organizational developments in the Army, particularly the establishment of General Headquarters for the field forces in 1940, indicated this possibility was not viewed as a likelihood.

Marshall, of course, consulted not only Gerow, but all the officers of his staff division, and among them Lieutenant Colonel St. Clair Streett, one of two air officers on his staff, and the only air officer on the Joint Planning Committee of the Joint Board (Army and Navy).

"Streett," said Marshall, "take down your hair and tell me what's wrong with the Air Corps."

Streett had plenty to tell him, beginning with the fact that some time earlier the Army members of the Joint Planners had received orders to report in their recommendations to the Joint Board that their total requirements in heavy bombers were twelve planes.

"That," said Marshall, "is nonsense. We won't even consider it."

With that attitude of the new Assistant Chief of Staff, WPD, to guide its officers, the major problem of WPD at once became revision of the planning booklet, "Joint Action of the Army and Navy," to make it conform to the increasing performance capabilities of air power. The division of mission between sea and air forces was the point at issue, and although compromise would succeed compromise in tentative agreements, the question was to plague relations between the two services, not only during the period of preparation for war, but during the war itself. The Navy would resist bitterly any encroachment on its stubborn position that the mission of the Army—and that included the Air Corps—ended, and the Navy assumed complete control and authority for all operations, at a vertical projection of the shore line.

Marshall, however, was destined to remain in charge of WPD only three months. Shortly after he arrived in Washington, General Pershing went to see President Roosevelt, who had a profound respect for the general's opinions despite the fact that he had failed to follow the old warrior's advice in 1935, when Pershing recommended Major General Hugh A. Drum for Chief of Staff, and the President instead named Major General Malin Craig. In 1938, Craig had served three years of his four-year term, and the question of a successor not only was becoming one of the President's major concerns, but was getting to be a matter of intense campaigning on the part of officers who knew themselves to be decidedly eligible.

After the usual exchange of greetings and pleasantries, Pershing came to the point of his visit.

"Mr. President," he said, "you have a man over there in the War Plans Division who has just come here—Marshall. He's Chief of Staff material. Why don't you send for him and look him over? I think he will be a great help."

There was another advocate at work, meanwhile, within the War Department. The Assistant Secretary of War, Louis M. Johnson, had met Marshall several months earlier during a trip through the Northwest which took him to Vancouver Barracks for a review of the troops there and luncheon with the commanding general. For all of Marshall's reputation in the Army, Johnson had never heard of him, but he was deeply impressed as he talked with him at Vancouver. Remembering a remark by Roosevelt that the Army had "too many old fogies" at the top, Johnson called for Marshall's file as soon as he returned to Washington. After studying it, he was even more impressed, and a few nights later, during an informal after-dinner conversation in the President's study, suggested that Roosevelt put Marshall into the War Plans assignment.

The President must surely have been astonished. His administrative method, if it could be called that, appeared at times to amount to little more than tossing men of divergent views and clashing temperament into a government arena and allowing them to fight one another more or less publicly, while the President enjoyed the scrap, used such attitudes from any contender as pleased him, and actually ran—or attempted to run—the department himself. The disagreements of Assistant Secretary Johnson and Secretary Woodring in the War Department had by that time become more rather than less public, and Roosevelt probably derived a huge if secret amusement to find that Johnson had discovered Marshall, and now was repeating Woodring's recommendation that Marshall be brought to Washington to head the War Plans Division.

Woodring, in the spring of 1938, had sent for Major General Stanley D. Embick, the Deputy Chief of Staff, and asked him in plaintive exasperation, "Do I have to select Drum as Chief of Staff?" Embick replied that he did not—that any general in the Army was eligible for the appointment. Furthermore, the Deputy told the Secretary, there would be some vacancies in the list of general officers, and Woodring could select any likely colonel on the eligible list, promote him to brigadier general, and thus make him eligible for the job of Chief of Staff.

However, Embick suggested that Woodring bring Marshall to Washington. Brigadier General Walter Krueger's tour as Assistant Chief of Staff, War Plans, would expire in June. Marshall could be called in to fill that assignment, move into Embick's spot as deputy soon after, and thus be brought to the intended appointment as Chief of Staff by a succession of logical moves. Embick, with only two more years to serve before the statutory age limit of sixty-four years forced his retirement, already had asked for command of the 4th Corps Area, with headquarters in Atlanta. There, his less than arduous duties would leave him time to devote himself to the strategic studies which had been his chief interest throughout his career.

If Embick felt any qualms about suggesting that Marshall be slated to take over as Deputy Chief of Staff on his way to the top position, they were of sympathy rather than conscience, for he knew that the deputy's job, particularly in peacetime, was one no man in his right mind would want—preparing the budget, wrestling with appropriations problems, seeing to it that the Army lived within its money grant. It was an exacting and unpleasant task, but an obvious assignment if Woodring wanted to line Marshall up to succeed Craig.

Evidently, there was more than one "conspiracy" to make Marshall Chief of Staff.

In September, it was Johnson who followed through on the intention to move Marshall one step nearer the ultimate goal. Secretary Woodring was away from Washington, and Johnson as Acting Secretary had called a meeting of the War Council in his office.

"What about a Deputy Chief of Staff?" was his question to Craig as the meeting began.

"We'll get that worked out, Mr. Secretary," Craig replied.

"What about George Marshall for deputy?" Johnson insisted.

"We'll work that out, Mr. Secretary," said the general.

"There is not going to be any War Council until that thing *is* worked out," Johnson announced.

Craig left the room. When he returned a few minutes later, he smiled a little and said, "The orders have been issued." Apparently Craig, like the President, found it unnecessary to inform Johnson that in this matter, at least, the Assistant Secretary and the Secretary were in complete accord.

At about the same time, orders were issued assigning General Drum to command the 2d Corps Area, with headquarters in New York, a post which had been vacant since the retirement of Major General Frank R. McCoy in July. Drum, however, still hoped to succeed Craig, and during the winter his efforts to obtain the appointment accumulated strength. He was, in fact, the most obvious choice in the Army—a senior major general, with a distinguished World War record, an all but perfect score for his entire career.

The qualities which Marshall possessed above anyone else in the Army, however, made the junior officer the choice of those who saw the nation approaching a grave crisis and a probable war, and Drum failed to win the active support of some of those on whom he had counted. Pershing, for one, refused to support the officer who had served as his Chief of Staff in the First Army in France, reminding Drum that he had advocated his cause four years earlier, but that in the new situation his choice was Marshall. Later, when the campaigning for the post was at its height, Pershing went again to the White House, discussed at length with the President the qualifications of the several candidates, and reiterated his reasons for regarding Marshall as the Army officer best fitted to fill the post with distinction in a time of crisis.

A new hazard on Marshall's approach to the long-sought goal appeared—at least in Marshall's apprehensive mind—soon after he became Deputy Chief of Staff in September, and as the result of a stormy argument with the President. That September of 1938 was the month of the Munich conference, and Roosevelt was one of those Americans who knew better than to place any reliance on Hitler's assurance that with the acquisition of the Sudeten German regions of Czechoslovakia, he now had no further territorial ambitions. Accordingly, Roosevelt announced a few weeks after Munich that the United States would build ten thousand military airplanes.

Unhappily but characteristically, he made the announcement through the press, and without consulting the Secretary of War or the Chief of Staff. Having announced the policy, he summoned Craig to the White House to discuss how the goal would be reached. Craig took Marshall with him, and in a long and stubborn argument they tried to convince the President that the figure was fantastically out of line with Army programs or capabilities. The President refused to be swayed—he was going to have a 10,000-plane program. Marshall's old friend Hap Arnold was now a major general and Chief of the Air Corps, and his protest was added to the others— the Air Corps could not possibly handle that many planes. To that statement, the President retorted that if the Air Corps could not, the Royal Air Force could. As the hectic conferences and arguments continued, the President also suggested to the Air Corps chief that there were places like Guam for people like Hap Arnold. The hint was not lost on the officer who had been exiled to the provinces along with Brigadier General William Lendrum (Billy) Mitchell, but it did not change his insistence that planes without operating bases, pilots, and crews did not make an air force. Finally, Craig returned to the fray, again accompanied by Marshall.

This time, the discussion was more heated than ever, but the President would not be budged. After the meeting, Craig telephoned a member of Congress, long an informed and influential specialist in military affairs, and asked if he might call that evening at the congressman's home. After Craig arrived accompanied by Marshall, it developed that the two soldiers were afraid that Marshall's bluntness had jeopardized his chance to succeed Craig, and the congressman was sought as an ally who might exert some influence on the White House from the Capitol.

"You may not have noticed it in the papers," Craig explained, "but the President of the United States delivered himself at a press conference of a statement that the War Department would do something about the Air Corps.

"We had no warning of his statement, and we were very much disturbed by it, because on its face the President was wrong in his judgment.

"I was called to the White House, and I took General Marshall with me. We argued the matter with the President, and tried to persuade him to change his views, but we didn't get very far.

"Then, we went a second time. The conversation became quite emphatic, and came very near to table-pounding. General Marshall was backing me up, and he finally said to the President, 'Very well, sir. You are the Commander in Chief, and we will obey your orders. We find it difficult to do in this instance, because they are contrary to the considered judgment of the General Staff, but we will obey them. You will, of course, never question the integrity of the General Staff in this matter!'"

With that challenge, the two generals left the President's office. Not long afterward, the Marshalls attended one of the formal winter receptions at the White House. As they approached the President to shake hands, Marshall said quietly to his wife, "Now we'll see whether I broke my plate!" The impression he got was that the chief executive was "frigid," although it seems more likely that Marshall's imagination, stimulated by apprehension, was working overtime. At any rate, he worried for several days about whether he should broach the subject again with the President, and finally decided to say to him that he hoped he had not offended him with his bluntness.

"Hell, no!" Roosevelt replied. "I'm pleased to have someone who will speak an honest opinion!"

Courage, said Clausewitz, is of two kinds: courage in the presence of danger to the person, and courage in the presence of responsibility, whether before the judgment of external authority "or before that of the internal authority which is conscience." Marshall had shown in France that he was not lacking in the first variety. Now, in Washington, he had demonstrated how complete his courage was in the presence of responsibility. He was learning, also, a vast amount about President Roosevelt, and how that great man (if poor administrator) operated. As Marshall commented later to a friend, relating the quarrels over the plane program and his own part in them, "He doesn't call you over there to *ask* you, he calls you over there to *tell* you!"

That second kind of courage in Marshall—moral courage, and the loyalty which an Army officer places on a level with it, were put to the rack while he was Deputy Chief of Staff. He must have felt, at times, as if he had been deposited in a cage of Kilkenny cats. Because of the administrative chaos which Roosevelt had created, and which he allowed to continue, in the War Department, the work of the Army command and staff was made enormously more difficult, and the position of the top staff officers in particular became on occasion almost intolerable.

Woodring, the Secretary, was utterly unable to grasp the significance of world events, to understand the dangerous implications for the United States of the cynical and evil forces which Hitler in Europe and Japan's war lords in Asia had loosed upon the world. Honest and sincere, but unimaginative, he was the complete product of an inland America so withdrawn behind geographic barriers that it did not see or understand the demolition of those barriers by speed, and forgot that geography has never in history provided a barrier against ideas. He came from a region the attitude of which toward the war was summed up epigrammatically by another Midwesterner in the summer of 1942 with the comment, "On December 6 there wasn't any war, and on December 8 we had it won." Moreover, Woodring had been affronted in the dignity of his office by the appointment and the attitude of the Assistant Secretary.

Johnson, far more realistic and perceptive in his appreciation of the dangers threatening the country, entered the office of Assistant Secretary in the belief that he was to succeed Woodring as Secretary. That there was some such assurance from the President can hardly be doubted, although it may not have been the flat and definite promise it was taken to be by ears waiting to hear such a guarantee. Unfortunately, Johnson made no secret of his ambition, or of his belief that the President had promised Woodring's job to him. The not unnatural result was that the two men met with open hostility, which hardly made for smooth administration of a critical department in a critical time.

The President's proposal of the 10,000-plane program, if not suggested by Johnson, at least followed repeated and forceful arguments by the Assistant Secretary in behalf of a more ambitious air policy, and particularly for greater emphasis on heavy bombardment planes. The animosity between Woodring and Johnson became an open contest on many matters, and one of them was the question of heavy bombers, the striking force of air power.

This concept of long-range heavy bombardment as an instrument of the strategic offensive would prove to be the most important new military doctrine contributed by the United States to the war against the Axis, and one that none of America's enemies and few of its Allies understood. It had been many years in development, and its career had been stormy from the start. Only after a bitter controversy within the budding Air Corps itself, with certain farsighted "visionaries" bucking the dominance of the pursuit aviation enthusiasts, had bombardment aviation been defined in 1926 as the basic air arm, just as Infantry was the basic ground arm, with all others auxiliary to it. Then began the long controversy between the Air Corps and the War Department General Staff, which had produced a storm and several punitive transfers of officers just before Marshall came to Washington in the summer of 1938. Among others "busted" in the controversy, Major General Frank M. Andrews lost his command of the General Headquarters Air Force, was reduced to his permanent grade of colonel, and sent to Fort Sam Houston, Texas, as air officer of the 8th Corps Area. Perhaps it was only chance, but it was an extremely odd coincidence that this same assignment had been Billy Mitchell's post of exile years before.

The precipitation of the battle by the Air Corps's proposal to expand the production and purchase of the new Boeing B-17 bomber, the Flying Fortress, had caused another clash between Woodring and Johnson. The Navy was opposed to the development of the long-range bomber, deeming it a threat of interference with the Navy's mission at sea. Moreover, the War Department General Staff clung to the conception of the air force as an arm without a basically independent mission of its own, but exclusively auxiliary in its nature; and, so far as bombardment aviation was concerned, limited in its Army applications to a short-range mission of comparatively heavy hitting capacity—a fundamentally defensive weapon, for offshore bombardment of hostile fleets or close support of ground armies. This attitude governed the plane procurement program, limiting the purchase of B-17's to twelve planes, which was presented at a staff meeting called by Woodring early in 1938. (It was one aspect of this program which Streett reported to Marshall when the latter asked him to "take your hair down").

The program was drawn by the General Staff, and it reflected the approval of Craig, a man of many fine qualities, but extremely conservative. When it had been presented to the meeting, Woodring said, "That will be the plan."

"Wait a minute, Mr. Secretary——" Johnson broke in.

"Oh," said Woodring, "we all know you're opposed to it."

"Yes, I'm opposed to it," Johnson replied, "and I want General Andrews to be heard."

"I don't want to hear General Andrews."

"General Andrews," Johnson urged, "is the most brilliant man on bombardment aviation in the Army, and I insist that he be heard."

Craig leaned over toward the Secretary and whispered to him, and Woodring then asked Andrews to speak. The general made a cogent plea for emphasis on heavy bombardment. When he had finished, Woodring said, "This is still the program." Johnson, however, had more to say. As Assistant Secretary, he was clothed with statutory authority over Army procurement, and he now flung a reminder of this fact at Woodring.

"With all due respect to your office," Johnson taunted, "there is a statutory responsibility involved. This is *not* the program until the Commander in Chief approves it."

The Assistant Secretary then took the matter to the White House. The Commander in Chief apparently was not yet ready to take up the cudgels for what would certainly be an enormously expensive program, for the twelve-bomber program went through, and Andrews and some of his colleagues were exiled. However, the Munich appeasement altered the President's views, and he made his 10,000-plane announcement.

After the protests and pleas proved vain, the incredibly difficult job of planning the procurement began in earnest. The dismay in the General Staff became consternation when Johnson, who for nearly a year had been urging an air program expenditure of $1,400,000,000, announced to the planners that their cash limit was $300,000,000. The thing was impossible. Sweating out a plan within the prescribed limit, and including base construction and training schedules to bring some semblance of a true air force, the planners produced a roar of anger from the President. That money was to be spent for planes, and nothing but planes; he could not influence Hitler with barracks, runways, and schools for mechanics. Eventually an agreement was reached on the 5,500-plane program which the President recommended in his budget message to the Congress in

January 1939. It was an unbalanced, unsound program, even calling for more than 150 Douglas B-18's, a twin-engined bomber with a top speed far below 200 miles an hour, and already obsolete. The planners did manage to squeeze into it about 250 Flying Fortresses. The staff called the President's announcement and the frenzy that followed it the "numbers racket."

But Marshall's bluntness in protesting the unbalanced nature of the program had not jeopardized his scheduled appointment. Apparently Roosevelt meant it when he told the General he liked a man who spoke an honest opinion, for on April 27, 1939, jumping him over thirty-four senior officers, he nominated Marshall to be Chief of Staff, succeeding Craig when the latter retired on August 31.

XV

Fighting for an Army

The arrival of Marshall at the exalted dignity of Chief of Staff imposed on him a duty and a triumph, the last purely personal triumph the busy years of emergency and war would allow him. The home-town boy had made good, and Uniontown wanted to celebrate the fact with the General and his wife.

So, a few days after he took the oath of office on September 1, Marshall went back to Uniontown. A band, a parade, tea, banquet, and reception—and some of the old friends to talk to, and share the reminiscing. There was Alex Mead, now superintendent of the county farm, who greeted his former playmate with "Well, George, here you are Chief of Staff, and I'm in the poorhouse!" And Jap Shepler, one of his partners in the fightin' chickens enterprise, wormed his way through the crowd, clutching a small paper bag.

"I've got a little package here for you, George," he said.

Marshall looked at the bag, and a delighted grin spread over his face.

"It's licorice!" he shouted.

Marshall's sister came over from Greensburg. Helen Houston was at the dinner, and Alex Beeson, and a happy, chattering crowd of familiar old friends. And after dinner, Marshall slipped away from the crowd and walked from the hotel—the new White Swan which had risen on the site of the Brownfield's place—down the hill, past the theater that had replaced his own birthplace, past the Thompson home where the Thompsons no longer lived, and up the hill beyond to the old Gilmore place. There the General, like the

Signal Corps Photo

QUADRANT CONFERENCE

At this meeting in Quebec in August 1943, Marshall was selected to command the Anglo-American invasion of Normandy the following spring.

Signal Corps Photo

THANKSGIVING DAY IN CAIRO

By the time Churchill and Roosevelt met Chiang Kai-shek at this conference in November 1943, the

small boy, knocked at the back door, and was admitted by Fred Hallow to visit Mrs. Bliss and Mrs. Houston.

It was a pleasant interlude, but a brief one. He had to return to Washington, where the government and the public, beginning to be familiar with his name, would in the next few months take the measure of this junior brigadier who had been catapulted—the public, after all, did not know the long years of striving—into the nation's most important military position.

Between the two incredible but inexorable facts of the Nazi-Soviet pact of 1939 and the fall of France less than ten months later, George Marshall traversed the vast space between the status of an obscure Army officer, almost entirely unknown to a public traditionally distrustful of soldiers, to that of acknowledged military statesman, the repository of an all but universal trust.

It was an astounding growth in stature, and the explanation of it is to be found in a single word—character. Professional skill there was, in the highest degree, and it was recognized; but competence, no matter how brilliant, does not inspire such faith as was given Marshall. Intelligence? Marshall's intellectual capacity was equaled by that of few of his contemporaries, but intelligence is no more valid than skill as the explanation of that trust which transcended respect, and was more than confidence.

There was a deeper quality found in Marshall. It was a compound of self-discipline, of moral courage, of simplicity of speech and manner, of absolute and transparent honesty, of self-effacement and a disarming frankness. It was these attributes which confirmed in the minds of the people Marshall's right to the great position he held, so that the office and the public could be served by his intelligence and by a superb military competence, forged and tempered by the disappointing years.

The prestige would continue to grow—Marshall himself would continue to grow, in breadth of vision and depth of understanding—during the rushing and climactic years which followed; but it was established by the summer of 1940.

The effect that Marshall produced on Congressional committees, on the crowds of people at one of his rare public appearances, was one of unaffected simplicity, of unconscious candor and modesty. But was the simplicity unaffected in reality, were the candor and modesty unconscious? They were undoubtedly reflections of native attitudes, but there can be no doubt that there was art in the production of that effect. As Marshall's continued and demonstrated interest in the enlisted men who had served under him at any time was both a sincere and natural attitude and a calculated gesture, so were his simplicity and modesty at once natural and studied.

"Marshall is the most accomplished actor in the Army," said one official who was closely associated with him over a long period. "Everybody thinks MacArthur is, but he's not. The difference between them is that you always *know* MacArthur is acting!"

In Marshall, greatness appeared in the world, and greatness is never unconscious. It may be almost completely unselfish, and in Marshall it certainly was; but unconscious, never. In the words of a certain French officer and historical philosopher, still quite obscure when he penned them in 1932, "Nothing great is done without great men, and they are great for having willed it so." Charles de Gaulle might become a maladroit politician, and a difficult ally for reasons not chargeable solely to him, but as historical philosopher he had few contemporary peers, and this was a true thing well said.

The methods Marshall used to create this impact are difficult to trace, but his principal tool was knowledge—complete, detailed, demonstrable, irrefutable fact. One observant officer of his staff at Fort Benning came close to discovery of this method—but only close; and unfortunately, he probably cherished his false deduction as firm conviction.

Shortly after Marshall's departure from the Infantry School to take his brief command assignment at Fort Screven, a group of officers at the school were discussing him. Their comments were a mounting chorus of praise, until one dissenter spoke up. He, it developed, did not admire or respect Marshall, because he had noticed that Marshall never committed himself in conference on any controversial question until he learned the official War Department attitude on it. He was howled down indignantly. He was, in fact, wrong; but he had been on the verge of perception. It was true that Marshall frequently did not commit himself quickly on controversial planning questions; but it was not the "official" attitude from the War Department he waited for, it was the opportunity and the time to possess himself of sufficient knowledge of the subject on which to form a judgment he could support and defend with certainty.

For Marshall, throughout his career, was quite careful to commit himself only when he knew he was right, and could prove it. This was in great part the result of an inner necessity to know himself to be right, but it was also a calculated policy aimed at acquiring the respect and confidence of his colleagues and his superiors. It was by Marshall's conscious intent that his superiors never encountered a flaw in his reasoning, or in his judgments and decisions. He wanted not only to be right, but to have the reputation. How subtly he accomplished that purpose is indicated by the fact that only a very few officers who knew him for many years and in many situations were aware of it. And, of course, it was no mere vanity, for Marshall never offered the appearance of knowledge until he had the substance.

This reluctance to be forced into an intuitive solution, an offhand answer, was encountered by President Roosevelt soon after Marshall came to Washington, but before the unexpected 10,000-plane announcement. On that occasion, Marshall was pushed to a confession that he had no judgment of the matter at hand, a thing that rarely happened. The question was Assistant Secretary Johnson's recommendation that $1,400,000,000 be spent to expand the Air Corps, with emphasis on heavy bombers. The official War Department program was still to limit heavy bomber purchases to twelve B-17's. The President had not yet made up his mind, and the subject was under discussion at a White House conference. After protracted argument, he turned to Marshall and asked the attitude of the Deputy Chief of Staff.

"I don't go as far as Secretary Johnson's memorandum for $1,400,-

000,000," Marshall replied, "but I do go farther than Secretary Woodring's proposal."

"How much farther?" the President asked.

"I don't know."

It was a truthful answer. Marshall did not know. He was feeling his way through the morass of problems which had accumulated in the Army during years of neglect. He was remembering that Johnson's program would mean embarking on the expenditure of billions for an air force, while the Infantry lacked modern rifles. It would be easier to get appropriations for air power than for anything else the Army needed, but there was a limit on the ability of the small Air Corps to handle increase. Mere numbers did not mean an air force. Moreover, a powerful air force, without corollary development of other arms, meant imbalance and possible disaster, not a war team and probable victory if the United States should become embroiled in war. There were so many things, less dramatic and less photogenic than airplanes, which were no less vital to sound military preparation. The problem was one he described in a speech made about that time at the opening of the Air Corps Tactical School at Maxwell Field, Alabama, on October 1, 1938.

"Military victories," he told the students, "are not gained by a single arm—though the failures of an arm or service might well be disastrous—but are achieved through the efforts of all arms and services welded into an Army team. . . .

"The most difficult problem for the War Department is the determination of the best organization for the Army, within the limits of the funds available. . . . With us, geographical location and the international situation make it literally impossible to find definite answers for such questions as: who will be our enemy in the next war; in what theater of operations will that war be fought; and what will be our national objective at the time? These uncertainties lead inevitably to the conclusion that the only sensible policy for us to follow is to maintain a conservatively balanced force for the protection of our own territory against any probable threat during the period the vast but latent resources of the United States, in men and material, are being mobilized."

Few if any of the students in that first class at the Tactical School were aware of the controversy then in progress in Washington, and accordingly they did not realize how completely frank Marshall was being when he told them that "it is no exaggeration to state that the War Department is devoting more study to the size and composition of the Air Corps component of the Army team than to any other single subject. . . ." They were, however, trained officers, preparing to begin the consideration of advanced problems of the air arm, concerned with combined operations with other combat elements, and so able to comprehend the enormous responsibilities implied by the words that followed. These words, incidentally, presented in terms of current problems one of the most succinct statements of the reason for a general staff since the days of Elihu Root.

Marshall suggested to these airmen:

Sit down sometime and try to balance all the factors concerned with the national defense—including limited appropriations—and then attempt to outline the organization for a balanced army. Divorce yourself for the moment from the Air Corps and assume that the responsibility for the decisions regarding national defense rests solely on your shoulders. Conscientiously consider the limitations imposed by annual appropriations—and weigh carefully the necessity and requirements for each arm, including the present problem of archaic equipment for which there are no replacement funds. Having reached a general conclusion, which checks with probable appropriations and the basic law, then set up, within those limits, the air force that you feel will best meet our requirements. Be conservative as to the powers of aviation and honest as to its limitations.

Your first decision will probably be to equip your air organization with modern matériel. That is a sound decision, but how are you going to carry it out? Aviation matériel is extremely costly; it takes a long time to produce; and—remember this—is rapidly outmoded. Can you afford to discard the expensive matériel you have on hand for yet more modern types? Another consideration: the more costly the plane, the fewer of them you can have, and for each plane, guns, instruments, bombs, ammunition and maintenance must be provided. Study the emergency situations you think we may be required to meet, and then decide on the proportion of plane types to meet those situations. Is it more desirable to have a large number of small planes or a small number of large planes? Consider the major emergency problem of training of pilots rapidly, or rather, the use of rapidly trained pilots; and that your air force may be required to operate in theaters where airdromes are limited in number and size. In view of these factors, are combat planes, simple to operate and rugged in construction, indicated? Is it wise to sacrifice desirable technical features in order to obtain planes with special characteristics? There are almost unlimited permutations and combinations to resolve into an accepted solution.

You must set aside funds for research and development, and for the maintenance of training and personnel, year in and year out. We have a very fine commercial air system and splendid naval aviation. What effect will these have on the solution of your problem? The questions I have outlined are not academic—far from it, they are before the War Department for consideration every day.

This was one of Marshall's first public appearances after he became Deputy Chief of Staff. A month later, he reviewed for an Armistice Day crowd at Brunswick, Maryland, some of the failures of the United States in its past wars due to lack of public understanding of the time required to equip and train armies. He reminded his listeners that a year or more was required to manufacture most of the weapons of war—"no matter how many billions of dollars Congress places at our disposal on the day war is declared, they will not buy ten cents' worth of war matériel for delivery under twelve months, and a great deal of it will require a year and a half to manufacture."

Addressing the National Rifle Association in Washington on February 3, 1939, Marshall spoke of the unprecedented situation created in the world by the fact that Germany, rearming since 1935 after being completely stripped of armaments by the Treaty of Versailles, became the first great power in history possessing vast forces equipped entirely with the newest and most modern devices. The penalty of enforced disarmament had become a boon, freeing the Nazis of those financial economy considerations which impelled other nations to cling to outmoded but still serviceable supplies. He stressed, also, the danger of forgetting that all of Germany's rearmament was not concerned with those spectacular new weapons which showed up in the picture supplements—"We have all heard how many planes Germany has and what vast numbers she can produce, but I doubt if very many have learned that for more than two years she has turned out a million rounds of artillery ammunition a week!" This led him to the imperative need of first-class men and thorough training for the infantry, the foot soldiers on whom the final decision rested.

". . . I think the common belief is that the most quickly created instrument of war is the infantry regiment. Yet, I would say that we have lost more lives and been delayed more in battle by the acceptance of this doctrine than for any other purely military reason." The most thorough and rigorous training was essential, not because training could approximate battle conditions or actually send a soldier into battle completely prepared for it, but because it could produce the discipline and leadership which enabled infantry to meet the terror and conquer it. "In ordinary training little that the infantryman does closely simulates what actually happens on the battlefield, and what is more important, the most serious errors or lacks of the peacetime training can seldom be made apparent in that training, or even in maneuvers; because until the leader or individual has once been submerged with hostile fire—bullet, shell and bomb—and left apparently unsupported in an exposed position, and has found himself utterly unable to secure any artillery fire or machine-gun fire, or other supporting action, he will never appreciate the special importance to infantry—above all other arms of services—of discipline and leadership, and of communications; and their absolute determining effect on the battlefields."

During this preparatory period, when the contest was on to succeed Craig, and Marshall was being pushed to the fore by his many advocates, his work as Deputy Chief of Staff was to a very large extent concerned with those essential matters of supply procurement and industrial mobilization which appealed very little to this man who wanted to command troops. But some of his public speeches of necessity dealt with the urgency of these questions, and when the emergency expansion appeal of the President in January 1939 was being considered by the Congressional committees, Marshall appeared before them to make a thorough exposition of the need for orderly development of the industrial program and the need for appropriations to supply both immediate requirements and "educational orders" to give manufacturers preparatory experience in the production of equipment to meet exacting military standards.

In an appearance before the Senate Military Committee toward the end of February 1939, Marshall detailed some of the glaring deficiencies in matériel, particularly in antiaircraft guns, field artillery, and modern rifles for the initial protective force—the screen of Regular Army and National Guard behind which the country could mobilize for war.

"I repeat," he told the senators, "that it is of vital importance that we have modern equipment for this initial protective force of the Regular Army and the National Guard; that we modernize our artillery; that we replace our 34-year-old rifles with more modern weapons; that we have the antitank and the antiaircraft matériel in the actual hands of the troops; that we have the necessary reserves of ammunition; and that these matters be regarded—and I should like to make this as emphatic as possible—as fundamental to the entire proposition of national defense."

Marshall also did some skillful ducking of senatorial questions on the Army's attitude toward the purchase of American military equipment by foreign governments. A considerable flurry of excited questioning had been raised by the news that a French purchasing agent had been killed in the crash of an experimental Douglas attack bomber in California. Because it was expedient politically to make it appear that the military departments were not concerned with such foreign missions, an elaborate scheme had been devised under which the foreign missions operated in the United States under the formal aegis of the Treasury's procurement division. Much of the Congressional disturbance was, at least on the surface, due to fears that American military secrets might be given away. The truth was that the United States possessed almost no military secrets except the carefully guarded Norden bombsight, and the military departments welcomed the foreign purchases which expanded the nation's munitions capacity. They could not say so frankly, but they approved any British or French contracts which did not interfere with actual deliveries to the Army.

None of these speeches and statements by Marshall received any widespread attention, although the groundwork for future confidence was laid during this period at the White House and in Congress. Marshall was still a virtual stranger to the public when the President nominated him in April to succeed Craig. After that, the attention of the public and Congress was focused more directly on the Deputy Chief of Staff, and by the time he returned from his good-will mission to Brazil in June—the United States already was gravely concerned about Nazi infiltration in South America and the danger to the Panama Canal—his name had become familiar, if his great abilities had not. Then, on July 1, 1939, Craig began his terminal leave before retirement, and Marshall became Acting Chief of Staff. The authority and the responsibility were now his, and the actual assumption of the title of Chief of Staff and its temporary rank of general on September 1 would be a mere incident.

What was the job? Marshall's speeches and statements during the preceding months had outlined its fundamentals—the orderly development of a balanced combat team, the selection and training of leaders, the prompt acquisition of full equipment for the initial protective force of 400,000 men, the acquisition of critical reserves for the larger general mobilization, the planning of industrial mobilization, and the education of key industries in military production by means of small orders.

It is worth while to examine the machine he inherited as the means for accomplishing this job. At the top—his planning, advisory, and co-ordinating group—was the War Department General Staff of one hundred eighteen officers, including ten from the Officers' Reserve Corps and the National Guard. There were the arms and services, six arms or combat branches, and nine services, or supply and administrative branches, each headed by a chief with direct access to Marshall. There were the National Guard Bureau, the nine Corps Areas, the General Headquarters Air Force, the overseas Departments—Hawaii, Panama, and Puerto Rico—directly under the Chief of Staff. It was a complicated mechanism to control, and would grow even more complicated before it was subjected to drastic overhaul.

Even the semblance of control over this intricate device to which the national safety was anchored would have been impossible without the General Staff. Plagued by the anomalies inherent in a purpose to co-ordinate without the possession of command authority, the Staff nonetheless had functioned so well that by the time Marshall became its chief the last semblance of distrust of this body had disappeared and its value was taken for granted. A tendency to compartmented planning which would have produced chaos in mobilization had been discovered and checked by Woodring as Assistant Secretary in 1933, and the basic problem of industrial mobilization restudied and closely integrated to man-power and training proposals on a sound basis.

The planning had even extended to complete integration of civilian as well as military resources for national defense, the Staff avoiding the political dangers implicit in such thinking by the conclusion that, while the national policy on such subjects was completely outside the jurisdiction of the military establishment, study of techniques and methods to implement any policy the Congress and the President might be likely to adopt was a proper and necessary activity. If, in the end, industrial mobilization would not follow the General Staff plan, the planners in the early thirties could hardly have been expected to foresee such extraordinary developments as the lend-lease program; and their work was not wasted, for it supplied exhaustive advance studies which were invaluable in the programs actually adopted. It was well for the United States that the War Department General Staff had done this work; for while industrial mobilization is indubitably the responsibility of the civil rather than the military authorities, the unfortunate fact was that no civil agency existed to assume it, and none of sufficient scope would appear on the scene until well after the mobilization program had been accomplished and production was in high gear.

General MacArthur, while Chief of Staff, had noted also the tendency of the five General Staff divisions to grow into self-contained small bureaus, and by initiating the General Council, at which the principal staff officers met occasionally for the pooling of ideas, had begun the same kind of integration of military planning as Woodring had initiated in the industrial mobilization phases. The five divisions, each headed by an Assistant Chief of Staff, were responsible for the top-level planning and co-ordination of all Army activities. Personnel (G-1) formulated policies on the enlistment, promotion and discharge of all Army personnel, on supervision of enemy aliens and prisoners of war, on such things as decorations and awards. Military Intelligence (G-2) collected, assessed, and distributed military information, formulated the policies on military topographical surveys and maps, supervised the military attachés at foreign capitals, governed the use of codes and ciphers, had charge of military censorship, and at this time was responsible also for public relations. Operations and Training (G-3) planned the organization of Army units, their disposition, determined the types and allowances of equipment, prepared the policies for and supervised training. Supply (G-4) had the planning job for real-estate purchases, construction, manufacture, and distribution of equipment and supplies, disbursement of War Department funds, and preparation of appropriations estimates, transportation. War Plans Division was responsible for all planning for the use of the Army in theaters of operations; in the event of war, the Chief of Staff was expected to take the field as commanding general of the field forces, and this division would go with him as his General Headquarters Staff. The greatest defect of General Staff planning in the years between the two great wars probably was the failure to foresee that this GHQ plan would not work in a war on more than one front, and to envision the possibility of such a war. The least effective of the General Staff divisions was

G-2, and the shortcomings of intelligence would prove to be the country's gravest failure, not only prior to the second World War, but throughout its course.

In sum, however, the General Staff which Marshall took over in 1939 was a smoothly operating and very effective organization. Its conservatism could be altered to a wide degree by changes in personnel, and Marshall moved promptly to make those changes. Little more than a month after he became Acting Chief of Staff, for the most outstanding instance, the heavy bombardment expert who had been "busted" a year earlier for his advocacy of ideas not approved by Woodring and Craig was promoted again and brought back to Washington, and Brigadier General Frank M. Andrews became Assistant Chief of Staff, G-3. That appointment signalized Marshall's preoccupation with what was to be for the next two years his primary interest, the creation of a modern and balanced fighting team. Holding procurement to be the problem of the Assistant Secretary, who was charged by statute with that responsibility, Marshall would pay less attention than they deserved to supply matters. Logistics, that science of the transportation and supply of troops in military operations, concerned him greatly; but the procurement phases he left willingly—when he could—to other hands and minds.

Shortly before Marshall's nomination was announced in April, he went to the office of Brigadier General Lorenzo D. Gasser, then G-1, to tell Gasser that the appointment was going to be made and to ask him to become his deputy when he took over Craig's post. Gasser protested that he was too old, that he had only a year left to serve before his retirement, but Marshall insisted that his experience would be invaluable in helping the new Chief of Staff get started, and Gasser finally consented.

After Marshall assumed active charge of the Army, Gasser found the new Chief was dissatisfied with the Army organization. There were too many officers, representing too many and varied activities, reporting to the Chief of Staff and burdening him with details. Marshall wanted an organization which would provide him with a few channels through which he could receive the broad picture of

Army affairs necessary to arrive at decisions on general policy. His first attempt to arrive at this, following Gasser's retirement the next April, would be to appoint two more deputies; this would prove to be unsatisfactory, and would be followed by a drastic reorganization, but even in 1939 Marshall already was thinking in terms of simplifying the Staff and the command structure.

For Marshall was not only a superb staff officer, he was also a commander. It is a rare combination. The men around him were discovering that the office of Chief of Staff was occupied by a man who could see both the forest and the trees. He could turn from a staff problem of great detail to the immediate consideration of a broad policy, and make a prompt decision. On matters of action and operations, the decision would come with a lightning rapidity that contrasted sharply with his old habit of deliberation before committing himself to a planning theory. Men whose capacities were such that they found themselves assigned repeatedly to staff details frequently lost the capacity for command because they could not drop the staff habit of carefully balancing minutiae. This was not true of Marshall, and the reason probably was that, while most of his career had been spent on staff work, his desire always had been to command, and his staff work accordingly had invariably been accomplished in the light of his own knowledge of command realities.

The little methods and idiosyncrasies began to impress themselves on the officers around him this autumn and winter of 1939. They discovered, for instance, that Marshall's letters, no matter to whom addressed, must without exception be subscribed "Faithfully yours." They learned that the Chief preferred to have problems reduced to their barest essentials and presented to him orally. He would consider the problem a moment in silence, then give an oral decision. The officer receiving the decision would retire soberly and with dignity, then throw the office staff into a frenzy as he dictated precisely what the Chief had said before he could forget a single word, and see to it that sufficient copies were typed immediately to get one to every individual who might conceivably ever be involved or interested in the matter; for the General had a comprehensive and finite memory, and the unlucky officer who presented to him as a problem any question on which he had once given a decision was in for something akin to a verbal flaying.

The staff found, particularly, that the Chief was capable of truly explosive wrath if he was peeped at. Not only did he forbid the tiny peephole through which most secretaries in the War Department could check on the comings and goings in the boss's office; but it soon became known that anyone who opened the door of his office was expected to open it far enough to walk through and close it behind him. It made no difference if Marshall was in conference, and it made no difference with whom he was conferring; the newcomer could seat himself quietly near the door and wait until the conversation ended or the Chief called him over to the desk. But if he opened that door so much as a crack, it was at his own peril that he failed to complete the entry.

The sheer rapidity of Marshall's thinking gave many people the initial impression that he was "playing things off the cuff," but the actual instances in which he did so were extremely rare. Gradually the staff began to realize that Marshall's mental processes were not only brilliant; they were also thorough. This man who had taken so much knocking around not only examined technical aspects of the situations referred to him, but thought of motives behind the actions and recommendations, of the methods which would be required in any solution which occurred to him, of the individuals to whom it would be necessary to appeal to clinch his decision, of what prejudices they might have which he would need to overcome. It was the staff officer's thinking of every detail, but thinking at a fantastic speed, and with unmatched powers of analysis. The decision arrived at, it was stated in lucid terms of the greatest simplicity, the General speaking rapidly but plainly. With such clarity of thought and speech at his command, it was not surprising that Marshall grew impatient at the slightest sign of muddled thinking or verbose presentation. When a conference threatened to deviate from sense in this fashion, Marshall was likely to interrupt with an almost deferential and half-apologetic "Would it not be fair to state . . . ?" and then proceed to formulate the other man's idea with a precision the original speaker could not attain.

Marshall was obsessed with the need to rid staff studies, reports, orders, and all Army paper of excess verbiage, and the staff noticed with secret amusement that the first thing he did when a paper was presented for his consideration was to pick up a pencil. As he read, he edited it with all the speed and skill of an accomplished newspaper copy editor. Yet, for all this attention to details—sometimes apparently petty details—Marshall never lost sight of the proportions of the main task, and he was a brilliant administrator. That is, he had the capacity to choose able assistants, assign their jobs, and leave them alone as long as they performed the jobs properly. If they failed in important respects to measure up to his exacting standards, they were removed; but if their work pleased him, there was no interference from Marshall in the details of their operations. Equally important, he backed their decisions with his authority.

The wary alertness which America's military leaders had trained on the affairs of Europe for several years changed into a grim dread when the Soviet-German ten-year nonaggression treaty was signed on August 23, 1939. To the majority of Americans, this might be merely a couple of unpleasant dictatorships agreeing to carve up the coast of the Baltic between them, but to the military leaders it was as clear and ominous an announcement as a declaration of war. They, at least, knew that what Hitler had accomplished was to dispel the perennial German fear of a two-front war, to guarantee that the eastern border would be tranquil while the Nazi military machine was turned against Western Europe. That the first blow fell—on the day Marshall became Chief of Staff, September 1—against Poland and crushed that nation in five weeks did not alter the fact, plain to Marshall and his staff, that Hitler's objective was in the West. When France and Britain declared war on Germany after the invasion of Poland, it was merely the belated acceptance by them of an obvious and inescapable fact.

The fact was obvious and inescapable to Marshall, and also to

President Roosevelt. The latter, on September 8, declared a limited National Emergency and authorized the expansion of both the Regular Army and the National Guard. When Marshall became Acting Chief of Staff on July 1, the Regular Army consisted of 13,808 officers and 174,079 enlisted men. To build up the Air Corps and strengthen the Panama Canal garrison, Congress already had authorized an enlisted strength of 210,000, and a ten-year program to bring the officer strength to 16,716. Now in September, the President by executive order directed that the Regular Army be brought to an enlisted strength of 227,000, and the National Guard recruited to a total of 235,000.

In the light of later expansions, these appear pathetically small; but they were of incalculable value. They permitted Marshall and the staff to reorganize four incomplete square divisions of the Regular Army into three of the new and smaller triangular divisions which the Army had been studying for two years (the "square" division contained four infantry regiments and the "triangular" three). The streamlined division lacked some of the supporting artillery and other units which were an organic part of the square division, and so there was an urgent necessity to set up these units as corps troops. Fortunately, the emergency proclamation permitted this also, and for the first time in its peacetime history, the United States Army actually was able to assemble the peace complement of corps troops for one army corps. The emergency proclamation increased the number of armory drills for the National Guard, and more importantly, permitted the Guard units to be called out in the fall for an extra week of field training.

The next vital need was for maneuvers, and Marshall and his staff went after the money for them. While the division is the basic army organization, the basic battle unit is the army corps, consisting of two or more divisions with auxiliary arms and services—the "corps troops"—and the purpose of the maneuvers was not so much to harden the men in the ranks and accustom them to operating in large groups, although that was a useful and desirable aspect of them, but to give the higher commanders and staffs essential training in the technique, tactics, teamwork, and supply of large units in the field. The maneuvers were battle practice, but their purpose was not primarily to toughen the GI; it was primarily to give Marshall a chance to select the Omar Bradleys, the Dwight Eisenhowers, the George Pattons, the Joseph Stilwells—that unparalleled series of commanders which led American divisions, corps, armies, and army groups to victory—and to test the men who would comprise their staffs. In the spring of 1940, the war in Europe and the adroit and persuasive arguments of the Chief of Staff before the Congressional committees had made it possible to assemble 70,000 troops of the Regular Army in the field for the first genuine corps and army maneuvers in the history of the United States. The Command Post Exercise was dealing at last with men, trucks, guns, tanks, hospitals, supply dumps, and all the paraphernalia of troops in action, and not just with words and ideas.

By February 1940, Marshall was explaining to Congress that while the War Department's current objective was confined to completing the equipment for the Regular Army and the National Guard, it was urgently necessary to think immediately of providing critical equipment—ammunition, rifles, tanks, and artillery particularly—for the Protective Mobilization Plan Force of 750,000 men. Furthermore, he said, the procurement of this matériel "should take precedence over desired increases in personnel."

"As to the existing crisis abroad," he told the House Appropriations Committee, "we must face the facts. Any major developments there should be paralleled by added precautions in this country. If the situation grows more desperate, we should add to the numbers of seasoned troops in the Regular Army and to the strength of the National Guard. If Europe blazes in the late spring or summer, we must put our house in order before the sparks reach the Western Hemisphere. These should be but temporary measures, but they should be taken definitely, step by step, to prepare ourselves against the possibility of chaotic world conditions.

"To put it in another way, I am opposed to plunging into a sudden expansion of personnel to the limit of present authorizations, and I am equally opposed to the policy of waiting until the last moment and then attempting the impossible, from the viewpoint of the dominating time factor."

He was planning, with his staff—and he was warning the committee that his plans would call for more money—to complete a sixth triangular division, to transform the Army's one mechanized brigade into an armored division (he was already planning the Armored Force, also), to provide the special troops—heavy and antiaircraft artillery, engineers, signal, and so forth—for a second Army corps. "But," he added, "I repeat—this increase should come after the matériel requirements for the Protective Mobilization Plan Force have been provided."

Since the previous year, when Marshall as well as others had been skittish and evasive in discussing foreign munitions purchases in the United States, the outbreak of the expected war in Europe had altered the situation to the point that Marshall spoke boldly of the desirability of such purchases, and of the fact that they were closely co-ordinated with American military procurement and planning although still handled directly by the Treasury. In aircraft particularly, Marshall had taken the initiative in reducing planned purchases in order to avoid accumulating planes that might rapidly become obsolescent in the Air Corps reserve pool. The Army permitted Britain and France to take delivery on various combat types, in exchange for combat information which could be applied as improvements when the Air Corps stepped in again. Accordingly, he cut the budget estimate for 496 replacement planes to 166. Unfortunately, the House was impressed by the "phony war" of the winter instead of by Marshall's suggestion that Europe might blaze in the late spring or summer, and cut this minimum requirement to 57 planes.

But if Marshall did not get all he asked for from Congress that winter and spring, he got a very important and critical portion. More important, his incredible command of all the facts involved in the War Department planning and operations, his simple and unassuming manner, his patience under questioning that was not always sympathetic or even intelligent, built during that first year of his administration of the Army the esteem and trust which all factions in Congress gave to him in a measure unequaled by that accorded any other official of the government. Marshall never demanded, never threatened, never posed. He explained lucidly the problems confronting him and the responsibilities laid on him, asked for what he considered necessary to enable him to carry out his mission, and explained in detail the reasons for his requests. The congressmen before whom he appeared as witness, and more slowly the public at large, gradually became aware that this man was completely devoted to the public welfare, that here, in truth, was a democrat. He did not talk about the rights of man and the privileges of free citizens, but he showed by his every act and word that he deemed himself the servant of the civil government and the instrument of its policies. He did not suggest to the legislators where their duty lay. He gave them a complete and comprehensive report on their army, and took them into his confidence about his problems. The result was a universal confidence in him.

Those first painful months of the beginnings of preparation were the last—because of that confidence—in which he would have to plead for a minimum. The blaze in Europe which he had expected flared in April 1940, and the next crisis Marshall would have to face would not be concerned with getting an Army, but with holding it together.

On April 9, the phony war came suddenly alive. Denmark and Norway were overrun by the dictator with no further territorial ambitions in Europe. At dawn on May 10, the Nazi armies and *Luftwaffe* struck on the West Front. It took them just five brutal days to shatter and subjugate the Netherlands, just eighteen days to crush Belgium. On the first day, the Germans breached the French defenses at Sedan, and by May 21 they were on the Channel at Abbeville. Six days later, the British Navy, under a canopy of Royal Air Force fighters, began the evacuation of a beaten army of 320,000 men, one-third of them French, from the beaches of Dunkerque. Winston Churchill had succeeded Neville Chamberlain as Prime

Minister, to offer to his own people nothing but "blood, toil, tears and sweat" and to the French people an organic union with Britain. Paul Reynaud took over from Daladier, and Weygand from Gamelin; but it was too late. On June 16, Marshal Pétain became Premier of France, rejected a proposal to withdraw the government to North Africa and continue the struggle, and on June 22, his representatives signed a humiliating armistice at Compiègne while Hitler danced a gleeful jig. France, the heart of Western European civilization and regarded as the strongest land power on the continent, had ceased to exist as a power at all in just forty-four days.

The jolt of that collapse shook even the military leaders in America. The nation awoke suddenly to a realization that the Atlantic might not, after all, be a sufficient barrier; but to the President and his military advisers, the frightening aspect of this disaster was that Britain was, except for morale, in little better case than France. She had rescued most of her expeditionary force and a large number of French soldiers as well, but she had lost all of her heavy military equipment—nothing heavier than a machine gun had been brought away from Dunkerque—and much of her other equipment also. An urgent appeal came from the Prime Minister to the President for any arms that could be supplied for the defense of England and—since the appeal came after Dunkerque and before the French armistice—for the defense of what was left of France, if it held out.

Action was prompt. To Marshall, and to Admiral Harold R. Stark, the Chief of Naval Operations, the one immediate imperative was to prevent the fall of Britain. That bastion was essential to the defense of the United States. However much Americans might like or dislike the British, there was no sentiment whatever involved in the strategic consideration. Britain was essential, first as a base from which the British fleet could control the Atlantic (most of the American fleet was in the Pacific), and second as the base from which Anglo-American air forces and armies could get back to the continent in a war in which it was now almost beyond question that the United States would eventually become involved. It was absolutely beyond question if Britain were conquered.

While arguments at high levels sought to settle the question whether a nonbelligerent government could legally sell arms to a belligerent, or should turn them over to a private corporation to sell, Marshall ordered Major General Charles M. Wesson, Chief of Ordnance, and Major General Richard Moore, Assistant Chief of Staff, to go over the entire list of reserve ordnance and munitions stocks. The result was the sale of 500,000 Enfield rifles, 900 75-millimeter field guns, 80,000 machine guns, 130,000,000 rounds of ammunition for the rifles, 1,000,000 rounds for the 75's, some bombs, and small quantities of TNT and smokeless powder to the United States Steel Export Corporation, which in turn sold them to the British government. The Army did not wait for the contracts to be signed—by the time that was done, the material was waiting on the docks at Raritan, New Jersey, to be loaded aboard the ships which the British ordered there.

The strict legality of the transaction was a matter of considerable doubt. Woodring would not assume the responsibility, and resigned as Secretary of War. Assistant Secretary Johnson, as Acting Secretary, approved the necessary orders, and averred later that the only authority he had was a "chit" from the President promising a pardon if he should go to jail for the action. But the material was on its way within a week, and it enabled Britain partially to rearm her field forces, and arm the Home Guard, while British factories worked overtime to make up the equipment losses in France.

A few days later, Colonel Myron C. Cramer, who in another eighteen months would become the Judge Advocate General of the Army, came to Johnson and suggested that the equivocal legal position could be cleared by the process of declaring the transferred material to be surplus. This suggestion was passed along to the President, and the matter was argued at a conference in the White House. Would it not be better, suggested Johnson, just to defend the action on the basis that it had saved Britain?

"Oh, go ahead and declare it surplus," the President replied. "That's easier to defend."

Johnson expected to become Secretary after Woodring's departure; but the President, with a shrewd eye on the political value of a coalition cabinet for the emergency—particularly in a presidential campaign year; but also with a profound insight into the character of man needed in the position, asked Henry L. Stimson to take Woodring's place. So, in July 1940, a man who was Marshall's equal in character and in devotion to the public interest became Secretary of War. Intrigue and clash of purpose and intent disappeared from the Department, and an almost perfect team of statesmen began to pull together.

XVI

The Blow Falls

The destruction of France and the peril of Britain loosened at once the purse strings that Congress had been reluctant to untie. Two recommendations by the President in May for emergency supplemental funds totaling approximately $2,000,000,000 for the military establishment, far from being whittled by Congress, actually were revised upward by the Senate and the House to raise the authorized strength of the Army to 375,000.

The War Department, led by Marshall and Stimson, already was seeking not only to bring the National Guard into Federal service promptly, but to initiate compulsory selective service. The increase of authorized strength permitted Marshall to organize the skeleton units into which the selectees would be fed, and the money permitted early orders to manufacturers for clothing and equipment to be ready by October.

The request for federalization of the Guard was made in May, with the intent to train its units in summer camps while cantonments were being built for the expanded Army. By the time cold weather set in, the semipermanent quarters would be ready for the first increment of selectees, and the Regular Army and the Guard would be in position to supply training cadres for later increments. However, to quote the admirably restrained words of Marshall himself on the subject, "the democratic processes of legislation resulted in a prolonged debate on these two measures, which continued throughout the summer." When Congressional approval finally was given, everything had to be done at once—induction of the Guard, hasty and even frantic construction of camps, and induction of selectees. One or two of the hurriedly selected camp sites proved to be errors of judgment, and the Army came in for some criticism, but the astonishing aspect of that winter's building was that so little was wrong with a program undertaken so late and carried to completion with such urgency. Marshall and his advisers considered seriously the possibility of postponing Selective Service inductions, but decided that such a delay, following their urgent requests for the legislation, would jeopardize their relations with Congress. The inductions accordingly began before the Army was ready for them.

Without minimizing the work, particularly of public education, accomplished by civic-minded groups in preparing the country for peacetime compulsory service, the conclusion is inescapable that Congress finally approved this extraordinary step in military preparations because Marshall was Chief of Staff. It was the complete and towering integrity of the General which made that essential program possible.

Marshall was making other plans, also. In July 1940 the General Headquarters of the Army were established at the War College in Washington, and charged with planning and directing the training of the expanding Army, under the direction of Major General Lesley J. McNair. This appointment was a notable example of Marshall's capacity to use to the fullest the abilities of men who disagreed completely with his military philosophy. McNair was known not only as perhaps the most brilliant intellectually of all regular officers, but as a complete advocate of the professional military force, with a cold contempt for those citizen forces of which Marshall was the advocate and champion. He was to write, later, a scathing condemnation of National Guard officers in a report to the Chief of Staff. Marshall suppressed the communication, but kept McNair in the training assignment which he filled superbly.

Significantly, no commanding general was named for the General Headquarters. Major General McNair became its Chief of Staff—the clear implication was that Marshall would be Commanding General when GHQ advanced from its training responsibilities to its theater of war operations. But Marshall never got the title of Commanding General, largely because Stimson, onetime law partner of Elihu Root and thoroughly imbued with Root's concept of a Chief of Staff who was an adviser with none of the attributes of the traditional General in Chief of the Army, blocked the double title for Marshall. He felt strongly on the subject, and never suspected that Marshall felt equally strongly that the title, as well as the fact of command direction, should be given him—particularly in view of the later development in which Admiral Ernest J. King held the titles of Chief of Naval Operations and Commander in Chief of the Fleet.

Marshall was an "operator," and thought consistently in terms of command. If, however, he wanted a Commanding General of the Army, he wanted this job combined with that of Chief of Staff in the War Department, not used to establish a dual control of the military forces. Oddly enough, such a dual control was seriously contemplated by President Roosevelt, who wanted General MacArthur to return from the Philippines and take the commanding general's job. He had started trying to entice MacArthur to return soon after the former Chief of Staff went to Manila, and MacArthur had finally applied for voluntary retirement in 1937 to make sure that he could not be ordered to return to the United States. As the situation in Europe grew grave and finally exploded in war, the President returned to the idea of bringing MacArthur home. He was reported to have gone so far as to prepare an order which in effect, if not in name, would have re-established the office of Commanding General. In this proposal he had the support of Assistant Secretary Johnson, who argued that the excellence of the A.E.F. in the first World War was directly attributable to the conflict between General Pershing and General March. Roosevelt was a poor enough administrator to find merit in that argument, when in fact the reverse was true—the final excellence of the A.E.F. came about in spite of, not because of, that conflict. At any rate, the order never was issued, for what reason there can be at present only surmise—MacArthur's reluctance, Marshall's opposition, or possibly the discovery by the President that the National Defense Act made its legality questionable. Whatever the reason, it was the nation's great good fortune that the idea was abandoned. Nothing could possibly have been more disastrous to the national defense than a dual control of the Army, particularly if vested in those two able and positive officers.

As the vast expansion program developed impetus, the tasks involved in maintaining control over the Army multiplied enormously. The Corps Areas were relieved of their command functions over tactical units in order to permit them to devote their full time to the increasingly complex administrative duties, and the tactical control passed to GHQ and, under it, to the four field armies. Four Defense Commands were set up also, and the air force setup underwent successive changes. The top organization, although it functioned extremely well under the sure control of such a master as Marshall, was entirely too complex, and burdened him with unnecessary details. As early as the spring of 1940, the matter had been the subject of serious staff discussions. Some officers proposed three deputies. General William H. Bryden already was scheduled to succeed Gasser as deputy, and it was suggested that General Richard C. Moore be moved up from his G-4 spot to become a second deputy in charge of supply and construction planning, and that General Arnold be named a third deputy for air matters, in addition to his job of Chief of Air Corps. Gasser opposed the suggestion, countering with a recommendation that the four "G's" be promoted from brigadier to major generals, and given command authority. Marshall's temporary solution was the three-deputy plan, but it was unsatisfactory, particularly when Bryden, the senior deputy, proved unsuited for the primary job of a deputy—that of the ruthless "hatchet man" who keeps problems from reaching his chief unless they involve questions of basic policy that no one else can determine. The search for an organization which would serve Marshall as he wished to be served would continue all through 1941.

Internal organization was a pressing problem, but there were others equally pressing. Marshall and Stark were seeking throughout that year a formula for unity of command in the overseas theaters, but with the best intent in the world finding themselves unable to bridge the artificial gap created by vested interests of the Army and Navy, and particularly that mysticism of the quarter-deck which held that only an admiral could exercise even strategic command over a fleet.

Marshall's complete grasp of the whole problem of creating and equipping an army drew men with problems and suggestions to him, and the gravitation placed on his desk many matters he was reluctant to decide. On the procurement side, particularly, there were many who felt that he failed to act promptly and vigorously on supply questions because he lacked personal interest in them. It seems more likely that Marshall, who was careful always to refrain from invasion of what he held to be prerogatives of the civilian secretariat (and by the same token was decidedly disinclined to accept suggestions from them on what he deemed strictly military questions), made it a point to keep his advice on procurement matters within the strict confines of correct protocol. The determination of requirements was a General Staff responsibility; but procurement to fill those requirements was the responsibility of the Assistant Secretary.

An instance was the Munitions Program of June 1940. Colonel James H. Burns was executive officer to Assistant Secretary Johnson, and he drafted a memorandum suggesting a basis for munitions procurement planning, sending it direct to Marshall. The Chief of Staff took no action on it until the matter was raised again some time later by Johnson. Johnson and Burns attended a munitions conference at the White House on June 11, 1940. One of the others present was William S. Knudsen, of the National Defense Advisory Commission, and Knudsen brought the conference down to bedrock with the question, "How much munitions productive capacity does this country need, and how rapidly must it become available?"

Johnson asked his executive officer for the answer to that one, and Burns got out the memorandum he had prepared and sent to Marshall, dusted it off, and gave it to the Assistant Secretary. Designed, not to gear a production program directly to a man-power induction schedule, but to create a reservoir of munitions strength, it proposed that the planning goal should be a rate of production sufficient to meet the needs of a ground army of 1,000,000 men and an air force with 9,000 planes a year by October 1, 1941, double that rate by January 1942, and double the second goal by April 1, 1942. It went to Knudsen with this endorsement from Marshall: "I concur in the above quantity objectives, but I consider it of imperative importance that means be found to advance the date for the needs of the first million, herein scheduled for October 1, 1941."

On June 18, Johnson told Knudsen that detailed programs had not been calculated, but a total cost of $11,000,000,000 was indicated, with a minimum appropriation of $5,000,000,000 needed to launch it. The program was whipped into shape during several succeeding conferences until a final meeting at the White House—attended by Johnson, Marshall, Knudsen, and Burns—agreed on procurement of all items needed to equip and maintain a million men on combat status, reserve stocks of important long-range items for a force of 2,000,000; to create facilities permitting production to supply 4,000,000; to procure approximately 16,000 airplanes with spare engines, parts, guns, ammunition, radios, and other equipment, and to provide productive capacity for 18,000 planes a year. After that decision on June 28, the staff worked day and night for three days to complete the detailed program which was delivered to Acting Secretary Johnson on July 1 by memorandum from Marshall. It called for expenditures of nearly $6,000,000,000, with almost $2,000,000,000 to be provided in cash. The President approved it July 3, and the work of drafting a message to the Congress was begun immediately. Some officials have criticized Marshall for failure to initiate action more promptly on this matter; it would appear, however, that he deliberately refrained from initiating action, leaving that to the Assistant Secretary whose responsibility it was, but endorsing the size of the proposed program and urging greater speed once the first step had been taken by the proper official.

When Stimson became Secretary, Johnson reluctantly resigned as Assistant Secretary, and Judge Robert P. Patterson left the Federal

Circuit Court of Appeals in New York to take the vacated post. In December 1940, Patterson became Under Secretary when that office was created to take over the duties of the Assistant Secretary concerning procurement, but this time by delegation of the Secretary's authority, not by statute. Under this reorganization and enlargement of the Department, the office of Assistant Secretary became one of general assistance to the Department chief, and the long-vacant office of Assistant Secretary of War for Air was filled again. In the event, John J. McCloy, who filled the first of these two positions, became the chief civilian official between the Secretary and the General Staff, and operated in the many politico-military fields which the growth of the Army and the progress of the war were to develop; while Robert A. Lovett, who took over the air job, became the driving force behind the augmentation of the long-range, heavy bombardment striking force.

Lovett came to the War Department in the autumn of 1940 as a Special Assistant to the Secretary. Member of a Wall Street banking firm, and a naval aviator in the first World War, he had come back from a 1940 summer trip to Europe with strong convictions about air power, and had equipped himself with a wealth of statistical ammunition in a subsequent tour of American aircraft factories. The first of his convictions was that air power would be the dominant factor in the war, and the second was that the strength of air power was in its offensive characteristics—there was no effective defense against air power except greater striking power which could halt the enemy air force at its source. Having observed them, he was convinced that the British and French approached air war, as they approached ground war, with a defensive bias.

Toward the end of December, Lovett prepared a memorandum embodying his ideas about the proper employment of air power, and suggesting a greatly enlarged heavy-bomber program to implement them. Stimson approved his proposal, and Lovett then tackled the Chief of Staff. To his delight, Marshall not only was convinced of the desirability of offensive striking power in the air, but was receptive to new organizational ideas to make it effective and became a tremendous help in piloting the big bomber program to completion. An army reorganization plan worked out in the summer of 1941 by the Air Staff became the basis for the reorganization which was effected later, giving the Army Air Forces virtual autonomy.

The expansion, and the shift of emphasis to long-range striking force, was not accomplished without opposition from the Navy. Naval representatives at a showdown conference in 1941 predicted that any attempt to produce as many as 500 heavy bombers a month would break the country and destroy industry. Naval opposition to the enlarging sphere of the Air Forces became strident when the employment of Army planes against enemy submarines came up for discussion. Nevertheless, an antisubmarine air patrol eventually was started, offensively to hunt the submarines down, instead of defensively to protect against them by convoy operations.

Early in 1941, guarded conversations were begun with British officials and military representatives concerning the probable nature of American operations in the event the United States was drawn into the war. The possibility of Japanese action in the Pacific was recognized by that time, and the chance—still considered remote—that the United States might find itself involved in war in both oceans. No commitments were made at these meetings, but when they ended it was generally understood that, in the event of involvement in both directions, Germany was the greater danger and the weight of American effort would be applied first to Europe.

As the threat to the United States grew graver with Germany's increasing dominance in Europe and the danger that she might move into Africa, particularly Dakar, and thus present an immediate menace to Brazil, Marshall's primary concern became the planning of expeditions to seize vital outposts quickly if the threat became more active. It was not easy to do, since there were restrictions on the use of Selective Service men and the National Guard outside the United States. The 5th Division was scheduled to go to Iceland, and the 1st Division was kept ready for expeditionary purposes also. In both, the number of selectees was kept at a minimum, the plan being to substitute regulars or volunteers for the selectees promptly if the need arose. The Panama garrison also could be used, and National Guard troops be sent to replace it in the Canal Zone. With these, Marshall figured he had approximately 40,000 men available for emergency expeditions, and suggested to Stimson this was a sufficient number to make a secret troop poll for volunteers—with the danger of leaks which would imperil security—unnecessary. In the event that the Nazis moved into Dakar, the Marines and the Army were poised to seize the Vichy-French island of Martinique in the Caribbean. An expedition commanded by Admiral Ernest J. King also was planned to seize the Azores, so that the United States would have a base for invasion if Britain succumbed, and Marshall was concerned with security measures on the sailing dates for the Army combat team which would be a part of this force, as well as the fact that the Army would have to lend six transports to the Navy to carry it.

By June Marshall was deep in planning for an expeditionary force to Europe—in 1943. The staff was at work on a strategical study of the capabilities and probable lines of action of Axis and friendly powers, which would provide a troop basis and a production basis for the Army of the United States. Shipping was the key problem in these studies—the bottoms on hand and scheduled for construction already were insufficient to keep up with British shipping losses. Shipping would govern the size of the expeditionary force, because shipping would determine how many tons of equipment and supplies could be carried to maintain it.

"How large an expeditionary force are you counting on in your estimate?" Stimson asked during one conference on the subject.

"I'm not sure—probably 500,000," the General replied.

By June it had been decided to use Marines instead of Army troops for the occupation of Iceland, but the Marines' equipment had to come from Army stocks—the virtually nonexistent Army stocks.

"My main battle is equipping the Marines," said Marshall dryly. "Whether we will have anything left after the British and the Marines get theirs, I do not know!"

There were the exasperations created by reports from industry that their planning for production could be made more efficient if the Army ordered in larger quantities, received in the knowledge that those same industries were resisting all pressure to reduce their normal commercial business so as to increase the current output of equipment already ordered, and desperately needed by an Army still less than half armed. There was the arrival of a Frenchman of dubious status and even more dubious information, although vouched for by Admiral Leahy, with suggestions that Weygand would join the Americans if they invaded North Africa in force. There was the mounting concern over morale of the Army, and the necessity to decide whether to keep the National Guard in Federal service and get rid of its overage and inefficient officers, or release the Guard and so avoid the political troubles to be expected from the weeding-out process. Inefficiency was not confined to the Guard, and Marshall was after legislation to let him get rid of Regular officers who failed to measure up to the standards required by grave emergency.

In mid-June of 1941, the question of aid to China was taking immediate precedence. Chennault's Flying Tigers organization was nearly a year old, but the Chinese were about to ask the United States to train 500 military pilots for them, and Marshall asked MacArthur about the possibility of doing the job in China. The Army was releasing more trained pilots to China, was using so many others in ferry services around the world that Lovett said the Air Corps could not reach either its twenty-five group program or its fifty-four group program unless some of these trained pilots were brought back. One hundred P-40 fighters had been allocated to the Chinese, but they required .30 caliber and .50 caliber ammunition, and the Army had none in either category to send with the planes. All of these points, and many others concerning the delivery of planes and the training of pilots for China, were thrashed out at a conference on June 10, the upshot of which was a report to the President informing him that the program he had approved fitted in almost none of its details. In the middle of the discussion, Stimson turned to Marshall.

Signal Corps Photo

TEHERAN CONFERENCE

Accompanied by Field Marshal Dill, Marshall greets Sir Archibald Clark-Kerr, British Ambassador to Moscow, while Harry Hopkins talks with Stalin and Voroshilov in the garden of the Soviet Embassy. During this four-day conference, Roosevelt named Eisenhower to the invasion command.

Signal Corps Photo

BEACHHEAD IN NORMANDY

Elated and smiling, Marshall warmly congratulates General Bradley as General Arnold looks on just after the invasion of France in June 1944.

"General Marshall," he asked, "what have you on this?"
"I have just a headache on this question," Marshall retorted.
Stimson nodded.
"Somewhat like mine!" he snapped.

Then, on June 22, the whole aspect of the war changed. Hitler, instead of launching the invasion of England which had been expected since the fall of France, attacked the Soviet Union. With that involvement, it seemed likely that the immediate danger to the United States in Europe and the Atlantic had been diverted—but there was no certainty as yet how long Russia could last. At an off-the-record press conference, the colonel in charge of the Intelligence Branch—that is, foreign intelligence—of G-2, explaining glibly that while the Russian was an excellent fighting man there was no indication his leadership "is any less moronic than it has been for many generations past," predicted flatly that "barring an act of God, of course Germany is going to win." That particular officer disappeared from the Washington scene with truly astonishing rapidity. Marshall was, in Marshall fashion, less dogmatic when he discussed the German attack on Russia at a meeting of War Department officials the day after it began.

"The question is," said the General, "whether or not the Russians are wise enough to withdraw and save their army, abandoning their own people if necessary; and whether they have arranged in an efficient manner for sabotage of the oil properties. . . .

"It is going to take some little time to determine just what the Russian set-up has been. We know that the Germans have taken every means they could for rapid conquest, rapid grabbing of the oilfields and other critical areas.

"We will not be able to determine anything positively for a number of days, particularly as to whether the Russians have learned any lessons in the way of controlling their large groups. They are lacking in qualified higher officers, and their lower ranking officers lack in education."

If the imminent danger of war seemed to have abated on the Atlantic side, the tension in the Pacific was mounting. Admiral

Nomura, the Japanese ambassador, had initiated "conversations" in Washington as early as March, but their continued campaigns in China and movements south along the eastern coast toward Indo-China made it abundantly clear that the Japanese would not consider the only solution of the Pacific trouble acceptable to the United States—cessation of Japanese hostilities in China, and withdrawal from the territory already seized.

In the midst of such pressing concerns, Marshall found the time to write the first of those three great biennial reports which have become a basic history of the American war effort. This first one was no ordinary report from a Chief of Staff—Marshall had, in fact, refused a year earlier to follow the established precedents and submit an annual report. Now, however, he had a pressing reason for writing one—this would be the cornerstone of his efforts to keep his Army from disintegrating as the one-year term of selectees, National Guardsmen, and Reserve Officers expired.

Congressional leaders already had informed the President that extension of the period of service was impossible—there were not enough members of Congress willing to face an angry and unrealistic constituency the next year with such a vote on their records. That meant it was impossible for the War Department to get a formal request to the Congress from the White House for an extension, which had been sought since April with the backing of Grenville Clark and the National Emergency Committee, and other public-spirited individuals and groups.

In the circumstances, Marshall could not send a direct formal appeal to the Congress. Yet some vigorous appeal must be made, and quickly, if the Army, created with such difficulty and trial, was not to be wrecked in September. It was while he was horseback riding one afternoon that the thought occurred to him that, this being June, he still had time to prepare a report to the Secretary of War and have it ready for publication by the end of the fiscal year, June 30. It would then appear that he had dropped the annual reports only to undertake more comprehensive biennial summaries, and it was a proper and legitimate medium which did not involve going around the President to the Congress—a procedure used freely by some military figures, but impossible for a man like Marshall who held himself bound in his official actions by the decisions—political as well as military—of the Commander in Chief.

With the help of the staff, and working at top speed, he prepared in five days the report covering the period June 1, 1939, to June 30, 1941, and on July 1 it was released to the press. It was a comprehensive survey of the problems encountered and the growth achieved in two years, and the plea for extension of Selective Service was only a part of it. However, all the rest lent weight to that part, which itself was a vigorous and forthright statement of the peril which would result from disintegration of the Army. Unfortunately, the heading of this section was widely interpreted as indicating an intention to dispatch expeditionary forces overseas, and created a hubbub in the Congress. Marshall blamed this misinterpretation on a hastily and poorly prepared press handout of the Bureau of Public Relations, but whatever the cause, the impression had to be corrected.

On a Sunday morning in July, Marshall was called to the White House for a meeting with nine Congressional leaders. The President briefed the senators and representatives with a ten-minute summary of the military and political situation, then turned the meeting over to Marshall. The General asked if he could be completely frank, and when the President assured him anything less would be unsatisfactory, he became frank to the point of bluntness. For an hour Marshall dissected the problems he was facing. Finally, he said that public opinion had been formed to a large extent by newspaper headlines, not by the content of his report; worse, that the Congressional leaders present had formed their opinions the same way and had commented on the report without actually reading it; and that "the times are so serious that such procedure is devastating." He pointed out the absurdity of some of the senatorial suggestions that volunteer recruiting be substituted for selective service, when the man power involved totaled 600,000.

"The time has passed for ordinary political maneuvering," Marshall told the group. "You must decide one or the other of two things: One, we are not in a serious situation, and then go ahead with the usual political maneuvering; or, two, we are in a very critical situation, and we have no choice but to go ahead frankly and deal with this thing in a straightforward manner."

The members got into an argument as to which should lead off, the Senate or the House, on considering the resolution to extend the period of service, and while most of them agreed that the resolution was necessary, some doubted that it could be passed. Speaker Rayburn and House Majority Leader McCormack in particular were reluctant to take up the cudgels, although in the event it would be these two men who rounded up the support which got the resolution through the House by a margin of a single vote.

Hesitant as he was to invade the civil prerogative, Marshall moved firmly to preserve the Army so newly created and so desperately needed as a force in being. When Representative May, the chairman of the House Military Committee, showed a reluctance to hold hearings on the matter, Marshall forced him into agreement—as Marshall phrased it to Acting Secretary Patterson: "I had to invite somewhat the next procedure." And the Chief of Staff considered the advisability of issuing a statement that his recommendation had been made without the prior knowledge of either Secretary Stimson or the President.

"The more it is *my* proposal and not *his*," he explained, "the easier it will be to press this."

When Patterson suggested the War Department urge the removal of both time and territorial restrictions, Marshall replied, "To my embarrassment, I tried definitely in my report to deal with the one and not with the other, and did not succeed." Then he added: "The matter of where and when is a matter for the Commander in Chief and the Congress to decide."

When he appeared before the House Committee a few days later, Marshall reiterated his earlier statements before the Senate Military Committee that the Army was hamstrung by the restrictions on selectees—he cited the dispatch of Marines to Iceland instead of Army troops because shipping shortages forbade an Army garrison subject to constant turnover of personnel in such an outpost defense spot—and launched into a discussion of the morale of the Army as a result of the legislative uncertainty and the pressure on soldiers by outsiders to sign petitions opposing extended service.

"As you may have read in the press," said the General, "some of those young men were led into this business. We cannot continue to ignore such actions. We must treat them as soldiers; we cannot have a political club and call it an army. I regard these disturbing activities from outside the Army, gentlemen, as sabotage of a dangerous character. I do not wish to be held responsible for the development of the Army under such conditions. We must enforce disciplinary measures to offset such influences, if the Army is to have any military value or dependability as an army. Without discipline an army is not only impotent, but it is a menace to the state. . . .

". . . We asked you to reach a decision, to settle this matter, and leave us the opportunity to train and develop the Army for our national security. I realize the difficulties of your problem, but the logical solution, to my mind, is so unmistakable that I do not see how sound, acceptable arguments can be developed against it, unless you definitely determine to change our military system and maintain a large professional Army."

Marshall's eyes got cold and his voice developed an edge when, during this session before May's committee, one of the members called his attention to the fact that the Selective Service Law made released selectees members of the Reserves, and subject to immediate recall to active duty.

"That is correct," Marshall snapped, "but I think it would be most unfortunate to do that at this time, because the soldier would feel that he had been victimized by a maneuver, by sharp practice, under the cover of the law. . . .

"We must not indulge in such procedure.

"I want to go straight down the road, to do what is best, and to do it frankly and without evasion."

While this struggle for preservation of the Army was in progress, the growing menace in the Pacific led Marshall to ask the President to approve the establishment of a theater of operations in the Far East, and to recall MacArthur to active duty to command it. Legally, the retired officer could be recalled only in the grade of major general, but Marshall wanted him a step higher, and the President approved the order giving the former Chief of Staff the grade of lieutenant general. The requests and demands which started flowing in from Manila sometimes exasperated Marshall, indicating as they did a lack of understanding of—or rather, lack of sympathy for—the critical difficulties the Army still was encountering in the creation of a fighting team and in the procurement of equipment and supplies. Marshall was as worried as MacArthur about reinforcements for the Philippines, but the restrictions on use of troops, the shipping shortages, and the willfulness of a large and important segment of industry which was disposed to expand military production only if new facilities were built for it and commercial output was not reduced posed infinite and maddening problems.

If Russia under assault had eased slightly and temporarily the danger of immediate war with the Axis, it also brought new problems. A Russian military mission arrived to ask for help in the form of munitions. At the first meeting, Marshall made no commitments—the Russians, he said, reported that they had stopped the Germans, but that they could not hold them unless they got a lot of help, and got it fast. The day after that meeting, Marshall designated Brigadier General Joseph T. McNarney to accompany Harry Hopkins on a special trip to Moscow. The question of possible intervention in South America had come up again, largely because of renewed hostilities between Peru and Ecuador, and the War Plans Division under General Gerow had made an exhaustive study of the situation. Marshall was certain that the Axis was involved in the Peru-Ecuador dispute, but declined to tell even War Department officials on which side because "I can't prove anything."

"WPD made this study," Marshall told Stimson. "They are fearful that our government will get involved in something."

"They," replied Stimson, "are not half so fearful as the State Department is!" He added that he thought the State Department was watching the situation closely, but Marshall remarked that "they have scared me before."

The last week of July, McCloy reported that Prime Minister Churchill had at last come through with firm figures on British production, to be integrated with American schedules. Stimson immediately warned the War Council not to let anyone get enthusiastic and go to the President with those figures until the Staff had balanced them against demands and requirements, and the Deputy Chief of Staff, General Moore, broke in with the comment that he had found it impossible to get the Navy's ammunition production figures until he promised they would not be shown to OPM.

The morale situation in the Army was getting worse, and Marshall, who had been giving this considerable attention, finally suggested that Frederick H. Osborn, who had been working as a civilian in the Department, be appointed as brigadier general and placed in charge of a morale and education program for the Army. Entertainment would be a part of the program, but Marshall's particular concern was that the men in the ranks be told why the nation was in peril, and why it was necessary to preserve the Army. It was a bitter commentary on the education of American youth for the responsibilities of citizenship that the Army had to plead with Congress to keep the Army in existence, and then divert a part of its attention from its only proper job—getting ready to fight—in order to transform itself into an educational institution to tell its enlisted men why an Army was necessary. The Army would be criticized later for not doing a more adequate job of this educational work. In simple truth, it did a remarkable job with a program which should not, properly speaking, have concerned it at all.

This same feckless willingness to use the Army for nonmilitary purposes and demand of it an ideal solution of nonmilitary problems was to crop up in many ways, the most notable being concerned with the status of Negroes in the army.* With the noblest of purposes, many people sought to utilize the Army as an agency of social

---

* See the *Report of Board of officers on Utilization of Negro Manpower in the Post-War Army*, distributed by the Press Branch, Bureau of Public Relations of the War Department, for release in morning papers, Monday, March 4, 1946. Up to this writing, no other official reports have been made available for public use.

reform (there were some, of course, whose purpose was less noble). In a condition of man-power shortages, only one thing prevented the free and willing use by the Army of as many Negroes as it could induct—the fact that the Army's experience of combat failures of Negro troops made their assignment and employment a complicated, time-consuming, and harassing problem. That was not theory, but fact; and fact not removed by the notable exceptions to the rule. The popular conception of the Army is of an organization in which everything is done by rote, on order from above. Nothing could be more fantastically wide of the truth. The rigid discipline is an essential means, but not an end. The end is self-discipline, and responsible behavior as an individual by even the lowliest private soldier. That performance could not be obtained from Negro combat troops—from certain Negro individuals, yes—but not from Negroes generally. The reason is not difficult to discover: no one, white or black, becomes fit to exercise responsibility except by exercising responsibility, and Negroes in the United States have been systematically deprived of the opportunity for that experience, deliberately kept in a state of dependence by the society which uses but does not accept them. The fact of their irresponsibility is not their fault, but to ignore it, to pretend that what was true was not true, was to invite disaster. So another disheartening and exasperating problem was added to the many already plaguing the Army. The Army accepted Negroes in the ratio of population proportions, but the success of operations made it necessary to restrict their use largely to noncombat duties, and imperative that the maximum ratio not be exceeded. The problems posed by this question entered into the smallest details of planning. Thus, when Marshall proposed in the late summer of 1941 to release men over twenty-eight, allowing any over that age who wished to do so to remain in service, he found it necessary to order that only noncommissioned and commissioned officers over twenty-eight be allowed to remain lest all the Negroes over that age elect to stay.

Meantime, the relations with the Japanese were becoming more and more critical. Marshall's efforts to achieve unity of command over the operating forces in any potential theater, but particularly in the outlying bastions of Hawaii, Panama, and the Caribbean, were intensified, but to no purpose. The sessions of the Joint Board of the Army and Navy gradually arrived at agreement that there should be unity of command instead of mutual co-operation—what the Joint Congressional Investigating Committee would later call command by "joint oblivion"—in the three critical outposts, but they could not agree on the form that unity should take. The Navy proposed that the Navy command in the Caribbean, and the Army in Panama and Hawaii except when major naval forces were based there—the general idea was that at no time would any respectable portion of the fleet ever come under Army command. The Army countered with a proposal that unity of command be established in all coastal frontier regions, the Army to command except when a major portion of the fleet was operating against comparable forces within range of possible Army aviation support and when the respective Army and Navy commanders should agree to transfer the command from one to the other.

That was the impasse reached on November 17, two days after Saburo Kurusu arrived in Washington on his dramatic "peace" mission, and the very day that he called formally on Secretary of State Hull. Ten days later Marshall sent the following telegram to Major General Walter C. Short, commanding in Hawaii—the only message to Short signed personally by Marshall during the weeks preceding the attack on Pearl Harbor:

"Negotiations with Japan appear to be terminated to all practical purposes with only the barest possibilities that the Japanese government might come back and offer to continue. Japanese future action unpredictable but hostile action possible at any moment. If hostilities cannot, repeat cannot, be avoided the United States desires that Japan commit the first overt act. This policy should not, repeat not, be construed as restricting you to a course of action that might jeopardize your defense. Prior to hostile Japanese action you are directed to undertake such reconnaissance and other measures as you deem necessary but these measures should be carried out so as not, repeat not, to alarm civil population or disclose intent. Report measures taken. Should hostilities occur you will carry out the tasks assigned in Rainbow Five so far as they pertain to Japan. Limit dissemination of this highly secret information to minimum essential officers."

Gerow, chief of War Plans, later assumed complete responsibility for failure to examine the unlikely possibility that Short's response announcing an alert against sabotage meant he had taken no other measures—an unlikely possibility that proved to be tragically true. Short also reported that he was in liaison with the Navy in Hawaii, and the War Department knew that Admiral Kimmel had received repeated warnings that war was probable. Unfortunately, the claim of liaison was overstated. A closer watch should have been maintained by the War Department on the actions of the Hawaiian department commander, perhaps, even if Hawaii was not considered to be the most likely target of the first Japanese attack. But Short had been warned, the responsibility and the authority were his, he had been directed to undertake reconnaissance and any other action he deemed necessary to prevent surprise, and it was not the responsibility of the Chief of Staff to behave, under such circumstances, like a multiple company commander issuing the detailed orders for all the platoons in Hawaii.

The blow fell on December 7, and the only good thing that came from it was the shock that ended all quibbling about unity of command in theaters of operations. In a broad sense, Pearl Harbor was a failure of intelligence. If all the information available in Hawaii and in Washington—available to the State Department, the Army, and the Navy—had been brought together in one spot, studied, analyzed, and assessed, the attack could not have been successful. Pooled and correlated, the information was sufficient. Scattered, it permitted disaster.

XVII

Grand Strategy

STRATEGIC decisions are simple to make. The difficulty comes in implementing them, and the truly complicated problems occur on the field when battle is joined. These are the reasons the armchair amateurs are so glib about grand strategy, but when they turn to tactics or logistics become either fatuous or silent.

Grand strategy, being war's largest aspect, shares more completely than others its basic political nature. The political objective of the war is the first and heaviest factor governing the strategy of its conduct. For the United States, the first great strategic decision had been made before Pearl Harbor: that Germany was the most dangerous enemy, and must be defeated first.

This decision, tentative in the cautious exploratory conversations early in 1941, definite in August at Argentia Bay, confirmed in December in Washington, took account not only of the greater military force of Germany compared with Japan, but of the flaming and evil motive behind that force which constituted a greater threat to democratic institutions than any idea propagated by the Japanese. The decision, in other words, did not overlook the immutable fact that ideas are stronger than weapons.

Thus it was that, although the United States became a belligerent because of a blow struck in the Pacific by the Japanese, the American strategy was to remain defensive in the war with Japan until Germany was crushed. The question then became how and where to apply the Allied strength, and Marshall supplied the primary answers to both questions: as to how, under unified command; and as to where, in France and Germany.

Both decisions involved important political considerations, immediately and recurrently throughout the war. It has become the fashion among many articulate but superficial Americans to criticize the British for their preoccupation with the Mediterranean and the Balkans, to bandy harsh words about the inevitable political considerations which entered into British military decisions. Such reactions are unavoidable among a people just beginning to understand the age-old truism that war itself is a political act; but they contribute too little to the general enlightenment when they ignore or obscure the truth that America's war decisions were equally governed by politics.

Marshall was freed to press the invasion of France—as he did insist upon it—by a political decision. That decision was President Roosevelt's, his so-called "great design." The President believed that Soviet Russia could be drawn fully back into the community of democratic nations. What that meant to American military strategists was, to put it bluntly, that it made no difference to the world future whether Red Army or Anglo-American troops stood upon any indicated area of the European map when the conflict ended. The one consideration to govern the deployment of American forces was the quickest and surest destruction of German might. With that mandate, Marshall and his staff could insist, not only that the main blow must be struck in Germany through France, but that it must be struck as promptly as the necessary forces could be assembled. They won the first point, but lost the second—for reasons both political and military.

There is evidence that Marshall lacked a complete understanding of the manifold political and social implications of the war until some time had elapsed after Pearl Harbor, and also that even Marshall did not comprehend the true magnitude of the strictly military task facing the United States before the Japanese attack changed preparation to combat. Certainly, his progressively greater recommendations for men and material followed each other in such rapid succession that on at least one occasion the President lost his temper.

"I wish they'd make up their minds what they want over there!" he roared as a relayed message reached him that a new upward revision of estimates was on its way. "They're changing these figures on me faster than I can pass them on to Congress!"

Marshall was only sending to the White House, in the form of new proposals, his growing understanding of the immensity of the war task facing the country; and he was among the first to understand it. Marshall himself was shifting from the task of organizing and training a minimum force for the protection of a nation which still hoped to stay out of the war, and doing it under relatively limited appropriations and freedom of action, to the task of directing the Allied forces to victory over their enemies, with all the vast resources of the United States now unequivocally behind him. The time required for him to make this shift was lengthened by the urgent necessity to devote attention to many small matters, detailed operational matters which normally should never have come to the attention of the Chief of Staff, but which were essential to salvage what could be salvaged of the situation in the Pacific. Immediate tactical decisions were required in the Atlantic, also—among the first being that Army troops would relieve the British and the Marines in Iceland. General Emmons had replaced General Short in Hawaii, but his reinforcement requests had to be whittled. In Australia, on the other hand, General Brett had to be told that he needed—and would get—more troops than he thought he needed. Marshall even had to take the time to support, in the proper quarters, MacArthur's view that President Quezon should not leave the Philippines in January, lest Philippine resistance collapse. These are samples—the Chief of Staff still was trying to struggle out of a welter of details.

The step he took to free himself of the details required tremendous courage. It was the complete reorganization of the Army while that Army was in process of completion and deployment in a world-wide war. The impetus had come from Marshall's dissatisfaction with the complicated staff and command system he had inherited, but which he had found impossible to alter materially until a disaster demanded drastic action, and also provided the opportunity. The Air Staff's War Plans Division had drafted a proposed reorganization which

Arnold submitted to Marshall late in the summer of 1941, and General Gerow, War Plans chief, and General Embick, recalled to active duty as chairman of the United States-Canada Permanent Joint Defense Board, had examined the plan and recommended that it be given further study and development. A comprehensive General Staff study had been initiated before Pearl Harbor. After the war began, Marshall detailed General McNarney to take charge of the final planning. McNarney, after his return from the trip with Hopkins to Moscow and Britain, had gone with Justice Roberts to Hawaii for the investigation of the Pearl Harbor attack. Tall, dark, and saturnine, he was an air officer of great organizing and administrative capacity, with firm convictions against trying to run a war with a debating society.

On January 31, 1942, he gave Marshall a memorandum recommending that all activities of the Army in the United States be grouped in three major commands—the Army Ground Forces, the Army Air Forces, and the Services of Supply (later renamed Army Service Forces). The old General Headquarters would disappear, its tactical and strategic responsibilities for theaters of war being transferred to War Plans Division of the General Staff, and its training responsibilities to the Commanding General, Army Ground Forces, who would absorb also the jobs of the Chiefs of Arms—Infantry, Cavalry, Field Artillery, and Coast Artillery. Functions of the Commanding General, GHQ Air Force, and of the Chief of Air Corps would be taken over by the Commanding General, Army Air Forces. All the services concerned with procurement, storage, and issue of equipment and supplies—except the aircraft procurement, which remained a function of the AAF—would come under the control of the Commanding General, Services of Supply. A greatly reduced General Staff would confine itself to the strategic direction and control of operations, the determination of over-all Army requirements, and basic decisions and policies on organization, administration, training, and supply.

In his memorandum, McNarney told Marshall that if the plan were submitted to the various staff divisions and other interested parties, "the result will be numerous non-concurrences and interminable delay." He recommended that Marshall approve the plan in principle, name the three major commanders, and then appoint an executive committee responsible only to Marshall to work out details and prepare the regulations. The plan was frankly an organization to fight a war, it departed in notable particulars from the theoretical ideal of a command and staff system (it would be inevitable that AGF assume many G-3 functions, and SOS invade the sphere of G-1 and G-4), and it ruthlessly overrode the traditions of many established offices and bureaus. Marshall immediately undertook the delicate job of convincing the Secretary and the President of its desirability, and succeeded so well that the President signed the executive order authorizing the reorganization on February 28, making it effective March 9, 1942.

General McNair, the brilliant and devoted Chief of Staff GHQ, was the obvious choice to command the Ground Forces, as General Arnold, flamboyant and undisputed leader of the airmen, was the inevitable choice for Commanding General AAF. To head the Services of Supply, Marshall personally picked General Brehon Somervell. This officer had been WPA administrator in New York City when he came down in the autumn of 1940 and asked Marshall to terminate the loan of his services to WPA and Mayor LaGuardia, and let him come back to military duty. Marshall had agreed, provided LaGuardia released him, and Somervell reported in the office of the Inspector General in November that year. In a few weeks he was given the task of bringing order into the Army's chaotic and frenzied construction program, and his brilliant success in the assignment resulted in his appointment as Assistant Chief of Staff, G-4 (Supply). His vigorous administrative abilities and determined purpose were precisely what Marshall wanted in someone to take the supply and procurement burden off his shoulders and leave him free to run the war. McNarney, who had rammed the planning through, became Deputy Chief of Staff, and no superior ever had a more ruthlessly efficient hatchet man, or one with a colder objectivity or more emphatic and final "No!"

On February 16, before the executive order was signed, McNarney had presided at the first meeting of the staff committee—it contained sixteen members—charged with preparing details of the reorganization. No clearer insight could be obtained into the man's methods than that presented by his opening words at that meeting.

"Gentlemen," he said, "the Secretary of War has approved in principle the reorganization of the War Department as shown on the charts. This committee has been formed for the purpose of coordinating details and preparing the necessary directives to put the reorganization into effect. It is not a voting committee. It is not a debating society. It is a committee to draft the necessary directives."

That the reorganization was accomplished with an almost complete absence of personal friction, but more importantly without interruption of the war effort, was the measure not alone of the zeal and single-minded purpose of the Army's leaders, but of the great efficiency which had been reached by the General Staff. A lesser man than Marshall would hardly have dared tamper with the organization of the Army in the midst of war, much less alter it so drastically; but the new structure vastly simplified his problems, enabling him to delegate many responsibilities and maintain control through a small number of trusted subordinates, and so turn the greater part of his attention to the command function which was his primary interest. Marshall was steadily emerging as the dominant figure in the Anglo-American councils. He had created an Army, got it trained, seen it equipped; from this point forward, his concern was operations.

Unity of command—that was his first, and probably his greatest, contribution to the Anglo-American effort. When Prime Minister Churchill came to Washington after Pearl Harbor and brought his military advisers along, the Combined Chiefs of Staff were organized. This group was composed of the American Joint Chiefs of Staff: Marshall, Arnold, Admiral Stark, the Chief of Naval Operations, and Admiral King, the Commander in Chief of the Fleet—and the British Chiefs of Staff: Admiral of the Fleet Sir Dudley Pound, General Sir Alan Brooke, and Air Chief Marshal Sir Charles Portal. Its command post was established in Washington, where a British Joint Staff Mission represented the British chiefs. This group included Field Marshal Sir John Dill, former Chief of the Imperial General Staff; Admiral Sir Andrew Cunningham, later to command British naval forces in the Mediterranean; Lieutenant General G. N. Macready, and Air Marshal Douglas C. S. Evill.

Churchill's agreement to single command over all forces, land, sea, and air, in theaters of operations was harder to get, but Marshall succeeded even in that. At a secret meeting in Churchill's bedroom at the White House, the American Chief of Staff finally wrung from the Prime Minister the concession that even His Majesty's Navy—the senior service in Britain and extremely conscious of the fact—might be prevailed upon to accept the principle of unified command. Marshall's shrewd and valuable ally in this struggle to prevent a repetition of the Allied command failures of 1914-1918 was Field Marshal Dill.

As Marshall emerged the outstanding member of the American Chiefs of Staff, so Dill was the dominant member of the British group. The two men had much in common—the same reserve, the same simplicity of manner, the same qualities of human sympathy and interest. Each had served a long and disappointing career before emerging finally as unquestionably the greatest military figure of his country. Each had maintained the sense of battle actualities despite a tendency of his respective Army to theorize and formalize too greatly. Each was ahead of most of his contemporaries in appreciation of the possibilities of modern equipment. Both were partisans of offensive rather than defensive war. Dill was perhaps more aware of political and social realities than Marshall. They became firm friends—Dill came in time to be closer to Marshall than any American officer—and a magnificent team. Above all other qualities, they shared the ability to think and speak as Allied leaders, not as American or British officers. It would be difficult to overestimate Dill's contribution to the cause of Allied unity, and his death before the end of the war was a severe loss to both countries.

The insistence of Marshall upon unity of command fell upon more willing American ears after Pearl Harbor, and the Army and Navy promptly placed the Pacific and Hawaii under naval command. The first theater of Allied operations to receive attention was ABDA— American, British, Dutch, Australian. Before the Japanese onslaught overran Malaya and the Netherlands Indies, while there still was hope that this barrier could be held, it was decided to place it under the command of a single officer who would be responsible to the combined chiefs, who in turn were responsible to the President and the Prime Minister. That decision reached, the question was, who will command? It was the first test, and striving between the Americans and the British for national prestige might have wrecked the policy at the start. At this point in the meeting, Marshall spoke.

"My choice is General Wavell," he said. The American Chief of Staff had nominated a British officer to command the first Allied theater. It was a good beginning. The Japanese offensive split Wavell's theater before he could even get it organized, but the British would not soon forget that gesture of Marshall's.

If the main task was Germany, the first task was still in the Pacific. Marshall initiated extraordinary steps to get supplies to MacArthur through the use of blockade runners, but while a few of these actually got as far as Cebu in the Philippines, only a trickle of material, chiefly medical and surgical, got through by submarine to Corregidor and Bataan. With the Philippines doomed, and Wavell's ABDA theater already hopelessly split beyond the possibility of single-command control by Japanese conquest of Malaya and the Netherlands Indies, the President ordered MacArthur to leave the Philippines and report in Australia. The British, in effect, left the entire Pacific to the United States. The Joint Chiefs of Staff divided it into several theaters of operations, all of them under naval command except the Southwest Pacific, which was given to MacArthur.

If the decision to remain on the defensive in the Pacific was primarily political, reinforced by the military decision that this country lacked the resources of carrying on offensives in both oceans, the decision to hold Australia was almost entirely political. The battle in the Philippines had been magnificent enough to rub out some of the shame of Pearl Harbor, and MacArthur's arrival in Australia on St. Patrick's day in 1942 as Allied Commander in the Southwest Pacific started immediate speculation on the possibility that the Allies soon would undertake the offensive from that subcontinent. Such speculation was harmless enough until it began to appear that MacArthur shared the idea.

Marshall was astonished to find that MacArthur, leaving the Philippines, had taken his entire staff with him, leaving none of the senior staff officers with Major General Jonathan M. Wainwright. Incredulity and something akin to anger accompanied his next discovery. MacArthur had left Wainwright in command only in the Bataan Peninsula. Each of the other forces in the archipelago was to be a separate force, and each—including Wainwright's—directly under the command of MacArthur, two thousand miles away. Marshall, however, already had taken care of that situation. MacArthur was informed that the President already had promoted Wainwright to lieutenant general and placed him in command of all forces in the Philippines. Moreover, the Southwest Pacific commander was told that, by agreement with the British, an Allied commander was expressly prohibited from exercising the direct command of forces of his own nationality. MacArthur was directed to relinquish the command of the forces in the Philippines to Wainwright.

Meantime, the Australian Minister in Washington, Herbert Evatt, had called on Marshall with some bitter comments about the British, and an assortment of extraordinary demands. He wanted the United States to halt immediately all shipments to Russia, Libya, and assorted other localities, diverting everything to Australia.

It was precisely the kind of disheartened and desperate plea for help that the Chief of Staff had to resist from all sides—including those American cities demanding antiaircraft protection as far inland as Keokuk, Iowa—lest the whole plan of the war dissolve in a frantic, wasteful, and meaningless plugging of holes. The only reason troops were sent to Australia at all was the political, not military, decision that a courageous and generous ally could not be left ruthlessly to the fate that was obviously in store for it otherwise. A cold and hard military decision would have allowed Australia to fall to the Japanese. MacArthur's one responsibility was to use such forces as could be assigned to him to prevent the enemy from reaching the Australian east coast. The main attack against Japan, when it could be undertaken, must go west from Hawaii, and a major offensive northward from Australia was no part of Allied calculations when MacArthur went there.

Only MacArthur would not have it so. The newspapers began to carry strange stories about the absence of meaningful orders from Washington for the Southwest Pacific commander, about the neglected and equivocal position of the hero of the Philippines, stories hinting intrigue and semiconspiracy preventing the proper development of the theater and an offensive against the Japanese. The misleading phrase "island-hopping" appeared and gained currency, the implication being that the Navy proposed this mysteriously shortsighted kind of campaign in the Central Pacific, while in the Southwest MacArthur was being kept from bold strokes involving no such island-hopping nonsense. There was a bland ignoring of the rather numerous islands which lay between Australia and either the Philippines or Japan. There was no attention for the dangerously long line of sea communications from San Francisco to Brisbane, Sidney, and Melbourne, its entire length subject to attack by the Japanese unless those islands in the Central Pacific were taken or neutralized. There was a complete disregard of the fact that for years American strategists, Army as well as Navy, had known—partly because of that exposed sea lane to Australia—that if war came and the Philippines fell, the way to Japan lay through or north of the islands, and that it was at least a two-year road.

Of graver nature was the continual leakage of military information to the jeopardy of security, and Marshall sent a message to MacArthur urging closer control. MacArthur replied with a long discourse about the constitutional rights of Australia. If co-operation was not to be had, then flat orders would have to be issued; the next message was prepared for signature, not by Marshall, but by the President. While this was going on, the March of Death had occurred on Bataan, and Corregidor had surrendered.

Meantime, Lieutenant General Joseph Stilwell had been sent to China as Chief of Staff to Generalissimo Chiang Kai-shek and commander of U. S. Forces in China-Burma-India, had become an international hero in the lost battle for Burma, and had begun to train some Chinese troops in India in pursuit of the always elusive goal of effective use of China's man power. The contest for priorities in materials and munitions had produced a tangle of A-1-a's, the War Production Board, and Harry Hopkins' Munitions Assignment Board—which Hopkins insisted that the President place directly under the Combined Chiefs of Staff. The Desert Training Center had been established in California, under the command of Major General George Smith Patton, Jr. Marshall had found so much of his time being consumed by the greeting of foreign officials and military missions that he had bucked this necessary but exasperating detail to McNarney. The old War Plans Division had become, with the advent of war and reorganization, the Operations Division—OPD—and the most important of the General Staff divisions, being Marshall's command post for the war. The man at the head of it that spring of 1942 had been tested as Lieutenant General Walter Krueger's chief of staff in the Louisiana maneuvers the previous autumn, proved further as Gerow's assistant in WPD, and not found wanting—Major General Dwight D. Eisenhower. The Inter-American Defense Board had been established with General Embick as chairman, and to the delighted astonishment of the skeptical Embick and Marshall had turned out to be, not a vehicle for more embarrassing demands for American men and materials, but an instrument of wholehearted support of the Allied efforts by the Latin American republics.

And, in April, Marshall and Harry Hopkins had gone to London to sell the cross-Channel invasion to a reluctant Prime Minister and a less than enthusiastic group of British officers. Against the British preoccupation with the Mediterranean, they posed the inescapable fact that Germany could be defeated—not stalemated, but defeated—only when Allied armies stood on German soil; that, plus the obvious fact that the most direct route to German soil lay across the Channel and through France. Marshall had a powerful team mate in Hopkins. If Hopkins possessed no military competence, he was a complete master of all the other aspects of the war, and he thought just as fast and just as far as the Chief of Staff. Moreover, he had the same complete and passionate devotion to a cause beyond self which characterized Marshall, and a shrewd and stubborn Americanism which the General found invaluable. Marshall approached the British as a military master set free of any requirement but the quickest route to victory. Hopkins approached them as an American statesman completely immune to those subtle blandishments of pomp and circumstance with which the British could beguile too many Americans. Marshall leaned heavily on Hopkins throughout the war, and one official cited as a principal reason for this the fact that Hopkins "doesn't give a damn for the Most Noble Order of the Bath!" Another and probably stronger reason was the extraordinary relationship between Hopkins and the President.

For Marshall himself, resisting the President's efforts to draw him into the Christian name intimacy that provided the atmosphere in which Roosevelt preferred to work, remained dignified, aloof, and uncharmed in his relations with his Commander in Chief. Nettled when even he could not penetrate the Marshall reserve, Roosevelt complained to Hopkins, and asked him to try to get the Chief of Staff to drop in casually and informally, as did Admiral Stark and others from the Navy, to talk over problems in an easy atmosphere. The word was passed along by Hopkins through Colonel Walter Bedell Smith, then a liaison officer between the War Department and the White House, and Marshall told Smith the thing was impossible "because I would be stepping completely out of character." Marshall was wise enough to understand, also, that his counsel would carry more weight if he kept it strictly professional. If the Navy found it useful to have its Chief of Operations on such a footing of intimacy at the White House that the President called him by his nickname, Marshall noticed that the affectionate raillery was just as frequently a medium for denying the Navy the things it needed and asked for—that it was, for instance, not "Betty" Stark, but General Marshall, who convinced the President that the sea train for fleet supply was a vital necessity and not a military pleasantry conceived in Navy playfulness. The course of the war proved the wisdom of Marshall's attitude, and no other officer received such absolute confidence from Roosevelt as this Army Chief of Staff who refused to become another puppet in the master's hands.

Marshall had convinced the President on the cross-Channel operation, and now had gone with Hopkins to the more difficult matter of convincing the British. The Russians, in desperate straits and expecting them to become more desperate when the Germans launched their summer campaign, were demanding a second front to draw off some of the enemy divisions. Marshall believed that a major assault could be launched across the Channel by the spring of 1943, and the British agreed—at least in principle—to this idea. The projected operation was given the code name "Roundup," and the build-up of American forces in Britain to make it possible, "Bolero." This was only part of the question, however. Marshall had considered—and now asked the British to consider—the possibility that the desperate gamble of a cross-Channel operation before the end of 1942 might have to be taken. As it became a plan, this 1942 invasion was called "Sledgehammer." This was no reckless willingness to plunge into an offensive without preparation, but a calculated proposal to risk important strength and even eventual failure, if necessary, to prevent the collapse of Russia; and it should be noted that Marshall, at this time, believed Sledgehammer to be entirely feasible. The possibility that France would be invaded in the autumn of 1942 rather than the spring of 1943 thus entered the Allied plan.

With British agreement "in principle" to his proposals assured, Marshall returned to the United States just in time to share the elation over the bombing of Tokyo on April 18 by Lieutenant Colonel Jimmy Doolittle and a group of medium bombers which took off from the aircraft carrier *Hornet*—although, of course, the names of the fliers remained a closely guarded secret for weeks as the Army and the Chinese co-operated in the attempt to rescue the survivors of the crashes which marked the end of the flight. How the attack was launched was not disclosed for many months. The attempt had been suggested by the Navy, accepted eagerly by Arnold, and Doolittle had spent intensive weeks training the selected volunteer crews meticulously in take-off techniques for a mission of which they knew only that it would be extremely hazardous.

The next week Marshall took one of those trips by means of which he "educated" the British in the vast military effort of the United States, and particularly the training techniques which had been developed and were now working with the precision of a machine. Accompanied by Sir John Dill and members of Dill's staff, Marshall went to Fort Bragg, Fort Benning, and Camp Blanding. They saw a review of the 2d Armored Division which moved three thousand vehicles past the reviewing stand at Benning in twenty-four minutes. They inspected the Officer Candidate School, a paratroop training center, the Field Artillery Training Center, reviewed three infantry divisions and a regiment of combat engineers.

The fear that the Japanese might make a heavy attack on the West Coast, possibly using gas, in retaliation for the bombing of Tokyo led Marshall to order extraordinary precautions in that area, and late in May—when the Joint Chiefs already knew of the enemy's fleet concentration in the Pacific preparatory to moving toward Midway—Marshall went west to check defenses personally. He ordered the antiaircraft units on the coast brought to full strength immediately. Arrangements were made to improve barrage balloon screens around the vital aircraft plants, and to move partially completed planes to the interior as soon as they could be flown. Air Forces units scheduled for delivery to MacArthur's theater were ordered held in Hawaii, and sixteen Flying Fortresses earmarked for flight to Britain were pulled back and sent to Hawaii also. Alaska was reinforced by a group of P-38 fighters, and four B-17's—Marshall and General DeWitt wanted to send more B-17's, but there were no trained crews. Later, a pursuit group and a heavy bombardment group were ordered to the west, delaying Bolero, the build-up in Britain—but the Japanese danger was acute. Marshall took Dill with him on the West Coast trip, also.

While Marshall was on this trip west, his Operations chief, Eisenhower, took off for conferences in England. With him went Arnold and Somervell, as well as three brigadier generals—Mark W. Clark, John C. H. Lee, and William C. Lee—and Rear Admiral John H. Towers, Chief of the Navy's Bureau of Aeronautics. The arrival of this imposing mission fed the public speculation on a second front in 1942, which was not dampened by Roosevelt's remark at a press conference that the air offensive against Germany was not the exclusive topic of the London talks, nor extinguished by Marshall's flat assertion a few days later in a speech at West Point that American soldiers "will land in France." When Eisenhower returned with Arnold and Clark, they were accompanied by Lord Louis Mountbatten, and Washington correspondents did not overlook the "significance" of conversations between American military leaders and the commander of the Commandos, who presumably was then the leading Allied expert in amphibious operations. Sir Archibald Wavell, Commander in Chief in India, also was in Washington. Marshall, however, took Mountbatten off on one of the Chief of Staff's quick "educational" tours of Army posts.

If the Battle of Midway was a crushing defeat for the Japanese, the elation in the War and Navy Departments was changed to consternation when the Chicago *Tribune* published a story, used also by the other Patterson-McCormick papers, which not only reported the engagement, but a virtually complete order of battle of the Japanese fleet. A secret message from the Pacific command to the Navy Department was repeated almost word for word, naming many ships of the enemy force, not by category, but by name. There was, of course, only one way the Navy could have come into that information, and that was through possession of the Japanese code. This news story was the most flagrant violation of security of the entire war, and action against the *Tribune* was begun at once. A special grand jury was convened, the Federal Bureau of Investigation and the Office of Naval Intelligence converged on Chicago, and the Attorney General of the United States flew to Chicago to assume personal direction of the case. For a few days the press of the country was filled with reports of these extraordinary proceedings—although with no inkling of the reason for them—and then, as suddenly as it had been begun, the case was dropped without explanation. The mystery was not cleared, so far as the public was concerned, until the word "Magic" became familiar in the postwar investigation of Pearl Harbor; but what had ended the incipient prosecution of the *Tribune* was the discovery that no Japanese agent had seen the story, or noticed the extraordinary activity it provoked—the code was still being used by the enemy.

During that first week of June, Stimson approved formally the establishment of a European Theater of Operations by the Army, and on June 15 Marshall named Eisenhower to command it. This was the first, as it was the greatest, of those selections which marked Marshall's self-effacing willingness to advance other men to positions of great public prestige. He picked his men with great care, entrusted them with authority to operate freely in discharging their responsibilities, and gave them a magnificent and steady support. Eisenhower went to England because he shared Marshall's strategic concept with its emphasis on Western Europe, because he had the broad vision and the moral courage and integrity necessary for the direction and control of vast operations, and because he had to an extraordinary degree those simple but noble qualities of understanding which seemed to promise that fusion of joint purpose necessary in an Allied effort. The man whom the United States sent to Britain probably would be the Allied commander—or at least, *an* Allied commander. Eisenhower appeared to Marshall to be the one who could create a new type of command, and combine diverse national traits and methods into a unity.

Meanwhile, Churchill had come to Washington again, and Marshall was plunged into a new effort on the eve of Eisenhower's departure to preserve Bolero from the diversionary aims of the British. The German submarine warfare in the Atlantic also was examined thoroughly, but the main issue was Normandy or the Mediterranean, and the Prime Minister's arguments, always persuasive, became more urgent after Tobruk fell to the Germans. The British had launched a counterattack against Rommel's forces in Libya on June 6, but it became a disaster when it ran into a tank-trap at Knightsbridge, and the battered Eighth Army retreated into Egypt, leaving Tobruk under siege. The city and its thirty thousand troops fell to Rommel on June 20. In desperation, the Eighth Army dug in at El Alamein, a scant seventy miles from Alexandria. This gloomy situation, coupled with the German advance in the Crimea and the evident doom of Sevastopol, presented the distinct possibility that the vast German pincers aimed at a double envelopment of the Middle East might succeed. It was all very well to attempt to offset public concern by playing up the R.A.F.'s successes in 1,000-plane raids over Germany, and by announcing the new American ETO setup, with its implicit promise to future offensives; Churchill was eloquent of the threat to the Middle East, severing Britain's life line and the United States air routes to India and China, giving to the Nazis the oil of Arabia, Mesopotamia, and Iran.

Churchill was eloquent, but so was Marshall. The Chief of Staff would not be diverted from the main show by political involvements in the Mediterranean or the natural British desire for face-saving; although he hardly put it so bluntly in the conferences. If the Prime Minister was doubtful that the Allies could make an effort on the French coast in 1942, Marshall insisted that it was possible, and might yet be a necessity at no matter what risk. Churchill wanted an attack in North Africa. Marshall insisted that such a move would be a diversion of effort, whereas the only hope of defeating Germany lay in concentrated effort in the area which could be decisive. In the end, Marshall preserved the basic agreement on Bolero, but he also made certain concessions:

Air reinforcement of the Near East already had been planned, and this was now rushed. The Aircraft Carrier *Ranger* would ferry a load of pursuit ships to Africa, and they would be flown to Egypt. A heavy bombardment group was ordered to Africa immediately, and General Brereton, commanding the American Air Forces in China-Burma-India, was ordered to Egypt at once with all the planes he could take, despite the protests of Chiang, who was informed that the crisis in the Near East was serious, and that if the Germans should take Egypt, the air route to China would be finished. Three hundred medium tanks and one hundred self-propelled guns were taken away from the American armored divisions to which they had just been issued, and rushed in three fast ships to Egypt. The British wanted an armored division also sent, but there were no ships available except at the cost of a two-month delay in Bolero, and a compromise arrangement was agreed upon, with Marshall to send the cadres for training an armored division in England.

Then Churchill was taken by Marshall and Stimson on one of the educational visits—they went to Fort Jackson, reviewed three combat teams, and watched a firing demonstration in which machine guns and artillery used service ammunition.

With the decisive plan saved, and with the situation in Egypt beginning to show signs of improvement, Marshall went to the President and suggested, on the off-chance there might still be a disaster in the delta of the Nile, that he prepare a statement which would condition the American public and assure the British of sympathetic treatment in the press.

Only, the decisive plan had not been saved. Within a month, it would be placed in cold storage and the Allies would shift their strength to Africa.

XVIII

Global Attack

BEFORE the end of the second week in July, Roosevelt received a disturbing message from Churchill about Bolero. Despite the agreement reached when the Prime Minister was in Washington only two weeks earlier, the message made it obvious that the whole plan for invasion of France, whether Sledgehammer in 1942 or Roundup in 1943, was threatened.

In a desperate new attempt to save the plan, Roosevelt sent Marshall and a group of officers and advisers on a rushed trip to London for further conferences with the Prime Minister and his military staff. It was an imposing array of brains and brass that arrived in London on Saturday, July 18—Marshall, Admiral King, Harry Hopkins, Brigadier General W. B. Smith, now Army secretary of the Joint Chiefs, Brigadier General Charles P. Gross, Colonel Hoyt Vandenberg, and Stephen T. Early, secretary to the President, were the principal members of the party.

Eisenhower's staff had worked overtime preparing plans and studies for Marshall's use, and the development of these continued over the week end as the General, King, and their colleagues pored over the papers, absorbing the assembled facts and making suggestions for additional staff preparations. Then, on Monday, Marshall and King met the British Chiefs of Staff, and Marshall turned on the heat for an invasion of Normandy in September. For three days the arguments continued before Marshall was forced against his will to cable Roosevelt that, even if the British should be pressed finally into agreement, they would undertake the expedition with such reluctance as to make its success even more doubtful than ever. Accordingly, he asked permission to proceed with an alternative plan—the invasion of French northwest Africa. Sledgehammer was abandoned. Bolero would continue to the extent that the build-up could be maintained parallel with preparations for the North African move, and Roundup—the proposed landing in Normandy in the spring of 1943—remained a plan. But no one thought, really, that it could now become an actuality. North Africa would be a major campaign, and a major campaign is like a sponge—it always sucks up vastly more men, material, money, and time than its planners ever intended to give it.

The change of plan was forced largely by British staff studies, partly by British preoccupation with the Mediterranean. But it should be remembered that British political maneuvering in that area is the result, not the cause, of strategic considerations. The Mediterranean was the direct route to the Far East, an important and even compelling factor for Allied powers confronted with shipping shortages and the terrific losses to enemy submarines. Furthermore, Churchill's obsession with the Balkans was political only in part; for the rest, it reflected the strategic intent of a highly gifted military amateur to crush Germany with a huge and classic double envelopment, through the Balkans to the plains of Hungary and the Bohemian bowl and through the Low Countries to the plains of northwest Germany—aiming at the enemy precisely the same kind of strategic double threat that the enemy in the summer of 1942 was aiming at the Middle East. The fault in Churchill's strategy lay in his ignoring the difficulties of the Balkan route. He began talking about the "soft underbelly" of Europe; but there was nothing soft about a solid mass of mountain barriers without even the beginnings of adequate highway and rail systems to carry and supply the armies which would be necessary. Furthermore, the door to the Balkans lay farthest from the primary bases in Britain and the United States. Finally, the Allies lacked the men and the matériel to launch two great invasions of the continent—and even the persistent and eloquent Churchill was compelled to admit that a Balkan campaign could not be decisive without a simultaneous campaign in Western Europe, whereas the campaign in Western Europe by itself could be decisive. Marshall had to dig in his heels and refuse to budge, for the British never abandoned the Balkan attempt until they failed in their last effort to get the forces which were poised in the Mediterranean to invade southern France in August 1944 diverted to the Ljubljana Gap and an attack in Yugoslavia and Hungary.

Nevertheless, the invasion of North Africa had sound strategic reasons behind it, and Marshall accepted that alternative to Sledgehammer because he knew the reasons to be valid, if less weighty to his mind than the overriding need for decisive action in Western Europe. While the whole force of American argument was turned to the invasion of France, there was by no means unaminity of opinion in the American councils. A number of American officers and civilian advisers, among them the shrewd and energetic Assistant Secretary of War McCloy, believed that North Africa was an extremely important and desirable major target, not only because of the psychological impact success there would have upon France and other parts of occupied Europe, but also for the strategic gains to be made by sweeping the Germans from the southern shore of the Mediterranean. Stimson and Marshall, passionately at one on the invasion of France, felt that the shortest line of communications was essential to quick defeat of the Germans—and the shortest line was through Britain. They were fearful of the long supply lines, imposing heavier burdens on limited shipping, implied by the invasion of North Africa and an invasion of Europe from Africa. Nevertheless, one of the clearest outlines of the strategic advantages gained from the North African campaign was written by Marshall himself.

"The opening of the Mediterranean," he wrote in his second biennial report, "would facilitate Allied global operations, and the removal of the constant threat of German activities in western Morocco and at Dakar would add immeasurably to the security of the Allied position while gathering strength to administer the final punishing blows.

"Furthermore, if our occupation of North Africa could be carried out without fatally embittering the French troops and authorities in that region it would provide a setting for the reconstitution of the French Army in preparation for its return in force to the homeland. The psychological effect of the conquest of North Africa would be tremendous."

If, however, the British could have been persuaded of the soundness of an important American strategical concept, the North African invasion probably would never have occurred. This concept was that the advent of true strategic air power had altered irrevocably and drastically the strategic value and position of narrow seas. Reduced to its simplest terms, so far as the war in Europe was concerned it meant that the fate of the Mediterranean would be determined, not by what occurred on its shores, but by what happened north of the Alps. It was an extremely broad and long-range concept, and unhappily it had to be presented as theory to a group of officers and statesmen who had been fighting nearly three years against an enemy with whom the Americans had yet to come to grips, and whose accumulated facts of experience lent a weight to the logic of their arguments that American vision could not balance. The American theory was based on a firm belief that American heavy bombers could undertake daylight—and therefore, more accurate and efficient—bombardment of the enemy, but the belief had yet to be demonstrated. Meantime, the British had found their own R.A.F. bomber command unable to conduct daylight operations, and were understandably reluctant to discard that hard fact and adopt an American theory. The preponderance of fact and experience was with the British; but history was to add an ironic footnote to the decision, for if the British had accepted the American view the Russians not only would have had a true "second front" a year earlier, but it would have come when the German armies were still deep in Russian territory, and it would almost certainly have been the Anglo-American forces which first reached Central Europe.

Marshall discovered, on this trip to London, what many Americans were to learn during the war: that British staff planning was more thorough, and of a higher order, than the planning work of the

Signal Corps Photo

ITALIAN FRONT

His face grimy with dust, Marshall leaves an infantry company command post in the Grosseto area in June 1944. Behind him in the jeep is General Mark W. Clark.

Signal Corps Photo

FRENCH TRIBUTE

The General's affection for children is reflected in the glowing faces of two youngsters who brought him flowers during his trip to France in October 1944.

American staff. This thorough examination in detail of the requirements for Sledgehammer was convincing that invasion of France in 1942 was impracticable. Yet, when the British had planned well, they lost the lead; for their staff organization and system did not lend itself so well as the American to command, to the prompt and vigorous execution of plans. It was this fact, recognized on both sides, which suggested that an American rather than a British officer should command their joint operations, and this indication was made a certain decision for North Africa by the political necessity of having Americans meet the French. There was considerable bitterness toward the British among French officers and civilians, so much that the Allies went to great lengths to make the projected invasion appear as nearly as possible to be an all-American undertaking. When the question of designating a commander arose, this point had been settled, and there was a strong desire made evident that the commander should be Marshall. It was Admiral King who told the Combined Chiefs that the best man they could get was already in Britain—Eisenhower. Nevertheless, when the final decision was reached on North Africa—the operation was given the code name Torch—Marshall was scheduled as Supreme Commander, with Eisenhower the likely choice for his deputy. Marshall probably did not intend to take the command, preferring to wait for the later and decisive invasion of Europe; for he still regarded Torch, although recognizing its importance, as a sideshow. In the event, Eisenhower went to Africa, not as deputy, but as Supreme Commander.

Back in Washington, the Torch plan threw the staff into high gear. It called for three task forces, of which two would sail from Britain under British naval escort, one entirely American to land at Oran, and one British-American force to land at Algiers. The third, entirely American, was to sail from the United States. The attacks of all three were to be simultaneous. To command the third, the so-called Western Task Force, which was to strike from the Atlantic at Morocco while the two forces from Britain were landing in the Mediterranean, Marshall already had selected the impetuous Major General George Smith Patton, Jr., whom he had known since the first World War, and whom he regarded as one of the smartest tacticians in the entire Army.

When the plans for the task force had been worked out—shipping, as always, was the determining factor in considering the size and make-up of the force—Marshall ordered Patton, then commanding the Desert Training Center at Indio, California, to report to him in Washington. When Patton arrived, Marshall told him what his assignment was. He also told the flamboyant cavalryman and armored expert he must understand, if he accepted the command, that the job had to be done with the troops which the staff had allotted. It was impossible to give him more troops, because that would require more ships, and more ships simply did not exist. Patton nodded, and Marshall then told him to report to the War College, where the staff would show him the detailed plans and brief him thoroughly in the forthcoming operation.

Patton went to the War College, studied the plans, talked to the staff, and telephoned Marshall. He was informed that the Chief of Staff was in conference, and could not be reached, so he talked to McNarney, the deputy. He would have to have a great many more men, he told McNarney, and more ships—he could not possibly do the job without them. McNarney promptly reported this conversation to Marshall, and Marshall simply said, "Order Patton back to the Desert Training Center!"

Forty-eight hours later, Patton telephoned Marshall from California. Once more, it developed, the Chief of Staff was "engaged" and could not take General Patton's call, so once more Patton talked to McNarney. He had, he admitted to the deputy, been thinking the problem over, and he had decided that he could, after all, accomplish the task with the forces assigned. McNarney duly reported this conversation to Marshall, and Marshall told his deputy to "order him back to the War College."

"And that," said Marshall, telling this story later to a group of high-ranking Army officers, "is the way to handle Patton!"

Figuring out a method of making the assertive, self-conscious, and carefully self-schooled Patton obey instructions was not the only, or even the gravest, problem confronting Marshall that summer of 1942. Perhaps the most important was the organization of the Joint Chiefs of Staff, that essentially weak compromise of the proved need for unified control and single command of military forces, in order to make it furnish a relatively high degree of co-ordination of the efforts of the Army, Navy, and Air Forces. An Army officer, himself one of the most distinguished staff officers of the entire war, has said that Marshall's two greatest services to the nation were his early and wholehearted support of the Air Corps's doctrine of strategic air power, and the fact that by his ability, tact, patience, and strength of character "he made the Joint Chiefs of Staff a working organization."

Conceived as an advisory group to the constitutional Commander in Chief, the gravest defect of the Joint Chiefs of Staff was not that the group lacked inherent command authority as a group over all forces, but that it was unable to reach a decision except by unanimous consent. That weakness, Marshall felt, could be counteracted, although not overcome, if the organization included a Chief of Staff to the President. Such an officer would preside at the meetings of the JCS, and by speaking for the President on the total military problem, rather than for one of the three armed services on its portion, might exert a unifying influence that would be absent as long as four officers of equal rank met without a recognized head.

Accordingly, Marshall began trying to "sell" the idea to the President, as early as the spring of 1942. Roosevelt's first reaction was "Nonsense, George, *you're* my Chief of Staff." Marshall pointed out that he was Chief of Staff of the War Department, that as such it was inevitable that he become on occasion a special pleader for the forces directly under his authority, that what the JCS needed was someone at a higher level than even the highest military positions in the War and Navy Departments, to bring into their councils the views of the Commander in Chief, to consider all problems from a vantage point detached from initial bias for any service. Roosevelt resisted the suggestion, for in spite of the fact that his manifold responsibilities left him too little time to give them the attention they needed, he relished the duties of Commander in Chief and disliked the prospect of anyone interposed between him and the direct control of the various armed forces. Nevertheless, he finally accepted Marshall's recommendation.

The opportunity for such an appointment arose when Admiral Stark, Chief of Naval Operations, was designated commander of U.S. Naval Forces in Europe, and Admiral King took over as CNO while retaining command of the fleet. The question then became, whom to recommend for the new post of Chief of Staff to the Commander in Chief? The qualifications required in a candidate narrowed the field, and the choice was difficult. He must be a man of great military distinction, of vision and imagination, of sufficient flexibility of mind to free himself of any inclination to think primarily in terms of his own service—a kind of elder statesman among military officers. The inspiration came during a conference of Marshall and some of his staff. One of them suggested Admiral William D. Leahy, retired former Chief of Naval Operations and until very recently Roosevelt's ambassador to Vichy France. Marshall took the recommendation to Roosevelt, and the President agreed heartily. Leahy became Chief of Staff to the President on July 21.

The wisdom of the appointment became apparent as the JCS began to function more smoothly, but the device never was as effective as had been hoped, partly because it was impossible—and not the President's desire—to give Leahy any greater authority than his own wisdom and the prestige of his position could acquire for him, partly because Admiral King pressed the Navy view of many proposals with great vigor. King was probably one of the ablest strategists the country possessed, and his contributions to operational planning were tremendous. Marshall found him a forceful and convincing supporter of the Chief of Staff's ideas on European strategy, and they were in complete agreement also on strategy in the Pacific—as indeed on most matters. However, King's mind lacked the suppleness that marked Marshall's, and he was unable to rise as far as Marshall did above the interests and desires of his own service. Not long after Leahy became a member of the group and the presiding officer of its meetings, the Joint Chiefs were required to reach a decision on a matter which had been under study for several weeks— a reduction of the Navy's program of battleship and heavy-cruiser building in order to divert some of the steel to production of other types, particularly landing craft and convoy escort vessels. The change had been urgently recommended by the British, and as the discussion—it was a lengthy one—proceeded in the Joint Chiefs' meeting, it became apparent that King alone opposed the shift. When Leahy remarked that it looked to him as though "the vote is three to one," King replied coldly that so far as he was concerned, the Joint Chiefs was not a voting organization on any matter in which the interests of the Navy were involved. It was an accurate statement—the JCS was not a voting organization on any subject, except by mutual and unanimous agreement. King's judgment on military questions usually was sound; but there were many occasions when decision by the Joint Chiefs proved to be impossible—some, as in this case, were ultimately referred to the President for ruling— because once King had reached a decision, it was all but impossible to reopen his mind, even for the consideration of factors which might have altered his decision had they been known when it was made.

Next to this lack of inherent ability to reach a decision by majority vote, the greatest shortcoming of the Joint Chiefs' organization was its failure to include civilians in its make-up. So much of politics was involved in every aspect of the war—in co-ordination (if any) with the Russians, with the French in North Africa, with the Spanish as the North African invasion was planned and occurred, in the Chinese situation, concerning the Australians, the New Zealanders and the British in the Pacific, to name some of the more obvious aspects—that the Joint Chiefs beyond question should have included, not merely the top-ranking military officers, but members of the civilian secretariat of the War and Navy Departments and of the State Department. Marshall recognized that shortcoming, with the result that he constantly referred JCS papers and proposals to Stimson and other members of the War Department secretariat for study and suggestion. Marshall not only welcomed the political advice and guidance of his civilian chiefs; he sought it. But King held no such views, and it was not until the last year of the war that any comparable reference of Joint Chiefs' matters to the Navy secretariat occurred.

Whether such a broader organization could have prevented the political blindness of the American attitude toward General Charles de Gaulle and the Fighting French as the plans were laid for North Africa is extremely doubtful. The fortuitous discovery of Admiral Darlan's presence in North Africa when the landings were made, and the prompt—if less vigorous than seemed indicated—use of that prize of collaboration was an unforeseeable windfall, and military opportunism of the most completely proper and justifiable variety. To one Cabinet protest, Stimson made a wrathful—and Stimson could be thunderously wrathful—and very sound reply, the general tenor being that a lot of men were getting shot, and if the use of Darlan meant a cease-fire order, it was the thing to do.

But the incredible cloak-and-dagger intrigue of the babes in search of a leader, who turned up no more likely candidate than the brave but stupid General Giraud, was comic opera material. That was a State Department and White House operation, although there is strong evidence that many of the American military leaders were unable to free themselves of the sentimental memory of the Marshal Pétain of World War I, which added at least a small bit to the prejudice against De Gaulle. Leahy came back from Vichy to report that the Gaullists had no important strength in France that he could discern, and it appears to have occurred to few American officials that the ambassador to Vichy was not the most likely recipient of Resistance confidence.

The prejudice against De Gaulle was very real, and Roosevelt was its leader. There were some officials, including some in the War Department, who wanted to use him in North Africa and later in France, but they found that such suggestions made Roosevelt almost violently angry. The President had a possessive attitude toward France, and disliked De Gaulle. Accordingly, the leader of the

Fighting French was disregarded, even snubbed; and the busy search for a leader of the French went on until, when they had by ineptitude done a great deal to destroy his effectiveness and sabotage his policies, American leaders made the belated discovery that the much-sought leader had been at hand all the time. Stiff, overly sensitive of his dignity, difficult, and even exasperating, De Gaulle still was the only Frenchman with true prestige among the resisting French, the symbol of their hope of liberation.

In such circumstances, even a properly constituted Joint Chiefs of Staff organization, with political as well as military membership, probably could not have arrived at a rational solution of the French problem that faced them with the invasion of French Africa. The French military in North Africa were loyal to Pétain and distrusted De Gaulle, but the use of that knowledge to get into Morocco and Algiers with the least possible bloodshed and then, when firmly established, to throw Allied support to the Fighting French as the strongest group in metropolitan France would have been no more cynical than was the opportunistic use of Darlan.

As to the North African invasion itself, it failed of its immediate tactical aim—which was the seizure of Tunisia within a matter of weeks to cut Rommel's supply lines and clear the southern shore of the Mediterranean rapidly. Instead, as Marshall and the American planners had feared, it settled into a dragging campaign, a sponge which sucked up more and constantly more men and munitions, delaying Roundup indefinitely. The great triumph of the North African campaign was the manner in which Eisenhower justified the trust which had been placed in him—he had been definitely named as Commander in Chief of the Allied forces as early as August—by creating the pattern of a unified command. Between the assault landings on November 8, 1942, and the crushing of German resistance in Tunisia where the last Axis remnants in Africa surrendered on May 13, 1943, Eisenhower's consistent efforts and great diplomatic gifts had welded all the forces under his command—land, sea, air, and service units of American, British, and French nationality—into a truly unified combat team. It was the Axis powers which had claimed unity, but the Allies who actually had produced the first example.

Among the many other questions confronting Marshall and requiring his close watch in the summer of 1942 were command problems in Australia; arriving at agreements in the Joint and Combined Chiefs' groups for sufficient allocations to the Pacific and Asiatic theaters to check the Japanese advances and exert a constant pressure on that enemy while making certain that nothing developed in the Pacific that would drain critical means away from the European conflict; antisubmarine war on the East Coast of the United States; Stilwell's difficulties with Chiang; a new troop basis for the Army to raise the authorized strength from 4,300,000 to 7,500,000 in 1943; even the problem whether Reserve and National Guard officers should continue to receive leaves of absence in order to attend sessions of state legislatures!

In Australia, the problem of subordinate commanders under MacArthur gave Marshall considerable concern. Since most of the air force which the theater could expect to amass would be American, Major General George C. Kenney was agreed upon as MacArthur's air commander shortly before Marshall and Admiral King were dispatched to London on forty-eight hours' notice by Roosevelt in their attempt to save Sledgehammer. Because both the theater and the air commanders were Americans, political considerations dictated that an Australian have the ground command; but the ranking Australian to whom this command was given was General Sir Thomas Blamey, in whose capacity the Americans found themselves able to place less than complete faith. The difficulty was to find an American officer who could appear to subordinate himself to Blamey, yet give MacArthur the necessary expert control over ground operations. Lieutenant General Robert C. Richardson, who later commanded the Army forces in the Central Pacific under Admiral Nimitz, was the first choice for the Australian assignment; but Richardson reported such strong aversion to the situation that Marshall decided it would be unwise to send him, and Major General Robert Eichelberger was assigned instead.

Meantime, MacArthur had submitted in June a plan for an offensive to retake New Guinea and important surrounding islands in the Southwest Pacific. Marshall and his staff subjected this to close and continuing scrutiny, finally agreeing that while undoubtedly such an offensive would be helpful in the war with Japan, the resources needed simply did not exist. To undertake it, MacArthur had asked that he be given one amphibious division and two aircraft carriers, and it was the shortage of carriers which ruled out the proposal at that time. MacArthur would have to confine his theater to the purely defensive role originally assigned to it, of keeping the Japanese from reaching the highly developed and thickly populated east coast of Australia.

To maintain the Southwest Pacific even as a defensive theater, another purely defensive zone had been established as the South Pacific under the immediate command of Admiral William F. Halsey as part of Nimitz' command of the Pacific Ocean areas. The building of Halsey's wall against Japanese threats to the flank of MacArthur's communications line had involved the establishment of such bases as Bora Bora and Tongatabu, and the erection of strong points in Samoa and New Caledonia. But the enemy was persistent, and Admiral King finally suggested that Halsey undertake a limited offensive in the Solomons to block the Japanese approach. Agreement by the Joint Chiefs was prompt, instructions were sent to Nimitz, and on August 7 the Marines assaulted Guadalcanal and Tulagi.

So far as the main offensive against the Japanese was concerned, Admiral King at a session of the Joint Chiefs demonstrated that the route westward from Hawaii was the line it must follow, and that the Marianas Islands were the key to the entire Pacific. To seize the Marianas, it would be necessary to neutralize the Japanese positions in the strongly fortified Gilbert and Marshall Islands, lest the sea communications from Hawaii to the Marianas be exposed to flank attacks. General Marshall agreed emphatically with King as to the basic strategy in the Pacific, and the Joint Chiefs never deviated from that decision. When it became possible later to allocate additional men and equiment to MacArthur, sufficient to undertake an offensive, his campaigns developed as an additional and secondary offensive, ultimately becoming the left jaw of a vast pincers, or double envelopment, aimed at recapture of the Philippines to serve as the base for final assaults on Japan.

In the relations between China and the United States, Chiang Kai-shek kept matters in turmoil. He objected to Stilwell being his Chief of Staff and at the same time exercising control over lend-lease shipments to China. He objected to the retreat of Chinese forces from Burma into India—although this objection never reached Stilwell, and the American general took into India with him the Chinese troops which became the nucleus of the forces he proposed to train there. (The Generalissimo did not know, when he tried at the last minute to order them back to China, that Stilwell's final message to him after the defeat in Burma, announcing that the retreat to India had begun, had been followed by a personal announcement from the radio operator beginning the destruction of his equipment that "I'm taking an ax to this goddamned box!"). As already noted, Chiang had objected strenuously when Brereton was ordered to rush his 10th Air Force planes from the CBI theater to the Middle East. In July, he messaged Roosevelt that Chinese resistance might collapse, and asked that Harry Hopkins be sent out quickly for conferences (Lauchlin Currie was sent instead). By the end of July, Marshall had received the Generalissimo's urgent request for the immediate assignment to China of 500 planes, 5 divisions, and supply lines to deliver 500 tons of supplies monthly. The upshot of all these disagreements, discussions, pleas, and worries was the program under which Stilwell trained 100,000 Chinese troops at Ramgarh, the air line over the Himalayan "hump" was expanded until it was carrying not hundreds but thousands of tons a month to China, the building of the Ledo Road, the offensive which retook Burma (Marshall thought Stilwell's Hukawng Valley campaign the most brilliant tactically of the entire war, with MacArthur's operations which reconquered the Philippines ranking next), and the final bitterness which caused Stilwell's removal. All this was done, at the cost of lives and treasure which might have been spent to better purpose elsewhere, because it was deemed necessary to keep China in the war, and might make China's man power an effective military resource against the Japanese. That elusive goal was still a lure.

Marshall was concerned that year also with the organization and growth of the Women's Army Corps, and with getting the draft age lowered to eighteen years. The latter was a difficult struggle, but the Army had desperate need of younger men, and the Congress eventually approved the War Department request.

Despite the failure of the North African venture to accomplish its intended rapid seizure of Tunisia, all of Algiers and Morocco came into Allied hands, and Dakar joined up as well. The German threat to the Atlantic was removed—Hitler, having failed to invade England, and having attacked Russia in the summer of 1941, now had made his second great error when he failed to move promptly through Spain and crush the Anglo-American invasion of French Africa as he might have done. Tunisia was not yet taken, but it was between the jaws of the nutcracker formed by Eisenhower's forces on the west, and the British Eighth Army advancing across Libya under Montgomery. It was high time to map the next moves, and accordingly Roosevelt and Churchill met at Casablanca with their military advisers on January 14, 1943.

The probability, as seen by Marshall, that the North African campaign would delay Roundup beyond 1943 had now become a certainty. The invasion of Normandy was still accepted as the basic operation for the defeat of Germany, but there was no indication when it could be undertaken. To begin with, the fall of Tunisia—when that occurred—would not end the Mediterranean problem. The inland sea with its important short shipping lines to the Middle East and India would not be safe to the Allies when the southern shore was cleared of the enemy. It would be necessary, as well, to knock the Axis out of the Mediterranean islands and Italy. Operation Torch had become a sponge, indeed. But it had produced one strategic advantage of incalculable value: it had wrested the initiative from the Germans and given it to the Allies. From now on, it was the Axis which was on the defensive, not Britain and the United States. It was Hitler and Mussolini, Jodl and Von Rundstedt, who were wondering where the next blow would fall, not Roosevelt and Churchill, Marshall and Dill, Arnold and Portal, King and Cunningham.

But North Africa itself had become a means, not an end; and at Casablanca the Combined Chiefs decided to instruct Eisenhower to launch an attack on Sicily in July as a necessary preliminary to a knockout blow against Italy. It was decided to continue Bolero, the accumulation in Britain for the assault on France, against the day when that invasion should become possible. And it was decided to undertake a great strategic bombardment of Germany to weaken the military and industrial might of the enemy as an essential prelude to the invasion of Normandy.

The strategic air offensive provided the most contentious arguments at Casablanca. The British were convinced that the daylight bombing planned and then being developed by the American 8th Air Force under Major General Ira C. Eaker could not succeed. Eaker's force still was small, although growing rapidly, and it had not yet demonstrated to British satisfaction that the Flying Fortress, unlike the British bombers, could meet the enemy fighters in daylight combat without prohibitive losses. The Americans realized that, when the 8th built its attacking force to such strength that it became a serious threat to Germany, the *Luftwaffe* would turn its full force against the bombers unless they could be escorted, and work was proceeding feverishly on the development of fighters with longer tactical radius to provide escort for the heavies. It still was largely theory, however, and the British clung to the facts of their own experience. Spearheaded by Churchill, they fought their last battle at Casablanca to get the American heavy bombers diverted to night attacks of the British variety, abandoning the daylight precision attacks which were the core of the American strategic air bombardment concept. Marshall and Arnold fought stubbornly and persistently, but Churchill was a master phrasemaker, and he painted such vivid pictures of the ghastly casualties in store that they saw they were losing the struggle. Arnold summoned Eaker down from England—Brigadier General Carl Spaatz already was at Casablanca.

When Eaker stepped off the plane which brought him to the conference, Arnold was waiting for him, and told him that the conference had reached an agreement to assign the Fortresses to night bombing missions, abandoning the daylight bombing. The Americans had put up a good fight, and they had lost. Eaker decided to have one more try, on his own; and so he went to Churchill's villa. There he argued at length with the man who was not only one of the greatest, but also one of the most stubborn leaders of the war. Finally Churchill capitulated.

"You haven't convinced me you can do it," he told Eaker. "But you have convinced me that you ought to have a chance!"

What had torpedoed Churchill was a phrase. The Prime Minister not only was a master of phrases, but he was vulnerable to them, too; and Eaker had come up with one of the best—"Bombing around the clock," the 8th by day, the R.A.F. by night. And so the great bomber offensive was approved.

XIX

Too Good for Command

The extraordinary place of absolute trust that an American soldier had come to have in the hearts of the American people was revealed in dramatic fashion by the universal distress and protest which followed the disclosure late in the summer of 1943 that Marshall would leave his position as Chief of Staff to take the field command of the invasion of Europe.

That Marshall did not, in the end, get this command was to him a personal disappointment which he concealed beneath that willingness to serve unselfishly where he was most needed which had marked his entire career. For forty-one years he had wanted only the command of troops, and for most of them he had been denied it. Now he was given, and then lost again, a command such as no soldier in history had held.

Yet there was triumph in the deprivation; for what brought it about was the demonstration that the American public, traditionally distrustful of its military men, had an unshakable faith in this one. Marshall, who had consciously and deliberately effaced himself, who had refused interviews and discouraged writings about himself, who was contemptuous of self-dramatization and self-seeking, whose biennial reports gave no slightest hint of the tremendous part he had played in the events he recorded, emerged not only as the most important figure of the war, but acknowledged as such. He could not have the field command because the job he was doing was more important, the people of America recognized it as more important, and recognized that there was no one to take his place in it.

The decision that Marshall would command the invasion was not made until August 1943, although it had been a generally accepted likelihood among Allied leaders since July 1942. The decision that, instead of Marshall, Eisenhower should command was made in December at Cairo and Teheran. Meantime, before the question of a commander arose, the operation itself had been fixed.

That decision was made in Washington in May 1943, at the so-called Trident Conference of the President, the Prime Minister, and their staffs. Some extraordinarily important decisions were made at that meeting. The first was that, after Sicily had been taken, the Mediterranean campaign should be pushed so far that Italy would be forced out of the war. Another was to bring the important German oil refineries at Ploesti in Rumania under bombardment by American strategic bombers until they were destroyed or so crippled as to be worthless to the enemy. The Allied leaders agreed to build up the air transport route from India to China, and initiate aggressive land campaigns to clear North Burma and reopen a ground supply route to Chungking. Admiral Nimitz and General MacArthur, as a result of the Trident Conference, were directed to move against the outer Japanese defenses—drive the enemy from the Aleutians, seize the Marshalls, some of the Carolines, the remainder of the Solomons, the Bismarck Archipelago, and all of New Guinea. American mobilization and production had reached the point at which the Allies could undertake offensives, not just on two fronts, but on several. Finally, the invasion of France and a direct assault on Germany were confirmed. The code name was changed from Roundup to Overlord, and the target date for the assault landings in Normandy was set for early in May 1944.

The agreement that, after Sicily, Italy was to be knocked out by exploiting whatever advantage Eisenhower should decide he possessed was made by the Americans with the reservation that nothing should interfere with Overlord, but by the British with one eye on the capture of all Italy and the other on Yugoslavia and the Ljubljana Gap—the Balkans again. From Washington, Churchill set out for Algiers to sell his ideas to Eisenhower, and it was the Prime Minister himself who suggested to Roosevelt that, since his desires hardly coincided with those of the United States, the President had better send Marshall along to argue the opposite view. The upshot was that Eisenhower, to whom the decision was to be left—subject to Combined Chiefs of Staff approval—whether to hit Italy or stop in Sicily, declined to commit himself until he had learned in Sicily what kind of fight he might expect on the mainland. One firm decision made at these Algiers talks was that Churchill would urge the British Chiefs of Staff, and Marshall the American, to authorize Eisenhower's air forces to bomb the railway yards in Rome.

The attack on Sicily was made July 10, and largely through the boldness of General Patton's Seventh Army the island had been conquered and all organized resistance obliterated by August 17. The fall of Sicily was accompanied by the fall of Mussolini, and Marshal Badoglio began negotiating with Eisenhower's headquarters for a surrender by the Royal Italian Government. The invasion of Italy was launched, but—as in most campaigns—the best-laid plans did not come off as hoped, and Italy became to some degree what Marshall had feared it might—"a vacuum into which the resources of the cross-Channel operation would be dissipated. . . ." The Germans reacted strongly, and instead of accomplishing a quick seizure of Rome, the Allies in the south of Italy had to fight a long and bloody and terrible campaign to get the Eternal City—as they had been forced to fight an entire winter for Tunisia, instead of seizing it within the first few weeks after North Africa was invaded.

The Italian campaign brought terrible personal tragedy to the Marshalls. On the morning of May 29, Mrs. Marshall was startled to see the General return to his quarters hardly an hour after he had left for his office in the Pentagon. He had come back to tell his wife that her son, Second Lieutenant Allen Tupper Brown of the Armored Force, had been killed that morning on the Anzio beachhead.

The initial phases of the Italian campaign were accompanied by one of the Army's worst scandals. Despite the ill-advised efforts to suppress it, the story that General Patton had slapped an enlisted man hospitalized in Sicily for "battle fatigue" became public property, and the most sensational news story of the war. The public reaction was the more violent because of the bumbling attempts at suppression, launched from the untenable premise that publication of Patton's indefensible action would jeopardize the security of operations in the Mediterranean theater.

It was true that Patton, whom the Germans feared mightily and with reason after his dazzling Sicilian campaign, was being used for an elaborate "cover" or deception plan, seeking to draw off German forces from the south of Italy by making it appear that Patton and his Seventh Army—by that time merely a headquarters, an Army without troops—which had become the great mystery force of the area after Sicily, were preparing to launch an attack against the Italian coast north of Rome from the islands of Corsica and Sardinia. But for all that the "security" plea was used to justify the suppression, the fact remains that Eisenhower proposed to relieve Patton of command, and probably would have done so if Marshall had failed to intervene, not with orders, but with a strong reminder of Patton's unmatched usefulness as a combat leader and tactician.

"Georgie's in trouble again," Marshall remarked to some officers at the War Department. "He's always in trouble. But I'm not getting rid of Patton. He was solely responsible for Sicily."

The decision to keep Patton in a command capacity, while reprimanding him severely for so flagrant a violation of Army Regulations and the code of an officer, was a sound one—Patton was too valuable to lose. He was also too valuable to have his usefulness impaired by the scandalous controversy which raged after the disclosure of his action. That was a public relations failing. The scandal was largely because of the attempted suppression, and since it was the most notable incident resulting from a shortsighted public relations policy in the War Department throughout the war which Marshall failed to correct, the Chief of Staff's attitude towards public relations merits examination.

Certainly Marshall's own understanding of public relations purposes and methods was profound. His impact upon Congress when he appeared before its committees was extraordinary, and this was because he knew exactly what to say, when to say it, and in what tone. He had, also, an engaging way of taking listeners into his confidence, telling them little things that they had no right to know, and which they knew they had no right to know. He achieved the same kind of results at his press conferences, which were fairly frequent before the war. After Pearl Harbor, he occasionally appeared at "off the record" general news conferences, and he instituted a series of monthly briefings for a carefully selected group of reporters and editors which continued more or less regularly throughout the war. The story of his press conference in Algiers—at which he accepted a question from each of some sixty correspondents, thought for a moment, then began a beautifully organized discourse which reviewed for them the entire course and progress of the war, and as he talked answered every question which had been asked, nodding slightly to the man who had asked it as he reached that part of his talk—the story has become one of the classic Marshall anecdotes.

Part of his personal success in public relations was due to a shrewd assessment of the lengths to which his listeners could be trusted. More of it was due to the fact that it was obvious to the listeners that Marshall believed, without affectation, that they were entitled to every scrap of information which he could give them without endangering the security of operations. And he did believe that. How firmly he believed it, and how thoroughly he understood the reason why free access to information should be restricted only by security requirements, was indicated early in the war when General Staff intelligence officers, suspicious of the validity of the code of voluntary censorship adopted by the American press, proposed to Marshall that he issue orders under the espionage laws imposing a strict and compulsory military censorship for the duration of the war. His reply to them, delivered not harshly but simply and with conviction, might be paraphrased thus: "We have the fate of the nation in our hands. We could fail, and it would be disastrous. We think we are competent—we would not be human if we did not think so; but suppose we were not here in Washington. Suppose we were out in the field, in the Army, and some other group was here exercising the responsibility that we hold. If they were doing something we thought was disastrous, and we heard they had done what you have just proposed to me, how do you think we would ever make them understand how we felt about it?"

Yet that attitude did not prevail in the Army's public relations establishment, and all too frequently the plea of "security" was used to cover nothing more important than embarrassment. The director of public relations in the War Department once told a reporter, during a discussion of the Patton incident, that he saw his job as one of two primary responsibilities, the first to "protect" the Secretary of War from criticism, the second to "protect" the Chief of Staff from criticism, and that accordingly "I have to set up resistances against the press!" Because of the lack of fundamentally sound public relations policies at the War Department level, those "resistances" extended to every theater. Since the attitude was completely at variance with Marshall's own views, why did he not make his views prevail?

The answer lies in the fact that the Bureau of Public Relations was established, not as a part of the Army, but as a part of the Office of the Secretary of War. Until the summer of 1940, public relations had been a stepchild activity of the Military Intelligence Division of the General Staff. In that year, after Stimson became Secretary of War, the need for expansion of this service beyond the scope of the old G-2 Press Branch was recognized, and the Bureau was created. Because it was intended primarily to serve civilian individuals, groups, and organizations, it was placed in the Secretary's office, rather than under the Chief of Staff. If Stimson had been as appreciative as Marshall of the true purposes of public relations, this would have been in fact—as it was in theory—the proper place for the Bureau. Unfortunately, he was not so appreciative; the "resistances" had Stimson's approval. Marshall made one unsuccessful effort to bring the Bureau back under General Staff aegis. When he failed, he maintained thereafter his carefully correct detachment from the duties of the Secretary's office. He deliberately refrained from any major effort to change the personnel or the methods of the Bureau; and the Army suffered in public esteem as a consequence.

By the time the Quadrant Conference was held in Quebec in August 1943 by Roosevelt and Churchill, accompanied as usual by their respective batteries of military experts, Badoglio was negotiating with Eisenhower for the Italian surrender, and the theater commander was instructed from the conference to seize Sardinia and Corsica, and proceed to the Italian mainland, but making his program in the knowledge that any commitments he made in Italy must not interfere with the now well-advanced plans for the invasion of Normandy.

"Compelling reasons had developed for the invasion of the Italian mainland," Marshall explained in his last biennial report. "The operation (Avalanche) would enable us to capitalize on the collapse of Italian resistance; it offered a field for engaging German divisions which otherwise might operate against the Red Army and later against the forces in France; it would provide airfields from which the German homeland and the Balkans could be bombed from substantially shorter range; it would complete Allied control of the Mediterranean."

Marshall did not say so, but the secondary sponge was still sucking up primary resources.

To create a diversion and help draw off German strength which otherwise might be thrown against the Normandy beachhead, and to do it in a fashion that would permit a development and exploitation as part of the whole campaign in France, the Quebec conference planned an invasion of the French Riviera, to occur simultaneously with the Normandy invasion. The Normandy plan had been renamed Overlord, but the old name Sledgehammer was remembered when the Southern France operation was given the code name "Anvil."

At the Quebec conference also, the Southeast Asia theater was created and placed under the command of Admiral Lord Louis Mountbatten. Stilwell became Mountbatten's deputy, and the theater was directed to begin an offensive in North Burma that winter, to extend the Ledo Road to a juncture with the old Burma Road as rapidly as the projected campaigns could clear the route, and to build a pipeline from Calcutta to Assam and another paralleling the Ledo Road to build up the supply of motor fuels to China.

The expansion of air transport operations over the Hump was agreed upon at Quebec, and the Combined Chiefs decided to accept the Army Air Forces' plan to establish bases in China from which their new giant bomber, the B-29, could operate against the Japanese home islands. Superfortress bases also were planned for Pacific islands still to be conquered. And all these proposals had to be coordinated, by the most detailed and meticulous division of means, to care for allocation of ocean tonnage, the possibility of airborne operations to break a stalemate in Italy, the increasing build-up for the invasion of Normandy, assistance to MacArthur in his Southwest Pacific campaigns, the Navy's needs for the campaigns in the Pacific Ocean areas, and dozens of other pressing requirements.

And at Quebec Marshall was designated to command the European invasion. To make certain that this appointment went to Marshall, whom he regarded as the ablest officer the Allies had and whose passionate desire for command he knew, had been the principal reason for Stimson's trip to London that summer of 1943, although the ostensible reason was an inspection by the Secretary of American forces stationed in the United Kingdom. He found Churchill reluctant to shift Marshall from the Combined Chiefs level, not because the Prime Minister disliked Marshall, but because he thought that Eisenhower's command organization was working smoothly, and Marshall was more valuable in the supreme staff assignment. Nevertheless, he yielded to Stimson's insistence that Marshall had a right to the greatest field command of the war. Churchill could understand that—and he not only regarded Marshall as the greatest military figure of the war, but mixed considerable affection with his great respect for the American general.

However, there was potent American opposition—and for very sound reasons—to the Marshall appointment. After the decision had been made, discussing it with long faces and shaking heads, Admiral

Leahy, General Arnold, and Admiral King each discovered that both the others had gone to Roosevelt, privately and on his own initiative, during the conference to urge him to keep Marshall in Washington. They told him that they believed the part Marshall was playing as a member of the Joint and Combined Chiefs organization was so important that they hoped the President would not consent to his removal from those councils. When the President asked King who else was available, the Admiral replied, "General Eisenhower is a natural!"

Secretary of the Navy Knox, as well as Stimson, came to Quebec during the conference, and he impressed upon his Chief of Naval Operations and Commander in Chief of the Fleet his desire that Marshall have the Overlord command. Knox cited the fame of Pershing, the obscurity of March, in the first World War. King retorted that the two situations were not comparable—the first World War was fought on a single front, the second on as many as nine—and he reiterated his belief that Marshall's work in Washington was vastly more important to the country.

Back in Washington, the following weeks saw the development of a determined campaign to keep Marshall in Washington. The reason so many people dreaded the thought of Marshall's departure was their knowledge that Marshall not only was the dominant figure on the Joint and Combined Chiefs organization, which decided the strategy of operations and—more importantly—dictated the allocations of men and equipment to implement the strategic decisions; but that he was the only eligible officer who could achieve and maintain some semblance of unity in the American forces. One of those most keenly aware of this fact was General Embick, still chairman of the Inter-American Defense Board but also chairman of the Joint Chiefs' Joint Strategic Survey Committee (this was one of several committees which gave the Joint and Combined Chiefs a measure of that extremely valuable British institution, the permanent secretariat of government ministries).

Embick, when he learned of the designation of Marshall to command Overlord, decided to attack the decision through the White

House influence of Harry Hopkins, chairman of the Munitions Assignment Board. Hopkins' executive officer in this job was Major General James H. Burns, who as a colonel and Assistant Secretary Johnson's executive had initiated the munitions program of June 1940. Embick asked Burns to intercede with Hopkins, and Burns returned with word that the decision was a firm one, past changing.

But Embick was not satisfied. He next approached General Malin Craig, the retired Chief of Staff who had returned to active duty as chairman of a personnel board in the War Department, and asked Craig to arrange an appointment for both of them with Pershing to discuss the problem with the aged General of the Armies. At this meeting, the three agreed that Embick would prepare a letter to the President, which Pershing would sign—the letter, rather than a personal call and interview, being chosen so as to make the protest a matter of written record. The letter expressed the conviction that Marshall's transfer "would be a fundamental and very grave error in our military policy." The President replied that he thought the only fair thing to do was to give "George" a chance in the field—that he wanted him to be the Pershing of the war against the Axis, which he could not be if he remained in Washington.

Craig then went to seek help from Colonel John Callan O'Laughlin, editor and publisher of the *Army and Navy Journal* and old friend of Pershing and most of the senior officers of both the Army and the Navy. Word of the appointment already had "leaked" to the press, and the *Journal* began an editorial denunciation of the transfer of Marshall to the field which fed a rapidly growing public protest.

Stimson, meanwhile—and even before the appointment became generally known—had realized that a controversy probably would follow the news, and had moved to build a backfire against it. Sending for a member of Congress—the same to whom Craig and Marshall had gone after the 10,000-plane episode—Stimson informed him that a decision had been made concerning Marshall, that it was made purely on the basis that Marshall was the man pre-eminently fitted for the new assignment, that the news probably would "leak" and protest follow, possibly with charges that Marshall was being moved to make room for another officer, and that he wanted him to begin, in guarded cloakroom conversations, to create a state of mind in the Congress which would make this opportunity for Marshall acceptable on Capitol Hill.

Marshall kept silent through all this. He never indicated to anyone, unless it was to his wife, what his own desires were in the matter; and he never knew any of the extraordinary intrigue initiated by others. Arnold, Leahy, King, Embick, Craig, Pershing, O'Laughlin, Stimson all acted without prior consultation with the Chief of Staff, or later disclosure to him of their action. To add to Marshall's embarrassment as the controversy developed, Senator Johnson of Colorado chose this period to air a suggestion that Marshall should be the next Democratic nominee for President, and a new wave of speculation was started.

The hubub was at its height when Marshall left at the end of November for the Cairo conference of the Anglo-American leaders with Generalissimo Chiang Kai-shek and their Teheran meeting with Stalin and the Russian military leaders. At Cairo, where the Generalissimo's demands collided with the hard fact that every Allied resource already was committed to paramount operations, the decision was made reluctantly that it would be impossible to increase the speed and scope of the Burma campaign just getting under way by adding an amphibious assault in the Bay of Bengal—the men and guns, but particularly the ships and landing craft, could have been made available only at the cost of abandoning the invasion of France in the spring of 1944. The only promise the Americans could make to the Chinese was that the operations in Burma would be pushed with the greatest vigor possible in order to reopen overland communications with China.

The vigorous and convincing, but considerate and diplomatic, part which Marshall played in these meetings apparently brought to a head the misgivings of the President about losing Marshall from the strategic-diplomatic councils of the Allies, for he sent Harry Hopkins to the General. Hopkins said the President was worried about the situation at the top level, and was now uncertain about the wisdom of assigning Marshall to command Overlord. He wanted to see Marshall the next evening. When the General reported for that appointment, Roosevelt asked him whether he thought he would be of greater value as Chief of Staff or in command of Overlord. Marshall declined to evaluate his own services, leaving that to the Commander in Chief. He told Roosevelt, however, that he thought the war made personal preferences of no account, and he wanted the President to know that, whatever his decision, it would be "all right" with Marshall. Thus it was that at Teheran the President informed his Allies that it would be Eisenhower, not Marshall, who would command Overlord the next spring.

It was not characteristic of Roosevelt to change his mind when he had reached a major decision, and the public outcry is not sufficient explanation of this change on the score of Marshall's assignment. Actually, what Marshall had said ruefully to a friend four years before was the President's method had now been completely reversed so far as the Chief of Staff was concerned—Roosevelt now called Marshall over not to *tell* him, but to *ask* him. It was a reflection from the White House of the extraordinary influence of Marshall's character, and of that air of reserve wisdom and reserve authority which pervaded the War Department and dominated the Army to an astonishing degree. During the first World War, Peyton March had compelled obedience in the Department by strict methods, but Marshall obtained a higher degree of it, and almost without method. Not only did officers put his orders into effect, but all of them—from Somervell, McNair, Eisenhower down to junior officers, including those who did not quite know what Marshall wanted and could not follow his imagination and ideas—had an unhesitating desire to make even his thoughts effective. It was a palpable if intangible quality which prevented Marshall's differences with Admiral King from developing into a schism, which enabled him to keep the British, Eisenhower, MacArthur, the War Department, all in line, which had an immense impact upon industrial leaders, editors and publishers throughout the United States. Even the President wanted very much to do what George Marshall thought it wise to do.

The Combined Chiefs of Staff came back from Teheran—where

the Anglo-American team had told the Russians that Overlord would come the first week in May—and issued the directive to Eisenhower on his new job: "You will enter the continent of Europe and, in conjunction with the other Allied nations, undertake operations aimed at the heart of Germany and the destruction of her armed forces."

Then Marshall, without informing the President lest the Commander in Chief protest the dangerous trip, returned to the United States by air through India, Australia, and the Pacific Ocean areas. When he reached Australia after a flight of 3,400 miles from Ceylon, he found MacArthur's aide, Colonel Lloyd Lehrbas, waiting with arrangements made for a day of relaxation—surf bathing, and an unsuccessful chase in jeeps after kangaroos—before proceeding to MacArthur's headquarters in New Guinea by air. At this time the Solomons campaign was far advanced, and operations were going forward on Bougainville at the northern end of the archipelago under Halsey's command. MacArthur's leapfrogging up the New Guinea coast had reached Finschhafen and the grip on the Huon Peninsula was being consolidated. Operations linking the two Southwest Pacific drives, Halsey's through the Solomons, MacArthur's on New Guinea, had been started with co-ordinated attacks on New Britain.

As Marshall moved eastward across the Pacific, he got a firsthand briefing from the commanders at all headquarters on the other operations, particularly the invasion of the Gilbert Islands. Baker, Nukufetan, and Nanomea Islands had been occupied in September, and in November had come the operations in the Gilberts, with the bloody tragedy of Tarawa, and the seizure of Makin in another difficult and stubborn fight. The invasion of the Marshalls was at hand—Namur, Roi, and Kwajalein. With a fantastic force of men and equipment now building up in Britain for Normandy and the campaign which would decide the war and the fate of the world, with the world's most powerful air force—which meant another heavy drain on shipping—hammering at the enemy and headed for the climactic battles of February 1944 which wrecked the *Luftwaffe*, with a major campaign devouring men and material in the cold mud of Italy, with MacArthur's forces on the move in major operations and Stilwell's on the move in Burma, the Allies still possessed the resources to begin the great Pacific campaign.

But all was not well in the Pacific, and Marshall returned to Washington perturbed by what he had seen. The General himself would rather have forgotten the bitterness of the spiteful episodes that marred the American Pacific campaigns, and it is unnecessary and undesirable to dwell at length upon them. Yet they cannot be ignored, for their effect has gone beyond the personalities involved and fed a controversy obscuring the fact that some basic issues were brought to the fore in the Pacific, and never settled. The Joint Chiefs of Staff performed a tremendous service for the nation, attaining a degree of unified purpose and accomplishment without precedent. But the Joint Chiefs drew closest to complete failure when they came to the question of unity of command for the last great campaign against Japan itself. That question was never settled, and the reasons are to be found in what happened earlier in the Pacific.

An intense dislike of MacArthur pervaded the Navy. The vast majority of those Navy men who shared it had never seen MacArthur, had never been near his theater of operations, knew nothing of the actions or words which may have created the attitude, but nevertheless fed on the gossip and adopted the dislike. The attitude appears to have had its beginning in the Philippines in the summer of 1941 in a quarrel between MacArthur and Admiral Thomas C. Hart, commanding the Asiatic Fleet, whose headquarters were at Cavite on Manila Bay. It was fed by resentment of MacArthur's failure even to mention the sailors and Marines on Bataan in a communiqué (the expendable PT boats and crews, for instance, never were identified in MacArthur's announcement as a Navy group, but always as "MacArthur's PT boats"). It became a Navy cult, this resentment, during the months when the news stories emanating from MacArthur's theater built up the fiction that the Southwest Pacific would have been the major area of operations against the Japanese except for the Navy's preoccupation with "island-hopping" and a queer notion that the war with Japan was the Navy's exclusive property. Some of that propaganda was blatant, some of it extremely subtle, but the effect was uniformly unfortunate.

Another personality involved in the discord was that of Lieutenant General Holland M. Smith, United States Marine Corps. He came to be disliked by Army men almost as intensely as MacArthur was disliked by Navy personnel. Some of the reasons concerned certain operations in the Gilberts and the Marianas, while others are indicated by those characteristics which conferred on him the nickname "Howling Mad."

The third major factor involved in the dissensions which marred the developing Pacific campaigns was the differences in purpose, organization, and method between the Army and the Marine Corps. The Marines exist to support the fleet in the accomplishment of fleet missions, and are used as well for landing forces to protect American lives and property in disturbed foreign areas, or as occupation forces to preserve order and maintain peace in strife-torn lands. Their wartime duties envision their employment as expeditionary forces to serve the fleet. Their peacetime organization involves no unit larger than a division, and no training for extended land campaigns. In essence, their technique is that of the landing party, a beach assault force, and no troops in the world are the equals of the United States Marines in amphibious assault tactics.

The Army, on the other hand, is intended to conduct extensive land campaigns, and its organization and training reflect that mission. Its basic battle unit is the corps, formed of two or more divisions plus detached units of heavy artillery, engineers, signal troops, tanks, and other forces which are manipulated by the corps commander. The next higher unit is the army, consisting normally of two or more—frequently more—corps, with perhaps additional unattached divisions, and a complement of army troops and reserves. How great a part these corps and army units, as distinct from divisions, play in battlefield calculations is indicated by the Army's rule-of-thumb figure that an army commander has in his force 35,000 men per division. The division numbers approximately 16,000, so it can be seen readily that the corps and army troops greatly outnumber the actual division troops. To maneuver and supply such a force is an exceedingly complicated task, calling for rigorous training, and this training is the goal of the entire Army educational system. Marshall's plea to the Congressional committees in 1940 and 1941 for funds to conduct extensive maneuvers was predicated on the necessity to develop corps commanders and staffs.

Such training of corps commanders and staffs is not done by the Marine Corps, precisely because the Marines' mission does not contemplate extensive land campaigns requiring battle units of that size. But the Marines were engaged in the creation of a corps when Marshall made his Pacific trip, and the General expressed on his return some doubt of the ability of Marine officers to handle units of that size. Such ability is not a matter of native talent, but of training. Admiral King resented the suggestion.

"Well, General," he said, "when you have two or more divisions, what do you call it? To my mind it is a corps, even if it lacks the units in the Army's tables of organization!"

The Admiral had asked a rhetorical question, and answered it with a fallacy. It was ominously indicative of the misconception prevailing in the Navy, and to some extent in the Marine Corps, which was an unhappy augury of things to come. Some of them had already come, in fact. "Howling Mad" Smith, who viewed the inexpertly planned and tragically costly battle for Tarawa as new glory for the Marines, had been caustic about the combat team of the Army's 27th Division on Makin.

He became more caustic the following June when the 27th participated in the bitter struggle on Saipan, and a correspondent writing from his headquarters fed the public a mass of misinformation about that battle which provoked a savage inter-service tension that marred Army-Navy relations for the remainder of the war. The truth was that the 27th Division fought on Saipan with magnificent courage and great skill. During the battle, General "Howling Mad" Smith, U.S.M.C., removed Major General Ralph B. Smith, U.S.A., from the command of the 27th, and the hysterical and slanderous account filed by a correspondent whose outlet was unfortunately a news medium of national circulation appeared to be designed to justify that action.

However, no justification was necessary. The repercussions of the Saipan incident reached the level of the Joint Chiefs of Staff, but it was not the removal of General Ralph Smith which provoked an incident. In war, it is and must be the unquestioned and absolute prerogative of a superior commander to remove any subordinate, for any reason at all, even if it be no more than that he does not like the man, and finds his presence disturbing. Marshall knew that as well as any military man, and while he may have thought that the action was unjust to General Ralph Smith, he never questioned the right of the corps commander to remove him. What disturbed Marshall, and disturbed him very much, was that the information reaching the public—and so getting back to the soldiers—from General Holland Smith's headquarters was obviously destroying in the Pacific the unity of purpose which he had struggled so hard and so long to create in all theaters. Furthermore, he did not respect General Holland Smith's abilities as a commander. And so it happened that he lost his temper—one of the very rare occasions of the entire war. At a meeting of the Joint Chiefs, Admiral King made a slighting reference to Army commanders. He probably had MacArthur in mind, but the Saipan incident was fresh, and Marshall turned to the Admiral and told him harshly that, if he had his way, no Army troops would ever again serve under General Holland Smith.

The version of that incident which "leaked" into the gossip of Washington had Marshall saying Army troops would never again serve under Marine or Navy command. This was not so—Marshall said Holland Smith, and meant that officer alone. The account of an unfortunate episode and the bitterness which followed Saipan would not be complete without adding that Admiral Chester W. Nimitz, commanding the Pacific Ocean areas, cleared the 27th's record of the charges of failure and cowardice which had been disseminated, and tried unsuccessfully to have the offending correspondent's credentials revoked.

There were other causes of irritation in the Pacific, where Navy and Army forces in great numbers were engaged in joint operations. One of the major efforts of the Joint Chiefs was to change the Navy's habit of using supply ships as warehouses, immobilizing important amounts of shipping instead of unloading the cargoes and returning the vessels to the global but inadequate shipping pool. Most of the differences, however, were those little and unimportant things which slowly added up to large resentments. They were inevitable when men engaged in the same or similar tasks wore different uniforms, lived in different and unequal quarters, ate different and unequal food, enjoyed markedly different privileges. Such trivial matters, involving many men in many places, tend to create jealousies and antagonisms, not unity.

When Marshall returned on Christmas Eve from the Cairo-Teheran conferences and his Pacific trip, he found that the Army had taken over the railroads, and a steel strike was threatened. In view of the enormous production needed to make the great European and Pacific campaigns possible—it was already becoming evident that landing craft and other auxiliaries would not be available in time for Overlord, which would have to be postponed from May to June and could be mounted then only at the cost of delaying the diversionary invasion of southern France—he was both worried and angry. His anger became intense when his Military Intelligence Division gave him a report showing that German propagandists were using the strikes and labor troubles of the United States in broadcasts to their Balkan satellites, counteracting the Allied moves to split those countries away from the Axis. On his birthday, December 31, 1943, he held one of his off-the-record conferences with a picked group of reporters, who saw, not the suave and reticent Marshall they had known, but a new Marshall shaking with fury. They did not know, and he could not tell them, all that was at stake; but they heard a scathing denunciation of the conditions which fed Axis propaganda, and a warning of the fatal effect that additional strikes would have on the war.

The General's statement was important news, and stories were written immediately by those at the conference—of course, without attribution to Marshall or any hint which might identify him as the source. There was an immediate and violent reaction from organized labor, and considerable unfavorable comment in the press. Then, when Marshall asked for the monitored Axis broadcasts to substantiate the summary which had been given to him, they did not exist. The summary contained some G-2 assumptions, and rather overstated the facts. Marshall was identified several days later as the source of the story, but by that time the Army already had a new Chief of its Military Intelligence. Then a statement from William Green, demanding a presidential investigation of the mysterious Marshall incident and a reprimand for the individual responsible, set the tide of opinion running the opposite direction.

While the threatened steel strike did not occur, the incident was Marshall's worst, and almost his only, personal public relations failure. It was a failure because the General failed to take account of the difference between his usual off-the-record conference, which was an informative background narration of the war's progress for the guidance of commentators and news bureau managers, and a statement of vigorous opinion on a current domestic problem. The latter is the kind of statement which should never be made "off the record," but openly and boldly.

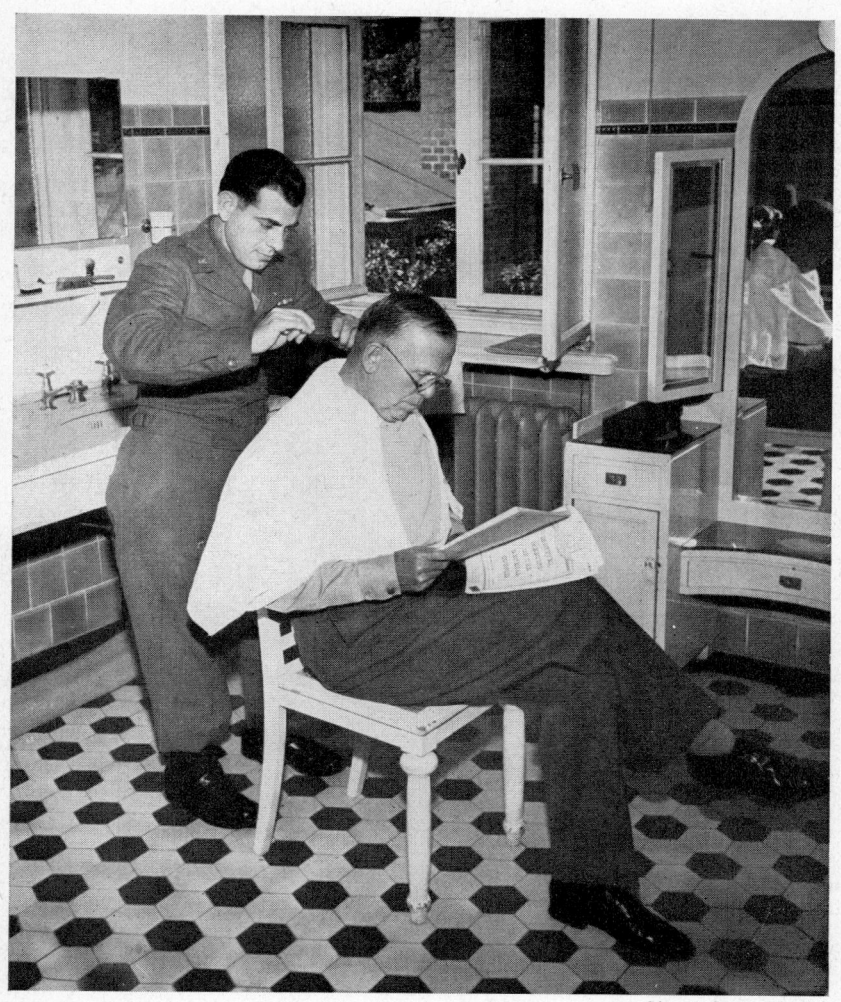

HAIRCUT AT POTSDAM

While Private First Class Nicholas Totalo trims his hair, Marshall catches up on the minutes of the General Council of the War Department staff during the Potsdam Conference in July 1945.

Photograph from Wide World Photos, Inc.

KATHERINE TUPPER MARSHALL

XX

Code of a Citizen Soldier

MILITARISM has been called the danger latent in the two great programs which claimed a constantly increasing share of Marshall's attention during the last years of the war: universal military training, and unification of the War and Navy Departments.

The word has been tossed around glibly by diverse groups in wondrous strange association, from college presidents banded together to prevent even twelve months' delay of their opportunity to instill in the young every idea except the responsibilities of citizenship, to admirals frantic at the thought of national necessity infringing the privileges of the quarter-deck.

Against the one program has been argued the suggestion, in many guises, that militarism lodges of necessity in military size and in military strength; against the other, the notion that concentration of authority and co-ordination of plan is militaristic. Both arguments are nonsense. Militarism is not power, but the use of military power unchecked by civil authority to flout the civil will—as exemplified, for instance, by admirals defying the Chief Executive to lobby in the Congress against the budget limitations imposed upon them; or, for earlier instances, General Miles and General Ainsworth lobbying with the Congress to resist the imposition of the civil executive's authority upon their independent privileges and prerogatives. The concentration of authority, the single central command, is military, but not militaristic; it is the inescapable necessity of military organization, and when technological advance made it impossible to separate sharply the missions of the arms, it became folly to allow their command to remain split. The immediate safeguard against militarism is to lodge the immediate command of the forces in a civilian, as it has been lodged in the War Department for forty-five years (Army orders are issued "by direction of the Secretary of War," Navy orders "by command" of the appropriate Navy officer); and the general safeguard is the will for peace of the citizens.

If Marshall was able, or felt compelled, to devote increasing attention to these great questions of future policy, it was not because he was free of operational concern. Yet, at the beginning of 1944, most of the great strategic decisions had been made, and the operational problems were primarily those of seeing that the limited means were divided carefully to implement them, of guiding the theater commanders so that the decisions could be carried out, of participating in the tactical decisions which altered the speed or the detailed course of the strategic plan.

When the Allies invaded Normandy on June 6, 1944, the main effort had been assigned to General Sir Bernard Law Montgomery, the spectacular and unpleasant commander of the magnificent British Eighth Army which had routed Rommel's Afrika Korps at El Alamein and in the Libyan desert.

That is to say not merely that Montgomery was in command of all ground forces until a beachhead could be consolidated and a breakthrough achieved; but that the strategic plan was for Montgomery's own Army group—the 21st Army Group composed of the British Second and Canadian First Armies—to break out of the beachhead, cross the Seine, and race for Germany across the Low Countries. Unhappily, the Germans spotted the plan correctly, and threw the full weight of their forces in Normandy against Montgomery at Caen. Furthermore, the old deliberative nature of the British command and staff system, which made them so much better planners than the Americans, once more put a brake on British action.

Much has been made of Montgomery's insistence that every detail of a projected operation be settled in advance of the attack, that every small aspect of the administrative plan be "tidy," that precise orders be issued for every phase, and that no attack begin until such a mass of artillery, equipment, and supplies has been accumulated as to guarantee that nothing can interfere with the orderly unfolding of the meticulous blueprint. This has been heralded as Montgomery's great contribution to the art of war, but in simple truth it is not new. It is, in fact, as old as Quintus Fabius Maximus, Cunctator. This cautious approach to battle, this willingness to bet only on a sure thing, is admirable and even necessary for the contender who is weak and on the defensive; but for the man on the offensive and in possession of the initiative, it flings a cloying net around boldness, palsies the intent to exploit advantage.

The campaign for France and for Germany was Eisenhower's campaign, yet Marshall had a part in it. There was an incessant interchange of messages between these two great officers, and Marshall exercised a more direct influence on Eisenhower's theater than he did on others. Partly this was the result of the mutual trust between them, partly it was a kind of natural development of a counterweight against Churchill's enthusiastic overseeing of the campaigns closest to him. To what degree Marshall influenced Eisenhower's decisions will remain a question until all the official records—and some of the personal papers—are open to examination. Some of his influence already has become evident.

It was Marshall who recommended that Lieutenant General Omar N. Bradley, a corps commander under Patton in Sicily, be advanced to command the Twelfth Army Group, consisting originally of the American First and Third Armies, when the build-up on the Norman beachhead became sufficient to make that group of armies operational. There is strong evidence that it was at least with Marshall's approval that the eight American divisions originally allotted to Montgomery for the thrust northeastward were withdrawn when Lieutenant General J. Lawton Collins' VII Corps broke through at St. Lô, and used to develop what became one of history's most dazzling campaigns.

Certainly it was Marshall who impressed upon Eisenhower that SHAEF's denial that Bradley now held equal status with Montgomery as an Army Group commander, with Eisenhower himself in direct command of ground forces in the field, had produced in the United States an even more unfortunate reaction than the unofficial disclosure of the new command structure had produced in Britain, and had "confused" both Marshall and Stimson. A formal announcement from Eisenhower's headquarters followed. Marshall's attitude in this was neither anti-Montgomery nor anti-British. It was merely his understanding that Allied harmony was a two-way proposition, and his knowledge that the morale of the American soldier would suffer unless he and his own commanders got public acknowledgment of their work.

It was Marshall who sent General McNair to Britain and Normandy as part of that elaborate and successful cover plan which so deceived the enemy that a German army remained immobilized in the Pas-de-Calais, waiting in apprehensive idleness for the "main" invasion there until Eisenhower had won Normandy. (And it was a bitter grief to Marshall that McNair was killed by American bombs which fell short in the attack that opened St. Lô.)

The supply of the Allied armies across the beaches of Normandy, thanks largely to the secret and ingenious artificial harbors of British invention and construction, had been so vastly greater than any historic precedent would lead a military staff to think possible that Eisenhower's forces were able to consolidate their beachhead, break out of it, and shatter the German forces in northwest France. The supply over the beaches, however, was not enough to keep both Army Groups in full speed toward Germany. A choice had to be made, and the choice which Eisenhower made in August was to resume the original plan for Montgomery's 21st Army Group to use what supplies there were to keep driving for Germany and a crossing of the lower Rhine before the Nazis could recover from the demoralization of their defeat in France. The First Allied Airborne Army was assigned to reinforce 21st Army Group, and spearhead its crossing of the Rhine. There followed, in the middle of September, the heroic failure of Arnhem.

Now both Montgomery's and Bradley's Army Groups were halted, and the enemy had a chance to dig in along the German border. It became imperative to have a port. Cherbourg, which Collins' corps had taken in the first month of the invasion, was too far away to supply the front lines. Other French and Belgian ports were blocked by the last-ditch stand of German garrisons. But on September 3, Antwerp, one of the largest ports in Europe, had fallen into Montgomery's hands, with its facilities virtually intact. To use it, however, it was necessary to clear the mouth of the Scheldt, particularly the strongly fortified island of Walcheren. Montgomery was reluctant to undertake the operation, and wanted to abandon the American idea of a campaign for the Frankfort corridor and a double envelopment of the heart of Germany, diverting all supplies from France to the northern thrust. This was to become the bone of the last great contention between the American and British members of the Combined Chiefs of Staff. But meantime, Eisenhower insisted that Montgomery undertake to clear the Scheldt, and in October Marshall, visiting the European headquarters, went to Montgomery and told the Field Marshal that the use of Antwerp was an absolute necessity if the campaign for Germany was to continue. It was still hoped to mount two great attacks and crush the Nazis by the end of 1944.

"Oh, I'm getting along pretty well," was Montgomery's reaction to Marshall's request that he clear the mouth of the Scheldt immediately to make Antwerp usable.

"Yes," retorted Marshall, remembering the diversions of supplies from the south to Montgomery's group of armies, "and the First Army is in fair shape. So is Patch in the south—he's being supplied through Marseille. But Patton, in the center, is starved and immobilized. We've got to have Antwerp."

Montgomery, magnificently assisted by the Royal Navy and the Royal Air Force, finally undertook the Scheldt estuary campaign, and on November 27 the first convoy bringing Allied supplies from Britain docked in the harbor of Antwerp.

Marshall was behind the decision to maintain unrelenting pressure against the Siegfried line until it was breached, and some of his public utterances disclose that in September he thought it was possible to terminate the war before the end of the year. But he had to combat once again the British preoccupation with the Balkans. General Sir Henry Maitland Wilson, the Allied commander in the Mediterranean, proposed to abandon the idea of an invasion of Southern France, and to launch instead an amphibious assault on the Istrian Peninsula which could be exploited through the Ljubljana Gap in Yugoslavia and put Allied forces into the plains of Hungary. The strategic argument—and it had great merit—in favor of this was the likelihood that it would knock Hungary out of the war, and present a sufficient new threat to the German rear to make the enemy pull divisions away from Eisenhower's front. However, when Wilson talked of this proposal with Marshall during a meeting of the Combined Chiefs in London about ten days after the invasion of Normandy, Marshall told him that the port of Marseilles was essential if the Allied armies in France were to receive sufficient reinforcement and support—the harbors likely to be available in northwest France were inadequate. Wilson continued for several weeks to recommend the alternative, but on July 2 he received orders from the Combined Chiefs to make preparations for the invasion of Southern France, with the target date to be August 15. The operation had to be delayed that long because it could be mounted only with assault craft which Eisenhower was able to release from Normandy when the Allied position there was secure.

By the time the Combined Chiefs gathered at Malta to discuss Eisenhower's plans for the final blows on the West Front, the great attack by Field Marshal Von Rundstedt's armies—the last mobile reserves of the Wehrmacht—had ended the hope of victory in 1944. Only heartbreaking bad luck had prevented a massive Allied attack at the very time Von Rundstedt struck. Patton's Third Army was massed beyond Metz, poised to exploit the result of what was to have been the most enormous close-support air bombardment ever attempted. The entire 8th and 9th Air Forces were ready to blast through the German positions with a concentration of high explosive and new-type incendiary bombs in an attack which would have dwarfed even the bombardment which prepared the way for the

St. Lô break-through. The Siegfried line would have been ruptured, and the whole German West Front flanked. But several successive days of fog and heavy overcast grounded the Allied air forces, and gave Von Rundstedt the chance to maneuver unobserved the mobile Army which up to that time the Allies had kept under close observation. The result was the Battle of the Bulge, which wrecked the Wehrmacht, but also delayed the Allied victory by several months.

Shortly after the Battle of the Bulge began, Under Secretary Patterson suggested to Stimson that the size of the Army be increased to provide a number of new divisions, and said the increase could be accomplished without interfering with production—manpower resources could be combed more thoroughly than they had been. Stimson agreed, and presented the recommendation to Marshall. The Chief of Staff rejected it, and remained adamant in his opposition despite the vigorous urging of the Secretary. Marshall agreed that a larger reserve of divisional strength was desirable for the campaign now inevitably prolonged through the winter, but said that it would be obtained only at the cost of the immediate weakening of the field forces by the withdrawal of veteran and skilled enlisted and commissioned personnel for training cadres for the proposed new units. That step he flatly refused to take. Instead, he ordered the 86th and 97th Divisions, already on the West Coast awaiting shipment to the Pacific as reinforcements for MacArthur, to be sent to Eisenhower instead.

On his way to Malta in February 1945, Marshall met Eisenhower near Marseilles and discussed with him the SHAEF plan to reach the Rhine—an attack by the First Canadian Army southeastward from the Nijmegen bridgehead between the Meuse and the Rhine, another by the American Ninth Army eastward from Aachen across the Roer River to the Rhine at Düsseldorf, and a third by Patton's Third Army above the Saar. The main effort beyond the Rhine was to be north of the Ruhr, a joint attack by the British Second and the American Ninth Armies, but Eisenhower planned to get across farther south also and strike for the Frankfort corridor into central Germany.

At Malta, where the Combined Chiefs met prior to accompanying Churchill and Roosevelt to the Big Three conference at Yalta, the British Chiefs of Staff proposed, first that the Combined Chiefs issue instructions to Eisenhower confining his Rhine crossing to the northern effort, and second that an over-all commander of ground forces under Eisenhower be appointed. A determined contest was being waged when Marshall, delayed by his meeting with Eisenhower, arrived at the island in the Mediterranean. King and Arnold had been adamant in their opposition to both proposals, and Marshall now told the British chiefs categorically that the American Joint Chiefs of Staff would in no circumstances become a party to instructions telling Eisenhower that he was not at liberty to exploit any opportunity that came to his armies.

As to the second proposal, that an officer be designated under Eisenhower to command all ground forces, the opposition of the American Chiefs of Staff was consistent, but less categorical. Marshall argued that Eisenhower's plan of campaign was sound, that his command structure was excellent, and that there was no reason to disturb either. The over-all ground command argument was reminiscent of Montgomery's injured sensibilities in Normandy, but Montgomery was not suggested by the British Chiefs of Staff to fill the proposed assignment. Instead, they wanted General Sir Harold R. L. G. Alexander, for whose abilities the Americans as well as the British had a high regard, to be transferred from the Mediterranean to the ground command under Eisenhower. The Combined Chiefs finally agreed that they would await developments, to see whether such a step might become necessary.

The disagreement about the British proposal to instruct Eisenhower that his attack north of the Ruhr must be, not only the main effort beyond the Rhine, but the only one, was not settled until the President and the Prime Minister arrived at Malta. Then the military men gathered before the chiefs of state for a showdown, and Marshall won. The proposed instructions were not issued.

At Yalta, a studied and successful effort was made to allay any Russian suspicions that the Soviet military leaders were faced by an

Anglo-American coalition. The conferences were carefully kept tripartite, and the groundwork was laid for co-ordinating the Red Army offensives to some extent with those of Eisenhower's forces. Yalta marked the first real gain toward correlation of the Soviet campaigns with those of Russia's western allies. The Russians were reluctant, however, to inform the British and Americans of their plans, and as the Anglo-American Chief of Staff came to realize that this was due largely to a fear that British and American security measures were inadequate, they were forced to admit to themselves that the Russians had substantial reason for the fear. They noticed, too, that the Russian generals would answer few questions without consulting Stalin.

Meantime, the Pacific campaigns had been moving swiftly to a climax, long before the Joint Chiefs of Staff or the commanders had thought possible. At the Octagon Conference in Quebec in September 1944, decisions had been reached on the basis of communications from Halsey, Nimitz, and MacArthur which moved the invasion of the Philippines up by three months and shortened the war with Japan by a longer time.

But before they went to this conference, Marshall and Arnold disappeared for a week, taking elaborate precautions to conceal the fact that they were together, and to prevent any indication where they might be. They took a vacation, the nearest thing to a complete and extended relaxation that either of them had during the war. Equipped with sleeping bags, fishing rods, and food, and accompanied by some forest rangers with a radio set, they went into the High Sierras for a camping and fishing trip. A special plane flew over their general vicinity each day, the pilot knowing neither what it was he was going to drop nor who was there on the ground to receive it, and the Chief of Staff of the Army and the Commanding General of the Army Air Forces lighted signal flares to indicate the drop zone. The bag which the pilot then tossed out contained the daily operations reports and other summaries which Marshall and Arnold needed to know, or problems they had to decide. When necessary, they could communicate with headquarters by means of the forest service radio. There was one frantic morning when a new pilot on the mystery run overshot the drop zone, and flipped the precious bag a mile or more away, beyond a wide ravine and a high ridge. There was a rapid if rough triangulation by Marshall and one of the rangers, and then the whole party scrambled off in search of the day's top secrets, lodged somewhere on a mountainside in the Sierras. The bag was found, but it gave two very high-ranking generals a bad hour.

When the Combined Chiefs met with Roosevelt and Churchill at Quebec in September, MacArthur was attacking Biak, and he planned to move to Talaud to bring his ground-based air support closer for an invasion of the south coast of Mindanao. Nimitz' forces had taken Saipan and Guam in the Marianas—the key to the Pacific was in American hands. It had not been possible to go directly there because of the flank threat from the Marshalls, and the Gilberts had been selected in 1943 as a preliminary to the seizure of key islands in the Marshalls for three reasons: to get on the flank of the Japanese threat to Samoa, to provide land-based air support for the Marshalls operations, and to keep the covering naval forces in position to be diverted to New Guinea should they be needed there. Now the strategy was paying off, and converging offensives were moving toward the Philippines.

There had been some disagreement as to whether the objective should be the Philippines or Formosa, the Navy favoring Formosa because its possession would cut Japan's sea communications with her forces in Indo-China, Malaya, and the Indies. Marshall favored the Philippines, and MacArthur's vigorous presentation of the more favorable conditions in the Philippines for a base of operations against Japan, made at a conference in Hawaii, coupled with the President's decision that political considerations dictated a return to the Philippines, swung the decision.

Toward the end of August, Admiral Halsey began probing the enemy's strength in the western Carolines and the Philippines. On September 7 and 8, his carrier planes bombed Yap and the Palau Islands, and on the next two days they attacked Mindanao. On the morning of September 12, Halsey hit the central Philippines. The next day the Joint Chiefs, in conference at Quebec, received a copy of a message from Halsey to Nimitz, announcing his belief that the enemy air strength in the Philippines was a myth, and suggesting that instead of carrying out the projected intermediate operations against Yap, Mindanao, Talaud, and Sangihe, joint forces attack Leyte in the Philippines immediately. Nimitz offered to place an Army corps then loading in Hawaii for the attack on Yap at MacArthur's disposal. The information was relayed to MacArthur, and his reaction requested. Two days later, he replied that he was already prepared to shift his plans so as to attack Leyte on October 20 instead of three months later. Marshall, King, Arnold, and Leahy were the guests of Canadian officers at a formal dinner when MacArthur's reply arrived. They left the table for a hurried conference, and less than an hour and a half after MacArthur's message was received in Quebec, Nimitz and MacArthur had been instructed to land in Leyte on October 20, abandoning the intermediate operations.

Of the few great strategic decisions left to be made, one, whether to invade the Japanese home islands with an amphibious assault force or accomplish the Pacific victory by blockade and air bombardment, was made in the spring of 1945 after the unconditional surrender of the shattered remnants of the German military machine had ended the war in Europe. President Roosevelt had died, and President Truman asked his military advisers if the casualties of an amphibious invasion could be avoided. They were unanimous in their advice that blockade and air bombardment could not be relied upon to produce certain victory. It was agreed to mount an invasion of Kyushu Island before November 1, but the decision on a second amphibious assault—tentatively planned to take the Tokyo plain in the spring of 1946—was postponed.

Another decision was to use the atomic bomb against Japan. That was made during the Potsdam conference, upon the advice of Marshall and the other members of the Joint Chiefs, to shorten the war. The Joint Chiefs had known since spring that the efforts to achieve nuclear fission were nearing success, and it was only after long and searching discussions that they reached the fateful decision to recommend the terrible new weapon's use against Japan after the New Mexico test. They even gave careful consideration to the question of announcing the atomic bomb to the enemy, giving Japan an opportunity to surrender before this frightful device was turned against a Japanese city. Unfortunately, the Joint Chiefs were unable to escape the military man's concern with secrecy about weapons, and they recommended against prior announcement.

The question of a supreme commander in the Western Pacific for the invasion of Japan was never settled. The resentments and the petty rivalries had produced an impasse. MacArthur was given command of all Army forces in the Pacific in April 1945, but despite the fact that the invasion of Japan would involve primarily great land armies and require the closest co-ordination of all forces, no over-all commander was selected. Instead, the old vertical projection of the shore line came into play, with the Navy to command until the troops were established ashore, and then MacArthur was to take over. King came to feel that Marshall believed MacArthur was always right, but the truth was not that simple. With MacArthur, as with many others, the question to Marshall's mind was never "like" or "dislike." It was a mark of his great character and steady wisdom that personalities entered into his command decisions to an amazingly small degree. Flamboyance was alien to Marshall's nature, arrogance offensive to him, the seemingly arbitrary order without staff consultations not his method; but Marshall could free himself of irrational and extraneous factors to a degree unmatched by any of his contemporaries, and with MacArthur he merely accepted the incontrovertible evidence that here was one of the great captains of history.

Beside these problems, accompanying them and gradually taking precedence over them, were the problems of the future. His speeches and writings show that Marshall was more than soldier, he was statesman; more than statesman, he was historical philosopher. He examined this great army he had constructed upon the foundations so painfully but surely built through forty years by Elihu Root, Franklin

Bell, Major Morrison, Leonard Wood, Henry L. Stimson, John McAuley Palmer, Pershing, and the others—himself among them. The General Staff had been created in 1903, and it had begun to serve immediately; but it had required more than thirty years for the idea to reach mature actuality, to produce a sure skill and smooth efficiency in just one of the nation's two great military services.

Now the instruments of warfare had so altered the factors of time and space that the barriers of land and sea had lost meaning. The growth of air power particularly had created such overlapping of function that it was no longer possible to consider the mission of one arm without considering all three. None was able to operate alone. Land, sea, or air, each required the services of the two others. Combined operations were the inescapable need. In this war now reaching a triumphant conclusion, the failures had been scored by separate services, the victories by a team.

Single command in a theater of operations had been accepted by all services as a minimum necessity. Yet how could theater command be truly effective unless it had at its disposal forces educated and trained in combined operations? Joint planning, not debate, would produce a team. Single authority over single purpose, not compromise of separate interest and jealously guarded prerogative, was the only hope of achieving the soundest possible military establishment at a minimum cost. It was not necessary to merge the services, but it was necessary to unify their strategic and policy staffs and to set over them a single civilian authority charged with none but military responsibilities, so that debate could end in decision.

Marshall looked at the organization of which he was a member: the Joint Chiefs of Staff—Marshall, Leahy, King, Arnold. Their achievements had been great; but there had been failures, too, and the weakness of the group was that, despite himself, each member had been caught by the fears and ambitions of service prestige and made an advocate of special, instead of national, interest. When that happened, there was no one short of the President to render a decision on what was, after all, a purely military problem. Marshall knew that the Army no more than the Navy, the Navy no more than the Air Forces, should be allowed to reach a decision on its own mission and the means required to accomplish it, without the critical examination and ultimate approval of the other services. The positions on the Joint Chiefs organization should be filled only by strong men, and strong men do not readily accept others' views. But the strong men should be able to come to a decision, by majority vote, and after exhaustive study by a staff representing all services. If the history of the Army was the criterion it appeared to be, unification was just a beginning; for it would be many years before joint planning, combined operations and integrated training produced staffs and commands which thought and acted consistently in terms of co-ordination, of teamwork, rather than as reluctant and suspicious associates in a common enterprise forced on them by deadly peril. So Marshall became an advocate of the unification of the War and Navy Departments.

"The national security is a single problem, and it cannot be provided for on a piecemeal basis," was his rational summation.

Closer to his heart was the citizen army, and the last and most brilliant of his great biennial reports led through a recital of victorious campaigns to a vigorous recommendation that the United States adopt universal military training so that its historic policy of citizen forces become a constant reality, not a neglected dream to be transformed again—when there might not be time—into the fact of power by a harassed staff and command which had been deprived of all but idea for their peacetime training.

Nettled by the folly of those who accused him of a "mass army" complex, he called to the public's attention that, in its total military mobilization of 14,000,000 men, the number of infantry troops—Army and Marines—was less than 1,500,000. Technological warfare required more, not fewer, men; and aircraft, tanks, radar demanded more, not less, training. The absurd and dangerous assumption that atomic missiles ushered in push-button warfare was understandably disturbing to a military statesman who had seen the advent of military aircraft produce the same bland assurance that the nature of war had changed. Unless war was to become mere wanton destruction without purpose, even the guided missiles carrying atomic bombs would be only the shock-assault weapons striking the first paralyzing blows to prepare the way for the invading forces.

Early in the war, he had become concerned with this postwar planning. Somervell had established a postwar planning group in the Army Service Forces, largely to program demobilization, and Marshall had brought it into the War Department Special Staff and broadened the scope of its studies. To guide its thinking on the postwar military establishment, he had recalled Brigadier General John McAuley Palmer to active duty. Palmer discovered, to his humiliated surprise, that the citizen army idea was, even at this late date, an unwelcome doctrine to these professional soldiers. "They did not even know what I was talking about," he complained. They listened courteously, but went right on with their efforts to achieve a large professional army. To force their hands, Palmer finally conceived the idea of writing a directive for Marshall's signature, with the suggestion that it be published in the official War Department Circular as a statement of basic policy. Marshall approved the suggestion, and that was the origin of the celebrated directive of August 1944 to postwar planners that they formulate a program to include a minimum of professional troops supplemented by adequate citizen reserves, because the large standing army "has no place among the institutions of a modern democratic state."

Marshall wrote in his last report:

We must start, I think, with a correction of the tragic misunderstanding that a security policy is a war policy.

War has been defined by a people who have thought a lot about it—the Germans. They have started most of the recent ones. The German soldier-philosopher Clausewitz described war as a special violent form of political action. Frederick of Prussia, who left Germany the belligerent legacy which has now destroyed her, viewed war as a device to enforce his will whether he was right or wrong. He held that with an invincible military force he could win any political argument.

This is the doctrine Hitler carried to the verge of complete success. It is the doctrine of Japan. It is a criminal doctrine, and like other forms of crime, it has cropped up again and again since man began to live with his neighbors in communities and nations. There has long been an effort to outlaw war for exactly the same reason that man has outlawed murder. But the law prohibiting murder does not of itself prevent murder. It must be enforced. The enforcing power, however, must be maintained on a strictly democratic basis. There must not be a large standing army subject to the behest of a group of schemers. The citizen-soldier is the guarantee against such a misuse of power.

Marshall observed that the objections to universal training "often seem to give undue importance to restrictions on our freedom of life," but he did not point out sharply—as he might have done—to a presumably literate America that the whole process of civilized society is one of imposing restrictions on freedom of action. Superbly self-disciplined himself, he did not tell the public that unless they disciplined themselves, they placed themselves in deadly peril. He did not remind the nation that the privileges of democracy entail their inescapable obligations. These were matters a democratic society might be assumed to know. What, in effect, he told them was merely that, unless they adopted a system of constant readiness, they probably could never again get ready in time to stave off disaster. The United States had been saved, while it took from 1939 to 1942 to prepare itself, by the blood and suffering of Czechs, Poles, Norwegians, Danes, Dutch, Belgians, French, English, Chinese, Australians, Russians, and assorted others. In those fateful years, the oceans had still been a barrier. But the distance would not protect another time; and the next blow almost certainly would be launched directly, and first, against America.

"If this nation is to remain great," said Marshall, "it must bear in mind now and in the future that war is not the choice of those who wish passionately for peace. It is the choice of those who are willing to resort to violence for political advantage. We can fortify ourselves against disaster, I am convinced, by the measures I have here outlined. In these protections we can face the future with a reasonable hope for the best and with quiet assurance that even though the worst may come, we are prepared for it."

It was a mistake on Marshall's part that he did not push the program for universal training, and that for unification, while the agonies of actual war conditioned the minds of the Congress and the public to accept such measures. Or was it a mistake? The decision to postpone until peace the seeking of these measures in which he believed so strongly is the clearest proof of his profound and passionate belief in democracy, the conviction of a great man that a democratic people can solve its problems rationally. To have used emotion and fear to achieve what was to him a rational solution would have appeared to Marshall not only distasteful, but shameful.

It was his deep human sympathy which led him to approve a demobilization plan and schedule which wrecked the Army so carefully created. This man had known the loneliness of foreign service, had suffered the painful stresses it created in what should have been the normal and unbroken relationships of home and family. He worried less that the greatest army in the world would in the course of a few short months be no army at all, than about the distressing knowledge that while it remained an army, homes and marriages were disintegrating. It was this, more than any other thing, that put his signature on the plan which quite literally destroyed the greatest military machine in history.

After the surrender of Japan, Marshall wanted to retire immediately. He felt strongly that, while the planning must go on, he should not remain in office, determining by his decisions the course that his successor must follow. Eisenhower, the victor of Europe, was slated to succeed him, and Marshall, careful to get Eisenhower's approval for each new appointment or promotion that he made, still felt that the office should be turned over to the younger man at once. Moreover, he wanted Eisenhower to come home before the inevitable criticisms of any man who commanded the occupation forces in Europe might dim the luster of Eisenhower's fame. But the President wanted him to stay, for two reasons which made no slightest appeal to Marshall. One was a bill pending in Congress to strike a special medal in his honor. The other was legislation to exempt him from retirement law, keeping him on the active list in his new rank—that five-star rank of General of the Army which he resented as an absurdity.

The demand for that rank had come from the Navy. Suggestions that it should be conferred on the nation's topmost Army and Navy officers, to make them "equal" in rank to Britain's highest officers, had cropped up frequently during the war, and Marshall had resisted them as frequently as they appeared. But Navy prestige had to be served, and the House Naval Affairs Committee eventually introduced legislation to give the topmost admirals the new five-star rank of Admiral of the Fleet. The House Military Affairs Committee promptly prepared a bill to allow the Army to keep pace, and started trying to get Marshall's reaction to the legislation. Marshall would not react. Finally, Representative Wadsworth of New York, who was not a member of the Military Committe, brought the subject up at the end of a conference with the General on other matters.

"How do you feel about this?" the congressman asked.

"I'm against the whole thing," Marshall replied. "We don't need it. If I'm called to testify on the bill, I shall refuse to go. The important thing at a military conference is not your relative rank. The important thing is to know your story, and have lots of money and lots of men.

"If I know my position, and have the power to back it up, I can sit at the foot of the table as a brigadier and have as much influence as anybody there."

Nevertheless, the rank was conferred on him, and he remained Chief of Staff until it had been confirmed as a permanent active rank. In September, Stimson resigned, and there were tears in Marshall's eyes—and in Stimson's, too—when these firm friends and great colleagues said good-by. The Marshalls moved out of Quarters Number 1, Fort Myer, so that the old house could be made ready for its new occupants. And in November Marshall at last was allowed to retire, after an Oak Leaf Cluster to his Distinguished Service Medal had been presented by Truman in a public ceremony at the Pentagon.

The little private ceremony marking the departure of a ranking officer from the Pentagon is informal, but it has its established pattern. The officer's superior cites his services in a short speech, the officer himself makes a brief farewell address, and then his associates and assistants who have gathered to say good-by file past and shake his hand as he stands by the door. The line starts with the highest ranking officer present, and continues in order of precedence until the most junior has gripped the hand of the departing boss, and said, "Good-by and good luck, sir!"

The voice of Judge Patterson, who had moved up from Under Secretary to take Stimson's place, was none too steady as he talked simply of the climax and end of a devoted career. When he had finished, it was Marshall's turn, and it took the General nearly two minutes—minutes that seemed like hours to this wet-eyed collection of "tough" brass hats—to get a firm enough grip on his emotions to make his throat stop working up and down, and let him speak. The words were few, and they were simple, also—his affection for the old friends there, his pride in the work they had done together, his gratitude for the help they had given him. Then he turned, and walked quickly to the door. Nobody else moved. They stood reluctant and awkward—Somervell, Handy, all the "G's" of the General Staff, down to Buck Lanham, now a brigadier and the most junior officer present, and as such, nearest the door waiting for the rank to start moving from the other end of the room. Suddenly Marshall grinned, his eyes twinkled a little, and his voice was firm again. He held out his hand.

"Come on, Lanham!" And the scene ended. The tired man who had served his country well for nearly forty-four years was free to take the rest he had earned.

There was no question where he would go to take it. Home had always been his dream, and his desire. In 1940, he and his wife had bought Dodona Manor, a handsome Georgian brick house at Leesburg, Virginia, and they had spent as much time in it as the busy years would allow them. During the war Marshall had kept a felt hat and a tweed jacket in his office, and on Wednesday and Saturday afternoons he would slip those on, get into his own Plymouth, and drive down to Leesburg—drive furiously, to the terror of his staff, who were certain at every start that this trip would bring disaster. It was on these trips that Marshall picked up the hitchhikers whose conversations with the general in mufti have added to the store of Marshall anecdotes.

On the December day in 1945 when Marshall and his wife rolled up to Dodona in the Plymouth, intending to settle down for the quiet private life so long denied them, Mrs. Marshall started upstairs for a rest, and the General began unpacking the things brought along in the trunk of the car. Halfway up the stairs, Mrs. Marshall heard the telephone ring, heard the General answer it.

An hour later, she came back down, and entered the living room as a news broadcast came from the radio. It announced that Patrick Hurley had resigned, and that President Truman had appointed General Marshall a special ambassador to China. He would leave, said the broadcast, immediately. Mrs. Marshall stood motionless and silent, and tears trickled down her face. The General got up from his chair and came over to her.

"That phone call as we came in was from the President," he said quietly. "I could not bear to tell you until you had had your rest."

Rest? To seek in China a stability of turmoil would not be rest. He could hardly hope to succeed, but he could not refuse to go. When the President of the United States cannot find an American civilian willing to forget private ambition to serve a public need, he can always command a soldier. It was not because Marshall was a soldier, of course, but because he was Marshall, that Truman turned to him. Yet it is true that in the military services the Chief Executive knows that he possesses the only group of able individuals who consistently and without question place duty before self. The military career is the only one which not only permits devotion unswerved by politics or personal desire, but requires it.

Unhappy but unhesitating, Marshall went to China, just as, little more than a year later, he dramatically assumed the post of Secretary of State while on his return flight from the Orient.

It has become the fashion to present America's military leaders as triumphs of the average, the common men whom the accidents of time and circumstance have brought out of the mob. The log cabin and callused-palm label cannot be tied to Marshall. His heritage was aristocratic, his schooling disciplined, his intellect far above average, his deliberate choice of career the Army. Yet few Americans have believed so passionately in democracy, or served it so well. This was a citizen soldier, and a most uncommon man.

INDEX

INDEX

Aachen, Germany, 359
Abbeville, France, 275
ABDA, 306
Abercrombie, Maj. W. R., 86
Acropolis, the, 99
A.E.F., 165, 166, 181, 184, 281. *See also* American Expeditionary Force
Aero, 132, 133
Africa, 315, 316, 319
Afrika Korps, 354
Ainsworth, Maj. Gen. Fred C., 100, 101, 102, 103, 116, 353
Air Corps, 206, 245, 249, 252, 253, 259, 260, 272, 274, 288
Air Corps Tactical School, 260, 261
Air Forces, 286, 341, 366
Aisne-Marne operation, 145, 150, 153, 154
Alaska, 97, 238
Aleutian Islands, 335
Alexander, Gen. Sir Harold R. L. G., 360
Alexandria, Egypt, 315
Algiers, Algeria, 99, 321, 327, 331, 335, 336, 337
Allen, Corp. ———, 73
Ambulance Company 3, 131
American Expeditionary Force, 124, 135, 137, 144, 147, 161. *See also* A.E.F.
Amiens, France, 140
Andrews, Maj. Gen. Frank M., 253, 254, 268
Andrews, Capt. John A., 211
Ansauville, 136, 137, 138, 139, 140

Anti-Comintern pact, 243
Antietam, battle of, 47
Antwerp, Belgium, 357
Anvil, 340
Anzio, Italy, 336
Arabia, 315
Argentia Bay, 299
Argonne Forest, 157, 158, 161
Arlington Cemetery, 201
Armistead, Nina, 61
Army and Navy Journal, the, 100, 343
Army Service Forces, 367
Army Service Schools, 104
Army Staff College, 89, 92, 94, 95, 96
Army War College, 89, 90
Arnhem, Netherlands, 356
Arnold, Maj. Gen. H. H., 109, 110, 249, 282, 302, 303, 304, 312, 313, 332, 333, 342, 344, 360, 361, 363, 365
Artois Post of Command, 133
Assam, India, 341
Atlanta, Ga., 247
Augusta, Ky., 22, 23, 24, 26
Augusta College, 23
Australia, 301, 306, 307, 308, 328, 329, 346
Austria, 243
Avalanche, 340
Azore Islands, 287

Baby Corps, 46, 47, 56, 57
Badoglio, Marshal ———, 336, 340
Baker, Newton D., 116, 124

377

Baker Isl., 346
Balkans, the, 300, 318, 319, 335, 340, 351, 358
Baltic, the, 125
Baltimore, Md., 61, 215
Bamford, Brig. Gen. Frank E., 164, 165
Bar-le-Duc, France, 158, 159
Barnum, Col. M. H., 124
Bataan Isl., 83, 306, 308, 347
Bataan Peninsula, 307
Bataganis, 77
Batangas Province, 108, 109, 120
Bathelémont, France, 135
Battle of Midway, 313
Battle of the Bulge, 359
Bay of Bengal, 344
Beacon Rock, 238
Beauvais, France, 145, 153
Beeson, Alex, 256
Beeson mill, 33
Beeson's Town, 27
Belfort, France, 156
Belgium, 275
Bell, Sgt. ———, 90
Bell, Maj. Gen. J. Franklin, 86, 87, 94, 106-110, 114-120, 121, 124, 125, 126, 148, 171, 365
Bell, Mr. and Mrs. Lew, 39
Belleau Wood, 151
Benson, Sir Frank, 215
Bent, Capt. Charles I., 73
Béthune, France, 154
Biak Isl., 362
Bieghly, Katheryn, 36
Bieghly, Sid, 36
Big Three conference, 360
Bismarck Archipelago, 335
Blamey, Sir Thomas, 328
Bliss, A. W., 26, 28, 29, 33, 34, 35
Bliss, Mrs. A. W., 257

Bliss, Brig. Gen. Tasker H., 90, 104, 153
Bodley, Gen. Thomas, 19
Boeing B-17, 253, 259, 312
Bohemia, 318
Bolero, 311, 312, 314-318, 332
Bomb, the, 60
Booth, Maj. E. E., 108, 110
Bora Bora, Oceania, 329
Borah, Sen. William E., 195
Bordeaux, France, 150
Bordeaux, Gen. ———, 132, 135
Boston, Mass., 103
Bougainville Isl., 346
Bowman, Herb, 37
Bracken County, Ky., 23
Braddock, Gen. Edward, 18, 27
Bradford, Dr. Jonathan Johnson, 15
Bradford, Col. Joshua T., 24
Bradford, Dr. Joshua T., 16
Bradford, Laura, *see* Marshall, Laura Bradford
Bradley, Gen. Omar N., 205, 355, 356
Brandreth, 172, 173, 174, 180
Brandreth, Pauline, 172
Brandywine Creek, 18
Brazil, S. A., 265
Brereton, Gen. Lewis H., 315, 330
Breteuil, France, 145
Brett, Gen. George H., 301
Briey, France, 156
Brisbane, Australia, 308
Britain, 244, 271, 274, 276, 279, 302, 314, 317, 321, 332, 356
Broad St. (Nashville, Tenn.), 50
Brooke, Gen. Sir Alan, 304
Brown, Sgt. ———, 73
Brown, 2d Lt. Allen Tupper, 216, 336
Brown, Clifton S., 214, 216

Brown, John, 20
Brown, Katherine Tupper, 214, 215. See also Marshall, Katherine Tupper
Brown, Molly, 216, 241
Brown, Sam, 39
Brownfield, Mrs. ———, 36
Brownfield, Natty, 34
Brownfield family, 33
Brunswick, Md., 262
Bryan, William Jennings, 41
Bryden, Gen. William H., 282
Buck, Brig. Gen. Beaumont B., 136
Buckpond, 19, 21
Bugge, Capt. Jens, 108, 110
Bulalacao Isl., 77
Bullard, Gen. Robert L., 128, 135, 136, 138, 140, 142, 144-146, 149, 152, 162
Bureau of Public Relations, 291, 295, 339, 340
Bures, France, 133
Burma, 309, 330, 335, 344, 347
Burma Road, 341
Burnett, Maj. ———, 133
Burns, Maj. Gen. James H., 283, 284, 383
Burr, Aaron, 20
Buzancy, France, 170

Caen, France, 354
Cairo, Egypt, 335, 344
Cairo conference, 344
Cairo-Teheran conferences, 351
Calais, France, 16, 154
Calapan, P. I., 73, 74, 75, 79, 82
Calcutta, India, 341
Campbell, Rev. Archibald, 18
Camp Blanding, 312
Camp Grant, 229, 231
Camp Lafayette, 224, 225

Camp Perry (Ohio), 96, 99
Canal Zone, 286
Canby, ———, 237
Cantigny, France, 127, 140, 141, 142, 144, 149, 164
Caribbean Sea, 287, 297
Carignan, France, 158, 161, 162
Caroline Islands, 335, 362
Carranza, Pres. Venustiano, 114
Carrizal, Mexico, 114
Carter, "King," of Corotoman, 22
Carter, Sgt. William H., 75
Casablanca, Morocco, 331, 332, 333
Castelnau, Gen. de, 132
Castner, Brig. Gen. Joseph C., 197, 198
Cavite, P. I., 347
CBI theater, 330
CCC camps, 238, 240, 243
Cebu, P. I., 306
Cedar Mt., battle of, 47
Central School (Uniontown, Pa.), 36, 37
Century of Progress Exposition, 225
Ceylon Isl., 346
Chalk Hill, 38
Chamberlain, Neville, 243, 275
Champagne-Marne assault, 151
Chance, Capt. Robert H., 211
Chancellorsville in the Wilderness, 47
Chang Tso-lin, Marshal, 187
Chantilly, France, 149
Charleston, S. C., 224
Charleston, the, 129
Château de Tartigny, France, 145
Château-Thierry, France, 143, 151, 152
Chattahoochee River, 208
Chaumont-en-Bassigny, France, 128, 139, 144, 145, 147-151, 154, 175

Chemin des Dames, France, 142, 143, 151
Chennault, Gen. Claire, 288
Cherbourg, France, 357
Chicago, Ill., 225, 227, 228, 231, 234, 235, 237, 313
Chicago *Tribune*, 313, 314
Childs, Lt. ———, 219, 220
Chilkoot Barracks (Alaska), 238
China, Marshall's service in, 185, 186-200, 225, 372; aid to, 288; air routes to, 315, 316, 335; air bases in, 341; mentioned, 21, 97, 244, 290, 330, 331
China Sea, 76
Chinwangtao, China, 185
Chungking, China, 335
Churchill, Winston, succeeds Chamberlain, 275; in Washington, 304-305, 314, 335; visits camps, 316; at Casablanca, 331-332; at Algiers, 336; at Quebec, 340-341, 362; at Malta, 360; mentioned, 295, 309, 317, 318
Church St. (Uniontown, Pa.), 34
Cincinnati, Ohio, 24
Citizens' Military Training Camps, 185, 239
Civilian Conservation Corps, 222, 223, 224
Clark, Grenville, 290
Clark, Lt. Gen. Mark W., 313
Clausewitz, Karl von, 236, 251, 367
Clay, Henry, 21
Clemenceau, Georges, 153
Clermont-en-Argonne, France, 158
CMTC, 185, 239
Coal Lick Run, 29, 33
Cole, Capt. Edwin T., 90
Coles, Edmund Pendleton, 64

Coles, Elizabeth Carter, *see* Marshall, Elizabeth (Lily)
Collins, Brig. Gen. Edgar T. ("Windy"), 204, 205, 218
Collins, Lt. Gen. Lawton J., 355, 357
Columbia, S. C., 67
Columbia River, 237, 238, 239
Columbus, Ga., 208, 214
Combined Chiefs of Staff, 304, 321, 332, 336, 341, 345, 358, 360, 362
Comfort, Lt. ———, 133
Command and General Staff School (Fort Leavenworth), 211
Command Post Exercise (CPX), 202, 228, 229, 233, 273
Commercy, France, 154, 159
Company F, 16th Infantry, 134
Company G, 30th N. S. Infantry, 72, 73, 74, 81, 86
Compiègne, France, 276
Connellsville, Pa., 28
Connellsville vein, 24
Conner, Florence, 172
Conner, Gen. Fox, 125, 139-140, 145, 147, 148, 162, 163, 172, 174, 179, 180, 186, 187
Conner, Mrs. Fox, 172, 173
Connor, Brig. Gen. William D., 187, 194, 197
Conrad, Jim, 34, 38, 39, 40
Cooper, Effie, 39
Coronado, Calif., 235
Corregidor Isl., 83, 111, 306, 308
Corsica Isl., 337, 340
Country Club, Tientsin, China, 194
CPX, *see* Command Post Exercise
Craig, Maj. Gen. Malin, 164, 234, 236, 246, 249, 250, 253-255, 263, 265, 268, 343, 344

Cramer, Col. Myron C., 277
Crane's Store, 38
Crimea, 315
Crook, ———, 237
Culpeper Minute Men, 18
Cunel, France, 170
Cunningham, Adm. Sir Andrew, 305, 332
Currie, Lauchlin, 330
Czechoslovakia, 243, 249

Dakar, F. W. Africa, 286, 287, 319, 331
Daladier, Edouard, 243, 276
Danville Military Academy, 63
Darlan, Adm. ———, 326, 327
Davis, Col. ———, 239
Davis, Secy. ———, 214
Davis, Brig. Gen. George W., 70
Dawes, Charles G. ("Hell 'n' Maria"), 226, 227
Debeney, Gen. ———, 140, 141
Denmark, 275
Denny's Dump, 193
Dentler, Lt. Col. C. E., 110
Dern, Secy. ———, 234, 236
Desert Training Center, 322
Detachment No. 1, 108, 109, 110
Detachment No. 2, 108
De Witt, Gen. John L., 88, 312
Diamond Dick, 38
Dick, Sgt. J. R., 219
Dickman, Maj. Gen. Joseph T., 162, 164
Dill, Sir John, 305, 312, 332
Distinguished Service Cross, 171
Distinguished Service Medal, 171
Dodona Manor, 371, 372
Donaldson, Corp. ———, 73
Doolittle, Lt. Col. James, 311, 312
Douglas B-18, 255

Drum, Maj. Gen. Hugh A., 125, 155, 162-165, 235, 246-247, 248, 249
Dufuskie Isl., 221
Duke, Gen. Basil W., 24
"Dump parties," 193
Dunbar Furnace Co., 27, 28, 42
Dunbar Iron Co., 24, 26
Dunbar Manufacturing Co., 26, 28
Dunkerque, France, 154, 275, 276
Düsseldorf, Germany, 359

Eaker, Maj. Gen. Ira C., 332, 333
Eames, Capt. Harry, 78, 79, 82, 90, 218
Early, Stephen T., 317
Eastern Department, 116
Ecuador, S. A., 294
Edgehill, England, 17
Edinburgh, Scotland, 19
Egan, Martin, 195
Egypt, 315, 316
Eichelberger, Maj. Gen. Robert, 328
18th Division (French), 132
18th Infantry, 124
8th Air Force, 332, 333, 358
Eighth Army, 315
Eighth Army (British), 331, 354
VIII Corps, 165, 171
8th Corps Area, 234, 253
8th Infantry, 211, 218, 223
86th Division, 359
Einville, France, 132, 134
Eisenhower, Gen. Dwight D., heads OPD, 309; trip to England, 312-313; heads ETO, 314, 317; in Africa, 321, 327, 331-332; to Sicily, 335-337; negotiates with Badoglio, 340; commands Overlord, 345-346; his strategy in France and Germany 355-361; mentioned, 186, 341, 342, 369

El Alamein, Egypt, 315, 354
Elbow St. (Uniontown, Pa.), 27
Eleanor, Princess, 16
Ely, Maj. Gen. ———, 164, 168, 197
Embick, Maj. Gen. Stanley D., 247, 302, 309, 342, 343, 344
Emmanuel Episcopal Church (Baltimore), 215
Emmons, Gen. Delos C., 301
England, 316, 331
Enlisted Reserved Corps, 122
Enright, Pvt. Thomas F., 135
Epernay, France, 151
European Theater of Operations, 314, 315
Evatt, Herbert, 307
Evill, Douglas C. S., 305
Ewing, Elizabeth, 24
Ewing, John, 24
Ewing, William (Billy), 34, 38

Fairfax, Va., 18
Fauquier County, Va., 18, 22
Federal Bureau of Investigation, 313
Federal Circuit Court of Appeals, 285
Federal Home Guards, 24
Feng Yu-hsiang, Gen., 187
Field Artillery Training Center, 312
Field Hospital 3, 131
15th Infantry, 185, 187, 192, 194
Fifth Army (British), 141
V Corps, 162, 163, 164
5th Division, 164, 286
5th Infantry Brigade, 235, 236, 237
58th Infantry Brigade, 175
"Fighting First," see 1st Division
Fighting French, 326, 327
Fillmore, Pres. Millard, 21
Finschhafen Isl., 346

Fire Island, N. Y., 215
First Allied Airborne Army, 356
First Army, in World War I, 150-165, 168, 249; postwar activities, 171, 180; in World War II, 355, 357
First Army (Canadian), 354, 359
First Army (French), 140, 144
I Corps (American), 152, 153, 162, 163, 164
1st Division, in World War I, 124-126, 128-132, 135-136, 140-141, 143-145, 148, 151-152, 163-164, 172; in World War II, 286
First Expeditionary Division, 129
1st Infantry Brigade, 136, 137
1st Moroccan Division (French), 137
Fleming, John, 54
Flicker, nickname of Marshall, 33
Florence, Italy, 99
Florida Avenue (Washington, D. C.), 200
Flying Fortress, 253, 312, 332, 333
Flying Tigers, 288
Foch, Marshal Ferdinand, 153, 154, 156, 157, 158, 161
Forest, The, 22
Forêt de Compiègne, France, 145, 151
Formosa Isl., 362
Fort Benning, 200, 202, 204, 207-208, 210, 212, 213, 214, 215, 217, 218, 222, 258, 313
Fort Bragg, 312
Fort Clark, 86
Fort Douglas (Salt Lake City), 117, 118, 131
Fort Jackson, 316
Fort Leavenworth, 84, 86-98, 108, 109, 111, 204, 211, 237
Fort Lewis, 239

INDEX

Fort Logan H. Roots, Arkansas, 104
Fort McKinley, 82, 106, 107, 111, 112, 123
Fort Moultrie (S. C.), 223, 224, 225
Fort Myer, 370
Fort Necessity, 27
Fort Reno, 86
Fort Sam Houston, 253
Fort Screven, 211, 218, 219, 221, 222, 223, 258
Fourth Army (French), 162, 163
4th Corps Area, 247
4th Division, 153
4th Infantry, 104
Fourth Section (Infantry School), 211, 212
40th Division (French), 163
41st Division, 239
47th Division of Chasseurs (French), 130
Fox, ———, 195
France, in World War I, 121, 123, 126-128, 131, 172, 184; World War II, 244, 249, 251, 257, 271, 274, 276, 279, 311, 317, 332, 335, 357, *et passim*
Frankfort, Germany, 357, 359
Frankfort, Ky., 20
Frederick of Prussia, 367
French Africa, 327, 331
French Riviera, 340
Frick Co., H. C., 29, 30
Frost Works, 29
Funston, Gen. Frederick, 94
Fuqua, Maj. Gen. Stephen O., 88, 136, 218

Gadd, George, 33, 38
Gallatin, Albert, 27
Galveston, Texas, 104
Gamelin, ———, 276
Gardner, Contract Surgeon Fletcher, 73
Garrison School, 104
Gasser, Brig. Gen. Lorenzo D., 268, 269, 282
Gaulle, Gen. Charles de, 258, 326, 327
Gebhard, Sgt. ———, 73
General Council, 267
General Staff, beginnings of, 67, 69, 70-72, 87, 99-103, 116, 121, 122, 185; in World War I, 124, 131, 145, 160, 175, 176; after World War I, 184, 211, 243; World War II, 253, 254, 265-268, 283, 285, 302, 304, 309, 339, 365, 371
Georgetown, S. C., 224
Germantown, Pa., 18
Germany, 262, 271, 299, 300, 313, 315, 331, 332, 335, 355, 367
Gerow, Gen. Leonard T., 244, 294, 298, 302, 309
Gettysburg, Pa., 22, 51, 95
G-4, 267, 282, 303. *See also* Supply Division
Gibbon, ———, 237
Gibraltar fortress, 238
Gilbert Islands, 329, 346, 348, 362
Gillum, John, 47
Gilmore, Judge ———, 26
Gilmore place, 26, 29, 256
Gilmore's Field, 40
Gilmore's Hill, 34
Giraud, Gen. ———, 326
Gondrecourt, France, 129, 130, 132, 135, 137
G-1, 267, 268, 303. *See also* Personnel Division
Governors Island, 63, 120, 123, 148
Grant, Gen. Ulysses S., 56, 237
Grant, Lt. Col. Walter S., 156

Green, William, 352
Greensburg, Pa., 42, 214, 256
Greer, Col. Allen J., 177
Gresham, Corp. James B., 135
Gross, Brig. Gen. Charles P., 317
G-3, 126, 131, 136, 139, 144, 145, 147, 155, 160, 168, 180, 184, 267, 268, 303
G-2, 267, 268, 289, 352. *See also* Military Intelligence Division
G-2 Press Branch, 339
Guadalcanal Isl., 329
Guam Isl., 362
Guardsman, the, 239
Gypse, 133

Hagood, Lt. Col. Johnson, 106, 107, 117, 118, 119, 120, 126, 128, 234
Haig, Field Marshal Sir Douglas, 153
Haiti, 15
Haldane, Lord, 70
Haley, Maurice, 29
Hallow, Fred, 35, 257
Halsey, Adm. William F., Jr., 329, 346, 361, 362, 363
Halstead, Capt. Laurence, 105, 111, 123
Hamilton, Alexander, 20, 70
Handy, Gen. Thomas T., 371
Harding, Maj. E. F., 187, 188, 192, 193, 198, 199, 200, 204, 211, 215, 216, 217
Harding, Mrs. E. F., 192, 199, 200, 204
Harding, Pres. Warren G., 185
Harper's Ferry, battle of, 47
Hart, Adm. Thomas C., 347
Hatié, Lt. Col. Joseph C., 226
Havana, Cuba, 70, 71

Hawaii, 97, 297, 298, 301, 302, 306, 308, 312, 329, 362, 363
Hawaii, Dept. of, 266
Hay, Pvt. Merle D., 135
Hayne, Capt. Frank, 199
Hayne, Mrs. Frank, 199
Helnick, Maj. Eli A., 104
Herron, Lt. Charles D., 88
Hill, The, 21
Hindenburg line, 156
Hitler, Adolf, 243, 249, 251, 254, 271, 276, 289, 331, 332, 367
Hoboken, N. J., 126, 127, 129
Hollins College, 215
Home Guard (British), 277
Home Guards, 24
Honolulu, Hawaii, 72, 83, 186
Hopkins, Harry, 294, 302, 309, 310, 311, 317, 330, 343, 344
Horner, Gov. Henry, 229
Hornet, the, 311
Hospital Hill, 35
Hossfeld, Col. Henry, 75, 83, 237
Hotel de Ville, 153
House Military Affairs Committee, 116, 292, 370
House Mountain, 55
House Naval Affairs Committee, 370
House of Burgesses, 18
Houston, Helen, 34, 256
Houston, Mrs. ———, 257
Howell, Fanny, 39, 40
Howell, Col. Wiley, 171
"Howling Mad" Smith, *see* Smith, Lt. Gen. Holland M.
Hudson Bay Co., 237
Hudson River, 127
Hugo, Lt. ———, 132
Hukawng Valley, 330
Hull, Cordell, 297
Hump, the, 341

Index

Hungary, 318, 319, 358
Hunter, Lt. C. N., 241
Huon Peninsula, 346
Hurley, Patrick, 372
Hustead, Ed, 37

Iceland, 286, 292
Ilin, Ilin Isl., 76, 77
Illinois National Guard, 225, 226, 230, 239, 240
India, 315, 330, 331, 335, 346
Indio, Calif., 321
Indo-China, 362
Infantry and Cavalry School, 87
Infantry Drill Manual, 213
Infantry in Battle, 210, 211, 212, 213
Infantry Journal, the, 93, 181, 205
Infantry Journal Press, 213
Infantry School, 203, 204, 205, 211, 217, 218, 258
Innes, Harry, 21
Inter-American Defense Board, 309, 345
Invalides, the, 99
Iran, 315
Isla de Negros, 73, 75, 79, 80, 82
Istrian Peninsula, 358
Italy, 331, 332, 335, 336, 337, 340, 341

Japan, 108, 244, 297, 298, 299, 308, 329, 330, 347, 361, 362, 363, 364, 368, 369
Jackson, Thomas Jonathan (Stonewall), 46, 47, 60, 61
Jackson-Hope medals, 60
Jackson Memorial Hall, 44, 60
James River, 17
Jamestown, Va., 17
Jay Treaty of 1794, 20

JCS, *see* Joint Chiefs of Staff
Jehol Province, 244
Jodl, ———, 332
John, King, 16
Johnson, Asst. Secy. ———, 281, 283, 284, 343
Johnson, Sen. ———, 344
Johnson, Lt. E. C., 200
Johnson, Louis M., 246, 247, 248, 252, 253, 254, 259, 260, 277
Johnson, Rooster, 55
Johnson, Gov. William, 16
"Joint Action of the Army and Navy," 245
Joint and Combined Chiefs, 328, 332, 341, 342, 360, 364, 365
Joint Board of the Army and Navy, 245, 297
Joint Chiefs' Joint Strategy Survey Committee, 342
Joint Chiefs of Staff, 323, 325, 326, 327, 329, 347, 350, 351, 360, 361, 363
Joint Congressional Investigating Committee, 297
Joint Planning Committee, 245
Jumonville, Coulon de, 27

Kai-shek, Chiang, 194, 196, 309, 315, 328, 330, 344
Keehn, Maj. Gen. Roy D., 226, 227, 228, 229, 230, 237
Keith, Mary Randolph, 21
Kellogg-Briand Pact, 206
Kenney, Maj. Gen. George C., 328
Kennedy, O'Neil, 34
Kennedy, Ralph, 40
Kennedy, Mrs. Ralph, 40
Kenton, Simon, 23
Kentucky River, 20
Kernan, Gen. ———, 112

Kimmel, Adm. H. E., 298
King, Col. ———, 132
King, Brig. Gen. Campbell, 218
King, Adm. Ernest J., titles, 281; of Joint and Combined Chiefs of Staff, 304, 321, 325, 326, 350, 365; to London, 317, 328; as CNO, 324, *et passim*
Kiskiminetas School, 40
Knightsbridge, 315
Know-Nothings, 21
Knox, Frank, 342
Knudsen, William S., 283, 284
Kriemhild positions, 170
Krueger, Lt. Gen. Walter, 90, 247, 309
Kuomintang, the, 194, 195
Kurusu, Saburo, 297
Kwajalein Isl., 346
Kyushu Isl., 363

Lafayette, Marquis de, 224
La Ferté-sous-Jouarre, France, 155
La Guardia, Fiorello, 303
Laguna de Bay, 82
Laiguelot, Gen. ———, 163
"La Marseillaise," 224
Langres, France, 171
Lanham, Lt. Charles T. (Buck), 202, 203, 209, 210, 211, 212, 371
Leahy, Adm. William D., 288, 324, 342, 344, 363, 365
Ledo Road, 330, 341
Lee, John C. H., 313
Lee, Gen. Robert E., 47
Lee, William C., 313
Leesburg, Va., 371, 372
Lehrbas, Col. Lloyd, 346
Letcher Ave. (Lexington, Va.), 45, 63
Letterman General Hospital, 243

Leviathan, the, 166
Lewis, Maj. Robert, 139, 140, 144
Lexington, Ky., 23
Lexington, Va., 42, 47, 53, 55, 57, 59, 62, 63, 180, 201
Leyte Isl., 363
Libya, 307, 314, 331, 354
Liggett, Lt. Gen. Hunter, 113, 152, 162, 163, 164
Ligny-en-Barrois, France, 157
Lippincott Co., J. B., 160
Ljubljana Gap, 319, 335, 358
Llewellyn, Frank, 33
Lloyd George, David, 153, 154, 195
London, Eng., 99, 317, 320, 328, 341, 358
Lorraine, France, 132, 149, 150
Lost Battalion, 161
Lovett, Robert A., 285, 288
Lualjadi, Eduardo, 76
Luftwaffe, the, 243, 275, 332, 346
Lunéville, France, 132
Luray Caverns, 30
Luzon, P. I., 76, 107, 108
Lys River, 141, 143

McAdams, Col. John P., 226
McAndrew, Brig. Gen. James W., 135
MacArthur, Gen. Douglas, in World War I, 163; assigns Marshall to Ill. National Guard, 225, 226; appointed military adviser to Philippine Commonwealth government, 234-235; service in World War II, 306-308, 312, 328-330, 335, 341, 345-347, 350, 361-364; mentioned, 236, 258, 267
McCammon, Lt. J. E., 200
McCloy, John J., 285, 295, 319
McCoy, Maj. Gen. Frank R., 248

INDEX

McCormack, House Leader, 292
McKinley, Maj. Gen. James F., 225
McKinley, Pres. William, 74
McLaughlin, Lt. William H., 133
McNair, Maj. Gen. Lesley J., 280, 303, 345, 356
McNarney, Brig. Gen. Joseph T., 294, 302, 303, 304, 322
Macon, Ga., 222
Macready, Lt. Gen. G. N., 305
Madison Barracks, 99
Magic, 314
Main St. (Uniontown, Pa.), 27, 29, 34, 42
Makin Isl., 346, 349
Malahi Island Military Prison, 82
Malaya, 306, 362
Malta Isl., 359, 360
Manassas, battle of, 47
Manchuria, China, 187, 244
Mangarin, P. I., 72, 75, 76, 77, 79, 80, 81, 82, 218
Mangarin Bay, 75, 76, 79
Mangyan people, 76, 78
Manila, P. I., 72, 73, 82, 83, 105, 106, 108, 109, 111, 112, 235, 281, 294
Manila Bay, 347
March, Maj. Gen. Peyton C., 166, 174, 175, 176, 177, 178, 342
March of Death, 308
Marianas Islands, 329, 348, 362
Marine Corps, 287, 292, 349, 366
Mariveles, Bataan, 83
Markham, John, 17, 22
Marne River, 143, 150, 151, 152, 153, 154
Marseille, France, 150, 357, 358, 359
Marshall, Elizabeth Coles, courted by Marshall, 45, 46, 61; marriage to Marshall, 63, 64; at Fort Leavenworth, 85-86; to Europe, 99; to

Marshall, Elizabeth Coles—*cont.*
the Philippines, 105, 111-112; in China, 197; to Washington, 200; death of, 201; mentioned, 83, 95, 166, 167, 170, 172, 173, 183, 187, 191
Marshall, Elizabeth (Mrs. John Marshall), 17, 18
Marshall, Elizabeth, *see* Ewing, Elizabeth
Marshall, George C., Jr., ancestry, 15-24; birth and childhood, 25-43; at V.M.I., 44-61; courtship and marriage to Elizabeth C. Coles, 45, 46, 61-64; in Philippines, 64, 72-83; assigned to Fort Reno, 86; at Fort Clark, 86; to Fort Leavenworth, 86-89; to the War College, 89-96; with Massachusetts National Guard, 96; to Europe, 99; to San Antonio, 99; to Fort Logan H. Roots, 104; in the Philippines, 105-113; aide-de-camp to Maj. Gen. Bell, 114-117; to Fort Douglas, 118; to San Francisco, 120; to Governors Island, 120; service in World War I, 124-166; postwar activities, 170-185; in China, 185-200; in Washington, 200-204; to Fort Benning, 204-214; marriage to Katherine Tupper Brown, 214-216; at Fort Screven, 218-225; as instructor with the Illinois National Guard, 225-235; assigned to Vancouver Barracks, 235-243; to General Staff in Washington, 243-249; as Deputy Chief of Staff, 249-255; as Chief of Staff, 255-275; in World War II, 275-370; to London, 309; trip to West Coast, 312; second trip to London, 317-321;

Marshall, George C., Jr.—*cont.*
  designated to command European invasion, 341; attends Cairo conference, 344; visits European headquarters, 357; goes to Malta, 359; in the High Sierras, 361; at Quebec, 363; made a five-star general, 370; receives Oak Leaf Cluster, 370; and Mrs. Marshall go to Leesburg, Va., 372; appointed special ambassador to China, 372; assumes post of Secretary of State, 372
Marshall, George Catlett, Sr., 15, 23, 24, 26-30, 35, 38, 43, 64, 85, 98
Marshall, Humphrey (brother-in-law of James Marshall), 20, 21
Marshall, Humphrey (grandson of Humphrey Marshall), 21
Marshall, James, 19
Marshall, Capt. John (I), 16
Marshall, Capt. John (II), 17
Marshall, Chief Justice John, 18, 19
Marshall, John, of The Forest, 17, 18, 20
Marshall, Katherine Tupper, 215, 222, 223, 224, 225, 241, 250, 371, 372
Marshall, Laura Bradford, 26, 29, 30, 31, 32, 42, 43, 64, 85, 98, 214
Marshall, Louis, 19
Marshall, Marie, 30, 38, 40, 42, 64, 85, 214, 256
Marshall, Martin (cousin of George C. Marshall, Jr.), 56
Marshall, Martin (son of Thomas Marshall), 42
Marshall, Martin (son of Rev. William Marshall), 22, 23
Marshall, Mary (wife of Col. Thomas Marshall), 21
Marshall, St. Julien Ravenel, 60
Marshall, Stuart, 30, 34, 40, 42, 64
Marshall, Thomas (father of Martin Marshall), 42
Marshall, Thomas, (son of Capt. John Marshall), 17
Marshall, Capt. Thomas (son of John Marshall), 23
Marshall, Col. Thomas (son of John Marshall of The Forest), 18, 19, 20, 21
Marshall, Thomas (son of Col. Thomas Marshall), 21
Marshall, Thomas Alexander, 21
Marshall, Rev. William (great-great-grandfather of George C. Marshall, Jr.), 18, 20, 22, 23
Marshall, William, (son of Thomas Marshall), 17
Marshall, William Champe (son of Martin Marshall), 23
Marshall Islands, 329, 335, 362
Martin, Maj. Gen., Charles H., 239
Martinique Isl., 287
Massachusetts National Guard, 96, 97
Massachusetts Volunteer Militia, 104
Maximus, Quintus Fabius, 355
Maxwell Field, 260
May, Rep. ———, 292, 293
Maybank, Sen. ———, 224, 225
Mead, Alex, 33, 36, 37, 40, 256
Medal of Honor, 171
Mediterranean Sea, 300, 305, 309
Mediterranean theater, 314, 317, 319, 320, 321, 327, 331, 335, 340, 358, 360
Melbourne, Australia, 308
Mercier, Cardinal, 172
Merritt, Maj. Gen. Wesley, 70
Mesnil-la-Tour, France, 137
Mesnil-St. Fermin, France, 149

INDEX 389

Mesopotamia, 315
Metz, France, 150, 156, 358
Meuse-Argonne offensive, 127, 158, 160, 164, 170, 183
Meuse River, 157, 158, 161, 359
Mexico, 104, 114
Meyers, Susan, 23
Mézières, France, 158
Midway Island, 312
Miles, Gen. Nelson A., 69, 237, 353
Military Intelligence Division (G-2), 184, 339, 351
"Military Lessons of the War," 180
Military Plaza, 113
Military Policy of the United States, The, Upton, 91
Military Service Publishing Co., 213
Miller, Chaplain ———, 192
Milton and Exeter, 183
Mindanao Isl., 90, 108, 362, 363
Mindoro Island, 73, 74, 76, 77, 80
Mindoro Strait, 76, 79
Mitchell, Brig. Gen. William Lendrum, 91, 250, 253
Moana, the, 186
Molly Hole, 54
Moncure, Robinson, 60
Mongolian ponies, 192, 197
Monongahela City, Pa., 26
Monroe Doctrine, 244
Montdidier, France, 144
Monterey, Calif., 117
Montfaucon, France, 161, 170
Montgomery, Gen. Sir Bernard Law, 331, 354, 360
Montsec, Mt., France, 138
Moore, Maj. Gen. Richard C., 277, 282, 295
Morgan's Cavalry, 24
Morocco, 319, 321, 327, 331
Morris, Hester, 19

Morris, Robert, 19, 20
Morrison, Maj. John F., 88, 90, 94, 96, 365
Morton, Pvt. John N., 73
Moscow, Russia, 242, 294, 302
Moseley, Capt. George Van Horn, 91
Moselle River, 161
Mountbatten, Lord Louis, 313, 340
Mt. Hood, 238
Mount Vernon, 18
Munich, Germany, 243
Munich conference, 249
Munitions Assignment Board, 343
Mussolini, Benito, 332, 336
Muster Roll, 102
My Experiences in the World War, Pershing, 160

Nagasaki, Japan, 73, 83
Namur Isl., 346
Nancy, France, 132, 153
Nanking, China, 244
Nanomea Isl., 346
Nantassu, China, 193, 199
Nantes, France, 150
Nashville, Tenn., 50
Nashville Centennial Exposition, 48
National Defense Act, 177, 179, 184, 205, 217, 282
National Defense Advisory Commission, 283
National Emergency Committee, 290
National Guard, 115, 118, 122, 175, 177, 178, 206, 227, 228, 234, 264, 265, 272, 273, 279, 286-288, 328
National Guard Association, 230
National Guard Bureau, 266
National Guard camps, 95, 96, 99
National Pike, 27, 29, 32, 37
National Rifle Assn., 262
National Rifle Matches, 96

Naval War College, 183
Nave, Lt. William ("Spike"), 241
Navy, U. S., policies, 246, 253, 297, 306, 349, 362, 364, 365; action, 312, 341; mentioned, 287, 298, 308, 313, 325, 347, 370
Naylor, Col. William K., 187
Nazi-Soviet pact, 257
Negroes in the Army, 295
Netherlands, 275
Netherlands Indies, 306
Neufchateau, France, 130
Nevada, Mo., 93, 94
New, Sen. Harry, 177
New Britain, Oceania, 346
New Caledonia, Oceania, 329
Newell, Col. Isaac, 194, 199
New Guinea, Oceania, 329, 335, 346, 362
New Market, Battle of, 42, 46, 56, 57, 105
New Mexico atom bomb test, 364
New Orleans, La., 48
New Willard Hotel, Washington, D. C., 64, 69
New York, N. Y., 99, 124, 125, 172, 248, 303
Nicholson, L., 45, 48, 51, 52, 54, 58, 59
Nick Carter, 38, 39
Nijmegen, Netherlands, 359
Nile River, 316
Nimitz, Adm. Chester W., 328, 335, 350, 361, 362, 363
1916 National Defense Act, 115, 116, 122
97th Division, 359
9th Air Force, 358
9th Corps Area (San Francisco), 234
Ninth Army, 359
Nivillers, 145

Nomura, Adm. ———, 290
Norden bombsight, 265
Normandy, 314, 317, 318, 331, 332, 335, 340, 341, 346, 354, 356, 358, 360
North Africa, 276, 315, 317, 319, 320, 321, 325, 326, 327, 331, 332, 336
Northern Neck, Va., 17
North Pole, 242
Norway, 275
Noyon, France, 144
Nukufetan Isl., 346

Oahu, H. I., 186
Oak Hill, 18, 19, 21
Oak Leaf Cluster, *see* Marshall, George C., Jr.
O'Bryon, Mary Kate, 33, 34
"Observer," pseudonym of Humphrey Marshall, 20
Octagon Conference, 361
Office of Naval Intelligence, 313
Officer Candidate School, 312
Officers' Club, 242
Officers' Reserve Corps, 122, 265
Ohio River, 24
Oise River, 158
O'Laughlin, Col. John Callan, 343, 344
Old Billy, Marshalls' horse, 35
Oliphant Furnace, 29
Olwein's, 38
152d Division (French), 142
167th Division (French), 152
Operations and Training (G-3), 184
Operations Division, 180
Operations Officer, *see* G-3
Oran, Algeria, 321
Organized Militia of Massachusetts, 104
Organized Reserve, 115, 178, 185

Index

Osborn, Frederick H., 295
Ourcq River, 153
Overlord, 335, 340, 342, 344, 345, 346, 351

Palau Islands, 362
Palmer, Brig. Gen. John McAuley, 86, 91, 92, 118, 125, 174-179, 184, 200, 214, 365, 367
Palmer, Mrs. John McAuley, 200
Panama, 97, 186, 297
Panama, Dept. of, 266
Panama Canal, 179, 265
Panama Canal Commission, 129
Panama Canal garrison, 272
Panama garrison, 286
Panay, the, 244
Pandarukan, Mindoro Isl., 77
Paris, France, 19, 99, 130, 150, 153
Paris-Amiens railroad, 154
Paris-Avricourt railroad, 154
Parker, Brig. Gen. Frank, 136, 163
Pas-de-Calais, France, 356
Patch, Gen. Alexander M., 357
Patterson, Under Secy. ———, 292, 359
Patterson, Judge Robert P., 284, 285, 371
Patterson - McCormick newspapers, 313
Patton, Maj. Gen. George Smith, Jr., 309, 321, 322, 336, 337, 339, 355, 357, 358, 359
Pearce, Miss ———, 233
Pearl Harbor, 297, 298, 299, 300, 302, 304, 306, 307, 314, 337
Peiping, China, 244
Peking, China, 188, 196
Pembroke, Earl of, 16
Pendleton, Ore., 238
Percy Mining Co., 29

Pershing, General of the Army John J., in Mexican skirmish, 114-115; in World War I, 121-125, 128, 130-131, 136, 138, 142, 148-150, 153-160, 162-166; postwar activities, 171-180; becomes Chief of Staff, 184; best man at Marshall wedding, 215; visits Pres. Roosevelt, 246; mentioned, 65, 90, 185, 186, 187, 189, 190, *et passim*
Personnel Division (G-1), 184
Peru, S. A., 294
Pétain, Marshal Henri, 149, 150, 153, 157, 158, 161, 276, 326, 327
Peyton, Col. Philip B. (Buster), 45, 46, 48, 54, 55, 59, 168, 205, 207, 208, 223
P-40 plane, 288
Philadelphia, Pa., 27, 224
Philippine Commonwealth Government, 235
Philippine Constabulary, 214
Philippine Department, 106, 108
Philippine Islands, Marshall at, 64, 85, 86, 90, 97, 98, 105-113, 120, 127, 225, 237; in World War II, 294, 301, 306-308, 330, 361-363; mentioned, 281, 347
Philippine Republic, 235
Pickett, Gen. George E., 237
Pickett, Mary Ann, 22
Pierce, Lt. J. B., 200
Pittsburgh, Pa., 24, 98, 213
Plattsburg training camp, 116
Ploesti, Rumania, 335
Poland, 271
Pont-à-Mousson, France, 137
Pope, John, 237
Portal, Sir Charles, 304, 332
Portland, Ore., 239
Potomac River, 17

Potsdam conference, 363
Pound, Sir Dudley, 304
Presbyterian Church (Uniontown, Pa.), 40
Presidio, San Francisco, 114
Price, Col. ———, 50, 51
Princeton University, 40
"Profiting by War Experiences," Marshall, 181
Protective Mobilization Plan Force, 273, 274
Providence, R. I., 238
P-38 planes, 312
Puerto Rico, Dept. of, 266

Quadrant Conference, 340
Quartermaster Depot, New York City, 124
Quarters No. 1, 370
Quebec, Canada, 340, 341, 342, 361, 362, 363
Quekemeyer, Col. John G., 172
Quezon, Pres. Manuel, 301

Rainbow Division, 163
Rainbow Five, 298
Ramgarh, India, 330
Ranger, the, 315
Rappahannock River, 17
Raritan, N. J., 277
Rayburn, Sam, 292
Recoleto Friars, 76
Redstone Creek, 33
Reims, France, 142, 143
Report of Board of Officers on Utilization of Negro Manpower in the Post-War Army, 295
Reserve Officers' Training Corps, 115
Reynaud, Paul, 276
Reynolds, Capt. Russel B., 211
Rhine River, 156, 356, 359, 360

Rice, Pvt. William E., 73
Richardson, Lt. Gen. Robert C., 328
Rilea, Brig. Gen. Thomas E., 239
"Riley's Ridge," 231
Rinehart, Mary Roberts, 214
Roanoke, Va., 58
Roberts, Justice ———, 302
Robinson, Elsie, 172, 173
Rockbridge *County News,* 59
"Rock of the Marne," 151. *See also* 3d Division
Rockville, Ind., 47
Roer River, 359
Roi Isl., 346
Roller, Charles Summerville, Jr., 60
Romagne, France, 170
Rome, Italy, 335, 337
Rommel, Field Marshal Erwin, 314, 315, 327, 354
Roosevelt, Pres. Franklin D., plans CCC, 224; appointments, 234, 235, 246, 255, 265, 278, 294, 324, 344-345; plans defenses, 249, 252, 254, 259-260, 266, 272; in World War II, 276, 279, 290-293, 295, 300, 303, 306, 308, 309, 310, 311, 313, 316, 317, 323, 325, 328, 330, 336; at Casablanca, 331, 332; at Quebec, 340, 362; at Yalta, 360; death of, 363; mentioned, 264, 281, 282, 288, 326, 342, 343, 346
Roosevelt, Pres. Theodore, 72
Roosevelt, Col. Theodore, Jr., 163
Root, Elihu, 65, 66, 67, 68, 69, 70, 72, 89, 91, 100, 101, 116, 185, 261, 281, 364
Ross, Col. Tenney, 177
R.O.T.C., 122, 206, 239
Roundheads, 17
Roundup, 311, 317, 318, 327, 331, 335

INDEX

Royal Air Force, 249, 275, 315, 320, 333, 357
Royal Italian Government, 336
Royal Navy, 357
Ruhr River, 359, 360
Rundstedt, Von, 332, 358, 359
Russia, 289, 294, 307, 311, 331

Saar River, 359
Sablayan, Mindoro Isl., 77
Ste.-Menehould, France, 158
St. Lô, France, 355, 356, 359
St.-Mihiel, France, 127, 130, 137, 149, 154, 155, 156, 157, 158, 159, 160, 164, 183
St.-Nazaire, France, 129, 130, 131, 150
St. Peter's Parish, 26, 31, 37, 39, 41, 85, 98
St.-Quentin-Cambrai, France, 158
Saipan Isl., 349, 350, 362
Salem, Ore., 239
Salt Lake City, Utah, 239
Samoa Isl., 329, 362
San Antonio, Texas, 99, 100, 125, 234
San Diego, Calif., 117
San Francisco, Calif., 114, 120, 126, 127, 185, 186, 200, 239, 242, 243, 308
Sangihe Isl., 363
San Jose, Mindoro Isl., 76
Santa Mesa Barracks, 72, 82
Santo Tomas, P. I., 74
Sanz, Padre Isidro, 76, 78
Saranac, N. Y., 173
Sardinia Isl., 337, 340
Saulles, Maj. A. B. de, 29
Saunders, Judge ———, 60
Savannah, Ga., 218
Scarpe River, 158
Scheldt River, 357

Schofield, Lt. Gen. 70
School of the Line, 86, 87, 88, 89
Scott, Maj. Gen. Hugh L., 121, 122, 124
Searight, James A., 31, 41
Sebastian, Judge Benjamin, 20
2d Armored Division, 312
Second Army, 162, 171, 231, 239
Second Army (British), 354, 359
2d Corps Area, 248
2d Division, 104, 151, 152
2d Infantry Brigade, 136
Sedan, France, 158, 162, 163, 170, 275
Sedan-Mézières railway, 161
Seicheprey, France, 138
Seine River, 354
Selective Service Law, 293
Semirara Isl., 77
Senate Military Committee, 176, 264, 292
Services of Supply, 171
Sevastopol, Russia, 315
Seven Days' Battle, 47
Seventh Army, 336, 337
7th Brigade, 70
VII Corps, 355
7th Infantry, 237
SHAEF, 355, 359
Shanghai, China, 194, 244
Shanhaikwan, China, 187
Shenandoah River, 56
Shepler, Jap, 36, 256
Sheridan, Gen. Philip H., 237
Sherrill, Capt. Clarence O., 84, 90, 95, 111
Sherrill, Mrs. Clarence O., 112
Shiebert, Sgt. ———, 73
Shipp, Gen. Scott, 60
Shoreham Hotel, 185
Short, Maj. Gen. Walter C., 297, 301

Sibert, Maj. Gen. William L., 124, 125, 126, 128, 129, 135
Sicily, 332, 335, 336, 337, 355
Sidney, Australia, 308
Siegfried line, 357, 359
Sigel, Gen. Franz, 56
Sims, Sgt. Frederick A., 75
Singer, Dr. ———, 42
Singer, Sgt. Frank, 232, 233
16th Infantry, 124, 132, 133, 134
Sixth Army (French), 152
6th Field Artillery, 124
62d Virginia Regiment, C.S.A., 56
Skyscraper, the, 42, 98
Sledgehammer, 311, 317, 318, 319, 321, 328, 340
Smith, Sgt. ———, 73
Smith, Lt. Gen. Holland M. ("Howling Mad"), 348, 349
Smith, Prof. Lee, 38
Smith, Maj. Gen. Ralph B., 349, 350
Smith, Rev. Richard S., 31
Smith, Brig. Gen. Walter Bedell, 310, 317
Soissons, France, 142, 151, 152
Solomon Islands, 329, 335, 349
Somervell, Gen. Brehon, 303, 313, 345, 367, 371
Somme River, 140, 141, 142, 143
Sommerviller, France, 132
S-1 (adjutant), 203
Souilly, France, 159, 162, 163
Southern Dept., 124
Soviet airmen, 242
Soviet Embassy, 242
Soviet-German nonaggression treaty, 271
Soviet Union, 289, 300
Spaatz, Brig. Gen. Carl, 333
Spain, 243, 331
Spencer, Herbert, 46

Spokane, Wash., 238
S. S. *Tenadores,* 129
Staff College, 204
Stalin, Josef, 344, 361
Stark, Adm. Harold R., 276, 282, 304, 310, 324
Stars and Bars, 46
"Star Spangled Banner," 224
Steuben, Gen. Frederick von, 69
Stilwell, Lt. Gen. Joseph, 187, 204, 309, 328, 330, 340, 347
S-3 (operations officer), 203
Stimson, Henry L., as Secretary of War, 100, 102, 116, 278, 279, 284, 294, 295, 314, 316, 319, 325, 326, 339, 343, 359, 370; as Gov. Gen. of P. I., 214; as Secy. of State, 244; in pre-World War II defense plans, 287, 288-289; to London, 341; to Quebec, 342; mentioned, 281, 285, 292, 344, 356, 365, 371
Stockton Hill, 15
Stone, Lt. Edward R., 75
Streett, Lt. Col. St. Clair, 245, 253
Strongbow, 16
Stuart, Capt. E. R., 93
Stuart, Aunt Eliza, 26
Stuart, Maria Louisa, 15
S-2 (intelligence officer), 203
Summerall, Gen. Charles P., 162, 164, 186, 187, 204
Summerall, Mrs. Charles P., 186, 187
Sun Yat-sen, Dr., 187
Supply Division (G-4), 184
Supreme War Council, 153
Swift, Maj. Eben, 88

Tactical Section, 204, 205, 207
Taft, William H., 101, 103
Tagalogs, 77, 105
Taggart, Lt. Col. Elmore F., 104

INDEX

Talaud, P. I., 362, 363
Taliaferro, Matilda, 22
Talmadge, Gov. ———, 221
Tampa, Fla., 67, 72
Tanay, Rizal, 82
Tank School, 211
Tarawa Isl., 346, 349
Teach the Pirate, 17
Teheran, Iran, 335, 344, 345
10th Air Force, 330
Tenth Army (French), 152
10th Cavalry, 114
10th Pennsylvania Regiment, 42
Texas City, Texas, 104
Thayer, Capt. Arthur, 88
Third Army, 171, 242, 355, 358, 359,
Third Army (French), 144
3d Cavalry, 51
III Corps (American), 153
3d Division, 151, 152
Third Reich, 243
3d Virginia Regiment, 18
13th Infantry, 106
30th U. S. Infantry, 64, 72, 82, 83, 86
XXXVIII Corps (French), 152
38th Infantry, 151
32d Division, 153
33d Division (Illinois National Guard), 226, 229, 230, 231
Thompson, Alcinda, 34, 36, 37
Thompson, Andy, 33, 36, 38, 39, 63
Thompson, J. V., 30
Thompson, John, 33
Thompson home, 256
Tientsin, China, 185, 187-200, 217
Tillamook, Ore., 238
Tindall, Maj. Richard G., 211, 212
Tobruk, Libya, 314, 315
Tokyo, Japan, 311, 312, 363
Tongatabu Isl., 329
Topographical Section, 144

Torch, 321, 331
Torstrup, Sgt. August, 75
Toul, France, 140, 141, 143
Towers, Rear Adm. John H., 313
Transylvania College, 19
Treaty of Versailles, 262
Trident Conference, 335
Troyanovsky, Ambassador, 242
Truman, Pres. Harry S., 363, 369, 370, 372
Tulagi, Solomon Islands, 329
Tunisia, 327, 331, 336
Twelfth Army Group, 355
28th Division, 151
28th Infantry, 124, 141, 164
XX Corps (French), 151, 152
21st Army Group (British), 354, 356
24th Infantry, 99, 217
29th Division, 175
29th Infantry, 207, 208
27th Division, 349
26th Division, 151, 152
26th Infantry, 124, 163
201 File, 96

Uniontown, Pa., 15, 26, 27, 28, 29, 36, 37, 39, 42, 54, 63, 85, 88, 99, 256
University of Georgia, 220
Upatoie Creek, 208
Upperville, Va., 213
Upton, Brevet Maj. Gen. Emory, 91, 92
U.S.A.T. *Ingalls*, 82
U.S.A.T. *Kilpatrick*, 64, 72
U.S.A.T. *Sherman*, 83
U.S.A.T. *Thomas*, 200
U.S.-Canada Permanent Joint Defense Board, 302
U.S. Steel Export Corp., 277
Utica, N. Y., 173

Valley Forge, Pa., 18, 21
Vancouver, Wash., 239, 241, 242, 243
Vancouver Barracks, 235, 236, 237, 246
Vandenberg, Col. Hoyt, 317
Vauban, Marquis de, 151
Verdun, France, 150, 158, 159
Vesle River, 153, 156
Vichy, France, 324, 326
Vicksburg, Miss., 42
Vienna, Austria, 99
Villa, Pancho, 115
Virginia Military Institute, 40, 42, 44-64, 88, 105, 168, 180, 214
Virginia Militia, 18
Virginia Polytechnic Institute, 58, 59
Volunteer Army, 115
Vosges Mts., 158

Wadsworth, Rep. ———, 177, 178, 370
Wagner, Col. Arthur L., 88
Wagner, Capt. ———, 192
Wainwright, Maj. Gen. Jonathan M., 307
Walcheren Island, 357
Walker, Lt. Frederick, 106
Walter Reed Hospital, 200
War College, 197, 200, 204, 280, 322
War Council, 248, 295
War Dept. Circular, 367
War Dept. Special Orders No. 100, 185
War Dept. Special Staff, 367
War Game, 228, 229
War Plans Division, 90, 175, 176, 184, 243, 244, 245, 246, 247, 267, 294, 301, 309
War Production Board, 308
Warren, Sen. ———, 103, 124

Washington, D. C., War College in, 89, 280; 201 file, 96; Pershing in, 125, 172, 173, 175, 246; Marshall in, 179, 180, 185, 200, 204, 217, 236, 243, 247, 251, 253, 257, 259, 261, 262, 322, 342, 343, 347; Churchill in, 304-305, 314, 335; mentioned, 171, 176, 211, 227, 230, *et passim*
Washington, Gen. George, 16, 18, 69, 91
Washington, Ky., 21
Washington and Lee University, 19, 58
Washington Barracks, 197
Washington College, *see* Washington and Lee University
Washington, Lincoln, Wilson: Three War Statesmen, Palmer, 214
Washington *Post*, 195
Wavell, Gen. Sir Archibald, 306, 313
Weapons Section, 205
Wehrmacht, the, 210, 358, 359
Wells, Gen. Briant, 217
Wertenbaker, Capt. Clark I., 73
Wesson, Maj. Gen. Charles M., 277
Western Dept., 120
Western Task Force, 321
Western World, 20
Westmoreland Co., 17, 18, 21
West Point (U. S. Military Academy), 179, 180, 313
Weygand, Gen. Maxime, 153, 276, 288
Whig Party, 21
"Whistling Mac," 53
White, Gen. George, 239
Whitehead, Right Rev. Cortlandt, 41
White Swan, The, 32, 33, 34, 38, 256
Whittlesey, Maj. Charles W., 161

Wightman, Rev. John R., 26, 37, 41
Wilderness campaign, 56
Wilhelm, Harry, 40
Willard Hotel, 172
Willey, Pvt. John W., 74
William the Marshal, 16
Wilson, Sir Henry Maitland, 153, 358
Wilson, Pres. Woodrow, 114, 115
Woëvre plateau, France, 170
Wolf, Sgt. ———, 51
Women's Army Corps, 331
Wood, Gen. Leonard, 99, 100, 102, 103, 116, 365
Wood, Will, 33
Woodfill, Lt. Samuel, 161
Woodhead, ———, 195
Woodring, Harry, 235, 236, 237, 247, 248, 251, 252, 253, 254, 260, 266, 267, 268, 277, 278

Woodruff, Capt. James A., 95
Works Progress Administration, 241
World War I, 66, 121, 123-165, 175, 181, 205, 210, 212, 216, 225, 241, 285, 322, 326, 342, 345
WPD, *see* War Plans Division
Wu P'ei-fu, 187, 188

Yalta, Soviet Union, 360, 361
Yangtze Valley, 194
Yap Isl., 362, 363
York, Sgt. Alvin C., 161
York River, 17
Youghiogheny River, 27
Ypres, France, 158
Yugoslavia, 319, 335, 358

Zamboanga, P. I., 70